Compiling in Modula-2

Compiling in Modula-2

A first introduction to classical recursive descent compiling

Julian R. Ullmann

*Department of Computer Science,
King's College London,
University of London*

PRENTICE HALL

New York   London   Toronto   Sydney   Tokyo   Singapore

First published 1994 by
Prentice Hall International (UK) Limited
Campus 400, Maylands Avenue
Hemel Hempstead
Hertfordshire, HP2 7EZ
A division of
Simon & Schuster International Group

Typeset in 10/12 pt Times
by Columns Design and Production Services Ltd,
Reading, Berkshire

Transferred to digital print on demand 2001

Printed and bound in Great Britain by Antony Rowe Ltd, Eastbourne

Library of Congress Cataloging-in-Publication Data

Ullmann, Julian R. (Julian Richard), 1936–
    Compiling in modula 2: a first introduction to classical
recursive descent compiling/by Julian R. Ullmann.
        p.   cm.
    Includes bibliographical references and index.
    ISBN 0-13-088741-2
    1. Modula-2 (Computer program language) I. Title.
QA76.73.M63U45   1994
005.4'53--dc20

93–33826
CIP

British Library Cataloguing in Publication Data

A catalogue record for this book is available from
the British Library

ISBN 0-13-088741-2

1 2 3 4 5 98 97 96 95 94

Contents

Preface

There is already a formidable spectrum of textbooks on compiler theory and technology, differing from each other in size, breadth, depth, mathematical theory, implementational detail, and in their coverage of topics such as parallelism, objects, modules, and compilation of declarative languages. The present book is an initial introduction that belongs to the family of elementary texts which focus on just one compiling technique and do not attempt to cover the entire field. Specifically, this book focuses on traditional hand-crafted recursive descent which has retained its practical importance since the 1960s, for example in Pascal P-code compilers that emerged during the 1970s, and can be appreciated by students who have very little mathematical background and no knowledge of automata theory.

This book has been used as the basis for a self-contained introductory undergraduate compiler course, in a context where there is a separate introductory course on automata and formal languages. These two courses together provide a complementary background for broader and deeper study of compiling.

The starting point of this book is elementary knowledge of Modula-2, basic data structures, and simple assembly language programming. The end point is *not* detailed knowledge of a fully-fledged practical recursive-descent compiler, *but* readiness to commence the study of one. This is an initial introduction that stops far short of professional compiler writing. We use Modula-2 both as a source language and as an implementation language: Pascal programmers can easily cope with this. Gough and Mohay (1988) and Rechenberg and Mössenböck (1989) provide brief introductions to Modula-2 for Pascal programmers.

A well-proven strategy for the design of a software system such as a compiler is top-down stepwise refinement. This strategy is appropriate for use by software designers who have already mastered the abstract general concepts that are involved. For students who are new to a field, general concepts must first be made meaningful, and this may be best accomplished by working from the particular to the general, having first consolidated understanding of the particular by the study of examples.

To facilitate understanding of the intricate mechanism of a compiler, much of this book is evolutionary rather than top-down. For example, when compiling expressions and control structures we first use variables that are predeclared, then we use purely static storage without allowing procedures, then we introduce procedures with dynamic storage, and finally we introduce modules. We do not have to rewrite the whole compiler at each evolutionary step, but instead merely introduce or modify various constituent modules.

Finally, we have a compiler for a fairly substantial subset of Modula-2, which might perhaps be hard to comprehend if there were no such gentle stairway leading up to it.

Newcomers to compiling are often eager to see how a compiler translates from a high-level language into a fairly familiar low-level language. So that the reader can easily see what is being achieved, we compile directly into an assembly language named SAL, which stands for *Simplified Assembly Language*. SAL is a simplification and adaptation of 8086 Assembly Language, and is so much simplified that it is an archetypical assembly language, with practical refinements carefully omitted. A reader who has elementary knowledge of any fairly conventional assembly language will learn SAL easily, and will not need to come to terms with 8086 specialities such as segments. We certainly do not presuppose knowledge of 8086 Assembly Language: an elementary knowledge of any conventional assembly language will be sufficient.

This book includes chapters on assembling, linking and machine code interpretation, which provide a complete chain such that programs that have been compiled, assembled, and linked can be executed by interpretation. These chapters serve as an introduction to more elaborate technology. For example, understanding linking at machine code level is a prerequisite for understanding separate compilation at the Modula-2 level. Before studying linking at the machine code level it is desirable to have a clear understanding of the translation of labels into numeric addresses. Part of this translation is done by an assembler, and this is one reason why we have a chapter on a SAL assembler.

In so far as a program may be compiled and subsequently assembled, assembly comes after compilation, and a chapter on assembling might be expected to come after chapters on compiling. In this book the chapter on assembling comes earlier, because it helps to consolidate the reader's knowledge of our compiler target language, and because it provides practice in working with a lexical analyzer. Our assembler uses recursive descent, which is introduced in a subsequent chapter. Instead of using the abstract ideas of recursive descent to help explain the working of the assembler, this book uses an assembler to help pave the way to a subsequent understanding of recursive descent. Whether this is ideal is debatable, but it certainly helps real live students. It is often helpful to study simple things before more complex things, and a recursive-descent assembler provides a useful introduction to a recursive-descent compiler.

The aesthetic aspect of compiling is worthy of comment. For example, statements in Modula-2 may contain further statements that contain further statements, and so on to any depth, at least in principle. Similarly, data structures may contain further data structures that contain further data structures and so on. Some people see great beauty in the way a compiler uses recursion to deal with recursion. Although the technology in this book has been simplified it provides the reader with a glimpse of an extraordinarily beautiful technical landscape. Before reaching this the reader is taken through the very much less spectacular terrain associated with assembling, linking and relocation. The climb through arid foothills is rewarded by the view from higher up.

J.R.U.

Department of Computer Science,
King's College London,
Strand,
London WC2R 2LS, UK

Acknowledgements

Intel 8086 Assembly Language instructions are used, and Table 2.7 is reproduced, with the permission of the Intel Corporation. The author is also grateful to Prentice Hall reviewers for immensely helpful comments and suggestions.

Disclaimer

Care has been taken to ensure the correctness of all software included in, and associated with, this book. However, the author and publishers accept no responsibility whatsoever for errors of any kind, nor for any eventualities arising therefrom.

Chapter 1

Introduction

1.1 Why compile?

A compiler translates a *source* program written in a high-level language that has features such as

    expressions,
    real numbers,
    types and type checking,
    structured types such as records and multidimensional arrays,
    control structures such as IF and WHILE,
    procedures and functions with parameters, and
    standard functions such as square root,

into an *object* program in a lower-level programming language in which

    individual instructions,
    registers,
    a one-dimensional address space, and
    the internal representation of data

are visible to the programmer. A compiler is a software bridge across the *semantic gap* between viewpoints of programmers writing in high- and low-level languages. These viewpoints are different because high-level and low-level languages are subject to different design criteria. High-level languages are programmer-oriented and are designed to make programs concise, easy to read, and preferably close to the programmer's natural way of thinking. The lowest-level languages are machine-oriented and are designed to satisfy engineering requirements relating to hardware cost, speed and efficient support of many different high-level languages. High-level languages are machine-independent and are intended to help minimize programming errors. The lowest-level languages are machine-specific and provide very little comfort for programmers.

    There have been attempts to avoid the need for compiling by raising the level of machine code (Myers 1982). In some systems this can be accomplished by developing a processor's microprogram interpreter so that the semantic gap is bridged by microcode below the machine code level. However, this binds the computer to a single high-level language, which may be an unacceptable restriction. Another disadvantage is that the microprogram interpreter has to repeat many times during execution various analytical processes, such as syntactic analysis of expressions, which can be executed just once by a compiler prior to execution. Yet another disadvantage pointed out by Myers (1982) is that a compiler checks program correctness to some extent before execution: if the compiler is abolished we have a new problem of checking prior to execution. For these reasons compilers have not gone away.

Instead of raising the level of machine code, there was a trend during the 1980s to make it even more primitive, resulting in so-called *reduced instruction set* computers, which rely heavily on compilers to translate from programmer-oriented languages to processor-oriented languages. Compilers have become more important.

A compiler bridges the semantic gap by software implementation of high-level features of a language such as Modula-2. By studying one specific compiler, we deepen our understanding of these features, and we learn their possible cost, for example the cost of an assignment statement, a procedure call, or a multidimensional array access.

1.2 Why assemble?

In a machine code program derived from compiler output, many of the detailed programming decisions have been made by the compiler instead of the source-code programmer. In situations where the programmer needs to design the machine code in detail, it may be appropriate to program in the appropriate assembly language instead of a high-level language. Instead of programming directly in machine code we program in assembly language because this gives the same amount of control as machine code but is more programmer-friendly owing to the use of names instead of addresses, the use of mnemonics for opcodes and registers, and the availability of features such as pseudo-ops.

Many practical compilers translate into an intermediate code that is more abstract than a specific assembly language; subsequently the intermediate code output has to be compiled, assembled and/or interpreted. For introductory purposes this book does not use an intermediate code; instead we compile directly into a simplified assembly language in the hope that this will be more obviously meaningful to a reader who is new to the field. From the viewpoint of efficiency it would be better to compile directly into machine code as in Ammann (1977), but this would make it more difficult for the reader to follow the action.

The end-point of this book is a simplified compiler that has as its source language a subset of Modula-2, and has as its object language SAL, which stands for *Simplified Assembly Language*. SAL is a simplification and adaptation of 8086 assembly language: unexpurgated 8086 assembly language would be unnecessarily complicated for present purposes. At a more primitive level than Modula-2, SAL allows the programmer to write a single program composed of a number of modules that are assembled separately.

1.3   Why use modules?

In this book the assembler, linker and compiler software is multimodular. When progressing to more advanced topics we sometimes develop modules, or introduce new modules, while reusing various previous modules unchanged within a single program. Moreover, both our source code and object code are multimodular.

Usually the least important advantage of assembling or compiling modules separately is that this requires less memory than would be required for translating all the modules merged together seamlessly into a single program. This advantage arises because during assembly or compilation of a single module the assembler or compiler builds up various tables whose size tends to increase with the length of the module. These tables are destroyed as soon as the assembly or compilation of the module has been completed, and memory that they occupied can be reused for other purposes, for example in the assembly or compilation of subsequent modules.

This book usually, but not always, follows the tradition of putting a data structure and its associated procedures into a separate module. This improves the logical clarity of programs. By preventing unnecessary external visibility of a module's internal identifiers, we eliminate the risk of using them erroneously from within other modules. Separate compilation is incidental rather than essential for this deliberate control of scope.

Perhaps with a little modification, a data structure, or another object such as a file, together with its associated procedures, may be reusable in many different programs. If we put an object and its associated procedures into a separate module, we may find that this module can be reused more easily than would be possible by applying a text editor to a single long program that should have been subdivided into modules. In this book there are many examples of reuse of modules by linking them together with different collections of other modules to make up new programs. The reusability of modules is an important practical advantage of modular programming.

From the viewpoint of reusability, separate assembly or compilation of individual modules is obviously desirable. If a module is reused with absolutely no modification, there should be no need to recompile or reassemble it each time it is linked together in a new context of other modules.

It is scarcely necessary to say that if we make a programming mistake in a big program that has not been subdivided into modules, then the whole program has to be reassembled or recompiled after correction of the mistake. But if there is a mistake in only one module of a multimodule program we may need only to reassemble or recompile that module.

The creative process of writing a large program is facilitated if modules are implemented separately and tested at least for compilability before being linked together into a single program. Another advantage of modular programming is that it is easier for different programmers to write different modules than to write different parts of a single program that has not been subdivided into modules. Furthermore, various commercial systems allow multilanguage modular programming, wherein modules written for example in C, Modula-2 and an assembly language can be separately translated into object code and then linked together into a single program.

Modules for input/output, file access, memory management, string manipulation, mathematical functions, and others that are normally associated with a Modula-2 compiler provide an example of a *run-time support environment*. This is essentially a collection of library routines that can be called from within an object–code program. Library modules, which are good examples of reused modules, do not have to be recompiled when a client program is compiled.

Although the use of modules is of great practical importance, we cannot claim that the technology of intermodule linking is of equally great theoretical interest. In compiling there are some issues such as syntax analysis where practical importance appears to be roughly proportional to theoretical interest, and there are other issues where inverse proportionality is a truer characterization. The orientation of the present book is very much more practical than theoretical.

1.4 Machine code interpretation

Our assembler software can assemble our compiler's output code, and our linker software links multimodule programs into a single machine code program. For completeness this book includes an interpreter that can interpret machine code programs. After assembling and linking, this interpreter can execute code that has been produced by our compiler. In this sense we introduce a complete, but simplified, system. In end-of-chapter exercises we leave the reader to remove some of the simplifications.

1.5 Programs in this book

In programming there is often a conflict between readability, robustness, and run-time efficiency. For introductory purposes this book usually gives highest priority to readability. To reduce clutter our software sometimes lacks robustness because it contains inadequate checks, such as overflow checks. For these reasons, and because our compiler source language is only a subset of Modula-2, omitting characters, subranges, enumerations, sets, pointers, procedure variables, and other facilities, this book may be found less detailed than it appears to be at first sight.

It is our policy to include almost all our introductory software either in the main text of the book or in the Appendix, except in cases where programs are very minor modifications of earlier versions. This kind of completeness is hopefully more satisfying than a more sketchy introduction, but the inevitable price is that some parts are less instructive than others. Modules in the Appendix are in alphabetical order of their name, and running heads enable modules to be looked up in the Appendix like looking up a name in a telephone directory. Where repetition may facilitate comprehension and cross-reference, the Appendix may include a complete listing of a module whose procedures are introduced in detail in the main text. For the same reasons this book has no inhibitions about listing the whole of a procedure that differs only slightly from a previous version belonging to an earlier stage of evolutionary development.

Our programs are written in Modula-2 as in Wirth (1985), which is the subject of commentaries in Wirth (1988), Cornelius (1988) and Gough and Mohay (1988). Our software has been developed using a Shareware Modula-2 compiler on a personal computer under DOS. This compiler, which is available at low cost from Fitted Software Tools, P.O. Box 867403, Piano, Texas 75086, USA, uses library modules that are fairly consistent with those of Wirth (1985). Anderson (1984) has provided information about some earlier Modula-2 compilers. Although we have used DOS, we have avoided doing anything DOS-specific in this text, which is not tied to any particular operating system, nor to any particular hardware.

All of the software in this book is available on diskette, free to adopters, from Prentice Hall, Campus 400, Maylands Avenue, Hemel Hempstead, Herts HP2 7EZ, UK. It is also freely available via e-mail *ftp* from `julian@dcs.kcl.ac.uk`.

Chapter 2

SAL: Simplified Assembly Language and machine code

2.1 Introduction

SAL, which stands for Simplified Assembly Language, has been designed to serve as the object language for a simplified compiler, which in turn has been designed purely for tutorial purposes. For SAL the design criteria were that it should be reasonably comfortable as a compiler object language, that it should have no complications that are unnecessary for purposes of elementary introduction, and that it should bear an easily recognizable resemblance to a well-established practical assembly language. Although SAL is a simplification and adaptation of 8086 Assembly Language, it is not merely a subset, and its machine code and multimodular facilities are considerably different to those of the 8086.

There is no need for the reader to learn to program fluently in SAL: all that is required for later chapters is the ability to read and understand SAL assembly language fragments, perhaps using the present chapter as a reference manual. It is even less necessary to learn the details of SAL machine code, which are included in this chapter essentially for reference during the study of an assembler in Chapter 4. On the other hand, it may be worthwhile to learn the SAL binary symbolic machine code format that is introduced in Section 2.9.3.

In our introduction to SAL we will enclose names of families of symbols within angle brackets. For example, <operand> means any one of a set of possible operands. Another example is that <opCode> means any one of a set of possible op-codes. Each SAL instruction is written on a separate line, and must be in one of the three forms:

```
<opCode> <operand>, <operand>
<opCode> <operand>
<opCode>
```

In the first two of these there must be at least one space between the <opCode> and the <operand>, and in the first the two operands must be separated by a comma and any number of spaces so long as the entire instruction is on one line, for example:

```
ADD AX, 6
```

2.2 Memory and registers

Unlike the 8086, SAL does not have segments or segment registers. SAL works exclusively with 16-bit words, and we are not concerned with the byte-orientated facilities. The SAL main memory looks like a single one-dimensional array of words that have consecutive addresses $0,...,2^{16}-1$. Each of these addresses selects a unique 16-bit word (not just a byte) in memory. The restriction to 64K words would be severe for a practical system, but for present purposes simplicity is a strong advantage.

Like the 8086, SAL has four 16-bit data registers named AX, BX, CX and DX and four 16-bit index registers named SP, BP, SI and DI. Index register SP (which stands for *stack pointer*) normally holds the address of the 16-bit word in main memory that is at the top of a stack. When a 16-bit word is pushed on to this stack, SP is first *increased* by 1 and then the 16-bit word is stored in the memory location whose address is in SP. Conversely, after popping a word off this stack, SP is decreased by 1. Here we have a difference between SAL and 8086 Assembly Language, which decrements SP by 2 when a word is pushed on to the stack. The SAL stack grows upwards, with increasing addresses as the stack grows, whereas the 8086 stack grows downwards, with decreasing addresses as the stack grows.

In SAL the registers AX, BX, CX, DX, SP, BP, SI and DI are not all equivalent: some are usable for purposes that others cannot be used for. These differences are specified later. As well as these eight registers, SAL has a *flag register*, that is, a register whose bits are *flag* bits. For example, there is one flag bit that is set to 1 when overflow occurs, another that is set to 1 when carry-out is 1, another that is set to 1 when the result of certain operations is 0. For present purposes we do not need to consider the details.

2.3 Labels

An instruction may optionally be preceded by

    <label>:

on the same line. There may be any number of spaces before the label, between the label and the colon, and between the colon and the subsequent text on the line. In SAL a label is any sequence of up to 24 upper-case letters. A label must not include any character other than an upper-case letter. For example, LA is a label in

```
LA: ADD AX, 6
```

Because this instruction has been labelled LA, the programmer can use LA to mean the same thing as the numeric address of the first word of machine code that corresponds to this instruction. The label LA is the symbolic address of this word.

Instead of containing an instruction, a line of a SAL program may contain a *pseudo-*

op, which is a message to the assembler asking it to do something. The pseudo-op DW asks the assembler to reserve one or more words, as in the following examples. DW is a mnemonic for 'define word'. For the example

```
FRED: DW 1694
```

the assembler assigns the decimal value 1694 to a word. Because this pseudo-op has been labelled FRED, the programmer can use FRED to mean the same thing as the numeric address of this word which contains 1694. Incidentally, in SAL all numbers are in decimal.

For the example

```
MARY: DW ?
```

the '?' asks the assembler to reserve a word without assigning a value to it. Another possibility is that we can write, for example,

```
JOHN: DW 20 DUP
```

which reserves a one-dimensional array of 20 words, none of which has an initial value. The programmer can use JOHN to mean the same thing as the address of the first (i.e. lowest-address) word of this array. DUP stands for 'duplicate' and the number preceding DUP is the number of words reserved by this pseudo-op.

2.4 Comments

A line of a SAL program may contain a semicolon followed by any sequence of characters. The assembler ignores all text after ';' on a line and this text can serve as comment to facilitate human understanding. There is an example of a module with comments in Section 2.7.3. If a line starts with any number of spaces followed by a semicolon, the assembler ignores the entire line. A line of a SAL program may be entirely blank: again, the assembler does not produce any machine code corresponding to such a line.

2.5 Operands of instructions

An operand of a SAL instruction is always one of <register>, <memory>, or <immediate>. In this, <register> means one of AX, BX, CX, DX, SP, BP, SI or DI, subject to restrictions that we will introduce later, and <immediate> means a decimal integer value, such as 17, which must be composed of digits, and must not be a label. This integer can optionally be preceded by minus sign. The assembler translates an <immediate> operand in SAL into a 16-bit 2's complement integer in machine code.

A <memory> operand is a word of main memory specified by a 16-bit address that is called the *effective address*. The programmer can give the effective address in a number of different ways which are called *addressing modes*.

When the addressing mode is *direct addressing*, <memory> = <label>, and the effective address is the numeric address of the label. For example, the instruction

```
MOV MARY, 253
```

assigns 253 to the word whose address is the numeric address of MARY.

When the addressing mode is *register indirect addressing*, <memory> = [<indexRegister>] where <indexRegister> is BX, BP, SI or DI. The effective address is simply obtained from the indexRegister. For example,

```
ADD AX, [SI]
```

assigns to AX the sum of the contents of AX and the contents of the memory word whose numeric address is stored in SI.

When the addressing mode is *indexed addressing*, <memory> = <label>[<indReg>], where <indReg> is SI or DI. The effective address is the sum of the numeric address corresponding to <label> and the contents of <indReg>. For example, in the instruction

```
SUB JOHN[SI], DX
```

the effective address is the numeric address of the word labelled JOHN plus the contents of SI. The effect of this instruction is to subtract the contents of DX from the word whose address is the effective address, and to assign the result of this subtraction to this same word.

When the addressing mode is *based indexed addressing*, <memory> = [<baseReg>][<indReg>] where <baseReg> is BX or BP. In this case the effective address is the contents of <baseReg> plus the contents of <indReg>. For example, the effect of

```
MOV BX, [BX][DI]
```

is to assign to BX the contents of the word of memory whose address is the contents of BX plus the contents of DI.

When the addressing mode is *base addressing*, <memory> = [<baseReg><plusOrMinus><d>], where <plusOrMinus> means + or −, and <d> is a decimal integer constant such that <plusOrMinus><d> can be represented by a 16-bit 2's complement integer, which is an example of a *displacement*. The effective address is the contents of <baseReg> ± <d>. For example, the effect of

```
JMP [BP + 3]
```

is to jump to the instruction whose address is 3 plus the contents of BP.

2.6 The SAL instruction set

2.6.1 Instruction categories

It is expedient to place SAL instructions in categories such that any two instructions in the same category have the same set of possible operands. For these categories we use the names twoOperandInstructions, singleOperandInstructions, jumpInstructions, leaInstruction, **and** noOperandInstructions. **Details are** as follows.

2.6.2 Two-operand instructions

Instructions in the twoOperandInstructions category have two operands, of which the first is <destinationOp> and the second is <sourceOp>. The operand <destinationOp> is so called because it specifies where the result of the instruction goes to, that is, the destination of the instruction (except for CMP instructions). It also specifies where the first operand comes from (except for MOV instructions). For twoOperandInstructions the only allowed combinations for <destinationOp> and <sourceOp> are as shown in Table 2.1. It is very important that, for example, <memory><memory> is not an allowed combination. Also note that when <sourceOp> is <immediate> the source operand is an integer value. When <sourceOp> is <register> the source operand is the 16-bit contents of this register. When <sourceOp> is <memory> the source operand is the contents of the 16-bit word of memory whose effective address is determined by <memory> as explained previously.

Table 2.1. Permitted combinations of operands for twoOperandInstructions

<destinationOp>	<sourceOp>
<register>	<immediate>
<memory>	<immediate>
<register>	<register>
<register>	<memory>
<memory>	<register>

In SAL the operation that is carried out by an instruction is determined by the instruction's opCode. For twoOperandInstructions instructions the opCodes are listed in Table 2.2. All twoOperandInstructions except MOV affect flags (which are bits in the flag register), but the details need not concern us here.

Table 2.2 OpCodes of twoOperandInstructions

OpCode	Effect
MOV	destination:= source operand
ADD	destination:= initial contents of destination + source operand
SUB	destination:= initial contents of destination − source operand
CMP	subtract source from contents of destination; do not assign result to destination but do set appropriate flags
AND	destination:= bitwise AND of initial contents of destination with source operand
OR	destination:= bitwise OR of initial contents of destination with source operand

2.6.3 LEA instruction

There is only one instruction in the `leaInstruction` category and it has two operands which can only be <register> <memory>. Its opCode is LEA, which stands for *load effective address*. The effect is to assign to the register specified by the first operand the actual 16-bit numeric effective address specified by the second operand. For example

```
LEA BX, JOHN[SI]
```

assigns to BX the *address* that is the contents of register SI plus the numeric address of the word labelled JOHN. It is important to distinguish this from

```
MOV BX, JOHN[SI]
```

which assigns to BX the *contents* of the word whose address is the contents of register SI plus the numeric address of the word labelled JOHN. The LEA instruction does not belong to the `twoOperandInstructions` category because combinations of operands such as <memory> <immediate> are illegal.

2.6.4 Single-operand instructions

Instructions in the `singleOperandInstructions` category have a single operand which may be either <register> or <memory>. These instructions are listed in Table 2.3.

Table 2.3. OpCodes of `singleOperandInstructions`

OpCode	Effect
DEC	destination:= initial contents of word specified by operand - 1;
INC	destination:= initial contents of word specified by operand + 1;
NEG	destination:= -initial contents of word specified by operand;
POP	destination:= contents of word whose address is in SP; SP:= SP - 1;
PUSH	SP:= SP + 1; word whose address is in SP:= contents of word specified by operand;
MULT	multiply the contents of AX by the word specified by operand. Assign the most significant half of the 32-bit result to DX and assign the least significant half to AX. Set the carry flag to 1 if the resulting contents of DX are non-zero.
DIV	divide a 32-bit dividend by the 16-bit word specified by the operand. The most significant half of the dividend is initially in DX and the least significant half in AX. Assign quotient to AX and remainder to DX.

2.6.5 Jump instructions

Instructions in the `jumpInstructions` category have a single operand that can only be <memory>. The instruction JMP <memory> is an unconditional jump that transfers control to the instruction whose first word is at the address specified by <memory>. SAL also has a family of conditional jump instructions which we only use immediately after a CMP or SUB instruction or a MULT instruction, for example

```
CMP    AX, MARY
JG     FRED
```

The effect of these two instructions is to jump to the instruction labelled FRED if the contents of AX are greater than the contents of the word labelled MARY; otherwise the next instuction to be executed is that which immediately follows the JG instruction. SAL's conditional jump instructions are listed in Table 2.4, where firstop and secondop are the first and second operands of this preceding CMP, SUB or MULT instruction, not of the jump instruction itself. These are all conditional jumps to <memory>.

Table 2.4. Conditional jump instructions

OpCode	Effect
JE	jump to <memory> if firstop = secondop
JG	jump to <memory> if firstop > secondop
JL	jump to <memory> if firstop < secondop
JGE	jump to <memory> if firstop >= secondop
JLE	jump to <memory> if firstop <= secondop
JNE	jump to <memory> if firstop <> secondop
JC	jump to <memory> if carry flag = 1

The jumpInstructions category also includes the subroutine CALL instruction CALL <memory> which has two effects: it increments SP and then assigns the return address to the memory word whose address is in SP. The return address is the numeric address of the word immediately following the (last word of the) CALL instruction. The CALL instruction then causes an unconditional jump to the memory location specified by <memory>.

Another useful instruction in the jumpInstructions category is LOOP <memory> which decrements CX by unity and if the result is non-zero jumps to <memory>. If the result is zero, the next instruction to be executed is that which immediately follows the LOOP instruction.

2.6.6 No-operand instructions

One of the noOperandInstructions is RET. Its effect is an unconditional jump to the address stored in the word whose address is in SP. This is intended to be a jump to the return address at the end of a subroutine. After obtaining the return address via SP, RET decrements SP by 1. The only other SAL instruction that has no operands is NOP, which produces no effect.

2.7 Modules in SAL

2.7.1 IMPORT and EXPORT in SAL

In SAL the programmer can write modules that can be assembled separately and can subsequently be linked together to make a single executable program. A module that refers to a label in another module is said to IMPORT that label. On the other hand, a label is said to be EXPORTed if it is available for reference within other modules. All labels imported and exported by a module must be declared at the beginning of the module. The declaration of exported labels (if any) must precede the declaration of imported labels (if any).

The declaration of exported labels consists of the reserved word EXPORT followed by a list of exported labels, separated by commas, with end-of-line at the end of this list: there is no restriction on the length of a single line. Similarly, the declaration of imported labels consists of the reserved word IMPORT followed by a list of imported labels, separated by commas, with end-of-line at the end of this list. For example, the following is a SAL module that imports labels INTREAD, INTWRITE and NEWLINE which means that it uses these labels which do not label any word in this module. This module exports COPY and HOWMANY which do label words within this module and may be used within at least one other module.

```
EXPORT   COPY, HOWMANY
IMPORT   INTREAD, INTWRITE, NEWLINE
HOWMANY: DW ?
COPY:    MOV CX, HOWMANY
CLOOP:   CALL INTREAD
         CALL INTWRITE
         CALL NEWLINE
         LOOP CLOOP
         RET
```

This is a subroutine that has HOWMANY as a parameter. INTREAD reads an integer and INTWRITE writes an integer, as explained later, and this is done HOWMANY times. To call this subroutine from within another module, we would include HOWMANY and COPY within that module's IMPORT declaration. For example, to call COPY to read and write 10 integers we would write

```
MOV HOWMANY, 10
CALL COPY
```

2.7.2 SAL system calls

We will not discuss SAL's input and output instructions. Instead we will link into every SAL program a module named salSubs (which stands for *SAL subroutines*) containing (what can be regarded as) calls to the operating system to perform input and output and other basic services. Module salSubs exports, among others, the labels INTREAD, INTWRITE, NEWLINE and ENDPROG. We will use these by writing, wherever we wish in other modules, CALL INTREAD, CALL INTWRITE, and so on. The effect of these calls is shown in Table 2.5:

Table 2.5. Effect of calls of subroutines in module salSubs

Subroutine call	Effect
INTREAD	reads a (possibly signed) integer from the current input stream, increments SP by unity, and assigns the input integer as a 16-bit 2's complement number to the memory word whose address is in SP.
INTWRITE	writes the integer from the memory word whose address is in SP and decrements SP by unity. Outputs a single space character after the integer.
NEWLINE	outputs a newline carriage control character. Does not affect the stack or anything else.
ENDPROG	causes program termination (i.e. causes control to be returned to the operating system).

2.7.3 An example of a multi-module SAL program

The following is a very simple example of a four-module SAL program that reads ten integers into an array that has base address ARX, sorts them by calling a bubblesort subroutine BUBSORT, and then prints them out. It is not necessary for the reader to see in detail how these modules work. The first module contains input and output routines:

```
    EXPORT HOWMANY
    IMPORT ARX, BUBSORT, STKBAS, INTREAD, INTWRITE, NEWLINE, ENDPROG
            LEA SP, STKBAS
            MOV CX, HOWMANY
            MOV DI, 0      ; initialize to read HOWMANY
    INLOOP:  CALL INTREAD  ; integers into array AX
            POP ARX[DI]
            INC DI         ; for next integer
            LOOP INLOOP
            LEA BP, ARX
            CALL BUBSORT   ; bubblesort array AX
            MOV CX, HOWMANY
            MOV DI, 0      ; initialize to output 10 integers
    OUTLOOP: PUSH ARX [DI] ; from array AX
            CALL INTWRITE
            CALL NEWLINE
```

```
            INC DI
            LOOP OUTLOOP
            CALL ENDPROG
HOWMANY:    DW 10
```

If the IMPORT declaration were omitted the assembler would report that BUBSORT, ARX, STKBAS, INTREAD, INTWRITE, NEWLINE and ENDPROG were unknown labels, because no line of this module starts with any of these labels. The IMPORT declaration tells the assembler which labels label lines in other modules. In our example the second module is

```
        EXPORT BUBSORT
        IMPORT STOPAT, HOWMANY
BUBSORT: MOV AX, HOWMANY
         DEC AX
         MOV STOPAT, AX
RLOOP:   MOV CX, 1    ; initialize last swap to 1
         MOV DI, 1
         MOV SI, 0
FLOOP:   MOV AX, [BP][DI]
         CMP AX, [BP][SI]
         JGE NOSWAP   ; no swap if elements in order
         MOV CX, DI   ; CX records subscript of last swap
         MOV BX, [BP][SI]
         MOV [BP][SI], AX  ; swapping array elements
         MOV [BP][DI], BX
NOSWAP:  INC DI
         INC SI
         CMP DI, STOPAT
         JL FLOOP
         DEC CX
         MOV STOPAT, CX
         CMP CX,1
         JG RLOOP
         RET
```

This starts with EXPORT BUBSORT which tells the assembler that BUBSORT is a label declared in this module and is possibly referred to in one or more other modules. IMPORT STOPAT, HOWMANY declares that this module refers to labels STOPAT and HOWMANY which do not label any line in this module. In our example the third module consists only of data:

```
        EXPORT STOPAT, ARX, STKBAS
ARX:    DW 10 DUP
STOPAT: DW ?
STKBAS: DW 8 DUP
```

The fourth and last module is `salSubs` which was introduced in Section 2.7.2. Its source text is:

```
EXPORT INTREAD, INTWRITE, NEWLINE, ENDPROG
INTREAD:  DW 513
INTWRITE: DW 514
NEWLINE:  DW 515
ENDPROG:  DW 516
```

In Section 6.3 we will see how these `DW`s are used.

2.8 SAL machine code

2.8.1 Machine code format

In SAL machine code a single instruction consists of one or two or three 16-bit words. The first word is called the *opWord*: it contains the opCode of the instruction, together with associated information. If the instruction has an immediate operand, such as 23 in `MOV BX,23` then the second word of machine code contains the 16-bit 2's complement value of this operand. If the instruction has a displacement then this is always the last word of the instruction. A displacement is either the 2's complement integer that is used in base addressing or the numeric address that corresponds to a label in direct addressing or indexed addressing.

In SAL machine code an opWord is usually subdivided into a number of fields. The fields of the least significant byte convey information about operands. For all categories of instructions, the format, that is, the subdivision into fields, of the least significant byte is the same. The format of the most significant byte of the opWord is the same in all instructions in the same category, but differs for different categories.

2.8.2 Format of least significant byte of the opWord

To show how a byte is subdivided into fields, we write a sequence of letters such as *aabbbccc* in which successive letters correspond to successive bits. Bits that have the same letter belong to the same field. For example, the sequence *aabbbccc* shows that the first two bits belong to the first field, the next three bits belong to the second field, and the last three bits belong to the third field.

The sequence *aabbbccc* indicates the format of the least significant byte of the opWord. The two bits labelled *a* constitute the m field and the meaning of these two bits in SAL machine code is as shown in Table 2.6. The three bits labelled *b* in *aabbbccc* constitute the `register` field and they select a register as shown in Table 2.7. The three bits labelled *c* constitute the `r/m` field, which specifies how the effective address is to be computed for memory access other than direct addressing. Bit patterns are shown in

Table 2.6   Encoding of the m field of the least significant byte of the opWord

m field	Meaning
00	displacement word is absent.
10	displacement word is present and is used with indexing.
01	direct addressing. Displacement word contains an operand address that is used without indexing.
11	the 3 bits of the r/m field identify a register, as in the register field.

Table 2.7 Encoding of register and r/m fields

register field		r/m field	
code	register	code	operand address
000	AX	000	(BX) + (SI)
001	CX	001	(BX) + (DI)
010	DX	010	(BP) + (SI)
011	BX	011	(BP) + (DI)
100	SP	100	(SI) + DISP
101	BP	101	(DI) + DISP
110	SI	110	(BP) + DISP
111	DI	111	(BX) + DISP

Table 2.7, where (BX) means *contents of* BX, (SI) means *contents of* SI, and so on. DISP is the displacement.

2.8.3 Format of the most significant byte of the opWord

Whereas the format and meaning of the least significant byte differ only slightly from 8086 machine code, the format of the most significant byte of the SAL machine code opWord differs drastically. The instruction category is indicated by some bits of the most significant byte, as shown in Table 2.8. The leftmost of these bits is always the most significant bit and is always 0.

Table 2.8. Indication of opCode category

Most sig. bits	Category
01	twoOperandInstructions
001	jumpInstructions
0001	singleOperandInstructions
00001	noOperandInstructions
000001	leaInstruction

Table 2.9 OpCodes. (a) `twoOperandInstructions`. (b) `singleOperandInstructions` (c) `jumpInstructions`

(a)		(b)		(c)	
OpCode	Instruction	OpCode	Instruction	OpCode	Instruction
000	MOV	000	DEC	00000	JMP
001	ADD	001	INC	01000	JE
010	SUB	011	NEG	01100	JG
011	CMP	100	MULT	01001	LOOP
100	AND	101	DIV	01010	JL
101	OR	110	PUSH	01011	JNE
		111	POP	01101	JLE
				01110	JGE
				01111	JC
				10000	CALL

For *twoOperandInstructions* the format of the most significant byte is *01aaabcd*, in which the bits labelled *a* consitute the opCode field as shown in Table 2.9(a). The bit labelled *b* is the *immediate* bit which is 1 if the instruction has an immediate operand, as in ADD AX, 6, and 0 otherwise. The bit labelled *c* is the *destination* bit which is 1 if the register specified by the *register* bits is the instruction's destination, and 0 otherwise. The bit labelled *d* is the *memRef* bit which is 1 if one of the instruction's operands is <memory>.

For `singleOperandInstructions` the format is *0001aaab*, where the bit labelled *b* is the *memRef* bit which is the same as in `twoOperandInstructions`. The bits labelled *a* constitute the opCode as shown in Table 2.9(b). Table 2.9(c) shows the opCodes for `jumpInstructions`, for which the format is *001aaaaa*, wherein the *a*s label the opCode field. For LEA, RET and NOP instructions the most significant byte is not partitioned into fields. Instead, the whole byte can be regarded as the instruction's opCode. For LEA, RET and NOP the opCodes are, respectively, 00000100, 00001000 and 00001111.

2.9 Relocatable and binary symbolic machine code

2.9.1 Relocation

When a program is executed its instructions are normally stored in (perhaps virtual) immediate access memory. At the same time immediate access memory normally contains a memory resident part of the operating system. Moreover, if there is multitasking or multiprogramming the immediate access memory may contain at least part of more than one user program at the same time.

To allow for sharing the immediate access memory with part of the operating system and possibly with other user programs, it is generally not practical to have a machine code program occupy a fixed sequence of successive addresses such as 0,1, ... Instead it may be expedient to have the first word of a machine code program at a different absolute address each time the program is executed. For example, on one occasion the first instruction might start at absolute address 256, with successive words of machine code at 257, 258, and so on. (In some systems, absolute addresses 0, ... , 255 are reserved for special purposes, and no user program ever has its first word of machine code at an address less than 256.)

If we simply store a machine code program produced by our assembler starting at a variable address we will generally find that it will not work correctly unless we amend the program appropriately. Suppose, for example, that the program

```
          JMP BEGIN
COUNT:    DW 0
NUMBER:   DW 365
BEGIN:    MOV BX, 1
          MOV DX, 0
          MOV AX, NUMBER
BLOOP:    MOV CX, AX
          AND CX, BX
          CMP CX, 0
          JE ZERO
          INC COUNT
ZERO:     ADD BX, BX
          CMP BX, 0
          JNE BLOOP
```

is assembled on the assumption that successive words of machine code will be located at addresses 0, 1, 2, ... Thus the numeric addresses corresponding to COUNT, NUMBER and BEGIN will be 2, 3, and 4, respectively. For example, the machine code corresponding to JMP BEGIN will be the same as machine code corresponding to JMP 4.

Suppose now that during execution this program is stored at absolute addresses 256, 257, 258, ... In this case, execution of JMP 4 would be disastrous, because address 4 is now outside the program. To correct this, the numeric addresses in the machine code program must be updated so that COUNT, NUMBER and BEGIN correspond to numeric addresses 256 + 2, 256 + 3 and 256 + 4. After this amendment, the instruction JMP BEGIN will correspond to JMP 260, which gives the required effect. Another example is that after this amendment, MOV AX, NUMBER will correspond to MOV AX, 259, which is now correct.

Correction is achieved by adding the address of the first word of machine code to every numeric address that the program refers to. This process of correction is called *relocation*, and the address of the first word of machine code is called the *relocating constant*. Thus to achieve relocation we simply add the relocating constant to every numeric address that is held in the displacement word of an instruction. (Relative addresses do not require relocation, but SAL does not have relative addressing. All jumps in SAL are to absolute addresses).

2.9.2 Relocatable binary machine code

If an assembler simply outputs SAL machine code, this consists of a sequence of 16-bit words. By looking at these words, it is not possible to tell which of them contain *relocatable addresses*, that is, addresses to which the relocating constant should be added to achieve relocation. *Absolute binary* machine code is machine code that is not accompanied by an indication as to which words contain relocatable addresses. Absolute binary machine code can only be executed if it is stored in memory at successive addresses such that the numeric addresses to which it refers are already correct. For an absolute binary machine code program there is exactly one address that is correct for the first word of the program, and this cannot be changed.

If we wish to run the same machine code program on different occasions with the first word of the program at a different address each time, then this program will have to be relocated prior to execution. To make relocation possible, we associate with the program an indication as to which words contain relocatable addresses. One way of doing this is to use an array of bits, called a *bit map*, in which there is one bit corresponding to each word of machine code. If a word of machine code contains a relocatable address then the corresponding bit in the bit map is 1. Otherwise the corresponding bit in the bit map is 0. In examples in Section 2.9.3 each 16-bit machine code word is followed by the corresponding bit-map bit.

Machine code that is accompanied by a bit map, or by some other means of indicating which words contain relocatable addresses, is called *relocatable binary* machine code. Usually references to numeric addresses within a relocatable binary machine code program are as if the successive words of the program are to be located at 0, 1, 2, ... prior to relocation. As we have already explained, relocation enables the program to work correctly when the first word is located at some address other than zero.

If the machine code program is stored in an array `machineCode` of 16-bit words, absolute binary machine code can be produced by a relocating routine:

```
FOR numericAddress:= 0 TO non-relocated address of last word DO
 IF bitMap[numericAddress] = 1 THEN
  INC (machineCode[numericAddress], relocatingConstant)
 END
END
```

Here `relocatingConstant` is the numeric address of the first word of the module's machine code after relocation.

2.9.3 Binary symbolic machine code

Relocatable binary machine code does not contain explicit information about external references, that is, about labels that are exported and imported by different modules. If we wish the assembler to produce some kind of machine code for each module that can be linked together with machine code for other modules without reassembly, then this must not only be relocatable, but also contain information about external references. Machine code that consists of relocatable binary plus adequate information about external references is called *binary symbolic* machine code.

For a SAL module, binary symbolic machine code consists of relocatable binary machine code preceded by extra information in a standard format. The assembler assembles each module as if, prior to relocation, successive words of machine code will be stored at successive addresses 0,1,2, ...

The first character in a SAL binary symbolic module is 'N'. This is followed by a cardinal that is the total number of words of machine code program in this module. This cardinal is followed by end-of-line. The first character on the next line is 'E'. This is followed by a cardinal that is the total number of entries in the export table. If this cardinal is non-zero, then the following lines contain the entries in the export table, one entry per line. Each entry consists of a label, which is a text string, followed by a cardinal, which is the non-relocated numeric address corresponding to this exported label. The format of the import table is similar to that of the export table, except that it starts with 'I' instead of E. The import table (if any) is followed by the relocatable binary machine code program. For the first module of the four-module program in Section 2.7.3 the binary symbolic machine code is:

```
N  33        (* 33 words in this module *)
E  1         (* export table has one entry *)
HOWMANY  32  (* address of HOWMANY is 32 *)
I  9         (* 9 words in the import table *)
STKBAS  1    (* word 1 should contain address STKBAS *)
INTREAD  7   (* word 7 should contain address INTREAD *)
ARX  9       (* word 9 should contain address ARX *)
ARX  14      (* word 14 should contain address ARX *)
BUBSORT  16  (* word 16 should contain address BUBSORT *)
ARX  22      (* word 22 should contain address ARX *)
INTWRITE  24 (* word 24 should contain address INTWRITE *)
NEWLINE  26  (* word 26 should contain address NEWLINE *)
ENDPROG  31  (* word 31 should contain address ENDPROG *)
0000010001100000 0 (* 0 *)
0000000000000000 1 (* 1 *)
0100001101001000 0 (* 2 *)
0000000000100000 1 (* 3 *)
0100011000111000 0 (* 4 *)
0000000000000000 0 (* 5 *)
```

```
0011000001000000 0 (*  6 *)
0000000000000000 1 (*  7 *)
0001111110000101 0 (*  8 *)
0000000000000000 1 (*  9 *)
0001001000111000 0 (* 10 *)
0010100101000000 0 (* 11 *)
0000000000000110 1 (* 12 *)
0000010001101000 0 (* 13 *)
0000000000000000 1 (* 14 *)
0011000001000000 0 (* 15 *)
0000000000000000 1 (* 16 *)
0100001101001000 0 (* 17 *)
0000000000100000 1 (* 18 *)
0100011000111000 0 (* 19 *)
0000000000000000 0 (* 20 *)
0001110110000101 0 (* 21 *)
0000000000000000 1 (* 22 *)
0011000001000000 0 (* 23 *)
0000000000000000 1 (* 24 *)
0011000001000000 0 (* 25 *)
0000000000000000 1 (* 26 *)
0001001000111000 0 (* 27 *)
0010100101000000 0 (* 28 *)
0000000000010101 1 (* 29 *)
0011000001000000 0 (* 30 *)
0000000000000000 1 (* 31 *)
0000000000001010 0 (* 32 *)
```

In this the text within (* and *) is not part of the binary symbolic output of the assembler, but is comment intended to facilitate understanding. Each word of machine code is followed by its bit-map bit and then by its numeric address between (* and *).

For the second module of the same program the binary symbolic is:

```
N    32
E    1
BUBSORT   0
I    4
HOWMANY   1
STOPAT    4
STOPAT    22
STOPAT    26
0100001101000000 0 (* 0 *)
0000000000000000 1 (* 1 *)
0001000000000000 0 (* 2 *)
0100000101000000 0 (* 3 *)
```

```
0000000000000000 1 (* 4 *)
0100011000001000 0 (* 5 *)
0000000000000000 0 (* 6 *)
0100011000111000 0 (* 7 *)
0000000000000001 0 (* 8 *)
0100011000110000 0 (* 9 *)
0000000000000000 0 (* 10 *)
0100001100000011 0 (* 11 *)
0101101100000010 0 (* 12 *)
0010111001000000 0 (* 13 *)
0000000000010011 1 (* 14 *)
0100001011001110 0 (* 15 *)
0100001100011010 0 (* 16 *)
0100000100000010 0 (* 17 *)
0100000100011011 0 (* 18 *)
0001001000111000 0 (* 19 *)
0001001000110000 0 (* 20 *)
0101101101111000 0 (* 21 *)
0000000000000000 1 (* 22 *)
0010110101000000 0 (* 23 *)
0000000000001011 1 (* 24 *)
0100000101001000 0 (* 25 *)
0000000000000000 1 (* 26 *)
0101111000001000 0 (* 27 *)
0000000000000000 0 (* 28 *)
0010110001000000 0 (* 29 *)
0000000000000101 1 (* 30 *)
0000100000000000 0 (* 31 *)
```

In this the export table has one entry which says that BUBSORT is word 0 of this module.

For the third module all the machine code words are 0, and we will not show this fully. The binary symbolic for the third module starts:

```
N   19
E   3
STKBAS  11
ARX     0
STOPAT  10
I       0
0000000000000000 0
0000000000000000 0
0000000000000000 0

   . . .
```

The first entry in the export table says that STKBAS is address 11 of the module. The second and third entries in the export table say that ARX and STOPAT are, respectively, addresses 0 and 10 of this module.

For the fourth module, which provides the system calls, the binary symbolic is:

```
N   4
E   4
ENDPROG    3
NEWLINE    2
INTWRITE   1
INTREAD    0
I   0
0000001000000001 0
0000001000000010 0
0000001000000011 0
0000001000000100 0
```

2.10 Exercises

1. The SAL fragment

    ```
          MOV AX, X
          CMP AX, Y
          JGE LA
          INC P
          MOV AX, R
          ADD Q, AX
          JMP LB
    LA:   DEC P
    LB:   NOP
    ```

    corresponds to the following fragment in Modula-2:

    ```
    IF  X < Y THEN
         P:= P + 1; Q:= Q + R
    ELSE P:= P - 1
    END
    ```

    Similarly, write Modula-2 fragments corresponding to each of the following SAL fragments. In your Modula-2 fragments the only variables are to be P, Q, R, X and Y: register contents are not to be shown.

    (a)

    ```
          LA:     MOV     AX, X
                  CMP     AX, Y
                  JGE     LB
                  MOV     AX, R
                  ADD     Q, AX
                  JMP     LA
          LB:     NOP
    ```

(b)

```
            MOV     AX, X
            CMP     AX, Y
            JL      LA
            DEC     P
            JMP     LB
    LA:     INC     P
            MOV     AX, R
            ADD     Q, AX
    LB:     NOP
```

(c)

```
    LA:     MOV     AX, R
            ADD     Q, AX
            INC     Y
            MOV     AX, X
            CMP     AX, Y
            JL      LA
```

(d)

```
            MOV X, 1
    LA:     MOV AX, X
            CMP X, Y
            JG LB
            MOV AX, R
            ADD Q, AX
            INC X
            JMP LA
    LB:     NOP
```

(e)

```
            JMP LA
    LB:     DW LC
            DW LD
            DW LE
    LA:     MOV DI, X
            MOV BX, LB[DI]
            JMP [BX]
    LC:     INC P
            JMP LF
    LD:     INC Q
            INC Y
            JMP LF
    LE:     INC Y
    LF:     NOP
```

2. Given that the numeric address corresponding to symbolic address FRED is binary
    00000000 01000100, write the binary SAL machine code instructions that
    correspond to each of the following SAL instructions:

    (a) ADD BX, 33
    (b) SUB CX, DX
    (c) AND FRED, AX
    (d) OR [SI], BX
    (e) INC [BP][SI]
    (f) DEC [BX - 2]
    (g) JC [SI]
    (h) LEA BX, FRED[SI]
    (i) MOV FRED[DI], 33

Chapter 3

Lexical analysis

3.1 Introduction

We will assume that a source program will be read from a file as a stream of characters. It is easier to write an assembler or a compiler if the source program is first translated from a stream of characters into a stream of symbols. This translation is known as *lexical analysis*. A program that performs lexical analysis is called a *lexical analyzer* or, alternatively, a *scanner*.

For present purposes, a *symbol* is any sequence of characters excluding space, tab and newline characters. Moreover, a *symbol class* is a class of symbols of the same kind. For our assembler all labels are symbols that belong to the same class, which we call labelSy, which stands for *label symbol*. Another example is that all opCodes, such as ADD and MOV, are symbols that belong to the symbol class opCodeSy. Yet another example is that all register names, such as AX and SP, are symbols that belong to the symbol class registerSy. The only numbers that our assembler recognizes are decimal integers, and these all belong to the same class numberSy.

For our assembler, each punctuation character belongs to a separate symbol class. For example, a ',' belongs to the class commaSy, which is a singleton class containing only the comma symbol. Another example is the '?' which belongs to the singleton class questionSy.

The output of a lexical analyzer is actually a stream of symbol class names, together with associated information, which is most easily understood by considering examples. Before giving an example, we introduce the mechanism by which our lexical analyzer delivers its output to the assembler or compiler.

Exporting global variables from a module is usually regarded as bad practice. Nevertheless, our lexical analyzer follows the tradition of exporting its output via three global variables, which we name sy, ind and val. For our assembler the variable sy is of type symbolType which is declared in a separate module:

```
DEFINITION MODULE symbType;
TYPE
  symbolType = (opCodeSy, registerSy, labelSy, numberSy, leftSqBrktSy,
                rightSqBrktSy, commaSy, questionSy, colonSy, plussOp, minusOp,
                dupSy, importSy, exportSy, newLineSy, endOfTextSy);
END symbType.
```

27

The values of `symbolType` are names of symbol classes for SAL. The ideas involved in lexical analyis for SAL will, after a little modification and development, be useful to us in writing a compiler for a subset of Modula-2, but we will have to redeclare `symbolType` and renegotiate `val`. For SAL, `ind` and `val` are of type CARDINAL. When `sy = numberSy`, `val` is the magnitude of the number. A plus or minus sign that precedes a number is regarded as a separate symbol. When `sy` is not equal to `numberSy`, `val` is undefined, or simply retains its previous value which is ignored.

When `sy = labelSy`, `ind` has a value that distinguishes this particular label from all others being processed. Similarly when `sy = registerSy` the value of `ind` distinguishes this particular register from all others. Another example is that when `sy = opCodeSy` the value of `ind` distinguishes this particular opCode from all others. When `sy` is the name of a singleton class, and also when `sy = numberSy`, `ind` is undefined, or simply retains its previous value which is ignored.

For example, our lexical analyzer reads the SAL fragment

```
        IMPORT INTREAD, INTWRITE, NEWLINE, ENDPROG
                JMP START
ARX:            DW 10 DUP
START:          MOV CX, 10
                MOV DI, 0
INLOOP:         CALL INTREAD
                POP ARX[DI]
                INC DI
                LOOP INLOOP
```

from the source file as a stream of characters starting with a sequence of space characters, then 'I', then 'M', then 'P', and so on. The corresponding output of the lexical analyzer, i.e. successive values of `sy`, `ind` and `val` are shown in Table 3.1.

Table 3.1 Example showing lexical analyzer input and output

Input	sy	ind	val
IMPORT	importSy		
INTREAD	labelSy	0	
,	commaSy		
INTWRITE	labelSy	1	
,	commaSy		
NEWLINE	labelSy	2	
,	commaSy		
ENDPROG	labelSy	3	
	newLineSy		
JMP	opCodeSy	13	
START	labelSy	4	
	newLineSy		
ARX	labelSy	5	

:	colonSy		
DW	opCodeSy	26	
10	numberSy		10
DUP	dupSy		
	newLineSy		
START	labelSy	4	
:	colonSy		
MOV	opCodeSy	0	
CX	registerSy	1	
,	commaSy		
10	numberSy		10
	newLineSy		
MOV	opCodeSy	0	
DI	registerSy	7	
,	commaSy		
0	numberSy		0
	newLineSy		
INLOOP	labelSy	6	
:	colonSy		
CALL	opCodeSy	21	
INTREAD	labelSy	0	
	newLineSy		
POP	opCodeSy	12	
ARX	labelSy	5	
[	leftSqBrktSy		
DI	registerSy	7	
]	rightSqBrktSy		
	newLineSy		
INC	opCodeSy	7	
DI	registerSy	7	
	newLineSy		
LOOP	opCodeSy	24	
INLOOP	labelSy	6	
	newLineSy		
	endOfTextSy		

Although successive values of `sy` constitute a sequence of names of symbol classes, we will follow the tradition of regarding this sequence simply as a stream of symbols. Values of `val` and `ind` are regarded as attributes of symbols.

3.2 Looking up strings of letters

One of the tasks of a lexical analyzer is to translate a string of letters such as `JMP` or `START` into appropriate values of `sy` and `ind`. This can be done by looking up a string of letters in a table, called the *string table*, of which Table 3.2 is a simple example, where dots indicate parts that have been omitted. Our lexical analyzer calls a procedure `searchStringTable` to look up a string of letters in the string table. If the string is found in the table, `searchStringTable` assigns the corresponding values to `sy` and `ind`. For example, if the input string of letters is 'DI' then `searchStringTable` looks up 'DI' in this table and assigns `sy:= registerSy` and `ind:= 7`.

Table 3.2 Incomplete example of a simple string table

Text string	sy	ind
MOV	opCodeSy	0
ADD	opCodeSy	1
SUB	opCodeSy	2
CMP	opCodeSy	3
.	.	.
.	.	.
DW	opCodeSy	26
AX	registerSy	0
BX	registerSy	3
.	.	.
.	.	.
DI	registerSy	7
DUP	dupSy	0
IMPORT	importSy	0
EXPORT	exportSy	0
INTREAD	labelSy	0
INTWRITE	labelSy	1
NEWLINE	labelSy	2
.	.	.

For SAL, if the lexical analyzer looks up a string of letters in the string table and finds it absent, then the string is assumed to be a label. The lexical analyzer calls a procedure `insertString` which enters this new string into the string table with `sy = labelSy` and `ind = nextInd`. `nextInd` is a variable that is now incremented so that successive labels entered in this way have successive `ind` values 0, 1, 2, 3, ...

Our string table is encapsulated within a module `strinTbl` and the reader need not be concerned with the internal workings, which are introduced in Section 3.4 and are more elaborate than Table 3.2 may suggest. This module contains the string table data structure and exports the procedures `searchStringTable` and `insertString`. As can be seen from the definition module, `strinTbl` also exports procedures `stringText`, `outputName` and `nameIs`, which will be useful for dealing with imports and exports:

```
DEFINITION MODULE strinTbl;
FROM symbType IMPORT symbolType;
CONST
    stringUB = 23;
TYPE
    stringType = ARRAY [0..stringUB] OF CHAR;
    stringRec = RECORD
                    initialChar: CHAR;
                    stringStart, stringLength: CARDINAL
                END;
VAR
    stringInfo: stringRec;
PROCEDURE searchStringTable (inString: stringType;
    length: CARDINAL; VAR symbol: symbolType;
    VAR ind: CARDINAL; VAR found: BOOLEAN);
PROCEDURE insertString (inString: stringType;
    length: CARDINAL; symbol: symbolType; ind: CARDINAL);
PROCEDURE stringText (idString: stringRec);
    (* outputs a string specified by the parameter *)
PROCEDURE outputName;
    (* outputs the current string *)
PROCEDURE nameIs(VAR name: stringType; VAR length: CARDINAL);
    (* returns a string via the first parameter *)
PROCEDURE enter(str: ARRAY OF CHAR; symbol: symbolType; ind: CARDINAL);
    (* same as insertString except that length is not given *)
END strinTbl.
```

The exported procedure `enter`, which is used during initialization of the string table, enters a string and its associated `sy` and `ind` values into the string table. Initialization of the string table is accomplished by a separate module `alexInit`: this is separate so that we can later reuse module `strinTbl` with different initialization. Module `alexInit` is listed in the Appendix.

3.3 Procedure inSymbol

Module `assLex`, which is the main module of our lexical analyzer, includes a procedure `inSymbol` that is called by the assembler when the next assignment to `sy` is required. If the first character of the next symbol is a letter then `inSymbol` calls a procedure `inText` that reads a string of letters from the source file into an array `inString` and looks this up in the string table using procedure `searchStringTable`. Another possibility is that the first character of the next symbol is a digit: in this case `inSymbol` calls a procedure `inNumber` to read a string of digits and convert them to a value of the global variable `val`. Yet another possibility is that the first character of the next symbol is neither a letter nor a digit, but is '[', or some such character: in this case the appropriate assignment to sy is made by a CASE statement. Procedure inSymbol is one of three procedures exported from module assLex:

```
DEFINITION MODULE assLex;
FROM symbType IMPORT symbolType;
VAR
   sy: symbolType;
   ind, val: CARDINAL;

PROCEDURE error(errNo: CARDINAL);
PROCEDURE inSymbol;
PROCEDURE accept(sym: symbolType);
END assLex.
```

When required, procedure error is called to output a brief error message that includes the source-code line number. Procedure accept is called to check the current symbol: if the parameter of accept matches the current value of sy then accept calls inSymbol. Otherwise something is wrong and procedure accept accordingly calls procedure error.

Module assLex has a global variable ch that contains the next character of the input source text stream. Procedure skipToNextSymbol skips spaces and comments leaving ch containing the first character of the next symbol. The implementation module is:

```
IMPLEMENTATION MODULE assLex;
FROM InOut IMPORT Read, Write, WriteString, WriteCard, WriteLn,
        ReadCard, RedirectInput;
FROM symbType IMPORT symbolType;
FROM strinTbl IMPORT searchStringTable, insertString, stringType;
FROM alexInit IMPORT lexInitialise;
CONST
   endOfLine = 36C; endOfFile = 32C;
TYPE
   charSet = SET OF CHAR;
VAR
   ch: CHAR; nextInd, lineNumber: CARDINAL;
PROCEDURE error(errNo: CARDINAL);
BEGIN
   WriteString('error no: '); WriteCard(errNo,5);
   WriteString(' at line no: '); WriteCard(lineNumber, 4); WriteLn
END error;

PROCEDURE skipToNextSymbol;

BEGIN
   WHILE ch = ' ' DO Read(ch) END; (* skip spaces *)
```

```
  IF ch = ';' THEN (* skip comment *)
    REPEAT
      Read(ch)
    UNTIL (ch = endOfLine) OR (ch = endOfFile)
  END;
END skipToNextSymbol;

PROCEDURE inSymbol;
  PROCEDURE inNumber;
  VAR
    i, tenTimes: CARDINAL;
  BEGIN
    sy:= numberSy; val:= 0;
    LOOP
      i:= ORD (ch) - ORD ('0'); tenTimes:= val * 10;
      IF tenTimes <= MAX(CARDINAL) - i THEN
        val:= tenTimes + i
      ELSE error(1); EXIT
      END; Read(ch);
      IF NOT (ch IN charSet{'0'..'9'}) THEN EXIT END
    END
  END inNumber;

    PROCEDURE inText;
    VAR
      length: CARDINAL; found: BOOLEAN;
      inString: stringType;
    BEGIN
        length:= 0;
        REPEAT
          inString[length]:= ch;
          INC (length); Read(ch)
        UNTIL NOT (ch IN charSet{'A'..'Z'});
        searchStringTable (inString, length, sy, ind, found);
        IF NOT found THEN
          insertString (inString, length, labelSy, nextInd);
          sy:= labelSy; ind:= nextInd;
          INC(nextInd)
        END
    END inText;

BEGIN (* body of procedure inSymbol *)
    CASE ch OF
      '0'..'9': inNumber |
      'A'..'Z': inText |
        '[': sy:= leftSqBrktSy; Read(ch) |
```

```
            ']': sy:= rightSqBrktSy; Read(ch) |
            ',': sy:= commaSy;   Read(ch) |
            '?': sy:= questionSy; Read(ch) |
            ':': sy:= colonSy;   Read(ch) |
            '+': sy:= plussOp;   Read(ch) |
            '-': sy:= minusOp;   Read(ch) |
        endOfLine: sy:= newLineSy; INC (lineNumber); Read(ch) |
        endOfFile: sy:= endOfTextSy
      ELSE error(3);
      END;
      skipToNextSymbol
  END inSymbol;

  PROCEDURE accept (sym: symbolType);
  BEGIN
    IF sy = sym THEN inSymbol ELSE
      error(4); WriteString(' wanted '); WriteCard(ORD(sym),4);
      WriteString(' but got '); WriteCard(ORD(sy),4)
    END
  END accept;

  BEGIN
    lexInitialise; nextInd:= 4; lineNumber:= 1;
    RedirectInput('salAssin'); Read(ch); skipToNextSymbol
  END assLex.
```

It is important that (unless the end of the file has been reached) procedure inSymbol makes an assignment to sy and then calls skipToNextSymbol which ensures that ch contains the first character of the next symbol. Thus while the assembler is working with a particular value of sy, ch contains the *next* character that will be input to inSymbol. This way of working is called *one-character look-ahead*. The body of module assLex initializes this by reading a character and calling skipToNextSymbol before inSymbol has been called by the assembler.

Within procedure inSymbol, procedure inNumber reads successive digits of a number and assigns the corresponding CARDINAL value to val. If the number becomes too big to be assigned to val, procedure inNumber calls error to report this. Different values of the parameter of procedure error distinguish between different errors.

In procedure inText the REPEAT loop builds up a string in a local string variable. For SAL a string is terminated by any non-alphabetic character. If procedure searchStringTable does not find the string in the string table, procedure inText calls procedure insertString to make a new entry in the string table, assuming that the string must be a label.

The lexical analyzer reports errors in individual symbols but is not responsible for detecting syntax errors such as omission of the comma in MOV SI, 1. For example, lower-case letters 'a', ... , 'z' are illegal in SAL and assLex reports their occurrence as an error, with error number 3.

3.4 Implementation of the string table

In Section 3.2 we introduced a simple string table that requires development in several respects. One of these is that strings of characters such as AX and INTREAD are not all of the same length. If we make each entry in the table a record that stores one of these character strings in a field that is an array, this array must have enough elements for the longest string. For short strings, a number of these elements will be unused and therefore wasted.

To avoid this waste of memory space, we store all the strings in a single array named charArray. For our example the first few elements of charArray would contain MOVANDSUBCMPANDORDECINC..., which consists of strings MOV, AND, SUB, ... , simply placed end to end. Using this idea, the first few entries in the main string table are as shown in Table 3.3. For example, the second entry in this table says that the character string that starts at charArray[4] is three characters long and is an opCodeSy that has ind = 1. The next entry says that the character string that starts at charArray[7] is three characters long and is an opCodeSy that has ind = 2, and so on.

Table 3.3. A few entries in a string table that has an auxilliary array of characters

Start	Length	sy	ind
1	3	opCodeSy	0
4	3	opCodeSy	1
7	3	opCodeSy	2
10	3	opCodeSy	3
.	.	.	.
.	.	.	.

Given a string, such as CMP, the lexical analyzer could easily look it up in this table by linear search. The time taken for this look-up would on average be proportional to the number of entries in the table, and this would be too slow if the number of entries were large. To make the look-up faster, we reorganize the string table as a chained hash table that is an array of 52 pointers, one corresponding to each letter 'A', ... , 'Z', 'a', ... , 'z'. Lower-case letters are not required for SAL but we will use the same implementation of module strinTbl for a subset of Modula-2. We simply use the first character of a string as the hash function value, yielding a subscript for this array of pointers. This is generally a very poor hash function, and we compensate by having each pointer in the array point to a binary search tree, instead of a linked list, providing access to all the strings that have the same initial letter. By working with an array of trees instead of a single tree we hedge against the risk that a single tree might turn out to be very unbalanced. A minor advantage of using the initial letter as the hash function value is that we need not store the initial letter in the array charArray.

The implementation module `strinTbl` is listed in the Appendix. The details can be skipped because understanding the inner workings of this module is not a precondition for understanding anything else, and other implementations might be just as good or better.

3.5 Discussion

In the design of a substantial software system it is good practice to delegate appropriate tasks to separate encapsulated subsystems so as to reduce the complexity of the remaining central part of the system. An assembler or a compiler delegates to a lexical analyzer tasks such as the skipping of spaces and comments, the handling of individual characters within a string and the processing of individual digits within a number. Without this delegation an assembler or compiler would be unnecessarily complex and obscure.

When used with a SAL assembler, our four lexical analyzer modules `symbType`, `strinTbl`, `alexInit` and `assLex` are linked together with the modules of the assembler. Assembler modules import `sy`, `ind`, `val` and `inSymbol` from `assLex`, so as to be able to obtain successive symbols of the symbol stream. Our lexical analyzer works while, not before, the assembler translates the source program. The next value is assigned to `sy` when, not before, `inSymbol` is called.

An alternative way of working is to have the lexical analyzer output the entire symbol stream to a file. After completion of lexical analysis, an assembler or compiler obtains the source symbol stream from this file. Lexical analysis now constitutes a first pass through the data, and the lexical analyzer is a program that is itself separate from the assembler or compiler program: lexical analyzer modules are not linked with assembler or compiler modules. When working with limited memory, an advantage of doing lexical analysis in a first pass is that the string table can be destroyed at the end of this pass, and the lexical analyzer program can be removed from memory, so that more memory is available for subsequent passes of the assembler or compiler.

In this chapter we have have introduced a hand-crafted lexical analyzer without any supporting theory. Textbooks such as those by Bennett (1990) and Holub (1990) introduce theory that is the basis for producing software which automatically writes a lexical analyzer, given a full specification of the required functionality. This can be useful as well as demonstrating command of underlying theory that is beyond the scope of the present book.

3.6 Exercises

1. For the source text fragment

    ```
            JMP START
    ARX:    DW 10 DUP
    START:  MOV CX, 10
    ```

    write down the value of `ch` at each successive call of `inSymbol`.

2. For the source text

```
            MOV BX, 1;          initialize outer loop
   OUTERL:  MOV SI, 1
            MOV CX, 20;         initialize inner loop
            MOV DI, BX
   INNERL:  MOV AX, THAT[BX][SI]
            MOV BP, SI
            MOV THIS [BP][DI], AX; this[SI,BX]:= that[BX,SI]
            INC SI
            LOOP INNERL
            INC BX
            CMP BX,30
            JLE OUTERL
            CALL ENDPROG
   THIS:    DW 600 DUP
   THAT:    DW 600 DUP
```

write down the ouput of the lexical analyzer, in the form of a table as in Section 3.1, working by hand, and assuming that OUTERL will have ind = 4.

3. For the source text fragment

```
            MOVBX, 1;           initialize outer loop
   OUTERL;  MOV 1, SI
            MOV CX20;           initialize inner loop
            MOV DI BX
   INN3RL:  MOV AX, THAT[BX],[SI]
            MOV BP, 2, SI
            MOV THIS [BP][DI], AX this[SI,BX]:= that[BX,SI]
            INC SI 1
            LOOP INNIRL
```

write down the ouput of the lexical analyzer, working by hand, and assuming that OUTERL will have ind = 4.

Chapter 4

An assembler

4.1 Introduction

4.1.1 Translation of labels and intructions

The term *assembler* is sometimes used to mean an assembly language and is sometimes used instead to mean a program that translates from an assembly language to machine code. This book uses the term in the latter sense. Like a compiler, but at a more primitive level, an assembler translates from a programmer-oriented source language to a machine-oriented object language.

This chapter introduces an assembler that works line by line through a SAL source program, producing corresponding machine code instructions as it goes along. The output is binary symbolic machine code which can be linked by the linker that will be introduced in Chapter 5. The assembler's translation of a single instruction involves translating labels into corresponding numeric addresses, translating mnemonic opCodes such as ADD into binary opCodes, and assigning appropriate values to other fields of machine code opWords. Our assembler comprises the following modules:

machCode	in which the output machine code is built up;
labels	which contains a table used for translating labels into numeric addresses, along with associated procedures and the wherewithal for dealing with external references;
instrns	which translates individual instructions;
salAssem	which is the main module of the assembler and has overall control.

Lexical analyzer modules symbType, strinTbl, alexInit and assLex are linked together with these to make up the complete assembler. This chapter introduces the assembler modules in turn, with frequent reference to an example program that is introduced in Section 4.1.2.

4.1.2 Simple example of an assembled program

A SAL machine code program is a sequence of 16-bit words. Our SAL assembler builds up this sequence in an array machineCode: ARRAY [0..machineCodeUB] OF CARDINAL.

Although each element of this array is a Modula-2 CARDINAL, it is physically a pattern of 16 bits, and this is how we think of it. The upper bound of the `machineCode` array is `machineCodeUB`, in which the last letters UB stand for *upper bound*. Our assembler simply will not be able to assemble a machine code program that has more than `machineCodeUB` 16-bit words in it. (Later we will be working with various other arrays, and we will normally use the array name, or an abbreviation for it, with UB appended to indicate an arbitrary upper bound for the array.)

There is a one-to-one correspondence between words in our array `machineCode` and words of machine code in the memory of a computer that executes this machine code. Thus there is a one-to-one correspondence between subscripts of words in `machineCode` and addresses of words containing machine code instructions when the machine code program is executed. For introductory simplicity we will start by regarding the subscript of a machine code word in `machineCode` as the same as the address of this machine code word in memory when the machine code program is executed. Later we will consider relocation.

We use the Modula-2 CARDINAL variable `numericAddress` as the subscript of array `machineCode`. As was explained in Chapter 2, a machine code instruction may consist of one, two, or three 16-bit words. Table 4.1 shows a complete example, in which SAL instructions appear alongside corresponding machine code instructions in relocatable binary.

In Table 4.1, the opWord for `LEA SP, STKBAS` is in `machineCode[0]`, and this instruction's displacement is in `machineCode[1]`. The opWord for `CALL INTREAD` is in `machineCode[2]`, and this instruction's displacement will go into `machineCode[3]`. The opWord for `POP AX` is in `machineCode[4]`, and because `POP AX` does not have a displacement, the opWord for `CMP AX, 0` is in `machineCode [5]`. The bit map has a 1 corresponding to each relocatable address, and zeros corresponding to all other words of machine code.

4.2 Machine code module

Our assembler keeps the array `machineCode` encapsulated in a module named `machCode`, in which a global variable `numericAddress` is the address where the next word of machine code will be inserted. The definition module is:

```
DEFINITION MODULE machCode;
CONST
   machineCodeUB = 3000;
TYPE
   bit = [0..1];
   machineCodeRange = [0..machineCodeUB];
VAR
   numericAddress: machineCodeRange;
```

```
PROCEDURE incAddressBy (amount: CARDINAL);
  (* INC(numericAddress, amount)   *)

PROCEDURE enter(aWord: CARDINAL; b: bit);
  (* machineCode[numericAddress]:= aWord;
     bitMap[numericAddress]:= b; INC(numericAddress) *)

PROCEDURE enterAt(whatAddress: machineCodeRange; aWord: CARDINAL);
  (* machineCode[whatAddress]:= aWord *)

PROCEDURE backPatch(refAddress, displacement: CARDINAL);
  (* fills in forward references as explained below in the text *)

PROCEDURE putMachineCode;
  (* output contents of array machineCode *)
END machCode.
```

The implementation module is listed in the Appendix.

Table 4.1 Relocatable binary machine code corresponding to a SAL program

		machineCode[numericAddress]	bit map	numericAddress
IMPORT	INTREAD, INTWRITE, ENDPROG			
	LEA SP, STKBAS	0000010001100000	0	0
		0000000000011000	1	1
MLOOP:	CALL INTREAD	0011000001000000	0	2
		0000000000000000	1	3
	POP AX	0001111000000000	0	4
	CMP AX, 0	0101111000000000	0	5
		0000000000000000	0	6
	JE LSTOP	0010100001000000	0	7
		0000000000010001	1	8
	CMP AX, MAX	0101101101000000	0	9
		0000000000010111	1	10
	JLE MLOOP	0010110101000000	0	11
		0000000000000010	1	12
	MOV MAX, AX	0100000101000000	0	13
		0000000000010111	1	14
	JMP MLOOP	0010000001000000	0	15
		0000000000000010	1	16
LSTOP:	PUSH MAX	0001110101000000	0	17
		0000000000010111	1	18
	CALL INTWRITE	0011000001000000	0	19
		0000000000000000	1	20
	CALL ENDPROG	0011000001000000	0	21
		0000000000000000	1	22
MAX:	DW 0	0000000000000000	0	23
STKBAS:	DW 15 DUP	0000000000000000	0	24
		and succesive words all 0s up to		
		0000000000000000	0	38

4.3 Translation of labels

4.3.1 The label table

LEA SP, STKBAS means 'assign to SP the address of the word whose label is STKBAS'. In the example in Table 4.1, the word labelled STKBAS is at numericAddress 24, so the assembler translates LEA SP, STKBAS into a machine code instruction that means 'assign to SP the address 24'. This address, which is 011000 in binary, goes into machineCode[1]. Thus the assembler has translated STKBAS into 24. This translation is necessary because there are no labels in machine code: instead, when a program is executed, the CPU works only with numeric addresses. As another example, JMP MLOOP is translated into the machine code for 'jump to the instruction whose address is 2'. In this case, label MLOOP is translated into addess 2 because the word labelled MLOOP is at numericAddress 2. Accordingly in Table 4.1 machineCode[12] contains the binary equivalent of decimal 2.

The assembler translates a label into an address by reference to a table called the *label table*, which in our assembler is a one-dimensional array of records of type

```
labelTableRecord = RECORD
                      status: labelStatus;
                      address: CARDINAL
                   END
```

where

```
labelStatus = (notSeen, referenced, declared, imported)
```

The values of labelStatus are explained in Table 4.2. For each label the lexical analyser yields a unique ind value, and the assembler uses this to identify a label's entry in the label table. LabelTable[ind].address is eventually the address of the word that is labelled with the label whose ind value is ind.

Before starting to process the source code, entering numeric addresses into the label table, the assembler initializes all records in the table to have status = notSeen and address = endMarker. The use of endMarker will be explained later.

Table 4.2 Values of labelStatus

labelStatus	Meaning
notSeen	The label has not yet been encountered by the assembler.
referenced	The label has been referenced but a line labelled with this label has not yet been encountered.
declared	A line labelled with this label has been encountered.
imported	The label was included in the IMPORT list.

Numeric addresses are entered into the label table while the assembler processes the source program line by line. If the first sy on a line is labelSy, as it would be, for example, for the line

```
LSTOP:   PUSH MAX
```

then the assembler calls a procedure labelColon:

```
PROCEDURE labelColon;
BEGIN
  CASE labelTable[ind].status OF
    declared, imported: error(5) | (* duplicate label *)
    notSeen:    WITH labelTable[ind] DO
                   address:= numericAddress; status:= declared
                END |
     referenced: backPatch(labelTable[ind].address, numericAddress);
                WITH labelTable[ind] DO
                   address:= numericAddress; status:= declared
                END; DEC (unknownLabels)
  END;
  inSymbol; accept(colonSy)
END labelColon;
```

The assembler is written so that when labelColon is called we can be sure that sy = labelSy and ind is the ind value for the label. This is an example of *one-symbol look-ahead*, which is analogous to the *one-character look-ahead* used by the lexical analyzer. Procedures inSymbol, accept and error are included in the listing of the lexical analyzer module assLex in Section 3.3.

The action of procedure labelColon when the status is declared, imported or notSeen is self-explanatory. If the status is referenced then the label's numeric address was not available in the label table at the time when the label was referenced, and in this case procedure backPatch is called to fill in the missing information, as will be explained using examples.

We now consider how the assembler builds up the contents of the label table while processing the program in Table 4.1 line by line. When the assembler comes to

```
MLOOP:
```

procedure labelColon assigns 2 to labelTable[4].address. This is because the lexical analyzer gives ind = 4 for the label MLOOP, because MLOOP is the fifth label encountered by the lexical analyzer, and the lexical analyzer gives successive labels the ind values 0, 1, 2, ... , as was explained in Section 3.2. Thus label STKBAS has ind = 3, because it is the first label to be found by the lexical analyzer after the three imported labels INTREAD, INTWRITE and ENDPROG in the source text.

Label LSTOP has ind = 5 and numeric address 17 so procedure labelColon assigns labelTable[5].address:= 17. Continuing like this, it is easy to check that when the assembler reaches the end of the source program the address fields of records in the label table contain addresses as shown in Table 4.3.

Table 4.3. Example of addresses in the label table.

ind	labelTable[ind].address
0	
1	
2	
3	24
4	2
5	17
6	23
7	

The assembler works by calling procedures, and at the time of each such call, sy already contains the first symbol required by the procedure. At the time of termination of the procedure, sy is the first symbol to be dealt with by the next procedure. Thus procedure labelColon ends by checking that the label is indeed followed by a colon, and then calling inSymbol (from within the procedure accept in assLex) to assign to sy the symbol that immediately follows the colon.

4.3.2 Label references

A *label reference* is an occurrence of a label not followed by a colon. For example, MLOOP in the instruction JLE MLOOP in Table 4.1 is a reference to the label MLOOP. The second word of the instruction JLE MLOOP is a displacement, which is the numeric address corresponding to the label MLOOP. When the assembler encounters a label reference it calls

```
PROCEDURE labelReference (labelInd: CARDINAL);
BEGIN
  CASE labelTable[labelInd].status OF
    declared:   enter(labelTable[labelInd].address,1) |
    notSeen:    WITH labelTable[labelInd] DO
                   status:= referenced; address:= numericAddress
                END;  enter(endMarker,1);
                INC (unknownLabels) |
    referenced: WITH labelTable[labelInd] DO
                   enter(address,1); address:= numericAddress - 1
                END |
    imported:   WITH importTable[importReferences] DO
                   address:= numericAddress; enter(0,1);
                   whichLabelInd:= labelInd;
```

```
                    END;
                    INC (importReferences);
            END
        END labelReference;
```

LabelInd is the label's ind value, which is 4 for MLOOP in our example. LabelTable[4].status = declared because MLOOP labelled a previous line of the program. In this case procedure labelReference calls procedure enter (in the machCode module) which simply enters the label's address, obtained from the label table, into machine code as a displacement. Procedure enter also sets the associated bit-map bit to 1, signifying that this displacement is a relocatable address.

For the label reference MAX in a previous instruction CMP AX, MAX in Table 4.1, labelTable[6].status = notSeen; the ind of MAX is 6. In this case procedure labelReference assigns to labelTable[6].address the numericAddress of the machine code word that will eventually contain the displacement of the instruction CMP AX, MAX. The numeric address of MAX is not yet known, and instead procedure labelReference calls procedure enter to enter endMarker into the displacement word of the machine code instruction. endMarker is a constant CARDINAL value that is larger than machineCodeUB. Procedure labelReference also increments unknownLabels, which is the number of labels that have so far been referenced before having been found followed by a colon at the beginning of a line.

The label MAX is next referenced in MOV MAX, AX. This time labelTable[6].status = referenced, and what is entered into the displacement word of the machine code instruction is not the numeric address of MAX but instead the address of the previous displacement word that should eventually contain the numeric address of MAX. In this example this address is 10, as shown in Table 4.5. Procedure labelReference assigns to labelTable[6].address the numeric address of the displacement word of MOV MAX, AX. After the assembler has finished processing this instruction the contents of the label table are as shown in Table 4.4. At this intermediate stage the contents of array machineCode are as shown in Table 4.5.

When the assembler comes to LSTOP: PUSH MAX it calls procedure labelColon to deal with LSTOP: and because at this time labelTable[5].status = referenced, procedure backPatch is called:

```
PROCEDURE backPatch(refAddress, displacement: CARDINAL);
VAR
  thisEntry, nextEntry: CARDINAL;
BEGIN
  thisEntry:= refAddress;
  REPEAT
    nextEntry:= machineCode[thisEntry];
    machineCode[thisEntry]:= displacement;
    thisEntry:= nextEntry
  UNTIL thisEntry = endMarker
END backPatch;
```

Table 4.4 Contents of the label table after processing `MOV MAX, AX`

ind	Address	Status	Comment
0	endMarker	imported	
1	endMarker	imported	
2	endMarker	imported	
3	1	referenced	address STKBAS will go into word 1
4	2	declared	MLOOP: has been found
5	8	referenced	address LSTOP will go into word 8
6	14	referenced	address MAX will go into word 14
7	endMarker	notSeen	there is no label with ind = 7

Table 4.5 Relocatable binary machine code at an intermediate stage after assembly of `MOV MAX, AX`

		machineCode[numericAddress]	numericAddress
		Bit map	
IMPORT	INTREAD, INTWRITE, ENDPROG		
	LEA SP, STKBAS	0000010001100000 0	0
		endMarker 1	1
MLOOP:	CALL INTREAD	0011000001000000 0	2
		0000000000000000 1	3
	POP AX	0001111000000000 0	4
	CMP AX, 0	0101111000000000 0	5
		0000000000000000 0	6
	JE LSTOP	0010100001000000 0	7
		endMarker 1	8
	CMP AX, MAX	0101101101000000 0	9
		endMarker 1	10
	JLE MLOOP	0010110101000000 0	11
		0000000000000010 1	12
	MOV MAX, AX	0100000101000000 0	13
		address 10 1	14

The actual parameter `refAddress` is 8 which is `labelTable[5].address`. Table 4.5 shows that `machineCode[8]` = endMarker, which is assigned to `nextEntry` before the displacement is assigned to `machineCode[8]`. The displacement is the current value of `numericAddress`, which is the address of the first word of machine code for PUSH MAX: this is the numeric address that corresponds to the label LSTOP.

When procedure `labelReference` is called to deal with MAX in PUSH MAX, it enters 14, which is the address of the last word of machine code that should contain the numeric address of MAX, into `machineCode[numericAddress]`. Procedure `labelReference` also assigns this same `numericAddress` to `labelTable[6].address`. After completion of assembly of `PUSH MAX` the label table is as shown in Table 4.6. and the incomplete machine code program is as shown in Table 4.7. `labelTable[6].address` contains the address of a word of machine code that should contain the numeric address for MAX, and this word contains the address of another such word, and so on, as can be seen in Table 4.7. `MachineCode[8]` contains the numeric address 17 of LSTOP, and `machineCode[18]` contains the address of the previous word that will eventually contain the numeric address of MAX.

Table 4.6 Contents of the label table after processing `PUSH MAX`

ind	Address	Status	Comment
0	endMarker	imported	
1	endMarker	imported	
2	endMarker	imported	
3	1	referenced	address STKBAS will go into word 1
4	2	declared	MLOOP: has been found
5	17	declared	LSTOP: has been found
6	18	referenced	address MAX will go into word 18
7	endMarker	notSeen	there is no label with ind = 7

Table 4.7 Relocatable binary machine code at an intermediate stage after assembly of `POP MAX`

		machineCode[numericAddress]	bit map	numericAddress
IMPORT	INTREAD, INTWRITE, ENDPROG			
	LEA SP, STKBAS	0000010001100000	0	0
		endMarker	1	1
MLOOP:	CALL INTREAD	0011000001000000	0	2
		0000000000000000	1	3
	POP AX	0001111000000000	0	4
	CMP AX, 0	0101111000000000	0	5
		0000000000000000	0	6
	JE LSTOP	0010100001000000	0	7
		0000000000010001	1	8
	CMP AX, MAX	0101101101000000	0	9
		endMarker	1	10
	JLE MLOOP	0010110101000000	0	11
		0000000000000010	1	12
	MOV MAX, AX	0100000101000000	0	13
		address 10	1	14
	JMP MLOOP	0010000001000000	0	15
		0000000000000010	1	16
LSTOP:	PUSH MAX	0001110101000000	0	17
		address 14	1	18

When the assembler reaches the line labelled MAX: procedure `labelColon` calls procedure `backPatch` with parameter values 18 and 23, the second being the numeric address of MAX. Successive iterations of the REPEAT loop in procedure `backPatch` assign 23 to `machineCode[18]`, `machineCode[14]` and `machineCode[10]` by traversing the chain of addresses. `endMarker` is so called because it marks the end of a chain. The process of filling in addresses corresponding to labels referenced before they have been declared is known as *back-patching*. After completion of assembly of the source program the machine code is as shown in Table 4.1

4.3.3   External references

Our assembler has a module `labels` that contains the label table and associated procedures such as `labelColon` and `labelReference`. This module also looks after external references, including processing the IMPORT and EXPORT lists in the source code, and produces corresponding tables in the binary symbolic output from the assembler.

When starting to assemble a source code program, the assembler calls a procedure `commence`, of which an outline is:

```
PROCEDURE commence;
BEGIN
  make a list of exported labels;
  make a list of imported labels;
  FOR each imported label DO
    labelTable[labelind].status:= imported
  END
END commence;
```

When procedure `labelReference` is called to deal with a reference to an imported label such as INTREAD, it enters into a table called `importTable` a new record whose two fields are the `numericAddress` of the machine code word that will eventually contain the numeric address of the imported label, and the `ind` of the imported label. We have implemented `importTable` as a one-dimensional array of records, and a global variable `importReferences` is the subscript of the next free slot in this array. When the assembler reaches the end of the program in Table 4.1 the contents of `importTable` are as shown in Table 4.8.

When our assembler reaches the end of the source program it calls procedure `finalise` which in outline is:

Table 4.8 Final contents of `importTable`

whichLabelInd	Address	Comment
0	3	INTREAD referenced at address 3
1	20	INTWRITE referenced at address 20
2	22	ENDPROG referenced at address 22

```
PROCEDURE finalise;
BEGIN
  IF unknownLabels > 0 THEN
     report that at least one label has been referenced without being declared
  END;
  Output 'N' followed by the number of words of machine code;
  Output 'E';
  FOR each exported label DO
    output the label as a text string;
    output its numeric address obtained from the label table
  END;
  FOR each reference to an imported label DO
    output the label as a text string;
    output the address, obtained from importTable, of the machine code word
         into which the imported address should eventually be inserted
  END;
  output machine code and bit map
END finalise;
```

Detailed implementations of procedures `commence` and `finalise` are included in a listing of module `labels` in the Appendix.

4.4 Assembly of an effective address

So far we have only considered the translation of labels. We now turn our attention to the assembly of instructions, starting with operands in main memory. Our assembler uses a procedure `memoryOperand` to output machine code corresponding to <memory>. This procedure is in module `instrns`, which assembles individual instructions.

Module `instrns` has a global variable `displacement` which will contain the displacement, if there is one. For example, for the instruction MOV AX, FRED the displacement is a CARDINAL which is the numeric address corresponding to the label FRED. Another example is that for the instruction MOV AX, [BP - 2] the displacement is the 2's complement integer − 2.

Module `instrns` also has a global variable `displacementStatus` which is of an enumeration type that has value:

`displacementIsLabel`	if <memory> includes a label,
`displacementNoLabel`	if <memory> includes a displacement but not a label,
`noDisplacement`	if <memory> does not include a displacement, as for example in MOV AX, [SI].

Our assembler is written so that when procedure `memoryOperand` is called, we can be sure that `sy = labelSy` or `sy = leftSqBrktSy`. This is because a memory operand always starts with a label, as in MOV AX, FRED, or with a left square bracket as in MOV

AX, [DI]. Procedure memoryOperand has a VAR parameter that is the opWord of the instruction being assembled. When procedure memoryOperand is called some of the fields of the opWord have not yet had appropriate bit patterns assigned to them, and are initially filled with zeros. A much simplified outline of the procedure is:

```
PROCEDURE memoryOperand (VAR opWord: CARDINAL);
BEGIN
  IF sy = labelSy THEN
    displacementStatus:= displacementIsLabel;
    labelInd:= ind; (* labelInd is a global variable *)
    inSymbol       (* sy:= symbol that follows the label symbol *)
  ELSE  displacementStatus:= noDisplacement (* an initial assumption *)
  END;
  IF sy = leftSqBrktSy THEN (* at least one register referenced. For example,
             operand is FRED[SI] *)
    inSymbol; (* sy:= symbol that follows '[' symbol, which should be a
                 register *)
    obtain information about the first register;
    accept(registerSy); (* sy:= symbol that follows the register symbol *)
    IF sy IN symbolSet {plussOp,minusOp} THEN
      (* There is a numeric displacement. For example operand is [BP - 3] *)
      displacementStatus:= displacementNoLabel; inSymbol;
      (* an operand such as FRED[BX + 5] is illegal in SAL: if there is a
         numeric displacement there is no label *)
      displacement:= value of displacement;
      inSymbol (* should make sy = rightSqBrktSy *)
    END;
    accept(rightSqBrktSy);
    IF sy = leftSqBrktSy THEN (* based indexed addressing.  For example operand
                       is [BX][DI] and the second '[' has now been reached *)
      accept (leftSqBrktSy);
      obtain information about the second register;
      accept (registerSy); accept(rightSqBrktSy);
    END;
    assign appropriate bit pattern to r/m field of opWord
  END; (* of dealing with registers *)
  IF (displacementStatus # noDisplacement) THEN
      (* set appropriate bit in m field of opWord *)
  END;
END memoryOperand;
```

A bit pattern that should be assigned to the r/m field depends on the registers referenced by the instruction. The body of module instrns initializes global arrays rm1array and rm2array to contain r/m field bit patterns as shown in Table 2.7. Where our outline says 'assign appropriate bit pattern to r/m field of opWord' procedure `memoryOperand` actually adds a bit pattern to the opWord, which perhaps deserves explanation.

Suppose, for example, that the instruction is SUB AX, FRED[SI]. For SUB the opCode is 01010000 in the most significant byte of the opWord. When procedure `memoryOperand` is called, this is the most significant byte of its parameter `opWord`, and the least significant byte may be all zeros:

0101000000000000

From Table 2.7 we see that the r/m field bits for [SI] are 100. When `memoryOperand` has obtained this bit pattern from `rm1array` and added it into `opWord` the result is

0101000000000100

It is safe for procedure `memoryOperand` to add this bit pattern into the opWord, instead of bitwise ORing it in, because we can be sure that before the addition no bit in the r/m field of the opWord is a 1. (Modula-2 would allow us to OR 1s into a BITSET, but this is unnecessarily tortuous, and the traditional method of adding bit patterns to the opWord is satisfactory.)

While processing <memory>, procedure `memoryOperand` counts the number of registers that are used. For example, this count is one for MOV AX, [DI] and two for MOV AX, [BX][DI]. Procedure `memoryOperand` starts by zeroing this count. A more detailed outline of procedure `memoryOperand`, omitting various checks, is as follows:

```
PROCEDURE memoryOperand (VAR opWord: CARDINAL);
VAR
  noOfRegisters, reg1, reg2: CARDINAL;
  negative: BOOLEAN;
BEGIN
  noOfRegisters:= 0;
  IF sy = labelSy THEN
    displacementStatus:= displacementIsLabel;  labelInd:= ind;
    inSymbol
  ELSE  displacementStatus:= noDisplacement
  END;
  IF sy = leftSqBrktSy THEN (* at least one register referenced *)
    inSymbol;  noOfRegisters:= 1;
    reg1:= ind; (* of first register e.g in FRED[DI] *)
    accept(registerSy);
    IF sy IN symbolSet {plussOp,minusOp} THEN (* numeric displacement *)
      negative:= (sy = minusOp);
      inSymbol; (* should make sy = numbersy *)
      displacementStatus:= displacementNoLabel;
      IF negative THEN displacement:= -INTEGER(val) ELSE
          displacement:= INTEGER(val)
      END;
      inSymbol; (* should make sy = rightSqBrktSy *)
```

```
      END;
      accept(rightSqBrktSy);
      IF sy = leftSqBrktSy THEN (* based indexed address *)
         accept (leftSqBrktSy);
         reg2:= ind;  (* of second register e.g. in [BP][SI] *)
         noOfRegisters:= 2;
         accept (registerSy); accept(rightSqBrktSy)
      END;
      IF noOfRegisters = 2 THEN (* assign bits to r/m field *)
         INC (opWord, rm2array[reg1,reg2])
      ELSE INC(opWord, rm1array[reg1]) (* assign bits to r/m field *)
      END
   END; (* of dealing with registers *)
   IF (displacementStatus # noDisplacement) THEN (* set bit in m field *)
      IF (noOfRegisters > 0) THEN
        INC (opWord, 128) (* m field:= binary 10 *)
      ELSE INC (opWord, 64) (* m field:= binary 01 *)
      END
   END
END memoryOperand;
```

Procedure `memoryOperand` does not attempt to enter a displacement into machine code. If `memoryOperand` is called to deal with the first operand in, for example, MOV FRED, 7, the immediate operand must precede the displacement word that corresponds to FRED in machine code. The displacement must be entered into machine code after the assembler has dealt with the immediate operand after the return from procedure `memoryOperand`. As we shall see, at a later stage the assembler attempts to enter a displacement into machine code by calling:

```
PROCEDURE enterDisplacement;
BEGIN
   IF displacementStatus = displacementIsLabel THEN labelReference(labelInd)
   ELSIF displacementStatus = displacementNoLabel THEN
      enter(CARDINAL(displacement), 0)
   END
END enterDisplacement;
```

If there is a displacement that is a label, procedure `labelReference` deals with this as explained in Section 4.3.2. If the displacement is a number as in [BP + 3] procedure `enter` enters this into the next word of machine code.

4.5 Assembly of an individual instruction

Module `instrns` has a global array `opCodeTable` that is a one-dimensional array of records of type

```
opCodeRecord = RECORD
                    category: catType;
                    opCode: CARDINAL
               END;
```

When the lexical analyzer comes to an opCode such as ADD in the source text, it assigns `sy:= opCodeSy` and it assigns to `ind` a CARDINAL value that uniquely identifies this particular opCode. The body of module `instrns` initializes `opCodeTable` so that `opCodeTable[ind]` contains information about the opCode that corresponds to `ind`, specifically its instruction category, such as `jumpInsCategory` or `twoOperandCategory`, and its numeric opCode, as explained in Section 2.8.3. For example, for the opCode PUSH the lexical analyzer assigns `ind = 11`, and `opCodeTable[11]` is initialized to have `category = singleOperandCategory` and `opCode = 0001110000000000` (in binary).

To assemble an instruction the assembler calls procedure `instruction`, which is in module `instrns`. Procedure `instruction` obtains the instruction's opCode's category and numeric opCode from `opCodeTable` and calls a further procedure determined by the opCode category:

```
PROCEDURE instruction;
VAR
  opInd: CARDINAL;
BEGIN
  opInd:= ind; inSymbol;
  opWord:= opCodeTable[opInd].opCode;
  CASE  opCodeTable[opInd].category OF
     twoOperandCategory:     twoOp             |
     singleOperandCategory:  singleOp          |
     leaInstructionCategory: leaInstruction    |
     jumpInsCategory:        jumpInstructions  |
     noOperandInsCategory:   enter(opWord, 0)  |
     pseudoOp:               dw
  END
END instruction;
```

For the `noOperandInsCategory` procedure `instruction` simply calls procedure `enter` to enter the opWord into machineCode; because there are no operands there is no need to set any further bits in the opWord. Another simple case is that the pseudoOp DW is dealt with by:

```
PROCEDURE dw;
VAR
  number: CARDINAL;
BEGIN
  IF sy = questionSy THEN
    (* reserve a word without assigning a value to it *)
    incAddressBy (1); inSymbol
  ELSIF sy = numberSy THEN
    number:= val;  inSymbol;
    IF sy = dupSy THEN
      (* reserve this number of words *)
      incAddressBy (number); inSymbol
    ELSE  enter (val, 0) (* enter this number into machine code *)
    END
  ELSE error (19) END
END dw;
```

For the `jumpInsCategory` procedure `instruction` calls:

```
PROCEDURE jumpInstructions;
BEGIN
  diplacementStatus:= noDisplacement; (* initial assumption *)
  IF sy IN symbolSet {labelSy, leftSqBrktSy} THEN
    (* sy is the first symbol of a memory operand *)
    memoryOperand (opWord)
  ELSE error (15) (* only memory operands are legal for jump instrns *)
  END;
  enter(opWord, 0); (* enter opword into machine code *)
  enterDisplacement (* deal with the displacement, if any *)
END jumpInstructions;
```

Procedure `memoryOperand` is called to set appropriate bits in the `opWord` and to find out about the displacement, as explained previously.

The operand of single-operand intructions such as PUSH is either <memory> or <register>. A register operand such as AX in PUSH AX is dealt with by:

```
PROCEDURE registerOperand;
BEGIN
  INC (opWord, ind * 8); (* register field of opWord *)
  inSymbol
END registerOperand;
```

When the lexical analyzer comes to a register name, such as SI, in the source text, it assigns `sy:= registerSy` and it assigns to `ind` a cardinal value that is the same as that shown (in binary) in Table 2.7. For example AX has `ind = 0`, CX has `ind = 1`, DX has `ind = 2`, and so on. Procedure `registerOperand` simply enters this cardinal value into the register field of the least significant byte of the opWord, as explained in Section 2.8.2.

`registeroperand` multiplies `ind` by eight to move `ind` three bits left into alignment with the register field, which consists of the three bits labelled *b* in *aabbbccc*. For example, multiplication by 8 takes the ind value for `CX` from binary 00000001 to binary 00001000.

The procedure that assembles single-operand instructions is a little more elaborate than procedure `jumpInstructions` because it calls `registerOperand` to deal with a register operand, or `memoryOperand` to deal with a memory operand:

```
PROCEDURE singleOp;
BEGIN
  displacementStatus:= noDisplacement; (* initial assumption *)
  IF sy = registerSy THEN registerOperand
  ELSIF sy IN symbolSet {labelSy, leftSqBrktSy} THEN
    memoryOperand (opWord);
    INC (opWord, 256) (* memRef bit:= 1 *)
  ELSE error (14)
  END;
  enter(opWord, 0);  enterDisplacement
END singleOp;
```

The procedure that assembles two-operand instructions calls a separate procedure to deal with the second operand. This procedure has three parameters. The first is of the enumeration type `operandKind = (mem, reg)` and this indicates whether the first operand was a memory or a register operand. The second is BOOLEAN and indicates whether the second operand is immediate as, for example, in `MOV AX, 7`. The third operand is the value of the immediate operand, if any:

```
PROCEDURE secondOperand (firstOperand: operandKind;
    VAR immediate: BOOLEAN; VAR immedVal: CARDINAL);
BEGIN
  accept(commaSy); (* sy:= first symbol of second operand *)
  CASE sy  OF
    numberSy:  (* immediate addressing *)
        immediate:= TRUE; immedVal:= val;
        INC (opWord, 1024);  (* immediate bit:= 1 *)
        inSymbol |
    minusOp: inSymbol;
        IF sy = numberSy THEN (* immediate addressing *)
          immediate:= TRUE; immedVal:= CARDINAL(-INTEGER(val));
          INC (opWord, 1024);  (* immediate bit:= 1 *)
          inSymbol
        ELSE error(12) (* in SAL a sign must be followed by a number *)
        END |
    registerSy:
        IF firstOperand = reg THEN  (* r/m field will select second register *)
          INC (opWord, ind);  (* r/m field of opWord:= register's ind *)
```

```
          INC (opWord, 0C0H); (* m bits:= 11 in binary *)
          inSymbol
        ELSE  (* only one register operand *)
          registerOperand
        END |
    labelSy, leftSqBrktSy: (* second operand is <memory> *)
        IF firstOperand = reg THEN
          memoryOperand (opWord);
          INC (opWord, 256) (* memRef bit:= 1 *)
        ELSE error(12) (* cannot have two memory operands *)
        END;
    END
END secondOperand;
```

The procedure that assembles two-operand instructions starts by assuming that there is no immediate operand and no displacement:

```
PROCEDURE twoOp;
VAR
  immediate: BOOLEAN; immedVal: CARDINAL;
BEGIN
  immediate:= FALSE; displacementStatus:= noDisplacement;
  IF sy = registerSy THEN    (* destination is a register *)
    registerOperand;
    INC (opWord, 512);       (* destination bit:= 1 *)
    secondOperand(reg, immediate, immedVal)
  ELSIF sy IN symbolSet {labelSy, leftSqBrktSy} THEN
    memoryOperand (opWord); (* destination is <memory> *)
    INC (opWord, 256);       (* memRef bit:= 1 *)
    secondOperand(mem, immediate, immedVal)
  ELSE error (20)
  END;
  enter(opWord, 0);
  IF immediate THEN enter(immedVal, 0) END;
  enterDisplacement
END twoOp;
```

Module `instrns` is listed fully in the Appendix.

4.6 The body of the assembler

The line-by-line processing of the source text by the assembler is controlled by a WHILE loop:

```
WHILE sy # endOfTextSy DO
  IF sy = labelSy THEN
    labelColon;
    IF sy = opCodeSy THEN instruction ELSE error(6) END;
  ELSIF sy = opCodeSy THEN instruction
  END;
  accept(newLineSy)
END;
```

In SAL it is illegal for a line to start with a label and a colon and not contain an instruction or a pseudo-op. But a line does not have to start with a label, and may instead start with an opCode: in this case `instruction` is called to assemble the instruction. If a line of the source code program is blank, so that the first symbol on it is `newLineSy`, it is simply ignored.

A practical assembler should allow for the possibility that an error has occurred in a line of the source text. To allow recovery after an error, our assembler has a WHILE loop that is more elaborate than the one which we have just introduced. If `newLineSy` does not occur where it is expected, symbols are skipped until the next `newLineSy` is found. It is hoped that the assembler will be able to continue processing successive lines after this, without being upset by the error, in order to check for further errors.

The main module of our assembler is named `salAssem` and is listed in the Appendix. It starts by calling the procedure `commence` and ends by calling procedure `finalise` in module `labels`. In this version of the assembler the object code output goes to a file named `salAsout` and the source code comes from a file named `salAssin`.

4.7 Discussion

SAL is a simplified language and our SAL assembler is correspondingly simpler than an assembler for a practical assembly language. Our assembler is highly procedural: to change the output machine code we would have to rewrite many procedures, particularly in module `instrns`. An alternative approach is to have as much as possible of the machine-specific information in tables, so that changes can be made with minimal rewriting of the assembler's procedures. Another possible advantage is that machine-specific information in tables can more easily be checked for correctness.

Our assembler is an example of a one-pass assembler which reads through the source program file just once. It is convenient to have the whole of the machine code program in main memory while a one-pass assembler fills in forward references by back-patching. This may not be practical if memory is limited and source programs are not restricted to being fairly small modules. To make less demands on memory we can use a two-pass assembler. The first pass reads from a source file via a lexical analyzer and builds up a label table while writing the symbol stream to a temporary file. The second pass reads from the temporary file and uses the label table inherited from the first pass to translate the symbol stream into a machine code program. Successive machine code instructions can be output to an object code file as soon as they have been assembled: there is no backpatching and therefore no need to store the whole machine code program in main memory.

Two-pass assemblers allow more powerful macro facilities. A macro is a block of assembly language instructions that may have parameters somewhat like a procedure. The assembler copies this block of instructions into the program, making appropriate parameter substitutions, wherever the macro's name appears in the assembly language source. Macros are considered further by Pagan (1991). For a general overview of assemblers, including macros, the reader is referred to Barron (1978) and Calingaert (1979).

Sometimes it is not convenient to run an assembler on a computer whose machine code is the same as that of the assembler's output. A *cross-assembler* is an assembler that runs on one machine to translate an assembly language program into an object program for execution on another machine that has different machine code. For example, we could have a cross-assembler running on a 486-based PC to translate MC68000 assembly language into MC68000 machine code.

4.8 Exercises

1. Explain how a SAL assembler and lexical analyzer would have to be developed if SAL itself were extended to include the following instructions:

    (a) PUSHA ;   pushes contents of all registers on to the stack
        POPA ;   pops contents of all registers off the stack
    (b) SHL <destination> <count>; destination:= destination logically left shifted by
            <count> bits
        SHR <destination> <count>; destination:= destination logically right shifted by
            <count> bits

    In this, <destination> is <register> or <memory>, and <count> is a cardinal immediate operand or CX. When <count> is CX this means that the number of bits of shift is given by the contents of register CX. For example SHL FRED, 6 means 'shift the contents of word FRED logically left 6 bits', and SHR FRED, CX means 'shift the contents of word FRED logically right by a number of bits such that this number is the current contents of register CX'.

2. Develop the SAL assembler to allow the use of named constants defined by the EQU pseudo–op. For example, if a SAL progam includes the line

    ```
    LENGTH EQU 15
    ```

    then wherever LENGTH appears on a subsequent line the assembler will replace this by 15, for instance in MOV AX, LENGTH or MOV AX, [BP - length]. Assume that a named constant must be defined by an EQU before any line in the program in which this name is used. Obviously no two constants may have the same name and the name of a constant must not be the same as the name of any label. Assume that the name of a constant may comprise only upper case letters, just like a SAL label.

3. Modify the SAL assembler to accomodate the following revision of SAL. The only change in the assembly language is that conditional jump instructions JE, JG, JL, JGE, JLE, JNE and JC are now jumps to a relative address, and their single operand must simply be a label which must be within plus or minus 127 words of the jump instruction itself. This label must belong to a word whose address can be obtained by adding an 8-bit 2's complement number to the address of the conditional jump instruction. SAL machine code is revised so that a conditional jump instruction is a one-word instruction in which the most significant byte is as in Section 2.8.3 and the least significant byte is an 8-bit 2's complement number obtained by subtracting the address of this instruction from the address of the instruction that has the operand label.

Chapter 5

Linking and loading

5.1 Introduction

Address *binding* means mapping addresses within a program onto addresses within a computer system's memory space. Binding can be done by the assembler, which in this case produces an absolute binary machine code program that has no bit map and cannot subsequently be relocated. An assembler that binds the machine code program during assembly is called a *load and go* assembler.

More usually, an assembler produces relocatable binary or binary symbolic, and the program is bound during relocation some time after the time of assembly. Relocation may be done by a program called a *relocating loader* while it loads the program into memory for execution. An advantage of having a loader, instead of an assembler, do the binding, is that the binding can be changed without the program having to be reassembled.

When a program consists of many modules that are assembled (or compiled) independently, there are two possible times, between assembly time and execution time, for binding the program. One idea is to take the collection of binary symbolic modules and link them together into a single relocatable binary program. A program that does this linking is called a *linkage editor*. A linkage editor does not bind the program: binding is done subsequently by a relocating loader. This has the advantage that the linking need not be done again each time the program is relocated.

The other idea is to have a single program, called a *linking loader*, do both the linking and the loading, thus binding the program at the same time as linking the modules together (i.e. dealing with external references). The output of a linking loader is absolute binary machine code. A linking loader produces absolute binary more efficiently than a two-stage process comprising linkage editing followed by loading, but a program has to be relinked every time it is relocated.

So far we have considered binding at assembly time, at load time, and at link time. Another possibility is to bind at execution time, for example in a segmented memory system, which has the advantage that relocation prior to execution is unnecessary. Details will be found in textbooks on operating systems such as Deitel (1990) and Peterson and Silberschatz (1990).

The present chapter introduces a linking loader program, and we leave as an exercise the writing of a linkage editor together with a separate relocating loader program. The assembler that was introduced in Chapter 4 assembles an individual module and outputs binary symbolic to a separate file. Subsequently, each binary symbolic module that is linked by our linking loader is obtained from one of these separate files. Our linking loader first reads just the header part, skipping the relocatable binary part, of each of these files to build up a global label table that contains the relocated address of every label that is exported by any module. This process can be regarded as a first pass through the binary symbolic modules, in that each file is visited; but it is not a complete pass because only the header part of each file is read.

For a second time our linking loader visits each module in turn, now using the global table to translate imported references into relocated addresses, and also relocating all non-imported relocatable addresses. This produces a single relocated absolute binary program that is a concatenation of machine code programs of the individual modules.

The processing of export and import tables involves processing labels as strings of characters. It is convenient to handle these strings by using a string table in exactly the same way as in our SAL lexical analyzer, and indeed modules `symbType` and `strinTbl` are linked into our linking loader program.   Thus our linking loader can call `insertString` to insert a string into the string table, and `searchStringTable` to look up the `ind` of a label that is already in the string table. The actual string table used by the linking loader is entirely separate from the string table used by the lexical analyzer during the assembly of an individual module.

An advantage of using a string table is that this associates a unique `ind` with each label and we can use a label's `ind` as its subscript in the global label table. Thus we can look up a label's relocated address in the global label table without having to search this table serially.

5.2 The make file

A SAL binary symbolic module contains import and export tables but does not identify the modules whence imports are expected to come, so it is impossible to deduce which modules should be linked together. In this case a linking loader or linkage editor must be provided with a list of names of files that contain the binary symbolic modules that are to be linked. Traditionally this list is held in a further file that is called the *make* file. Our linking loader program assumes that the name of the make file is `McFile`.

As was explained in Section 2.7.2, SAL standard subroutines such as INTREAD, INTWRITE and ENDPROG are available in a module named `salSubs`. In our system the binary symbolic of this module is available in a file that is also named `salSubs`. If the binary symbolic for a single-module program that is to be linked together with `salSubs` is in a file called `salMain` then the contents of `McFile` will simply be

```
salMain
salSubs
```

`McFile` contains exactly one file name per line of text, and these files are in the same subdirectory as the linking loader.

To be consistent with Chapter 14, our linking loader reads the file names from `McFile` into a linked list that is encapsulated within a module named `mcModule` which exports three procedures:

```
DEFINITION MODULE mcModule;
PROCEDURE mcList;
PROCEDURE startFile(VAR noneLeft: BOOLEAN);
PROCEDURE restart;
END mcModule.
```

Procedure `mcList` transcribes file names from `McFile` into the linked list. Module `mcModule` includes a global pointer `currentModPtr` and procedure `restart` initializes this to be `NIL`. Procedure `startFile` makes `currentModPtr` point to the first record if `currentModPtr = NIL` at the time of the call and otherwise makes `currentModPtr` point to the next record in the list. If now `currentModPtr = NIL` procedure `startFile` returns `noneLeft = TRUE`, signifying that there are no more files in the list. Otherwise the file whose name is obtained from `currentModPtr^` is opened for reading. The implementation module is listed in the Appendix.

5.3 Building up the global label table

The first pass of our linking loader, which reads the export tables of all the modules and constructs the global label table `gLabelTable`, is handled by module `expTable`. The global label table is a one-dimensional array of CARDINALs organized so that `gLabelTable[ind]` will be the relocated address of the label whose ind is `ind`.

The definition module of `expTable` includes an exported constant `relocatingConst` which is the address of the first word of the absolute binary machine code program that is produced by our linking loader. For the first module listed in `McFile`, the relocating constant is `relocatingConst`. For the second module the relocating constant is `relocatingConst` plus number of words of machine code in the first module. The number of words of machine code in a module follows the letter 'N' at the beginning of the module's binary symbolic, and this number can easily be read during the first pass, enabling the linking loader to calculate the relocating constant for the next module. For the third module the relocating constant is `relocatingConst` for the second module plus number of words of machine code in the second module, and so on for successive modules.

Because the relocating constant is not the same for all modules, 'relocating constant' is not quite the right name for it, and instead we use `relocatingVar`, reserving the identifier `relocatingConst` for the relocating constant for the first module, which determines the relocation of the entire program. In a practical system this initial `relocatingConst` would be readable by the linker: we have made it a constant for simplicity. The definition module is:

```
DEFINITION MODULE expTable;
CONST
  relocatingConst = 64;   (* this is just an example *)
PROCEDURE getExports;
PROCEDURE whichAddress(letter: CHAR; ind: CARDINAL): CARDINAL;
END expTable.
```

Procedure `whichAddress` simply returns `gLabelTable[ind]`. Parameter `letter` is not used here but becomes important in Chapter 14. An outline of procedure `getExports` is:

```
PROCEDURE getExports;
VAR
  n, relocatingVar: CARDINAL;
BEGIN
  relocatingVar:= relocatingConst; n:= 0;
  FOR each module that is to be linked DO
    open this module's file;
    INC(relocatingVar, n); (* relocatingVar becomes relocated
      address of module's first word *)
    read from the module's header the number, n, of words of machine code in the
      module (* for use in initializing the relocating var for the next module *);
    FOR each entry in the module's export table DO
      read exported label as a text string;
      enter string into the string table and obtain a unique ind value for the
        label;
      ReadCard(refAddress); (* exported label's non-relocated address *)
      gLabelTable[ind]:= refAddress + relocatingVar (* =  relocated address *)
    END;
    close this module's file
  END
END getExports;
```

Upon termination of procedure `getExports` the first pass of our linking loader has been completed. For example, for the four-module program in Section 2.9.3 at the end of the first pass the relocated addresses in the global label table are as shown in Table 5.1. In this example the four modules start at absolute addresses 64, 97, 129 and 148, respectively.

5.4   Translation of imported labels

Normally a linking loader would leave the absolute binary program properly relocated in memory, ready for immediate execution. However, for the purposes of Chapter 6 our linking loader actually outputs absolute binary machine code in binary form to a file

Table 5.1 Global label table for the four-module example in Section 2.9.3

Label	ind	gLabelTable[ind]
HOWMANY	1	64 + 32
BUBSORT	2	97 + 0
STKBAS	3	129 + 11
ARX	4	129 + 0
STOPAT	5	129 + 10
ENDPROG	6	148 + 3
NEWLINE	7	148 + 2
INTWRITE	8	148 + 1
INTREAD	9	148 + 0

Table 5.2 For first module in Section 2.9.3: (a) binary symbolic import table; (b) contents of array importTable

(a)		(b)	
		where	refAddress
I 9			
STKBAS	1	1	140
INTREAD	7	7	148
ARX	9	9	129
ARX	14	14	129
BUBSORT	16	16	97
ARX	22	22	129
INTWRITE	24	24	149
NEWLINE	26	26	150
ENDPROG	31	31	151

named `absBinry` during the second pass. The second pass is handled by procedure `relocate` which uses a one-dimensional array:

```
importTable: ARRAY [1..importTableUB] OF RECORD
                          where, refAddress: CARDINAL
                        END;
```

For each module in turn, procedure `relocate` skips the export table and then makes an entry in `importTable` corresponding to each entry in the module's import table. For example, for the first module in Section 2.9.3 the import table in binary symbolic is shown in Table 5.2(a). This shows, for example, that imported label INTWRITE is referred to in word 24 of the module's non-relocated machine code. For each entry in the import table, procedure `relocate` obtains the imported label's relocated address from the global label table by calling `whichAddress` in module `expTable`. An outline of procedure relocate is:

```
PROCEDURE relocate;
BEGIN
  open file absBinry to receive absolute binary output;
  FOR each module that is to be linked DO
      open this module's file;
      initialize this module's relocatingVar;
      skip along the file's header to the start of the import table;
      FOR i:= 1 to number of entries in import table DO
        read the imported label as a text string;
        look up this string in the string table to obtain the label's ind;
        read non-relocated address into importTable[i].where;
        importTable[i].refAddress:= whichAddress(ch, ind) (* which returns
            gLabelTable[ind] *)
      END;
      FOR each word of relocatable binary machine code DO
        IF NOT relocatable then output word to absBinry file
        ELSIF word's address matches a where field value in a record in
          importTable THEN (* word should contain an imported address, so *)
          output to absBinry the refAddress from the same record in importTable
        ELSE add relocatingVar to this word and output the result to absBinry
        END
      END;
      close this module's file
  END; close absBinry
END relocate;
```

This outline indicates how procedure `relocate` builds up the contents of `importTable` separately and starting afresh for each module. For example, Table 5.2(b) shows the records in array `importTable` corresponding to Table 5.2(a). The first record in Table 5.2(b) shows that relocated address 140 should be inserted into non-relocated word 1 of the module's machine code. Word 1 refers to STKBAS (see Section 2.7.3). Another example is that the third record in Table 5.2(b) shows that relocated address 129 should be inserted into non-relocated word 9 of the module's machine code.

Because of the manner in which the binary symbolic import table has been constructed in Section 4.3.3 we can be sure that the contents of `importTable` will already be in sequence of increasing value of `where`. Relying on this sorted order, procedure `relocate` uses a merge-like technique, avoiding the need for serial search or non-trivial organization of the `importTable`. With this a detailed version of the second inner FOR loop

```
FOR each word of relocatable binary machine code DO ...
```

in procedure `relocate` becomes:

```
whichEntry:= 1;  (* whichEntry is subscript of importTable *)
FOR i:= 0 TO n-1 DO (* FOR each word of relocatable binary DO *)
```

```
ReadCard(machineCodeWord); ReadCard(bit); (* bit map bit *)
IF bit = 0 THEN WriteWord(absBinry, machineCodeWord)
ELSIF bit = 1 THEN (* word is relocatable *)
  IF whichEntry <= iNumber THEN (* at least one unused entry remains *)
    WITH importTable [whichEntry] DO
      IF i = where THEN
          (* word should contain an imported address, so *)
          WriteWord(absBinry, refAddress);
          INC (whichEntry) (* for next import *)
      ELSE  (* relocate *)
          WriteWord(absBinry, machineCodeWord + relocatingVar)
      END
    END
  ELSE  (* relocate *)
    WriteWord(absBinry, machineCodeWord + relocatingVar)
  END
ELSE WriteString ('Error. Bit map bit = '); WriteCard(bit,3);
  END
END;
```

Procedure `relocate` is in module `salLink`, which is the main module of our linking loader. The body of this module is:

```
BEGIN
  mcList; restart; getExports; restart; relocate;
END salLink.
```

5.5 Discussion

Our linking loader, which consists of modules `salLink`, `expTable`, `mcModule`, `strinTbl` and `symbType`, does not store more than one word of machine code at any one time. From this point of view it is more memory-efficient than a one-pass assembler, but this is only because the absolute binary program is output to a file instead of being left in memory ready for execution, as it would be in many practical systems.

Modula-2 checks types of imports and exports. At the very much more primitive level of SAL, our linking loader only checks that no two modules export the same label, and that every label which is imported is also exported. In Chapter 14 we will see that this linking loader requires development to allow proper linking of binary symbolic modules obtained via the assembler from separate compilation of modules written in a subset of Modula-2.

The present chapter has introduced just one example of a linking loader program. For a more general introduction to linking and loading, see Barron (1978) and Calingaert (1979).

5.6 Exercises

1. Working by hand, link and load the following three-segment binary symbolic
    program to produce a single absolute binary machine code program with the first
    word of the first segment at address 64.

    Module 1:

    ```
    N       27
    E       0
    I       8
    INTREAD     3
    MAX         5
    INTREAD     9
    PICKMAX     12
    MAX         16
    INTWRITE    18
    NEWLINE     20
    ENDPROG     22
    0000010001100000 0
    0000000000010111 1
    0011000001000000 0
    0000000000000000 1
    0001111101000000 0
    0000000000000000 1
    0100011000001000 0
    0000000000001001 0
    0011000001000000 0
    0000000000000000 1
    0001111000011000 0
    0011000001000000 0
    0000000000000000 1
    0010100101000000 0
    0000000000001000 1
    0001110101000000 0
    0000000000000000 1
    0011000001000000 0
    0000000000000000 1
    0011000001000000 0
    0000000000000000 1
    0011000001000000 0
    0000000000000000 1
    0000000000000000 0
    0000000000000000 0
    0000000000000000 0
    0000000000000000 0
    ```

Module 2:

```
N       8
E       2
MAX         7
PICKMAX  0
I    0
0101101101011000 0
0000000000000111 1
0010110101000000 0
0000000000000110 1
0100000101011000 0
0000000000000111 1
0000100000000000 0
0000000000000000 0
```

Module 3:

```
N    4
E    4
ENDPROG      3
NEWLINE      2
INTWRITE     1
INTREAD      0
I    0
0000001000000001 0
0000001000000010 0
0000001000000011 0
0000001000000100 0
```

2. Write a linkage editor program that links together a collection of binary symbolic modules and outputs a single relocatable binary program. Assume that the names of files containing the binary symbolic modules are in a further file named McFile, in which there is one file name per line of text.

3. Modify the linking loader so that it works without translating each label into a corresponding ind.

Chapter 6

Interpreting machine code

6.1 Introduction

A compiler or an assembler translates a source program into an object program. An *interpreter*, on the other hand, executes a source program directly, instead of producing an object program for subsequent execution. An interpreter works by looking at each statement or instruction in the source program, figuring out what needs to be done to execute this statement or instruction, and immediately doing what needs to be done. The sequence of statements or instructions that are executed in this way is exactly the sequence determined by the program. A well-known advantage of interpreters is that they can provide better debugging facilities than are available via a normal compiler or assembler, because they can enable the user to watch the process of execution step by step.

Unlike Modula-2 or an assembly language, machine code is normally interpreted: for reasons relating to memory requirements and efficiency, machine code is not normally translated into microcode. A programmer does not usually need to know exactly how a processor interprets machine code. Machine code interpretation could reasonably be studied as part of a course on computer design, but would normally be beyond the scope of a course on assembling, linking and compiling.

Nevertheless, the present chapter introduces an interpreter for SAL machine code. This interpreter executes programs produced by the linking loaders introduced in Chapters 5 and 14. Without this interpreter the practical execution of SAL programs would present a problem because CPUs that immediately execute SAL machine code are not on the market, although microprogrammable CPUs are available that could be microprogrammed to execute SAL machine code directly.

Details are different but the main ideas involved in interpreting machine code are similar to those involved in interpreting assembly language or compiler intermediate code such as p-code (Nori *et al.*, 1981). Interpretation of intermediate code has proved to be useful because a compiler's target processor can be changed simply by rewriting the intermediate code interpreter, without amending the main part of the compiler. Although run-time efficiency can be improved by translating intermediate code into machine code, it may be easier to write an intermediate code interpreter than to write a translator.

When run-time efficiency is not a strong requirement, interpretation of assembly language programs may in some situations be a sensible option. For example, to execute a VAX assembly language program on an MC68000 processor, it may be easier to write an interpreter than a translator. Moreover, it is easier to write an assembly language debugger if this is based on an interpreter.

This rest of this chapter can be skipped optionally, because it contains nothing that is a prerequisite for later chapters.

6.2 The machine code module

Our SAL machine code interpreter consists of two modules, named `progCode` and `interpret`. Module `progCode` contains the machine code program, which is not directly visible from the main module `interpret`. Module `progCode` also includes a global variable `ip`, which stands for *instruction pointer*. The role of `ip` is similar to that of the instruction pointer within an 8086 CPU. Thus `ip` contains the `address` of the machine code word that will next be accessed by the interpreter. The definition module is as follows:

```
DEFINITION MODULE progCode;
TYPE
   catType = (twoOperandCategory, singleOperandCategory,
                  leaInstructionCategory, jumpInsCategory,
                  noOperandInsCategory, extraCategory, errorCategory);
   opWordFields = RECORD
                     category: catType;
                     opCode: CARDINAL;
                     immediate, destination, memRef: [0..1];
                     lsByte, m, reg, rm: CARDINAL
                  END;

PROCEDURE getWord (VAR gotWord: CARDINAL);
   (* gotWord:= machineCode[ip]; INC(ip) *)

PROCEDURE getOp (VAR opRec: opWordFields);
   (* getWord(opWord); assign fields of opWord to fields of opRec *)

PROCEDURE jumpIP (newAddress: CARDINAL);
   (* ip:= newAddress *)

PROCEDURE dereference(numericAddress:CARDINAL): CARDINAL;
   (* RETURN machineCode[numericAddress]/*)/

PROCEDURE assignTo (numericAddress, operand: CARDINAL);
   (* machineCode[numericAddress]:= operand *)
```

```
PROCEDURE ipAddress(): CARDINAL;
  (* RETURN ip *)
END progCode.
```

For use by the interpreter, procedure `getOp` returns, via a VAR parameter, a record whose fields include the relevant fields of the opWord, including the instruction category, the opCode, the `immediate`, `destination` and `memRef` bits, the `m`, `reg` and `rm` fields, and the value of the least significant byte of the opWord. An outline of procedure `getOp` is:

```
PROCEDURE getOp (VAR opRec: opWordFields);
VAR
   wrd: BITSET; opWord, whichBit: CARDINAL;
BEGIN
  WITH opRec DO
     getWord (opWord); wrd:= BITSET (opWord);
     whichBit:= 15; (* most significant bit *)
     IF whichBit IN wrd THEN
       WriteString('Error: most significant bit cannot be 1')
     ELSE
       DEC(whichBit);
       IF whichBit IN wrd THEN (* most sig bits are 01 so *)
         category:= twoOperandCategory;
         opCode:= bits 13, 12 and 11 of opWord;
         IF 10 IN wrd THEN immediate:= 1 ELSE immediate:= 0 END;
         IF 9 IN wrd THEN destination:= 1 ELSE destination:= 0 END;
         IF 8 IN wrd THEN memRef:= 1 ELSE memRef:= 0 END
       ELSE
         DEC (whichBit);
         IF whichBit IN wrd THEN (* most sig bits are 001 so *)
           category:= jumpInsCategory;
           opCode:= bits 12, 11, 10, 9 and 8 of opWord;
         ELSE
           DEC (whichBit);
           IF whichBit IN wrd THEN (* most sig bits are 0001 so *)
             category:= singleOperandCategory;
             opCode:= bits 11, 10 and 9 of opWord;
             IF 8 IN wrd THEN memRef:= 1 ELSE memRef:= 0 END
           ELSE
             DEC (whichBit);
             IF whichBit IN wrd THEN (* most sig bits are 00001 so *)
               category:= noOperandInsCategory;
               opCode:= bits 10, 9 and 8 of opWord
             ELSE
               DEC (whichBit);
               IF whichBit IN wrd THEN
                 category:= leaInstructionCategory;
```

```
          opCode:= bits 9 and 8 of opWord
       ELSE
         DEC (whichBit);
         IF whichBit IN wrd THEN
           category:= extraCategory
         END
       END
     END
   END
  END
 END
END;
m:= bits 7 and 6 of opWord;     (* m field   *)
reg:= bits 5, 4 and 3 of opWord; (* reg field *)
rm:= bits 2, 1 and 0 of opWord   (* r/m field *)
  END
END getOp;
```

This finds out the instruction category by using the information in Table 2.8, and then extracts field values using knowledge of the machine code format for the instruction category, as in Sections 2.8.2 and 2.8.3.

The body of module `progCode` initializes `ip:= startAddress`, which is the relocated address of the first word of the absolute binary machine code program. If `salSubs` is listed as the first module in `McFile` things will go wrong.

6.3 The main module of the interpeter

An outline of the body of the main module of our interpreter is as follows:

```
halted:= FALSE;
REPEAT
  getOp(opRec);
  CASE opRec.category OF
    twoOperandCategory: twoOperandInstruction(opRec) |
    singleOperandCategory: singleOperandInstruction(opRec) |
    leaInstructionCategory: leaInstruction(opRec) |
    jumpInsCategory: jumpInstructions(opRec) |
    noOperandInsCategory: noOperandInstructions(opRec) |
    extraCategory: extraIns(opRec) |
    errorCategory: halted:= TRUE
  END
UNTIL halted
```

Each iteration of the REPEAT loop interprets a single machine code instruction by calling a procedure selected in accordance with the instruction category. `halted` is a global variable that is set to TRUE when `CALL ENDPROG` is interpreted.

The main module, which is named `interpret`, holds the contents of registers in a global variable array

```
register: ARRAY[0..7] OF CARDINAL;
```

and includes declarations

```
CONST
     AX = 0; CX = 1; DX = 2; BX = 3; SP = 4; BP = 5; SI = 6; DI = 7;
```

which have been chosen so that a register's contents are in array element `register[reg]`, where `reg` is the `reg` field of an instruction's opWord. For example, the SAL instruction `INC BX` can be interpreted by executing `INC(register[BX])`.

When module `interpret` finds that an instruction has a <memory> operand, procedure `formAddress` is called to compute the actual effective address of the operand. This involves looking at the `m` field of the opWord. If the value of the `m` field indicates that the effective address involves indexing, then procedure `indexing` is called to add the contents of one or more index registers into the sum that constitutes the effective address:

```
PROCEDURE formAddress (opRec: opWordFields): CARDINAL;
VAR
  refAddress: CARDINAL;
BEGIN
  WITH opRec DO
    CASE m OF
    0: (* there is no displacement *)
       refAddress:= 0; indexing(rm, refAddress)|
    2: (* there is a displacement and indexing *)
       getWord(refAddress); indexing(rm, refAddress)|
    1: (* there is a displacement and no indexing *)
        getWord(refAddress)   |
    3: WriteString('Error: attempting memory ref when r/m is a register'); WriteLn
    END
  END;
  RETURN refAddress
END formAddress;
```

Procedure `indexing` uses the `r/m` field to determine which register(s) to use in accordance with Table 2.7:

```
PROCEDURE indexing (rmField: CARDINAL; VAR refAddress: CARDINAL);
BEGIN
  CASE rmField OF
  0: refAddress:= refAddress + register[BX] + register[SI] |
  1: refAddress:= refAddress + register[BX] + register[DI] |
  2: refAddress:= refAddress + register[BP] + register[SI] |
```

```
     3: refAddress:= refAddress + register[BP] + register[DI] |
     4: INC(refAddress, register[SI]) |
     5: INC(refAddress, register[DI]) |
     6: INC(refAddress, register[BP]) |
     7: INC(refAddress, register[BX])
     END;
END indexing;
```

Among the procedures that interpret instructions in different categories, the simplest is leaInstruction, which interprets LEA instructions:

```
PROCEDURE leaInstruction (opRec: opWordFields);
BEGIN
  register[opRec.reg]:= formAddress(opRec)
END leaInstruction;
```

An LEA instruction certainly has a memory operand. The effective address of this operand is computed by procedure formAddress and is assigned to the register that is specified by the reg field of the opWord. When procedure leaInstruction is called, opRec already contains the fields of the opWord, and ip contains the address of the next word of machine code. If this word is a displacement, then the call of procedure getWord within procedure formAddress will obtain this displacement and leave ip as the address of the opWord of the next instruction. This illustrates the general fact that after interpreting an instruction, that is, at the end of the REPEAT loop in the body of module interpret, ip is always the address of the opWord of the next instruction.

Instructions that have no operands are interpreted by the following:

```
PROCEDURE noOperandInstructions (opRec: opWordFields);
BEGIN
  IF opRec.opCode = 0 THEN (* RET *)
    jumpIP(dereference(register[SP])); (* ip:= word whose address is
      in SP *)
    DEC(register[SP])
  END (* if NOP then do nothing *)
END noOperandInstructions;
```

In 8086 Assembly Language conditional jump instructions refer to the flag register. For simplicity our SAL interpreter refers instead to a global variable resultValue which stores the result of the previous two-operand instruction:

```
PROCEDURE jumpInstructions (opRec: opWordFields);
VAR
  jumpAddress: CARDINAL;
BEGIN
  jumpAddress:= formAddress(opRec); (* address to jump to *)
  CASE opRec.opCode OF
  0: (* JMP *) jumpIP(jumpAddress) (* ip:= jumpAddress *)       |
```

```
8: (* JE *) IF resultValue = 0 THEN jumpIP(jumpAddress) END |
12: (* JG *) IF INTEGER(resultValue) > 0 THEN jumpIP(jumpAddress) END |
9:  (* LOOP *) DEC(register[CX]);
    IF register[CX] # 0 THEN jumpIP (jumpAddress) END |
10: (* JL *) IF INTEGER(resultValue) < 0 THEN jumpIP(jumpAddress) END |
11: (* JNE *) IF resultValue # 0 THEN jumpIP(jumpAddress) END |
13: (* JLE *) IF INTEGER(resultValue) <= 0 THEN jumpIP(jumpAddress) END |
14: (* JGE *) IF INTEGER(resultValue) >= 0 THEN jumpIP(jumpAddress) END |
15: (* JC  *) IF carryFlag = 1 THEN jumpIP(jumpAddress) END |
16: (* CALL *) INC(register[SP]); assignTo(register[SP],ipAddress());
    jumpIP(jumpAddress)
ELSE WriteString('Error: illegal JUMPINSTRUCTIONS opCode')
END
END jumpInstructions;
```

A complete version of procedure `singleOperandInstruction` is included in the listing of module `interpret` in the Appendix. Just to give the flavour, the part of this procedure that deals with DEC, INC or NEG is as follows:

```
PROCEDURE singleOperandInstruction(opRec: opWordFields);
VAR
  operandAddress, opValue, result: CARDINAL;
BEGIN
  IF opRec.opCode < 4 THEN (* DEC, INC, or NEG *)
    IF opRec.memRef = 1 THEN (* memory operand *)
      operandAddress:= formAddress(opRec);
      opValue:=dereference(operandAddress) (* returns operand value *)
    ELSE (* register operand *)
      opValue:= register[opRec.reg]
    END;
    CASE opRec.opCode OF
      0: (* DEC *) result:= CARDINAL(INTEGER(opValue) - 1)|
      1: (* INC *) result:= CARDINAL(INTEGER(opValue) + 1)|
      2: WriteString('Illegal opCode for single-op instruction'); WriteLn|
      3: (* NEG *) result:= CARDINAL(-INTEGER(opValue))
    END;
    IF opRec.memRef = 1 THEN assignTo(operandAddress,result)
    ELSE register[opRec.reg]:= result
    END
  ELSE (* deal with other single-operand instructions *)
  END
END singleOperandInstruction;
```

If a two-operand instruction has an immediate operand, this precedes the displacement, if any. Therefore procedure `twoOperandInstruction` must read the immediate operand, if any, before dealing with the destination operand. This is why procedure `twoOperandInstruction` starts by obtaining the value of the source operand, which may possibly be an immediate operand. The next section of procedure `twoOperandInstruction` obtains the address and value of the second operand. A CASE statement applies the appropriate operation, for example ADD, and the final part of procedure `twoOperandInstruction` assigns the result of this operation to the destination:

```
PROCEDURE twoOperandInstruction(opRec: opWordFields);
VAR
  destinationAddress, destinationValue, sourceValue: CARDINAL;
BEGIN
  IF opRec.immediate = 1 THEN getWord(sourceValue)
  ELSIF opRec.destination = 1 THEN
    IF opRec.m = 3 THEN sourceValue:= register[opRec.rm]
    ELSIF opRec.memRef = 1 THEN
      sourceValue:= dereference(formAddress(opRec))
    END
  ELSIF opRec.memRef = 1 THEN sourceValue:= register[opRec.reg]
  END;
  IF opRec.destination = 0 THEN
    IF opRec.memRef = 1 THEN
      destinationAddress:= formAddress(opRec);
      destinationValue:= dereference(destinationAddress);
    ELSE WriteString('Error: memRefBit should be set'); WriteLn
    END
  ELSE destinationValue:= register[opRec.reg]
  END;
  CASE opRec.opCode OF
    0: (* MOV *)  resultValue:= sourceValue  |
    1: (* ADD *)  resultValue:= sourceValue + destinationValue  |
    2: (* SUB *)  resultValue:=
          CARDINAL(INTEGER(destinationValue) - INTEGER(sourceValue))  |
    3: (* CMP *)  resultValue:=
          CARDINAL(INTEGER(destinationValue) - INTEGER(sourceValue))  |
    4: (* AND *)  resultValue:=
          CARDINAL(BITSET(destinationValue) * BITSET(sourceValue))  |
    5: (* OR  *)  resultValue:=
          CARDINAL(BITSET(destinationValue) + BITSET(sourceValue))
  END;
  IF opRec.opCode # 3 THEN
      (* not CMP so assign result to destination *)
      IF opRec.destination = 1 THEN register[opRec.reg]:= resultValue
      ELSE assignTo(destinationAddress, resultValue)
      END
  END
END twoOperandInstruction;
```

Section 2.9.3 included a listing of the binary symbolic for module `salSubs`. For each subroutine, such as `INTREAD`, the binary symbolic simply included a single word, instead of an instruction sequence such as would normally be expected for a subroutine. Instead of a subroutine for `INTREAD`, module `salSubs` just has `DW 513`. Similarly, module `salSubs` has `DW 514` instead of a subroutine for `INTWRITE`, and so on for all the other subroutines in module `salSubs`. Procedure `getOp` recognizes `513`, `514`, etc. as opWords of instructions belonging to a new category `extraCategory`. Within module `interpret`, these instructions are executed by procedure `extraIns`. When the opWord is `513` procedure `extraIns` reads an integer and pushes it on to the stack, thus executing `CALL INTREAD`. Because `CALL INTREAD` is a subroutine call, procedure `extraIns` ends with a jump to the subroutine return address. For other subroutines in `salSubs` a CASE statement in `extraIns` selects the appropriate routine. For `ENDPROG` the routine is the single statement `halted:= TRUE`. In Section 2.7.2 we introduced only `INTWRITE`, `INTREAD`, `NEWLINE` and `ENDPROG`. Besides these, procedure `extraIns` also interprets further (pseudo-)subroutines that deal with real numbers.

In the Appendix the listing of module `interpret` includes a procedure `trace` which outputs the contents of registers, and some other information, after execution of each instruction. This procedure can be called after the CASE statement in the body of the module, enabling us to watch the execution of a program in detail, indeed for most purposes far too much detail. Exercises in Section 6.5 develop better debugging facilities.

6.4 Discussion

Each time our interpreter processes an instruction it unpacks all the instruction's fields. When an instruction is executed repeatedly, the same unpacking is repeated. To avoid this, we could translate every instruction into an unpacked form before commencing interpretation, which would work directly with an array of unpacked instructions. Unpacked instructions would occupy more memory but the interpretation of loops would be faster.

This illustrates the general point that interpretation can often be made more efficient by initial translation of a program into a form that facilitates interpretation. A practical example illustrating the same point is that in the Pascal P4 system p-code instructions are assembled into a convenient form before interpretation commences (Pemberton and Daniels 1986).

6.5 Exercises

1. As a preliminary to subsequent exercises, this exercise develops our interpreter to display the source text lines of a single module program that is linked with module `salSubs`. Module `salSubs` must come second in `McFile`.

(a) Amend a copy of the assembler introduced in Chapter 4 so that, in one-to-one correspondence to each word of relocatable binary in file `salAsout`, it outputs to another file `sLines` the line number of the assembly language program from which this machine code word was derived. For example, for the program in Table 4.1, if `LEA SP, STKBAS` is the second line of the source program, then the output to the file `sLines` would be 2 2 3 3 4 5 5 6 6 and so on, meaning that the first two words of machine code come from the instruction in line 2 of the source text, the next two words come from the instruction in line 3, the next word comes from the instruction in line 4, and so on.

(b) Develop the interpreter introduced in this chapter so that, as well as reading absolute binary machine code from file `absBinry`, it also reads from file `sLines` and reads the assembly language source code from a separate file. Assembly language text is to be read into a one-dimensional array like `charArray` in Section 3.4. Your program should set up

```
sourceLines: ARRAY [1..numberOfSourceLines] OF
                RECORD start, length: CARDINAL END;
```

so that `sourceLines[i].start` is the subscript in the character array of the first character of the source line whose line number is *i*, and `sourceLines[i].length` is the number of characters in this line. Instead of having machine code in an array `machineCode` of cardinals, your interpreter is to work with an array

```
mCode: ARRAY[startAddress..machineCodeUB] OF
          RECORD machineCodeWord, lineNumber: CARDINAL END;
```

which is to be set up so that `mCode[j].machineCodeWord` contains the same as `machineCode[j]` in Section 6.2, and `mCode[j].lineNumber` is the machine code word's source text line number obtained from file `sLines`.

(c) Write a procedure which, for debugging purposes, can be called at the start of the REPEAT loop in the body of module `interpret`, and will display the source text corresponding to the next instruction that is to be executed. (Preferably also display the source-text line number.)

2. Develop the software produced in Exercise 1 to allow the user to insert (using a text editor) an asterisk at the beginning of any line of the assembly language source program that is read by the interpreter (not the assembler). Whenever it executes an instruction corresponding to a source text line that starts with an asterisk, the interpreter is to display the source text of the line and call procedure `trace` to display the contents of registers after execution of the instruction. For this purpose the records in array `sourceLines` are to be given an extra field which is BOOLEAN and indicates whether or not a line has been marked with an asterisk by the user. Lines marked with an asterisk are known as *break points*. When the program reaches a break point it is to be held up (so that the user can read the screen) until the user types character `'C'`.

3. Develop the software produced in Exercise 2 to allow the user optionally to follow

an asterisk with +n or −n, where n is a cardinal value. For the first n times when it comes to an instruction for which the source has been marked *+n the interpreter is to display the source line and the contents of registers as in Exercise 2: thereafter this information is not to be displayed. For the first n times when it comes to an instruction for which the source has been marked *−n the interpreter is not to display the source line and display the contents of registers but for the (n+1)th and subsequent executions of this instruction the source line and register contents are to be displayed.

4. Develop the software produced in Exercise 2 so that when a program is held up at a break point, if the user types the textual name of a label followed by '=', e.g. FRED =, then if the program includes a data word labelled FRED then the contents of this word will be displayed. If the user types FRED + 3 =, the debugger is to display the contents of the word whose address is 3 plus the address corresponding to FRED. If the user types FRED − 3 = then the contents of the word whose address is the address corresponding to FRED minus 3 is to be displayed. If the user types e.g. 21 −> FRED then 21 is to be assigned to the word whose address is FRED. Similarly 21 −> FRED + 3 is to mean that 21 is assigned to the word whose address is three plus the address of FRED. And 21 −> FRED − 3 is to mean that 21 is assigned to the word whose address is that of the word labelled FRED minus 3. To achieve this it will be necessary for the debugger to obtain a label table from the assembler, or to build one up by reading the assembly language source file, and the label table will have to contain relocated addresses. If the user attempts to display the contents of, or assign a new value to, a word that is not a data word but an instruction, the debugger is to output an error message.

Chapter 7

An introduction to syntax analysis

7.1 Introduction

To translate from one programming language into another, a compiler or an assembler must determine the structure of the source program. The structure of a SAL program is so simple that we have been able to write a SAL assembler without discussing structural analysis explicitly: we have dealt with structure intuitively. To write a recursive descent compiler for a subset of Modula-2 we will need some formal understanding of program structure.

We will begin by considering expressions. For example, the structure of the expression U * V + X - Y * (W - Z) can be represented by the tree shown in Figure 7.1. This tree includes a subtree, shown separately in Figure 7.2(a), that indicates multiplication of U by V. In Figure 7.1 this subtree is part of a larger subtree, shown in Figure 7.2(b), which indicates that X is to be added to the product U * V. Figure 7.1 is consistent with traditional understanding of U * V + X - Y * (W - Z), for which Figure 7.3 is incorrect because it represents (U * V + X - Y) * (W - Z).

Part of the work of a compiler is to determine the intended structure of an arithmetical expression, or indeed of a complete program. In order to motivate the study of techniques for automatic analysis of structure we will start by illustrating how the results of this analysis can be used. We will subsequently consider how to achieve the analysis.

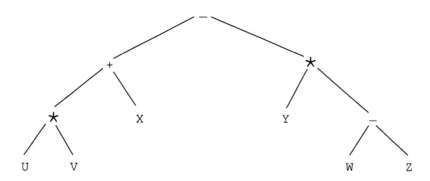

Figure 7.1 Structure of the expression U * V + X - Y * (W - Z).

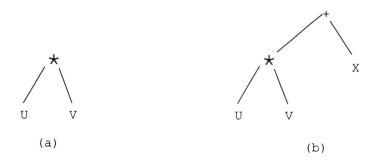

Figure 7.2 (a) Subtree for U * V. (b) Subtree for U*V+X.

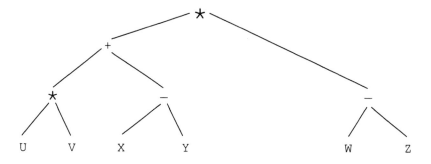

Figure 7.3 Incorrect structure of U * V + X - Y * (W - Z).

7.2 Generating object code from a tree

7.2.1 Postorder traversal of a binary tree

Chapter 8 introduces methods for constructing a tree such as that shown in Figure 7.1 to express the structure of an expression. In the present section we will assume that a tree such as this has already been constructed, and we will consider how to generate from this a SAL routine that will evaluate the expression, starting by re-expressing the tree as a linear string of symbols.

Traversing a tree means visiting every node of the tree. To express a tree as a linear (i.e. branchless) sequence we systematically visit every node in turn, inserting nodal information into the sequence. *Postorder* traversal means visiting the left child node then the right child node and then the parent node: postorder is so called because the parent is visited after both of its children. The result of postorder traversal of the tree in Figure 7.2(a) is the linear sequence UV*, which consists of *left child, right child, parent.*

If a child itself has children then these are visited first. For example, for the tree shown in Figure 7.2(b) postorder traversal takes us from the root '+' to the left child '*'. Before outputting the '*' we output its left child and then its right child, thus obtaining UV* which is the same as for Figure 7.2(a). At this stage we have finished with the left child of the root node '+'. Next we output the right child of '+', and finally we output the root node '+'. The complete result is the linear sequence UV*X+.

The general idea is that if we come to a child that is not a leaf node but is the root node of a further subtree, we do a postorder traversal of that subtree, and so on recursively. If the tree has nodes of type

```
node = RECORD nodeItem: CHAR; leftChild, rightChild: pointerToNode END
```

where `pointerToNode = POINTER TO node`, then postorder traversal can be achieved by calling the following recursive procedure:

```
PROCEDURE postOut(tree: pointerToNode);
BEGIN
  IF tree # nil THEN
    WITH tree^ DO
      postOut(leftChild);
      postOut(rightChild);
      Write(nodeItem)
    END
  END
END postOut;
```

Postorder traversal of a tree such as that in Figure 7.1 yields a linear sequence that tells us exactly what the tree tells us, that is, the structure of the expression, but because the sequence is linear it is easily translated into a sequence of SAL instructions that will evaluate the expression. The output sequence UV*X+YWZ-*- is an example of an expression in *postfix* notation, which is so called because an operator comes immediately after its two operands. This notation is sometimes known as *reverse polish*, because it was invented by a Polish mathematician. Any expression can be written in postfix notation. Ordinary notation, as for example in X + (Y * Z), is called *infix* because an operator is placed between its operands.

Important properties of postfix notation are that it does not require brackets to determine which operators to apply first, and it does not use a sense of priority, for example that * has priority over +. Instead the order in which operators are applied is determined *only* by the sequence in which the string is written. For example, postfix for P + Q * R is P Q R * +, whereas postfix for (P + Q) * R is P Q R + *. When two operators are adjacent, one of the operands of the second operator is the result of applying the first operator. For example, in PQ+* one of the operands of * is PQ+.

7.2.2 Generating code from an postfix expression using temporary variables

When producing a SAL routine from a postfix expression we will assume that the SAL object program already contains data words corresponding to the variables in the expression, e.g.

```
U:      DW 18
V:      DW 352
X:      DW 3
```

and so on. We will also assume that the SAL program includes a sufficient number of temporary variables:

```
T1:     DW ?
T2:     DW ?
T3:     DW ?
T4:     DW ?
```

and so on.

In a postorder sequence we can be sure that every operator is preceded by its two operands. We can read along the sequence until we come to the first operator and then produce SAL instructions to apply the operator to the operands that immediately precede it in the sequence. The first operator in UV*X+YWZ-*- is * and it is immediately preceded by its two operands U and V. SAL instructions for T1:= U * V are

```
MOV AX, U
MULT V
MOV T1, AX
```

We now need a sequence of instructions for the remainder of the expression which can be be written T1 X + Y W Z - * -, in which T1 replaces UV* in the original expression. The first operator in the revised version of the expession is +, and its operands must immediately precede it, so we produce instructions for T2:= X + T1 and our SAL fragment grows to

```
MOV AX, U
MULT V
MOV T1, AX
MOV AX, T1
ADD AX, X
MOV T2, AX
```

Continuing, we need a sequence of instructions for the remainder of the expression which can be written T2 Y W Z - * -. The first operator in this is - and its operands must immediately precede it. These are W and Z, so we append to our SAL program some instructions for T3:= W - Z:

```
MOV AX, U
MULT V
```

```
MOV T1, AX
MOV AX, T1
ADD AX, X
MOV T2, AX
MOV AX, W
SUB AX, Z
MOV T3, AX.
```

This leaves T2 Y T3 * -. Next we append instructions for T4 := Y * T3, which leaves T2 T4 -, and finally we append instructions for T5 := T2 - T4 completing the SAL routine:

```
MOV AX, U
MULT V
MOV T1, AX
MOV AX, T1
ADD AX, X
MOV T2, AX
MOV AX, W
SUB AX, Z
MOV T3, AX
MOV AX, Y
MULT T3
MOV T4, AX
MOV AX, T2
SUB AX, T4
MOV T5, AX
```

The value of the expresssion is assigned to T5. This is inefficient because there are too many MOVs, but it works correctly.

7.2.3 Generating code from a postfix expression using a run-time stack

We now introduce an alternative way of working in which an expression is evaluated by using a stack instead of temporary variables T1, T2, T3, etc. This way of working is so simple that we can very easily write a Modula-2 procedure to compile a postfix expression into SAL. As a preliminary step towards this, an outline of a SAL routine using a stack to evaluate UV*X+YWZ-*- is as follows:

```
PUSH U
PUSH V
pop top two words off stack, multiply them and push result on to stack
PUSH X
pop top two words off stack, add them and push result on to stack
```

```
PUSH Y
PUSH W
PUSH Z
pop top two words off stack, subtract and push result on to stack
pop top two words off stack, multiply them and push result on to stack
pop top two words off stack, subtract and push result on to stack.
```

It is easy to check that this will work correctly. After U and V have been pushed on to the stack, the multiplication has been executed and X has been pushed on to the stack, the stack contains:

```
value of U * V
value of X
```

In this the the contents of the top of the stack are shown *below* the next-to-top of stack, and so on. Continuing our example, after the result of addition has been pushed on to the stack and Y, W and Z have been pushed on to the stack, the stack contains

```
value of U * V + X
value of Y
value of W
value of Z
```

After the results of substraction and multiplication have been pushed on to the stack, the stack contains

```
value of U * V + X
value of Y * (W - Z)
```

After the result of the final SUB has been pushed on to the stack, the stack contains only the value of U * V + X - Y * (W - Z), as required.

To make our outline object-code routine into a detailed SAL routine we use, for example, the instructions

```
POP AX
POP BX
MULT BX
PUSH AX
```

to pop the top two words off the stack, multiply them, and push the result onto the stack. Moreover, we use the instructions

```
POP AX
MOV DI, SP
ADD [DI], AX
```

to achieve the same effect as would be achieved by popping the top two words off the stack, adding them and pushing the result on to the stack. Instead of three instructions we would like to use

```
POP AX
ADD [SP], AX
```

but [SP] is illegal as a memory operand for ADD in SAL, and this is why we use DI. The instructions that we use for subtraction and integer division are included in the CASE statement in the procedure applyOperator which is shown below.

This procedure, which translates a postfix expression into a SAL routine to evaluate the expression, assumes for simplicity that the postfix string is available as a string of characters without spaces between, with one character per variable and one character per operator. We assume that the sequence is terminated by a space character. The procedure is as follows:

```
PROCEDURE postfixToSAL;
TYPE
  charSet = SET OF char;
VAR
  ch: CHAR;
  PROCEDURE applyOperator(operator: CHAR);
  BEGIN
    CASE operator OF
    '+':      WriteString('    POP AX'); WriteLn;
              WriteString('    MOV DI, SP'); WriteLn;
              WriteString('    ADD [DI], AX'); WriteLn |
    '-':      WriteString('    POP AX); WriteLn;
              WriteString('    MOV DI, SP'); WriteLn;
              WriteString('    SUB [DI], AX); WriteLn |
    '*':      WriteString('    POP BX'); WriteLn;
              WriteString('    POP AX'); WriteLn;
              WriteString('    MULT BX'); WriteLn;
              WriteString('    PUSH AX'); WriteLn |
    '/':      WriteString('    POP BX'); WriteLn;
              WriteString('    POP AX'); WriteLn;
              WriteString('    DIV BX'); WriteLn;
              WriteString('    PUSH AX'); WriteLn
    END
  END applyOperator;

BEGIN
  RedirectInput('sorsText'); Read(ch);
  WHILE ch # ' ' DO
    IF ch IN charSet {'A'..'Z'} THEN WriteString('    PUSH   ');
      Write(ch); WriteLn
    ELSE applyOperator(ch)
    END;
    Read(ch)
  END
END postfixToSAL;
```

This procedure is very simple because it processes the operands and operators in the sequence in which if finds them in the postfix string. For example, for the postfix string UV*X+YWZ-*- this procedure outputs

```
PUSH U
PUSH V
POP BX
POP AX
MULT BX
PUSH AX
PUSH X
POP AX
MOV DI, SP
ADD [DI], AX
PUSH Y
PUSH W
PUSH Z
POP AX
MOV DI, SP
SUB [DI], AX
POP BX
POP AX
MULT BX
PUSH AX
POP AX
MOV DI, SP
SUB [DI], AX
```

This SAL routine works in exactly the same way as the routine that was introduced at the beginning of Section 7.2.3, using a stack that is called a *run-time* stack because it is used when the object program is executed.

7.3   A brief introduction to formal languages

7.3.1 Formal grammars

We have seen how a postfix string can be obtained from a structure-describing tree, and how a SAL routine to evaluate an expression can be obtained from a postfix string. Before we can see how a compiler can automatically generate a structure-describing tree, or a representation equivalent to this, we must first gain some elementary understanding of formal languages.

As in Section 3.1, it is sufficient for present purposes to say that a *symbol* is a string comprising one or more characters, and for simplicity we will say that none of these can be space, tab or new-line characters. What makes a symbol a symbol is that we have chosen to use it as such, just as we choose identifiers freely in Modula-2.

We will be concerned with three kinds of symbols: *start* symbols, *non-terminal* symbols, and *terminal* symbols. Technically, a string of terminal symbols constitutes a *sentence*. A formal language is a particular set of sentences, and a formal grammar is a means for defining a formal language. For example, a formal grammar exists that defines Modula-2, such that a legitimate program in Modula-2 is a sentence in the formal language that is defined by this grammar.

A formal grammar has a set of terminal symbols, a set of non-terminal symbols, and exactly one start symbol which is a special non-terminal symbol. We are free to choose what these symbols are, just as we can choose our own identifiers in a Modula-2 program. We are free to choose which symbols are non-terminal, which are terminal, and which is the start symbol.

To enable us to see at a glance which symbols are terminal and which are non-terminal, we can optionally adopt a convention that makes the distinction between terminal and non-terminals very obvious. For example, we can restrict terminals to be composed of lower-case (i.e. non-capital) letters and non-terminals to be composed of upper-case (i.e. capital) letters. Another idea that is often used is to restrict non-terminals to be any string starting with '<' and ending with '>', for example, <memory>. Restrictions like this may help us to see what is going on, but are otherwise unecessary.

A *formal grammar* consists of a set of productions as well as a start symbol, a set of non-terminal symbols, and a set of terminal symbols. Sometimes productions are called *rewrite rules*. For us, a *production* consists of a left-hand side and a right-hand side separated by an arrow ->. The left-hand side is a string that must include at least one of the grammar's non-terminal symbols or the start symbol. The right-hand side is a string comprising zero, one or more symbols which must be non-terminal symbols or terminal symbols belonging to this particular grammar. At least one production must have only the start symbol on the left-hand side; and no production may have only a terminal symbol on the left-hand side. The following are complete examples of formal grammars:

First example grammar
Start symbol: S
Non-terminal symbols: A, B, C, D
Terminal symbols: u, v, x, y
Productions:

```
S  ->  A C
S  ->  D
A  ->  B C
C  ->  x D
C  ->  y C
D  ->  v y x
B  ->  y
B  ->  u
```

Second example grammar

Start symbol: `Startit`
Non-terminal symbols: `N1, N2, N3, N4, N5`
Terminal symbols: `x736, !, AND, 88, Is`
Productions:

```
Startit -> N4 N2
N2   -> N1 N5 N3
N2 -> AND
N1 -> N3 88
N1 -> N3 ! N4
N3 -> 88 x736
N5 -> N2 Is
N4 -> 88 88 88
N4 -> AND N2
```

Third example grammar

Start symbol: `S`
Non-terminal symbols: `<expression>, <identifier>`
Terminal symbols: `+, *, a,b,c,d`
Productions:

```
S   ->   <expression>
<expression>  ->   <expression> + <expression>
<expression>  ->   <expression> * <expression>
<expression>  ->   <identifier>
<identifier>  ->   a
<identifier>  ->   b
<identifier>  ->   c
<identifier>  ->   d
```

Given a formal grammar, the following procedure generates strings of that grammar's terminal symbols:

```
PROCEDURE generate;
VAR
  workingString: stringOfCharacters;
BEGIN
  workingString:= startSymbol;
  REPEAT
    select at random any production that has its left hand side included in
          workingString;
    in workingString replace the left hand side by the right hand side of the
          selected production
  UNTIL  workingString contains only terminal symbols
END generate;
```

With our first example grammar, at successive iterations of the REPEAT loop in `generate`, `workingString` could, for example, contain what is shown on successive lines:

```
S
A C
B C C
B y C C
B y C x D
u y C x D
u y x D x D
u y x D x v y x
u y x v y x x v y x
```

By tracing through successive lines we can follow the derivation of the final line which contains only terminal symbols: a *derivation* is a sequence in which `generate` has selected productions. Procedure `generate` must stop at a line that contains only terminals because every production must have at least one non-terminal on its left-hand side. Terminal symbols are so called because further symbols cannot be derived from them, wheras further symbols can be derived from non-terminal symbols.

A string of terminals generated by procedure `generate` is a *sentence*. The set of all sentences that can be generated by procedure `generate` from a given formal grammar is the *formal language* defined by that grammar. Thus `uyxvyxxvyx` is a sentence in the formal language defined by our first example grammar. Another example of a sentence in the formal language defined by our first example grammar is `yyyxvyxxvyx`, which can be derived as follows:

```
S
A C
A x D
B C x D
y C x D
y y C x D
y y y C x D
y y y C x v y x
y y y x D x v y x
y y y x v y x x v y x
```

A string such as `yyyCxD` that may contain non-terminals and/or terminals is known as a *sentential form*. A sentence is a sentential form that contains only terminal symbols.

A formal grammar defines a particular language by specifying all of the sentences that belong to that language. It does this by specifying that this language consists of exactly the set of sentences that can be generated by applying procedure `generate` to its grammar. A formal language defined in this way does not necessarily have any real-world significance: it can be utterly meaningless. A formal grammar defines a formal language regardless of whether the strings have any meaning. Our second example grammar was chosen to emphasize this point. For our second example grammar a sentence could be derived as follows:

```
startit
N4 N2
N4 N1 N5 N3
N4 N3 ! N4 N5 N3
N4 N3 ! N4 N5 88 x736
88 88 88 N3 ! N4 N5 88 x736
88 88 88 88 x736 ! N4 N5 88 x736
88 88 88 88 x736 ! 88 88 88 N5 88 x736
88 88 88 88 x736 ! 88 88 88 N2 Is 88 x736
88 88 88 88 x736 ! 88 88 88 AND Is 88 x736
```

7.3.2 Parse trees

Instead of showing a derivation as a sequence of sentential forms, we can draw a tree to show the sequence in which the productions were, or could have been, selected by procedure `generate`. For the first example given in Section 7.3.1, Figure 7.4 shows that S was rewritten AC, A was rewritten BC, C was rewritten xD, D was written v y x, and so on. Because any sentence in a given formal language could have been generated by procedure `generate`, there must be at least one tree like this that shows how that sentence could have been generated. A tree like this that shows how a sentence could have been generated from a given grammar is known as a *parse tree*. To take another

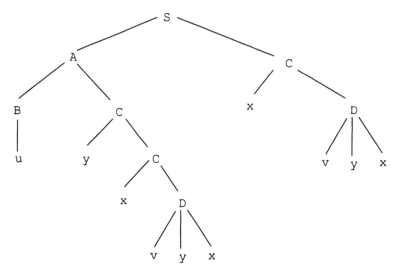

Figure 7.4 A parse tree for the sentence u y x v y x x v y x with the first example grammar.

example, with our third example grammar we can generate the expression a * b + c as indicated by the parse tree shown in Figure 7.5. Interpreting this tree as in Section 7.1, the structure is a * (b + c) : it is easy to see that the expression from which a is derived is multiplied by the expression from which b + c is derived. The fact that a * (b + c) is not the normal interpretation of a * b + c does not mean that formal grammars are hopeless. It just means that we did not define this particular grammar with sufficient care.

A grammar is said to be *ambiguous* if it defines a formal language in which at least one sentence has more than one derivation, and thus has more than one parse tree. Our third example grammar is ambiguous because the sentence a * b + c can be derived as shown above, and can also be derived differently as indicated by the parse tree in Figure 7.6. This indicates that c is added to the value of the subexpression a * b, which is consistent with the normal interpretation of a * b + c.

In each iteration, procedure generate selects *any* non-terminal in workingString for rewriting. We can modify generate so that it always selects the leftmost non-terminal for rewriting. If generate is modified in this way, then all its derivations are said to be *leftmost* derivations. Using the third example grammar, the following is an example of a leftmost derivation:

```
<expression>
<expression> + <expression>
<expression> * <expression> + <expression>
<identifier> * <expression> + <expression>
a   * <expression> + <expression>
a   * <identifier> + <expression>
a   * b   +   <expression>
a   * b   +   <identifier>
a   * b   +   c
```

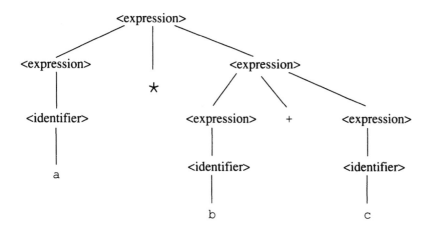

Figure 7.5 A parse tree for a * b + c with the third example grammar.

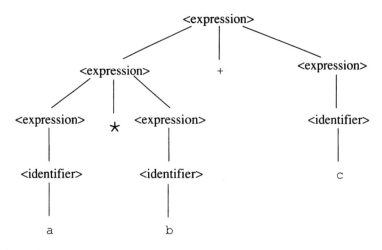

Figure 7.6 A second parse tree for a * b + c with the third example grammar.

A different leftmost derivation of the same sentence using the same ambiguous grammar is:

```
<expression>
<expression> * <expression>
<identifier> * <expression>
a * <expression> + <expression>
a * <identifier> + <expression>
a *  b  + <expression>
a *  b  + <identifier>
a *  b  + c
```

If procedure generate is modified so that it always selects the rightmost non-terminal for rewriting, then all its derivations are said to be *rightmost* derivations. Restriction to leftmost or rightmost derivation may not cure ambiguity, but will be of interest to us later.

Our fourth example grammar is an improvement on the third, in that it is not ambiguous, and its parse trees are consistent with the normal priority of multiplication over addition:

Fourth example grammar

```
Start symbol:  <expression>.
Non-terminal symbols:  <term>, <identifier>.
Terminal symbols:  +, *, a, b, c, d
Productions:
    <expression>  ->  <term> + <expression>
    <expression>  ->  <term>
```

```
<term>          ->   <identifier> * <term>
<term>          ->   <identifier>
<identifier> ->   a
<identifier> ->   b
<identifier> ->   c
<identifier> ->   d
```

With this grammar, a derivation of a * b + c is shown in Figure 7.7. This grammar defines the same language as the third example grammar, but is not ambiguous. Ambiguity has been removed by redesigning the grammar, but this is not always possible. A tree such as that in Figure 7.7 is of interest because we can generate object code from it, just as we did from Figure 7.1 via postfix, and we will return to this in Chapter 8.

7.3.3 Context-sensitive, context-free and right-regular languages

It is helpful to distinguish between different kinds of formal grammars. In a *context-sensitive* grammar the number of symbols on the left hand side of a production must not exceed the number on the right-hand side, and the left hand side of every production must include at least one non-terminal symbol or the start symbol. In a context-sensitive grammar a production such as Ax -> uvx says that A can be rewritten uv in any context in which A is immediately followed by x. This is why such a grammar is said to be context-sensitive.

Context-free grammars are a subclass of context-sensitive grammars in which the left-hand side of each production consists of exactly one symbol. A context-free grammar defines a context-free language. All of our example grammars are context-free.

Right-regular grammars are an important subclass of context-free grammars in which every production has on its right-hand side either exactly one terminal symbol or

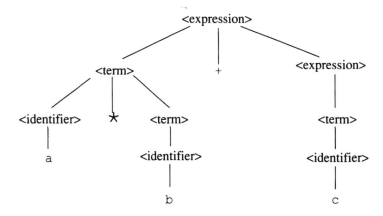

Figure 7.7 A parse tree for a * b + c with the fourth example grammar.

alternatively exactly one terminal symbol followed by exactly one non-terminal symbol. Parsing right-regular languages is very much simpler than parsing context-free languages, and this is one reason for their practical importance.

7.3.4 Extended Backus–Naur form

We can often write a context-free grammar more concisely by using | to separate alternative right-hand sides that have the same left-hand side. For example instead of writing

```
<identifier>  ->  a
<identifier>  ->  b
<identifier>  ->  c
<identifier>  ->  d
```

we can write more concisely

```
<identifier>  ->  a | b | c | d
```

In this sense | means *or*. Using this we can, for example, rewrite the productions of our fourth example grammar as follows:

```
<expression>    ->   <term> + <expression> | <term>
<term>          ->   <identifier> * <term> | <identifier>
<identifier>    ->   a | b | c | d
```

This does not change the grammar. As another example, the following productions define the set of all possible Modula-2 identifiers and reserved words:

```
<identifier>    ->   <letter> <N>
    <N>         ->   <letterOrDigit> <N>  | empty
<letterOrDigit> ->   <letter> | <digit>
    <digit>     ->   0 | 1 | 2 | ... | 9
    <letter>    ->   A | B | ... | Z | a | b | ...| z
```

The symbol empty is a terminal symbol that has the special property that it is invisible in a sentence. The use of this symbol, which is known as the *null symbol*, is essentially a technical trick that is sometimes convenient, as in the example just given. Some authors use the Greek letter epsilon, instead of the word empty, for the null symbol.

We can use the following abbreviated and more easily understood notation for exactly the same set of productions:

```
<identifier>        ->  <letter> {<letterOrDigit>}
<letterOrDigit>     ->  <letter> | <digit>
   <digit>          ->  0 | 1 | 2 | ... | 9
   <letter>         ->  A | B | ... | Z | a | b | ...| z
```

In this abbreviated notation, the curly brackets { } mean *zero or more occurrences* of what is enclosed between them.

To introduce further notation, the following productions define the set of all possible integers *optionally* preceded by + or –.

```
<signedInteger>  ->  <integer> | <sign> <integer>
<sign>           ->  + | -
<integer >       ->  <digit> {<digit>}
<digit>          ->  0 | 1 | 2 | ... | 9
```

We use square brackets [ ] to mean zero or one (but not more) occurrences of what is enclosed within these brackets. So in the example just given, instead of

```
<signedInteger>  ->  <integer> | <sign> <integer>
```

we can write

```
<signedInteger>  ->   [<sign>] <integer>
```

which is more concise and easier to understand. Another development is to use round brackets ( ) to group items together. These developments introduce the problem that brackets may be, or be included in, terminal symbols. To solve this problem it is usual to enclose terminal symbols between double quotes. Moreover, it is helpful to mark the end of every production with a period. When we use all of these developments we are expressing productions in an *extended Backus–Naur form* (EBNF). Instead of using an arrow as in

```
<signedInteger>  ->   [<sign>] <integer>
```

some authors write

```
<signedInteger>  ::=   [<sign>] <integer>
```

and it is not unusual to write = instead of ::= or ->.

As an illustration of the use of EBNF, the following set of productions defines all legitimate SAL programs, ommitting comments.

```
<program>   ->  [<exports>] [<imports>] {<line>} "endOfTextSy".
<line>      ->  [(<label>":" <instruction> | <instruction>)] "newLineSy".
<label>     ->  <letter> {<letter>}.
<labelList> ->  <label>{<label>}.
<exports>   ->  "EXPORT" <labelList>.
<imports>   ->  "IMPORT" <labelList>.
<cardinal>  ->  <digit> {<digit>}.
<digit>     ->  "0" |"1" |"2" | ... |"9".
```

```
<letter>    ->  "A" |"B" | ... |"Z".
<instruction>  ->  <twoOp> | <singleOp> | <leaInstruction> |
   <noOperandInstructions> | <jumpInstructions> | <pseudoOp>.
<twoOp>      -> <twoOpOpCode> <firstOperand> "," <secondOperand>.
<twoOpOpCode> -> "MOV" | "ADD" | "SUB" | ...
<firstOperand>  ->  <memoryOperand> | <registerOperand>.
<secondOperand>  ->  <memoryOperand> | <registerOperand> | <number>.
<singleOp>  ->  <singleOpOpCode> (<registerOperand> | <memoryOperand>).
<singleOpOpCode>  ->  "DEC" | "INC" | "PUSH" | ....
<jumpInstructions>    ->  <jumpInstructionsCode> <memoryOperand>.
<jumpInstructionsCode>  ->  "JMP" | "JG" | "JL" | ....
<leaInstruction>    ->  "LEA" <registerOperand> "," <memoryOperand>.
<noOperandInstructions>    ->  "NOP" | "RET".
<pseudoOp>  -> "DW" (<cardinal> | "?" | <cardinal> "DUP").
<registerOperand> -> "AX" | "BX"| "CX" | ....
<baseRegister>  ->  "BX" | "BP".
<indRegister>  ->   "SI" | "DI".
<indexRegister>  ->  <indRegister> | <baseRegister>.
<memoryOperand>  -> <label> ["["<indReg>"]"]|
              "["<indexRegister>"]" |
              "["<baseRegister>"]" "["<indRegister>"]" |
              "["<baseRegister> <plusOrMinus> <cardinal>"]".
<plusOrMinus>      ->   "+" | "-".
```

7.4 Backtrack parsing

7.4.1 Reversing the generative process

In Section 7.2.3 we saw that an assembly language routine for evaluating an expression can easily be produced from a postfix string which can be obtained by postorder traversal of a structure-describing tree. In Section 7.3.2 we were entirely concerned with generating sentences, at the same time generating parse trees, purely because this was easy. But this is the *opposite* of what a compiler has to do. Instead of being given a grammar and being free to generate any sentence in the language defined by that grammar, a compiler is given a grammar and has to determine the parse tree for any sentence (i.e. program) that a programmer has written. The compiler 'knows' the grammar and is given a sentence; what the compiler does not 'know' is which productions the programmer could have chosen in the generation of that particular sentence. If the compiler can figure out these productions then it can construct a parse tree, and/or produce an equivalent postfix string, and thence produce the required code.

The part of the work of a compiler that is an attempt to construct a parse tree, or an equivalent representation, is called *syntax analysis* or *parsing*. A program is syntactically correct if and only if it is a sentence in the programming language. If it does not belong to the language then syntax analysis will fail to produce a parse tree and will instead produce an error message.

We now begin to consider methods of parsing, starting with simple-minded methods that are too inefficient to be used in compilers. Later we will see how efficiency can be improved by imposing restrictions on languages. For introductory purposes we will use the following:

Fifth example grammar
    Start symbol: s
    Non-terminal symbols: A, B, C, D, E, F, G
    Terminal symbols: m, n, s, t, u, x
    Productions

```
S   ->   AB | CD
A   ->   Em | EF
B   ->   s  | n
C   ->   tn | EF
D   ->   uB | su
E   ->   sx | ty
F   ->   s  | u
```

Parsing algorithms are either *bottom-up* or *top-down*. A bottom-up parsing algorithm starts from the given sentence and attempts to match right-hand sides of productions to parts of it, and then works mainly from the right-hand sides to the left-hand sides of productions until the start symbol is reached and the entire sentence has been accounted for. A top-down parsing algorithm works in the opposite direction, starting from the start symbol and working mainly from left-hand sides to right-hand sides of productions until the entire sentence has been matched. *Bottom-up* means 'from sentence to start symbol'. *Top-down* means 'from start symbol to sentence'.

7.4.2 Bottom-up backtrack parsing

There are many possible bottom-up parsing algorithms and we will now briefly illustrate the working of a simple one. Using the fifth example grammar, suppose that the given sentence is sxusu. Our algorithm tries to find a production that has the first terminal s of sxusu as its right-hand side. It finds B -> s, and so tries replacing s by B, yielding Bxusu. It now tries to find a production that has B as the first symbol on its right hand side. None can be found, so B -> s must have been the wrong choice. So the algorithm looks for some other production with a right-hand side matching the first s in sxusu. It finds F -> s, and tries Fxusu. It tries to find a production that has F as the first symbol on its right-hand side. Again, none can be found. So the algorithm looks for some other production with a right-hand side matching the first s in sxusu, but none can be found.

So our algorithm next tries to find a production that has as its right-hand side the first *two* terminals of sxusu. It finds E -> sx and tries replacing sx by E, yielding Eusu. This could be all right because E is the first symbol on the right-hand side of at least one production. The algorithm goes on to try matching the first u in Eusu, and uses F -> u to obtain EFsu. It finds that EF matches the right-hand side of A -> EF, so it tries Asu and continues. The s in Asu matches the right-hand side of F -> s, so the algorithm tries AFu. It finds that neither A nor AF match the right-hand side of any production, so it looks for an alternative production with s as the right-hand side. None is found, so the algorithm takes the following u with the s and looks for a production with su as the right hand side. It finds D -> su and tries AD. Neither A alone nor AD together match the right hand side of any production. So the algorithm tries to find an alternative for D. Because none can be found, the algorithm backtracks further and tries to find an alternative for the A that was obtained from A -> EF. It finds C -> EF. Replacing the A in AD with this C, it tries CD, and finds that this matches S -> CD, thus completing the parse.

We will not write this algorithm out as a Modula-2 procedure because it is too inefficient to deserve such detailed study. This algorithm is inefficient because it tries a production, finds whether this could possibly be right, and if not tries another production and so on. A parsing algorithm should preferably produce a parse during a single pass through the given input sentence, never reaching a dead end that obliges it to go back, undo a previous tentative decision, and try out an alternative tentative decision to see whether this provides a satisfactory way ahead.

7.4.3 Top-down backtrack parsing

To illustrate the working of a simple inefficient top-down parsing algorithm we will again use the fifth example grammar and take sxusu as the string that is to be parsed. The algorithm starts from the top, which in this example means rewriting S -> AB, and then tries rewriting A -> Em and E -> sx, so that sxmB has been derived from S. In this string the first three terminals sxm do not match the first three terminals of the string sxusu that is to be parsed. The production E -> ty does not help, so the choice of A -> Em must have been wrong. Therefore the algorithm backtracks and instead of A -> Em tries A -> EF. Rewriting E -> sx this yields sxFB, in which the terminals match the terminals at the left end of sxusu, so it is worthwhile to continue. If F in sxFB is rewritten using F -> s this yields sxsB in which the third terminal does not match the third terminal in sxusu. The algorithm tries rewriting F -> u instead of F -> s, and this yields sxuB: so far, so good. But neither of the productions that have B on the left hand side yields a satisfactory match with sxusu, so the algorithm backtracks drastically and starts exploring S -> CD instead of S -> AB.

Rewriting C using C -> tn does not yield a match with the first two terminals of sxusu. So the algorithm tries C -> EF, and then tries E -> sx, which does match, yielding the sentential form sxFD. For F the algorithm tries F -> s. This s does not match the first u in sxusu, so the algorithm tries the alternative F -> u, which matches. The algorithm continues to explore the sentential form sxuD. It tries D -> uB and B -> s and B -> n, and does not find a match. So it backtracks, tries D -> su, and does find a match.

The whole of `sxusu` has now been accounted for, so the parse is complete. Knowing which productions were successfully selected by this algorithm we can construct a parse tree for `sxusu`. We will not give further details of this top-down algorithm because it is not practical.

7.5 Discussion

At the cost of imposing restriction on grammars, efficient backtrack-free parsers are available both for the bottom-up and the top-down approaches. In Chapter 8 we will give examples of practical top-down parsing algorithms which are surer-footed than backtrack parsers in that they do not explore alternatives which turn out to be fruitless. If we employ an appropriate grammar, parsing yields essentially the same structure-describing information as is illustrated by the tree in Figure 7.1, and in Chapter 8 we will say more about producing object code from this information. In Section 7.2 we considered going from a tree to an object code routine via postfix representation: it is not essential to go via postfix, but Section 7.2 has provided a useful introduction to the generation of object code, and we will build on this later.

This book is mainly concerned with recursive-descent compiling, which is a well-established traditional method that can be understood without extensive study of compiler theory. Section 7.3 is indeed a very cursory introduction to formal languages; we will add just a little more theory in Chapter 8. Further study of formal language theory and compiler theory is beyond the scope of this introductory book and the reader is referred to texts such as Aho *et al.* (1986); Barrett *et al.* (1986); Tremblay and Sorensen (1985); and Waite and Goos (1984).

7.6 Exercises

1. Check the equivalence of the following four pairs of infix and postfix expressions:

infix expression	postfix expression
`p + q + r - (s + t)`	`p q + r + s t + -`
`(p - q) * (r + s) / t + u`	`p q - r s + * t / u +`
`(p + q) * (r * s - t * (u + v))`	`p q + r s * t u v + * - *`
`p + q * (r + s * (t - u * (v + w )))`	`p q r s t u v w + * - * +`

2. Express the following infix expressions in postfix notation:

   (a) `p + q * r  - s * t`
   (b) `(p + q) * (r - s) * t`
   (c) `p * q + r - s * (t - u)`
   (d) `p + q * (r - s * (t - u))`

3. Write a SAL routine that will evaluate the expression `pqr-*s+` using a stack, making assumptions as in Section 7.2.3.

4. Write out all the sentences that belong to the language which is defined by the
    following grammar:

    Start symbol: Start
    Non-terminal symbols: SubjectPhrase, Article, Adjective, Verb, SubNoun,
         ObjNoun, ObjectPhrase
    Terminal symbols: a, the, boy, crocodile, fat, silly, wild, eats, chases,
         smells, biscuit, ostrich, banana
    Productions:

    ```
    Start            ->  SubjectPhrase Verb ObjectPhrase.
    SubjectPhrase    ->  Article {Adjective} SubNoun.
    Verb             ->  "eats" | "chases" | "smells".
    ObjectPhrase     ->  Article [Adjective] ObjNoun
    SubNoun          ->  "boy" | "crocodile".
    ObjNoun          ->  "biscuit" | "ostrich" | "banana".
    Adjective        ->  "fat" | "silly" | "wild"
    Article          ->  "a" | "the"
    ```

5. Write out five sentences, each having a different number of symbols, that are
    generated by the following grammar:

    Start symbol: Sigma
    Non-terminal symbols: Phrase, Noun, Verb
    Terminal symbols: this, is, the, that, wonderful, man, robot, house, builds,
                                 plans, protects
    Productions:

    ```
    Sigma   ->  "this is the" Noun {Phrase} "that is wonderful".
    Phrase  ->  "that" Verb "the" Noun.
    Noun    ->  "man" | "robot" | "house".
    Verb    ->  "builds" | "plans" | "protects".
    ```

6. The following is a well-known example of an ambiguous grammar:

    Start symbol: <start>
    Non-terminal symbols: <statement>, <condition>
    Terminal symbols: **"if"**, **"then"**, **"else"**, statement1, statement2, condition1,
         condition2
    Productions:

    ```
    <start>      ->  <statement>.
    <statement>  ->  statement1 | statement2 |
                            "if" <condition> "then" <statement> |
                            "if" <condition> "then" <statement> "else"
                                     <statement>.
    <condition>  ->  condition1 | condition2.
    ```

    Using this grammar, derive two different parse trees for the sentence:

```
if condition1 then if condition2 then statement1 else statement2
```

Without changing the language, change the grammar by replacing the non-terminal <statement> by two new non-terminals so as to eliminate the ambiguity.

7. Module `quads`, which is listed in the Appendix, reads a postfix expression and instead of producing SAL output code, produces compiler intermediate code of a kind known as *quadruples*. A quadruple is so called because it comprises an operator, a destination operand and two source operands. For the expression `UV*X+YWZ-*-` the output is

```
T1:=  U * V
T2:=  T1 + X
T3:=  W - Z
T4:=  Y * T3
T5:=  T2 - T4
```

where `T1, T2, ...,` are temporary variables as in Section 7.2.2. Module `quads` assumes for simplicity that the postfix string is available from a file as a string of characters without spaces between, with one upper-case letter per variable and one character per operator, except that we do not allow 'T' as an input operand because this is reserved for temporary variables. The sequence is terminated by a space character.

Amend module `quads` so that instead of producing quadruples it outputs triples. These differ from quadruples in that instead of using temporary variables explicitly, triples refer to the line numbers of lines where operand values were computed. These line numbers are traditionally enclosed within round brackets. If the input is `UV*X+YWZ-*-` the output is

```
U * V
(1) + X
W - Z
Y * (3)
(2) - (4)
```

For example, the last line says 'subtract the value computed in line 4 from the value computed in line 2'. (See Aho *et al.* (1986); Pyster (1988)).

8. Module `quads` can easily be modified to write its output to a text file. Write a program to read a sequence of quadruples from a text file and output equivalent SAL using temporary variables. For example, if the input is

```
T1:=  U * V
T2:=  T1 + X
T3:=  W - Z
T4:=  Y * T3
T5:=  T2 - T4
```

the output is be exactly the same as at the end of Section 7.2.2. (This can be made practical by reusing temporary variables and preferably also by making maximal use of registers for temporary variables.)

Chapter 8

Predictive parsing

8.1 Introduction

Efficient parsing is possible for various restricted classes of context-free grammars. This chapter is concerned with a restricted class that allows backtrack-free top-down parsing, using the following grammar as an initial example:

Sixth example grammar

Start symbol: S

Non-terminal symbols: A, B, C, D, E

Terminal symbols: t, u, v, w, x, y

Productions:

```
S  ->  AB
A  ->  xE | v
B  ->  C | D
C  ->  uw | tx
D  ->  A | w
E  ->  yE | empty
```

To explain the characteristic property of this grammar that makes efficient parsing possible, we need first to be more specific about the technical term *derivation* which we used in Section 7.3.1. For example, with the sixth example grammar, if we rewrite S -> AB and then AB -> vB, using the production A -> v, v is said to be *derived from* A. Furthermore, if we rewrite vB -> vC -> vtx, then tx is said to be derived from B. More generally, a string is said to be derived from a non-terminal if there is a production with this non-terminal in its left-hand side and by applying productions to non-terminals in the right-hand side and then applying further productions to non-terminals in the right-hand side of these productions, and so on, we can end up with this string.

For the sixth example grammar, because C can be derived from B, and uw and tx can be derived from C, then it is also true that uw and tx can be derived from B. Because D can be derived from B, A can be derived from D and xE and v can be derived from A, it follows that xE and v can be derived from B. It is also easy to see that w can be derived from B.

In this chapter we introduce efficient parsing algorithms that work with grammars, such as the sixth example grammar, which are specifically designed so that each string of terminals that can be derived from any given non-terminal starts with a different terminal symbol. By looking at this initial terminal symbol it is easy to see which production should be next chosen during parsing, and there is therefore no need for trial and error or for backtracking.

To illustrate this we will parse the sentence xyyxy$ using the sixth example grammar. In this sentence $ is not a symbol of the grammar, but is an end-of-string marker that is a helpful technical artefact. Top-down parsing of this sentence starts with S$ and tries to derive the given sentence xyyxy$. We will first work through this informally, and subsequently in Section 8.2 we will give a detailed algorithm and explanation. We will use a parsing process that always rewrites the leftmost non-terminal symbol of the current sentential form. When the parsing process has accounted for a terminal symbol we will move that symbol into the superscript position.

A top-down parse starts by rewriting the start symbol. For the sixth example grammar there is no choice: S must be rewritten AB. So we have to match AB$ against xyyxy$. Next the parser rewrites A, because this is the leftmost non-terminal of the current sentential form AB$. If the parser were to choose A -> v, this v would not match the leftmost terminal symbol, x, in xyyxy$ so this choice must be wrong, and therefore the parser does not make this choice. The only choice that could be right is A -> xE because the x does match the leftmost x in xyyxy$, so this is the choice that the parser makes, and A is rewritten xE. The parser now has to match xEB$ against xyyxy$. To show that the leftmost x has now been matched, we move it to the superscript position, so we can easily see that the parser has to match ^{x}EB$ against ^{x}yyxy$.

Continuing to work top-down, the parser must rewrite E, because this is the leftmost non-terminal in ^{x}EB$, choosing a production that is not inconsistent with ^{x}yyxy$. Again there is no freedom of choice because the y in E -> yE matches the leftmost y in ^{x}yyxy$. The parser must choose E -> yE instead of E -> empty because E -> empty would not account for the leftmost y in ^{x}yyxy$. So ^{x}EB$ has now been rewritten ^{x}yEB$ and because the leftmost y matches the leftmost y in ^{x}yyxy$ we move both of these ys to the superscript position to indicate that they have been accounted for. It remains for the parser to match the sentential form ^{xy}EB$ against ^{xy}yxy$.

In ^{xy}EB$, E must be rewritten next, choosing a production that is consistent with the leftmost non-superscript symbol in ^{xy}yxy$. For the same reason as before, the parser must choose E -> yE, and go on to match ^{xyy}EB$ against ^{xyy}xy$. The production E -> yE now could not possibly be correct, because the y does not match the leftmost non-superscript terminal, x, in ^{xyy}xy$. So the parser chooses E -> empty. The practical effect of this choice is to delete the E from ^{xyy}EB$ so that the parser goes on to match ^{xyy}B$ against ^{xyy}xy$.

The parser must next rewrite B. If it chose B -> C, the C would be rewritten uw or tx which would not match the leftmost non-superscript x in ^{xyy}xy$, so the parser must not choose B -> C. If the parser instead chose B -> D, the D could be rewritten using D -> A, which could be rewritten using A -> xE, which would match. Therefore the parse chooses B -> D and goes on to match ^{xyy}D$ against ^{xyy}xy$. D -> w would not yield a match, so the parser chooses D -> A, and procedes to match ^{xyy}A\$ against ^{xyy}xy\$.

The only possibility now is to rewrite A -> xE and then match ^{xyyx}E\$ against ^{xyyx}y\$. At the next step the only possibility is E -> yE, so the parser has to match ^{xyyxy}E\$ against ^{xyyxy}\$. The production E -> empty is the only possiblity: E is deleted from ^{xyyxy}E\$, and the parse has been successfully completed because ^{xyyxy}\$ matches ^{xyyxy}\$.

In our example we have used a method of parsing that is said to be *predictive* because it always correctly predicts the appropriate production by looking at the next terminal symbol that has to be accounted for in the input sentence. Section 8.2 introduces an iterative predictive parsing algorithm, and Section 8.5 introduces a recursive predictive parsing algorithm known as *recursive descent*, which is used in later chapters. Section 8.4 explains the restrictions with which a grammar must comply in order to allow predictive parsing.

8.2 An algorithm for non-recursive predictive parsing

Given the next non-terminal to be rewritten and the next terminal symbol to be accounted for, a predictive parsing algorithm knows exactly which production to select. The algorithm is provided with this knowledge before it begins to parse any sentence. For a non-recursive (i.e. iterative) predictive parsing algorithm this knowledge is expressed in a *parse table* that has one column corresponding to each terminal symbol and one row corresponding to each non-terminal symbol. The entry in row N and column m is the right-hand side of the production that should be applied when the next non-terminal to be rewritten is N and the next terminal symbol to be accounted for is m.

Table 8.1 Parse table for the sixth example grammar

	t	u	v	w	x	y	\$
S			AB		AB		
A			v		xE		
B	C	C	D	D	D		
C	tx	uw					
D			A	w	A		
E	empty	empty	empty	empty	empty	yE	empty

For our sixth example grammar the parse table is shown in Table 8.1. For example, the entry in row *A* column v indicates that if A is to be rewritten when the next terminal symbol to be accounted for is v then the parser must choose the production A -> v. The entry in row A column x tells us that if A is to be rewritten when the next terminal symbol to be accounted for is x then the parser must choose the production A -> xE. The blanks in row A for the other columns signify that the terminals corresponding to these columns cannot possibly be the next terminal to be accounted for when A is the next terminal to be rewritten. For example, when A is to be rewritten then the next terminal to be accounted for cannot possibly be w, and this is why the entry in column w for row A is blank.

Once the table has been constructed, the same table can be used for parsing all sentences defined by the sixth example grammar. The contents of the table do not have to be changed for different sentences.

During parsing it is convenient to keep the current sentential form on a stack, so that the symbol at the top of the stack is the next non-terminal that is to be rewritten. We implement this stack as in a one-dimensional array stack, and the symbol at the top of the stack is stack[top]. As in Chapter 4, sy is the current symbol, and inSymbol assigns the next terminal symbol to sy. An outline of the body of an iterative predictive parser is:

```
initialise;     (* sets up the parse table *)
inSymbol;       (* sy:= next symbol in input sentence *)
stack[1]:= endMarker; (* endMarker = $ *)
stack[2]:= S; (* start symbol *)
top:= 2;        (* top of stack initially is stack[2] *)
REPEAT
  IF stack[top] is a terminal symbol THEN
    IF stack[top] = sy THEN (* sy matches terminal at top of stack so *)
      DEC(top);          (* discard symbol at top of stack *)
      inSymbol
    ELSE error(2)
    END
  ELSE
    DEC(top);             (* discard non-terminal from stack top *)
    push on to the stack the symbols obtained from
    parseTable[stack[top],sy] so that the leftmost one of these
    symbols is at the top of the stack
  END
UNTIL (stack[top] = endMarker) OR syntaxError;
IF sy # endMarker THEN error(4)
ELSE WriteString('Successfully completed'); WriteLn
END;
```

Table 8.2 shows the stack contents and the remaining input string at the start of each iteration of the REPEAT loop during the parsing of xyyxy. The symbol at the top of the stack is shown on the left. Module nonRec in the Appendix is a detailed implementation of this parsing algorithm.

Table 8.2 Non-recursive parsing of xyyxy using Table 8.1

stack	sy	Remaining input string
S$	x	yyxy$
AB$	x	yyxy$
xEB$	x	yyxy$
EB$	y	yxy$
yEB$	y	yxy$
EB$	y	xy$
yEB$	y	xy$
EB$	x	y$
B$	x	y$
D$	x	y$
A$	x	y$
xE$	x	y$
E$	y	$
yE$	y	$
E$	$	
$	$	

8.3 Construction of a parse table

A parse table can be constructed using two functions FIRST(F) and FOLLOW(F), where F is any substring of any sentential form associated with a given grammar. FIRST (F) is the set of all terminal symbols with which any derivation of **F** might start. FOLLOW(F) is the set of all terminal symbols that occur immediately to the right of F in any sentential form associated with the given grammar. Detailed procedures for enumeration of FIRST (F) and FOLLOW(F) are given in textbooks such as Aho *et al.* (1986) and Barrett *et al.* (1986).

The following is a transcription of Algorithm 4.4 in Aho *et al.* (1986) which constructs a parse table from a given grammar:

```
FOR each production P -> Q in the grammar DO
  FOR each terminal, n, in FIRST(Q) DO
    enter Q in parseTable[P,n];
    IF empty is in FIRST(Q) THEN (* empty can be derived from Q *)
      FOR each terminal, m, in FOLLOW(P) DO
        enter Q in parseTable[P,m]
    END;
      IF $ is in FOLLOW(P) THEN enter Q in parseTable[P,$] END
    END
  END
END;
```

```
Mark every undefined entry in the parse table to indicate an error.
```

If P -> Q is a production and n is in FIRST(Q) then when P is the next non-terminal to be rewritten and n is the next terminal symbol to be accounted for, P -> Q is the production that must be selected, and this is why in this case the algorithm enters Q into parseTable[P,n]. If P -> Q is a production and *empty* can be derived from Q then any terminal, m, in FOLLOW(P) can be the first terminal in a string derived from P, so Q is entered into parseTable[P,m]. To illustrate this, consider the grammar whose productions are:

```
S -> AC
A -> B | D
B -> q | empty
C -> rs | tu
```

Both r and t are in FOLLOW(A). In the language defined by this trivial grammar, rs is a complete sentence. In parsing the sentence rs, the first step is to rewrite S -> AC. Next A must be rewritten, because this is the leftmost non-terminal, and the parse table must show which production should be selected. The parse table shows that A -> B should be selected, because after that the next production to be selected is B -> empty, which means that B is deleted from the sentential form BC$. The next production to be selected is C -> rs, which completes the parse.

8.4 LL(1) grammars

8.4.1 Definition of LL(1)

We have introduced a predictive parsing algorithm that is an example of an LL(1) parsing algorithm. In LL(1) the first L signifies that the input sentence is scanned from left to right. The second L signifies that the parsing algorithm yields a leftmost derivation: this is the case because non-terminals are rewritten in left-to-right sequence. The (1) in LL(1) signifies that the algorithm looks at the next *single* symbol of the input sentence when choosing the appropriate production. In Section 8.2 this single symbol was assigned to the global variable sy.

   LL(1) parsing works correctly only for a special class of context-free grammars that are called LL(1) grammars. A context-free grammar is an LL(1) grammar if and only if its parse table has not more than one entry for each (non-terminal, terminal) pair. For a non-LL(1) grammar the table-constructing routine outlined above would assign more than one entry for at least one (non-terminal, terminal) pair, and the parsing algorithm would not know which of these to choose.

8.4.2 Replacing a grammar by an equivalent LL(1) grammar

Sometimes a grammar that is not LL(1) can be replaced by an LL(1) grammar defining the same language, but this is not always possible. For example, the following grammar is not LL(1):

Seventh example grammar
> Start symbol: S
> Non-terminal symbols: A, C, D
> Terminal symbols: t, u, v, w, x, y
> Productions:

```
        S   ->  AC | AD
        A   ->  Ay | x | v
        C   ->  uw | tx
        D   ->  A  | w
```

One of its problems is that the parser cannot choose between S -> AC and S -> AD, because FIRST(AC) = FIRST(AD). This problem can be cured by introducing a new non-terminal, say B, and replacing S -> AC | AD by productions:

```
    S   ->  AB
    B   ->  C | D
```

which were all right in the sixth example grammar. This cure is known as *left factoring*. A more complicated example of left-factoring is that we could replace

```
    P   ->  TUVW | TUVX | TUYX
```

by

```
    P   ->  TUR
    R   ->  VZ | YX
    Z   ->  W | X
```

A general algorithm for left factoring is given by Aho *et al.* (1986, p. 178).

A grammar that includes any production of the form P -> Pq | n is said to be *left recursive*. FIRST(Pq) includes n, so the parser would not know whether to choose Pq or n in P -> Pq | n. This illustrates why no left-recursive grammar is LL(1). To cure left recursion we start by considering the strings defined by it. The production A -> Ay | x defines strings xy, xyy, xyyy, and so on. Exactly the same set of strings can be defined by introducing a new non-terminal, say E, and using:

```
    A   ->  xE
    E   ->  yE | empty
```

This was included in the sixth example grammar. The production E -> yE | empty is right-recursive, but this does not make any difficulty. The sixth example grammar was obtained from the seventh example grammar by left factoring and by changing left recursion to right recursion.

Another way of curing left recursion uses EBNF. For example, the set of strings defined by A -> Ay | x is equivalently defined by

```
A -> x{y}.
```

Using this idea the left recursion in our eighth example grammar has been avoided in our ninth, which defines the same language:

Eighth example grammar

Start symbol: `start`
Non-terminal symbols: `expression, term, factor, plusOrMinus, timesOrDivide`
Terminal symbols: `idSy, +, -, *, /, (, )`
Productions:

```
start  ->  plusOrMinus expression.
expression  -> expression + term | expression - term | term.
term  ->  term * factor | term / factor | factor.
factor -> "("expression")" | idSy.
plusOrMinus ->   "+"|"-".
timesOrDivide  ->  "*"| "/".
```

Ninth example grammar

Start symbol: `expression`
Non-terminal symbols: `term, factor, plusOrMinus, timesOrDivide`
Terminal symbols: `idSy, +, -, *, /, (, )`
Productions:

```
expression  ->  [plusOrMinus] term {plusOrMinus term}.
term        ->  factor {timesOrDivide factor}.
factor      ->  idSy | "("expression")".
plusOrMinus ->  "+"| "-".
timesOrDivide  ->  "*"| "/".
```

Here `idSy` stands for *identifier symbol.*

8.4.3 An example of a grammar that cannot be replaced by an equivalent LL(1) grammar

The parse table for an ambiguous grammar would not have unique entries, and therefore no ambiguous grammar is LL(1). For a grammar that is incurably ambiguous we will not be able to find an LL(1) grammar that defines the same language. The following is an example of a grammar that cannot be replaced by an equivalent LL(1) grammar:

```
S -> aSB | c
B -> bS  | empty
```

Ambiguity is illustrated in Figure 8.1 by two parse trees for the sentence `aacbc`. Corresponding to the production B -> bS, `parseTable[B,b]` for this grammar would contain bS. Because the grammar includes B -> empty, for each terminal, m, in FOLLOW(B), parseTable[B,m] would contain empty. From the derivation S -> aSB -> aaSBB we see that b is in FOLLOW(B). Therefore empty, as well as bS, would be in parseTable[B,b], so the grammar is not LL(1). Because parseTable[B,b] would not be unique the parser would be unable to choose between the two trees in Figure 8.1.

8.5 Recursive-descent parsing

8.5.1 Introduction

In Section 8.2 we used a non-recursive LL(1) parsing algorithm which used a *declarative* representation of the parse table. To change the grammar we would only have to change the declarations of symbols and the contents of the parse table, and the rest of the program would remain unchanged. We now introduce an alternative family of LL(1) parsing algorithms, in which a grammar's information is represented procedurally, not declaratively, and if we wish to change the grammar we have to rewrite various procedures. This alternative family of LL(1) parsing algorithms are known as *recursive-descent* algorithms. Instead of working iteratively with an explicit stack, a recursive descent parsing algorithm implicitly uses a run-time stack to achieve a similar effect recursively. We will use recursive descent parsers that call procedure inSymbol to assign successive input symbols to a global variable sy, as in Section 8.2.

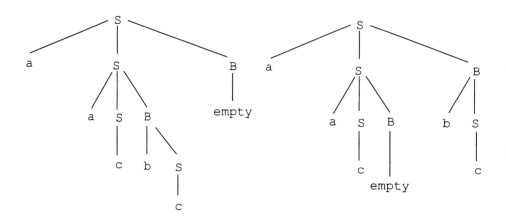

Figure 8.1 Two parse trees for the sentence aacbc.

A recursive-descent parser can be derived automatically from an EBNF LL(1) grammar, without producing or using a parse table. A recursive descent parser has one procedure corresponding to each non-terminal; this procedure has the same name as the non-terminal. Corresponding to a symbol sequence

```
symbolSequence = Symbol₁ Symbol₂...Symbolₙ
```

that is included in the right hand side of the production for non-terminal N, procedure N includes a sequence of statements:

```
StatementSequence =
    statementForSymbol₁; statementForSymbol₂; ... statementForSymbolₙ
```

If Symbolᵢ is a non-terminal then statementForSymbolᵢ is single statement that is a call of a procedure whose identifier is this non-terminal. If Symbolᵢ is terminal then statementForSymbolᵢ is

```
IF sy = Symbolᵢ THEN inSymbol ELSE reportError END
```

or equivalently accept (Symbolᵢ).

If the right hand side of the production for N is of the form

```
SymbolSequence₁ | SymbolSequence₂ | ... | SymbolSequenceₘ
```

then procedure N includes

```
CASE sy OF
    FIRST(SymbolSequence₁): StatementSequence₁ |
    FIRST(SymbolSequence₂): StatementSequence₂ |
    ...
    FIRST(SymbolSequenceₘ): StatementSequenceₘ |
END
```

Moreover, if the right-hand side of the production for N includes {SymbolSequence} then procedure N includes an iterative statement such as

```
WHILE sy IN FIRST(SymbolSequence) DO StatementSequence END;
```

If the right-hand side includes [SymbolSequence] then the procedure includes

```
IF sy IN FIRST (SymbolSequence) THEN StatementSequence END.
```

A more general formulation would show how these transformations can be compounded. For example, for the production

```
N -> [SymbolSequence₁] SymbolSequence₂ {SymbolSequence₃}
```

an outline of the corresponding procedure is as follows:

```
PROCEDURE N;
BEGIN
  IF sy IN FIRST (SymbolSequence₁) THEN StatementSequence₁ END;
```

```
    StatementSequence₂;
    WHILE sy IN FIRST(SymbolSequence₃) DO StatementSequence₃ END;
  END N;
```

As a first example, the following is a complete recursive-descent parsing program for the sixth example grammar:

```
MODULE recDec;
FROM InOut IMPORT Read, WriteString, WriteLn, WriteCard, Write;
CONST
  endMarker = '$';
VAR
  sy: CHAR;

PROCEDURE error(n:INTEGER);
VAR
  ch: CHAR;
BEGIN
  WriteString('Error number: '); WriteCard(n,3); WriteLn;
  HALT
END error;

PROCEDURE inSymbol;
VAR
  ch: CHAR;
BEGIN
  IF sy # endMarker THEN Read(ch) END;
  WHILE ch = ' ' DO Read(ch) END; (* skip spaces *)
  sy:= ch
END inSymbol;

PROCEDURE A;
BEGIN
  CASE sy OF
  'v':  WriteString('A  ->  v'); WriteLn; inSymbol |
  'x':  WriteString('A  ->  xE'); WriteLn; inSymbol; E
  ELSE error(2)
  END
END A;

PROCEDURE B;
BEGIN
  CASE sy OF
  't','u': WriteString('B  ->  C'); WriteLn; C |
  'v','w','x': WriteString('B  ->  D'); WriteLn; D
  ELSE error (3)
```

```
  END
END B;

PROCEDURE C;
BEGIN
  CASE sy OF
  't': inSymbol;
      IF sy = 'x' THEN  WriteString('C -> tx'); WriteLn
      ELSE error(4)
      END;  inSymbol |
  'u': inSymbol;
      IF sy = 'w' THEN  WriteString('C  ->  uw'); WriteLn
      ELSE error(5)
      END; inSymbol
  ELSE error(6)
  END
END C;

PROCEDURE D;
BEGIN
  CASE sy OF
  'w':     WriteString('D  ->  w'); WriteLn; inSymbol |
  'v','x': WriteString('D  ->  A'); WriteLn; A
  ELSE error(7)
  END
END D;

PROCEDURE E;
BEGIN
  IF sy = 'y' THEN WriteString('E  ->  yE'); WriteLn;
      inSymbol; E;
  END
END E;

PROCEDURE S;
BEGIN
   WriteString('S  ->  AB'); WriteLn;
   A; B
END S;

BEGIN
  inSymbol;  S;
  IF sy = endMarker THEN WriteString('Correct syntax'); WriteLn;
  ELSE error (1)
```

```
    END
  END recDec.
```

A recursive-descent parser uses one-symbol look ahead; for example, when procedure s calls procedure A, sy is already the first symbol that procedure A has to deal with. Procedure s calls procedures A and B because in the sixth example grammar the only production that has s on the left hand side is s -> AB. Procedure s prints out this production to show that it is been selected. Similarly, other procedures print out the selected productions. In procedure E there is an IF statement instead of a CASE statement because this is more appropriate. It is worthwhile to check that during the parsing of xyyxy$ the value of sy and the unconsumed part of the input string is as shown in Table 8.3 at the times of successive procedure calls.

Table 8.3 Steps in recursive-descent parsing of xyyxy$

Procedure	sy	Remaining input string
S	x	yyxy$
A	x	yyxy$
E	y	yxy$
E	y	xy$
E	x	y$
B	x	y$
D	x	y$
A	x	y$
E	y	$
E	$	

8.5.2 Recursive descent in the SAL assembler

The SAL assembler in Chapter 4 uses recursive descent. For example, corresponding to

```
    <leaInstruction>    ->   "LEA" <register> "," <memoryOperand>.
```

a recursive-descent procedure, which is called when sy is the first symbol after "LEA", is as follows:

```
    PROCEDURE leaInstruction;
    BEGIN
       registerOperand; accept(commaSy); memoryOperand
    END leaInstruction;
```

Procedure leaInstruction in assembler module instrns only calls procedure memoryOperand if sy is in FIRST(memoryOperand), which is symbolset{labelSy, leftSqrBrktSy}:

```
PROCEDURE leaInstruction;
BEGIN
  IF sy = registerSy THEN registerOperand ELSE errror(16) END;
  accept(commaSy);
  IF sy IN symbolset{labelSy, leftSqrBrktSy} THEN
    memoryOperand(opWord)
  ELSE error(17)
  END
END leaInstruction;
```

For single-operand instructions, a parser procedure corresponding to the production

```
<singleOp>   ->   <singleOpOpCode> (<registerOperand> | <memoryOperand>).
```

is as follows:

```
PROCEDURE singleOp;
BEGIN
  IF sy = registerSy THEN registerOperand
  ELSIF sy IN symbolset{labelSy, leftSqrBrktSy} THEN
    memoryOperand
  END
END;
```

Procedure `singleOp` in Section 4.5 is a little more elaborate than this because it does more than parse a single-operand instruction.

Near the beginning of Section 4.5 procedure `instruction` is only a slight development of the recursive descent procedure that corresponds to

```
<instruction>  ->   <twoOp> | <singleOp> | <leaInstruction> |
                    <noOperandInstructions> |<jumpInstructions>  | <pseudoOp>.
```

For example, FIRST(<twoOp>) = {MOV, ADD, SUB, ...} and the assembler recognizes these op-codes as belonging to the `twoOperandCategory`.

For the two productions

```
<lineSequence> -> {line} "endOfTextSy".
<line>  ->  [(<label>":" <instruction> | <instruction>)] "newLineSy".
```

a parser procedure would be as follows:

```
PROCEDURE lineSequence;
BEGIN
  WHILE sy IN symbolSet{labelSy, OpCodeSy, newLineSy} DO
    IF sy = labelSy THEN
      labelColon;
      IF sy = OpCodeSy THEN instruction ELSE error(6) END
    ELSIF sy = opCodeSy THEN instruction
    END;
```

```
    accept(newLineSy)
  END;
  accept (endOfTextSy)
END lineSequence;
```

At the beginning of Section 4.6 in the body of the main module salAssem of our assembler we have

```
WHILE sy # endOfTextSy DO
```

instead of

```
WHILE sy IN FIRST(<line>) DO
```

but the practical effect is the same.

8.5.3 Parsing simple expressions

We now introduce a recursive-descent parser for expressions defined by the ninth example grammar, except that we go a little further by having variables that are single-character identifiers A, B, ... Our program uses a primitive lexical analyzer module for which the definition module is as follows:

```
DEFINITION MODULE synLex;
TYPE
  symbolType = (idSy, plussOp, minusOp, timesOp, divideOp, negOp,
      leftRndBrktSy, rightRndBrktSy, endMarkerSy, empty);
VAR
  sy: symbolType; chOfSy: CHAR;
PROCEDURE error(n:CARDINAL);
PROCEDURE inSymbol;
END synLex.
```

When the current symbol is a variable or an operator symbol, procedure inSymbol assigns idSy or the appropriate operator symbol to sy and also assigns the actual single-character identifier or operator to the global variable chOfSy. Instead of outputting the productions that it selects, the following parser program outputs a postfix string that is equivalent to the input infix string:

```
MODULE toPostFx;
FROM InOut IMPORT Write;
FROM synLex IMPORT error, inSymbol, symbolType, sy, chOfSy;
CONST
  endOfFile = 32C;
TYPE
  charSet = SET OF CHAR;
  symbolSet = SET OF symbolType;
```

```
PROCEDURE expression;
VAR
  operatorChar: CHAR;
BEGIN
  IF sy IN symbolSet{plussOp, minusOp} THEN
    operatorChar:= chOfSy;
    Write('0'); inSymbol; term; Write (operatorChar)
  ELSE term
  END;
  WHILE sy IN symbolSet{plussOp, minusOp} DO
    operatorChar:= chOfSy;
    inSymbol; term; Write(operatorChar)
  END
END expression;

PROCEDURE term;
VAR
  operatorChar: CHAR;
BEGIN
  factor;
  WHILE sy IN symbolSet{timesOp,divideOp} DO
    operatorChar:= chOfSy; inSymbol;
    factor; Write(operatorChar)
  END
END term;

PROCEDURE factor;
BEGIN
  IF sy = leftRndBrktSy THEN
    inSymbol; expression;
    IF sy # rightRndBrktSy THEN error (2) END;
    inSymbol
  ELSIF sy = idSy THEN
    Write(chOfSy); inSymbol
  END;
END factor;

BEGIN
  inSymbol; expression;
  IF sy # endMarkerSy THEN error (3) END;
END toPostFx.
```

Write('0') is included in procedure expression so that if the input expression is −X+Y the output is 0X-Y+, which is appropriate if a unary minus operation is not available. It is worthwhile to check in detail that when the input is A * (B − C) the state of play at times of successive procedure calls is as shown in Table 8.4.

The final call of procedure `factor` outputs `'C'`. After the return from procedure `factor`, and then from procedure `term`, procedure `expression` outputs `'-'`. This call of procedure `expression` was within procedure `factor`. After the return from this call of procedure `factor`, procedure `term` outputs `'*'`, completing the postfix string `ABC-*`.

Table 8.4 Steps in recursive-descent parsing of `A * (B - C)`

Procedure	sy	Remaining input string	Output so far
expression	A	`* (B - C) $`	
term	A	`* (B - C) $`	
factor	A	`* (B - C) $`	A
factor	(	`B - C) $`	A
expression	B	`- C) $`	A
term	B	`- C) $`	A
factor	B	`- C) $`	AB
term	C	`) $`	AB
factor	C	`) $`	AB

8.6 Compiling simple expressions by recursive descent

Instead of having a parsing algorithm output a postfix string and subsequently compiling this string into SAL using a program such as `postfixToSAL` in Section 7.2.3, we will develop our program `toPostFx` so that it outputs SAL instructions directly. We will put into a separate module the procedures that output SAL instructions:

```
DEFINITION MODULE salOut;
FROM synLex IMPORT symbolType;
PROCEDURE applyOperator(op: symbolType);
   (* similar to applyOperator in Section 7.2.3 but including negOp which is a
      unary minus operator.  *)

PROCEDURE outPush(ch: CHAR)
   (* WriteString('   PUSH  '); Write(ch); WriteLn *)
END salOut.
```

As in Section 7.2.2 we assume that the output SAL instructions will be incorporated into a program in which all the required declarations such as

```
A:   DW ?
B:   DW ?
```

have already been made. Furthermore, the stack pointer is assumed to have been properly initialized. Procedure `applyOperator` is a less repetitive version of the procedure with the same name in Section 7.2.3 and does almost the same job. Note that we are (temporarily) using '/' to mean what `DIV` means in Modula-2. We will distinguish between integer and real division in Chapter 10.

The main module of a program that compiles an expression into SAL is:

```
MODULE toSAL;
FROM synLex IMPORT error, inSymbol, symbolType, sy, chOfSy;
FROM salOut IMPORT applyOperator, outPush;
CONST
  endOfFile = 32C;
TYPE
  charSet = SET OF CHAR;
  symbolSet = SET OF symbolType;


PROCEDURE expression;
VAR
  operator: symbolType;
BEGIN
  IF sy = plussOp THEN
    inSymbol; term
  ELSIF sy = minusOp THEN
    inSymbol; term; applyOperator(negOp)
  ELSE term
  END;
  WHILE sy IN symbolSet{plussOp, minusOp} DO
    operator:= sy; inSymbol; term;
    applyOperator(operator)
  END
END expression;


PROCEDURE term;
VAR
  operator: symbolType;
BEGIN
  factor;
  WHILE sy IN symbolSet{timesOp,divideOp} DO
    operator:= sy; inSymbol; factor;
    applyOperator(operator)
  END
END term;


PROCEDURE factor;
BEGIN
```

```
        IF sy = leftRndBrktSy THEN
          inSymbol; expression;
          IF sy # rightRndBrktSy THEN error (2) END;
          inSymbol
        ELSIF sy = idSy THEN
          outPush(chOfSy); inSymbol
        END;
      END factor;

      BEGIN
        inSymbol; expression;
        IF sy # endMarkerSy THEN error (3) END;
      END toSAL.
```

As a very simple example of the working of this program, suppose the input expression is A-B$. In this case procedure `expression` calls `term` which calls `factor` which calls `outPush` which outputs

```
        PUSH  A
```

and calls `inSymbol` to get the next symbol after the A. Procedure `factor` returns control to procedure `term` and because `sy` is now not * nor /, procedure `term` returns control to procedure `expression` which carries on where it had left off. The next statement to be executed in `expression` is the WHILE statement, which starts by assigning `operator:= sy` and calling `inSymbol` to get the symbol following the - in our example. Procedure `term` is called, and it works as before, except that

```
        PUSH  B
```

is now output. When control returns to procedure `expression`, procedure `applyOperator` is called and this outputs

```
        POP  AX
        MOV  DI, SP
        SUB  [DI], AX
```

which is code to subtract the stack top from the next to top and leave the result on the stack. The value of this result is A - B, which is correct.

8.7 Discussion

If a grammar does not belong to a restricted family such as LL(1) and we use a simple backtrack parser as in Section 7.4 then the time required for parsing may increase explosively with the length of the input string. LL(1) parsers are much better than this in that the time taken to parse a sentence is roughly proportional to its length. For restricted families of context-free grammars there are other parsers that are at least as efficient as LL(1) parsers. Among these, LR(1) parsers are widely used in practice and are also interesting from the theoretical point of view.

In LR(1) the L signifies that the input sentence is processed from left to right, the R signifies that the parsing algorithms yields a rightmost derivation, and the 1 means the same as in LL(1). LR(1) parsers are radically different to LL(1) in that they work bottom-up. LR(1) theory and technology are beyond the scope of this book; see, for example, Aho *et al.* (1986); Barrett *et al.* (1986); Fischer and LeBlanc (1988); Holub (1990); Pyster (1988); Tremblay and Sorensen (1985); and Waite and Goos (1984).

The non-recursive LL(1) parser in Section 8.2 is an example of a *table-driven* parser. In a table-driven parser information derived from a grammar is essentially stored in a table; the parse table in Section 8.2 is a simple example of this. A recursive-descent parser is not table-driven and instead grammatical information is embodied in its procedures. Many but not all practical LL(1) parsers employ recursive descent, whereas LR(1) parsers are usually table-driven.

Formal language theory has been developed to include vital aspects of compiling beyond syntax analysis. An *attribute grammar* formally associates *attributes* with symbols and *semantic actions* with productions (see Aho *et al.* 1986; Rechenberg and Mössenböck 1989; and Waite and Goos 1984). For example, we use val and ind which are attributes of the current sy. An example of a semantic action is the call of applyOperator in procedure term in module toSAL in Section 8.6: this call is not part of the syntax analysis. Instead it is an extra action associated with the production term -> factor {timesOrDivide factor} in the tenth example grammar. This extra action goes beyond syntax analysis to produce appropriate object code. In a practical compiler there are also semantic actions that perform housekeeping operations and non-syntactic checks.

A *compiler compiler* is a program which, given an attribute grammar, will automatically generate a parser along with software to deal with attributes and semantic actions. A well-known example of this is YACC, which produces a kind of LR(1) parser (Aho *et al.* 1986; Bennett 1990). YACC has been used as the basis of compilers for Modula-2 (Louden 1990; Powell 1984). Some further compiler compilers are catalogued by Rechenberg and Mössenböck (1989), and are mainly LR(1). The compiler compiler *Coco* (Rechenberg and Mössenböck 1989) is unusual in that it generates an LL(1) table-driven compiler written in Modula-2 and having Modula-2 as its source language.

Hand-crafted (i.e. hand-written) compilers have not been rendered obsolete by compiler compilers and can be more efficient. An Oberon compiler (Wirth and Gutknecht 1992) is a recent example of a hand-crafted recursive-descent compiler. To appreciate recursive descent it is not essential to study attribute grammars, although they provide a theoretical characterization of much of the work of a compiler. In this book we introduce details of actual attributes and specific semantic actions without systematization in a formal theoretical framework.

8.8 Exercises

1. Write an LL(1) grammar that defines a language which is the same as that defined by the grammar:

   Start symbol: S
   Non-terminal symbol: A
   Terminal symbols: a, b, c, d
   Productions:

   ```
   S -> A | a | b
   A -> Aa | Ab | c | d
   ```

2. For the input string A-B*D+E$ construct a table in which there is one row for each call and one row for each return from each of the procedures of module toPostFx in Section 8.5.3. For each call and each return, write down the name of the procedure, indicate whether this is a call or a return, show the whole of the unconsumed part of the input string, including the current symbol, and the whole of the output string produced so far.

3. For the grammar

   Start symbol: S
   Non-terminal symbol: L, M, N
   Terminal symbols: x, y, z
   Productions:

   ```
   S -> LMN
   L -> xM
   M -> yL | N
   N -> x | z
   ```

   (a) Construct a parse table.
   (b) At the start of each iteration of non-recursive parsing of the string xyxzyxxz$ show the contents of the stack, the current symbol, and the unconsumed remainder of the input string.
   (c) Write a recursive descent parser using '$' as an end-marker and assuming that there are no spaces before or between input characters. The only output is to be a message saying whether or not there is at least one syntax error in the input string.
   (d) For the input string xyxzyxxz$, each time the recursive-descent parser in (c) calls a procedure write down the name of the procedure, the current symbol, and unconsumed remainder of the input string.

4. This exercise is concerned with the grammar:

   Start symbol: Sentence
   Non-terminal symbols: Subject, Verb, Object, Qualifier, Article, Adjective
   Terminal symbols: a, the, lovely, green, hopeful, whale, snail, male, tin, pin

Productions:

```
Sentence -> Subject Verb | Subject Verb Qualifier Object |
                Qualifier Subject Verb Qualifier Object
Qualifier -> Qualifier Adjective | Article
Adjective -> lovely | green | hopeful
Article   -> a | the
Verb      -> finds | looses
Subject   -> whale | snail | male
Object    -> tin | pin
```

(a) Explain why this is not an LL(1) grammar.

(b) Write an LL(1) grammar that defines the same language.

(c) Write a parse table for the LL(1) grammar.

(d) Write a recursive-descent parser for the language defined by this grammar. The parser is to output the productions that it selects.

5. This exercise is concerned with the grammar:

Start symbol: `Program`

Non-terminal symbols: `StatementSequence, Statement, Assignment, WhileStatement, RepeatStatement, IfStatement`

Terminal symbols: `BEGIN, WHILE, REPEAT, IF, THEN, ELSE, END, DO, UNTIL, condition, expression, assignOperator, variable, ;`

Productions:

```
Program -> BEGIN StatementSequence END
StatementSequence -> Statement {; Statement}
Statement -> [Assignment | WhileStatement | RepeatStatement |
                IfStatement]
Assignment -> variable assignOperator expression
WhileStatement -> WHILE condition DO StatementSequence END
RepeatStatement -> REPEAT StatementSequence UNTIL condition
IfStatement -> IF condition THEN StatementSequence [ELSE
                StatementSequence] END
```

Assume that a procedure `inSymbol` is available, and you are not required to write it. This procedure assigns to a global variable `sy` the following value corresponding to the next symbol in the input:

Input symbol	Value assigned to `sy`
BEGIN	beginSy
WHILE	whileSy
REPEAT	repeatSy
IF	ifSy
THEN	thenSy
ELSE	elseSy
END	endSy

```
DO                    doSy
UNTIL                 untilSy
condition             conditionSy
expression            expressionSy
variable              idSy
assignOperator        assignOp
```

Note that for the purposes of this exercise, `condition`, `expression` and `variable` are terminal symbols. For example, a sentence generated by this grammar is as follows:

```
BEGIN
    IF condition THEN
            WHILE condition DO
                    variable assignOperator expression;
                    variable assignOperator expression;
                    REPEAT
                            variable assignOperator expression;
                            variable assignOperator expression
                    UNTIL condition
            END
    ELSE variable assignOperator expression
    END
END
```

Write a recursive-descent parser for this grammar. The parser is to output the productions that it selects: there is to be no attempt to output SAL code. You will find it helpful to use the procedure:

```
PROCEDURE accept(sym: symbolType);
BEGIN
    IF sy = sym THEN inSymbol ELSE error END
END accept.
```

6. Compiling directly into SAL may be helpful for purposes of elementary introduction, but there are practical advantages in compiling into an intermediate code, such as quadruples, and subsequently translating intermediate code to object code. Amend module `toSAL` in Section 8.6 so that instead of producing SAL it outputs quadruples like those in Exercise 7 in Section 7.6, except that ':=' is to be omitted, and the operator is to follow the second source operand. For example, if the input is `U*V+X-Y*(W-Z)$` the output is to be as follows:

```
T1 U V *
T2 T1 X +
T3 W Z -
T4 Y T3 *
T5 T2 T4 -
```

CHAPTER 9

Lexical analysis revisited

9.1 Introduction

In later chapters we will compile progressively larger subsets of Modula-2, using a lexical analyzer that is similar in principle to that which we used for the assembler. Instead of enlarging the lexical analyzer each time we enlarge the subset of Modula-2, we now introduce a lexical analyzer that is sufficient for all of our subsequent work.

To obtain the next symbol our compiler will call `inSymbol` in the lexical analyzer, and this will assign the next symbol to a global variable `sy`, as in Chapter 3. When the next symbol is either a standard identifier or a programmer-defined identifier, `idSy` (which stands for *identifier symbol*) will be assigned to `sy` by the lexical analyzer. For each different identifier a different distinguishing CARDINAL is assigned by the lexical analyzer to a global variable `ind`, which again is essentially the same as in Chapter 3.

The CARDINAL global variable `val` is now replaced by a global variable `valueRecord` which is of a record type that can accomodate REAL as well as CARDINAL values. When the next symbol is a number, the lexical analyzer assigns `sy:= numberSy` and assigns the number's REAL or CARDINAL value to appropriate fields of `valueRecord`.

9.2 Standard identifiers

It is necessary to understand the distinction between a *reserved word* and a *standard identifier*. Among the terminal symbols of Modula-2 are operators such as '+' and '−' and delimiters such as ';' and ')'. Terminal symbols such as BEGIN, END, ARRAY, IF, TYPE, UNTIL are an equally fundamental in-built part of the language and cannot be redefined by the programmer. All such terminal symbols that are words, such as BEGIN and END, are *reserved words* of the language. Our lexical analyzer outputs a different symbol corresponding to each reserved word: for example, the symbol that corresponds to BEGIN is `beginSy`, the symbol that corresponds to END is `endSy`, and so forth.

Our lexical analyzer also outputs a different symbol corresponding to each legitimate operator or delimiter: for example, the symbol that corresponds to '+' is `plussOp`, the symbol that corresponds to '−' is `minusOp`, the symbol that corresponds to ';' is semiColonSy, and the symbol that corresponds to ')' is closeRndBrktSy. Instead of module symbType in Chapter 3, we now use the following new module to export a definition of symbolType:

```
DEFINITION MODULE symbols;
TYPE
symbolType = (assignOp, plussOp, minusOp, timesOp, realDivOp, divOp, modOp,
   andOp, orOp, equOp, notEquOp, lessOp, greaterOp, lessEquOp, greatEquOp,
   negOp, notOp, periodSy, commaSy, semiColonSy, openRndBrktSy, openSqBrktSy,
   openCurlBrktSy, upArrowSy, dotDotSy, colonSy, closeRndBrktSy, closeSqrBrktSy,
   closeCurlBrktSy, barSy, arraySy, beginSy, bySy, caseSy, constSy, definitionSy,
   doSy, elseSy, elsifSy, endSy, exitSy, exportSy, forSy, fromSy, ifSy,
   implementationSy, importSy, inSy, loopSy, moduleSy, ofSy, pointerSy,
   procedureSy, qualifiedSy, recordSy, repeatSy, returnSy, setSy, thenSy, toSy,
   typeSy, untilSy, varSy, whileSy, withSy, numberSy, idSy, endOfTextSy);
END symbols.
```

ABS, BITSET, BOOLEAN, TRUE and CHAR are not reserved words but are examples of *standard identifiers*, also called *predeclared identifiers*, which the programmer can use without having to declare. It is convenient to have them as standard identifiers instead of reserved words because to an important extent standard identifiers are treated in the same way as all other identifiers. In particular, as will be explained in Chapter 12, standard identifiers as well as programmer-defined identifiers have entries in the compiler's identifier table, whereas reserved words do not.

Our new lexical analyzer uses a string-table module strinTab that is identical to module strinTbl in Chapter 3, except that it imports symbolType from symbols instead of symbType: thus it works with symbols appropriate for a subset of Modula-2 instead of SAL. Module strinTab is initialized by a new module lexInit to contain strings for reserved words and standard identifiers together with special identifiers READNUM, WRITENUM and NEWLINE which be will useful as a temporary expedient until we are ready to deal more authentically with input and output.

9.3　The main module of the lexical analyzer

The main module differs in detail from that of the assembler lexical analyzer. For instance, an end-of-line is an important symbol for an assembler, because it is an instruction delimiter, whereas for a compiler an end-of-line is more like a space character. A complete lexical analyzer for Modula-2 would cope with strings and would not allow an end-of-line within a string.

Modula-2 allows comments to be nested: that is to say, a comment may occur within an outer comment. To cope with this the procedure skipComment calls itself recursively when it finds a comment inside a comment. If '*)' is accidentally omitted at the end of a comment skipComment skips the rest of the program.

The following module allows constants to be of type REAL or of type INTEGER. Whereas the assembler lexical analyzer had a global variable `val` that took the value associated with `numberSy`, our new lexical analyzer has a global variable `valueRecord` that has fields giving both the type and the value of a numeric constant. The type is itself represented by a CARDINAL such that `tyInteger = 1`, `tyBoolean = 2` and `tyReal = 3`. If we were to omit the intial `ty` it would be easier to confuse the value of a type with a type standard identifier in a compiler program. `tyChar` is not included because we will not be dealing with type CHAR.

When `valueRecord.valType = tyInteger`, the unsigned integer value is assigned to `valueRecord.val1`. When `valueRecord.valType = tyReal`, the real value consists of two words which are assigned to `valueRecord.val1` and `valueRecord.val2`. If the object code produced by the compiler is to run on a real machine, the floating-point format of these two words will be that of the machine's arithmetical system. For present tutorial purposes SAL is interpreted as in Chapter 6, and we have taken a short cut using type conversion between a single real and an array of two words. This enables us to process a real number as a two-word object, to show how this can be done, without having to deal with the details of floating-point formatting. At a later stage we will need to be able to obtain the negative of a real number in two-word format; for this purpose the main module of the lexical analyzer exports a procedure `makeNegative`. The definition module is:

```
DEFINITION MODULE scanner;
FROM symbols IMPORT symbolType;
FROM FileSystem IMPORT File;
TYPE
  valRecType = RECORD
                          valType, val1, val2: CARDINAL
              END;
VAR
   valueRecord: valRecType; sy: symbolType; ind: CARDINAL;
PROCEDURE error(errNo: CARDINAL);
PROCEDURE accept(sym: symbolType);
PROCEDURE inSymbol;
PROCEDURE makeNegative(VAR v1,v2: CARDINAL);
PROCEDURE outSymbol;
PROCEDURE openInterFile;
PROCEDURE closeInterFile;
PROCEDURE switchStreamTo(newFile: File);
PROCEDURE restoreStream;
END scanner.
```

In Chapter 13 we will need to write the symbol stream from the lexical analyzer to a file. Procedure `outSymbol` outputs the next symbol and associated information to a file named `interFile` opened by procedure `openInterfile`. Procedure `inSymbol` assigns the next symbol to `sy`, as in Chapter 3.

In Chapter 14 our compiler will need to be able to read from a source file, then temporarily stop reading from this file and start reading from a definition module file, and then switch back to continue reading from the first file as if there had been no interruption. Procedure `switchStreamTo` makes the input come from a new file, and `restoreStream` switches back to the original file. Procedure `switchStreamTo` pushes information about the interrupted file on to a stack, and `restoreStream` pops this information off the stack and uses it to continue reading from the interrupted file from the exact point of interruption.

9.4 Discussion

The terminal symbols of a programming language can be regarded as sentences in a further language in which terminal symbols are individual characters. For some programming languages this further language is a regular language. By explicitly writing an attribute grammar that defines the terminal symbols of a programming language, we can systematize the design of a lexical analyzer, so that it is programmed in accordance with a guiding discipline instead of being freely hand-crafted.

Lexical analyzer generator programs are available which, given an attribute grammar whose language is the set of terminal symbols of a programming language, will automatically construct a lexical analyzer (Fischer *et al.* 1992; Grosch 1989). A well-known example is LEX, for which the input grammar has to be regular. For an introduction to LEX and its theoretical background, see Bennett (1990); Holub (1990); Pyster (1988); and Schreiner and Friedman (1985).

9.5 Exercises

1. Modula-2 allows the programmer to write an unsigned integer constant in decimal. Alternatively, an unsigned integer constant can be written as an octal number followed immediately by B. For example, 17B is decimal 15. Yet another alternative is that an unsigned integer constant can be written as a hexadecimal number followed immediately by H, so that for example, 0FH is decimal 15. A hexadecimal number must always start with a decimal digit, so that for example, instead of writing FH we must write 0FH. Also note that 17BH is a hexadecimal number, and the lexical analyzer must not interpret this B as meaning that this number is octal. Develop procedure `inNumber` so as to allow unsigned integers to be written in octal or in hexadecimal, as in Modula-2.

2. Modula-2 allows the programmer to append a scale factor to a real constant. For example, the programmer can write 0.0005 or alternatively 5.0E–4, where E means *times 10 to the power of*. Thus, to take another example, 0.0005E4 = 5.0. Develop procedure `inNumber` so as to allow a real number optionally to have a scale factor,

in accordance with the production

```
real -> digit {digit}.{digit}"E" plusOrMinus digit {digit}.
plusOrMinus -> + | -
```

3. As in Chapter 3, procedure `inNumber` should check that a numerical input value is not too great for the object-code representation. Develop procedure `inNumber` in `scanner` to check that input numbers are not too great, assuming that an integer will be represented by a 16-bit 2's complement number and a real will be represented by an 8-bit exponent and 24-bit 2's complement mantissa.

4. Develop the lexical analyzer so that when a character literal constant such as 'x' is read, `charSy` is assigned to `sy`, and the actual character is assigned to a field of a record `valueRecord` of an appropriately revised type `valRecType`. Modula-2 also allows the programer to write a character constant as an octal number followed immediately by C. When the lexical analyzer encounters a constant in this form, `charSy` is to be assigned to `sy`, and the actual character is to be assigned to the same field of `valueRecord` as is used when a character constant is a literal such as `'x'`.

CHAPTER 10

Compiling assignment statements

10.1 Introduction

We compile the right-hand side of an assignment statement by calling procedure expression, which produces object code to push the value of an expression on to the stack. If the right-hand side is a solitary constant or variable, its value is pushed on to the stack by the code produced by procedure expression. A single constant or a single variable is a simple special case of an expression. An assignment is implemented by popping the right-hand-side value off the stack into the left-hand-side variable.

In Section 8.6 we tacitly assumed that all operands of an expression were of type INTEGER. In the present chapter operands can be of type INTEGER, REAL or BOOLEAN, and we allow AND, OR and NOT operators. Moreover operands can be REAL or INTEGER numeric constants such as 77.914 or 77, and expressions can contain relational operators such as '>'.

A new version of procedure applyOperator and various other SAL-generating procedures are in a module putSAL for which the definition module is listed in Section 10.2.4. Section 10.2.3 introduces SAL for REALs, and Section 10.2.2 introduces an implementation of relational operations, which involves using SAL labels. Section 10.2.1 explains how our compiler generates SAL labels. In Section 10.5 compiling assignment statements involves type checking, and this is introduced in Section 10.3. Section 10.4 introduces a version of procedure expression that is more powerful than the version in Section 8.6.

10.2 Relational operations and real arithmetic in SAL

10.2.1 SAL labels

For many different purposes SAL object code includes jumps to labelled instructions. Because jumps are used in the implementation of >, >=, =, etc, using JG, JGE, JE, etc, we now consider how a compiler can generate labels. A SAL label used by our compiler is a string of four upper-case letters starting with 'Z'. Labels are generated by procedure genLabel in module putSAL:

```
PROCEDURE genLabel(VAR newLabel: labelString);
BEGIN
  newLabel:= currentLabel;
  IF currentLabel[3] # 'Z' THEN INC(currentLabel[3]) ELSE
    currentLabel[3]:= 'A';
    IF currentLabel[2] # 'Z' THEN INC(currentLabel[2]) ELSE
      currentLabel[2]:= 'A';
      IF currentLabel[1] # 'Z' THEN INC(currentLabel[1])
      ELSE error(0)
      END
    END
  END
END genLabel;
```

Type `labelString` is an ARRAY [0..3] OF CHAR. Within module `putSAL`, `currentLabel` is a global variable of type `labelString`, which is initialized to `'ZAAB'`. Successive calls of `genLabel` change `currentLabel` to `'ZAAC'`, `'ZAAD'`, and so on. Before updating `currentLabel`, `genLabel` returns the original label via its VAR parameter.

Another procedure in module `putSAL` is procedure `putLabel` that outputs a label followed by a colon:

```
PROCEDURE putLabel(pLabel: labelString);
BEGIN
  WriteString(pLabel); Write(':')
END putLabel;
```

The compiler calls `putLabel` to label an instruction that will be output after the ':'.

10.2.2 Relational operations on integers

In module `toSAL` in Section 8.6, procedure `applyOperator` outputs SAL code to apply an operator to the top two integers on the stack and leave the result on top of the stack. Our new module `putSAL` has a new version of `applyOperator` that allows AND, OR and NOT. Module `putSAL` also has a new procedure `applyRelationalOp` that applies a relational operator such as > or >= to the top two integers (or booleans) on the stack. These two operands are popped off the stack, and the boolean value of the result of the relational operation is pushed on to the stack. Throughout this work the boolean value FALSE is represented by integer 0, and TRUE is represented by integer 1. Procedure `applyRelationalOp` is as follows:

```
PROCEDURE applyRelationalOp(op: symbolType);
VAR
  skipLabel: labelString;
BEGIN
```

```
genLabel(skipLabel);
WriteString('     MOV AX, 1'); WriteLn;
WriteString('     POP BX'); WriteLn;
WriteString('     POP CX'); WriteLn;
WriteString('     CMP CX, BX'); WriteLn;
CASE op OF
  equOp:     WriteString('     JE   ') |
  notEquOp:  WriteString('     JNE  ') |
  lessOp:    WriteString('     JL   ') |
  greaterOp: WriteString('     JG   ') |
  lessEquOp: WriteString('     JLE  ') |
  greatEquOp: WriteString ('     JGE  ')
END;
WriteString(skipLabel); WriteLn;
WriteString('     DEC AX'); WriteLn;
putLabel(skipLabel); WriteString(' PUSH AX'); WriteLn
END applyRelationalOp;
```

For example, if `skipLabel = 'ZCBH'` and the relational operator is '>', then the code ouput by `applyRelationalOp` is:

```
      MOV AX, 1 ;   initially assume result TRUE
      POP BX    ;   second operand
      POP CX    ;   first operand
      CMP CX,BX ;   compare operands
      JG  ZCBH  ;   IF CX > BX THEN skip next instruction
      DEC AX    ;   AX:= FALSE
ZCBH: PUSH AX   ;   push result on to stack
```

Procedure `applyRelationalOp` only outputs the SAL instructions, not the explanatory comments.

10.2.3 Real arithmetic with SAL

In our system a REAL is represented by two 16-bit words, whereas an INTEGER is represented by a single 16-bit word. SAL does not have instructions for arithmetic with REAL operands. Instead, we incorporate into module `salSubs`, which was introduced in Section 2.7.2, a collection of SAL subroutines that do real arithmetic. These subroutines are as follows.

Subroutine `REALNEG` has as its operand a real number occupying the top two words of the stack. Execution of `REALNEG` pops the operand off the stack and leaves the negative of the real operand occupying the top two words of the stack. Subroutines `REALADD`, `REALSUB`, `REALMULT` and `REALDIVIDE` have the fourth from top and third from top words of the stack as their first real operand, and have the next to top and top words of the stack as their second real operand. Execution of any of these subroutines pops all four of the operand words off the stack, and subsequently pushes the two-word result back on to the stack. Module put SAL includes a procedure applyRealOperator that simply outputs a call to the appropriate subroutine, e.g. CALL REALADD.

Subroutines REALEQ, REALNOTEQ, REALLESS, REALGREATER, REALLESSEQ and REALGREATEQ evaluate relational operators =, <>, <, >, <=, and >= with real operands. These subroutines have the fourth from top and third from top words of the stack as their first real operand, and have the next to top and top words of the stack as their second real operand. Execution of any of these subroutines pops all four of the operand words off the stack, and the one-word result is pushed on to the stack. This word has the value 1 if the result of the relational operation is TRUE, and 0 if FALSE.

10.2.4 The module put SAL

The definition module is as follows:

```
DEFINITION MODULE putSAL;
FROM symbolsIMPORT symbolType;
TYPE labelString = ARRAY [0..3] OF CHAR;
PROCEDURE genLabel(VAR newLabel: labelString);
PROCEDURE putLabel(pLabel: labelString);
PROCEDURE putLine(aLine: ARRAY OF CHAR);
    (* WriteString(aLine); WriteLn *)
PROCEDURE putStrings(aString, etc: ARRAY OF CHAR);
    (* WriteString(aString); WriteString(etc); WriteLn; *)
PROCEDURE putStringAndVal(aString: ARRAY OF CHAR; v: CARDINAL);
    (* WriteString(aString); WriteCard(v,4); WriteLn *)
PROCEDURE applyOperator(op:symbolType);
PROCEDURE applyRelationalOp(op: symbolType);
PROCEDURE applyRealOperator(op: symbolType);
PROCEDURE newLabelSequence(VAR thisLabel: labelString);
    (* thisLabel:= currentLabel; currentLabel:= 'ZAAB'; *)
PROCEDURE restoreLabelSequence(thisLabel: labelString);
    (* currentLabel:= thisLabel *)
PROCEDURE standardImports;
    (* WriteString ('IMPORT INTREAD, INTWRITE, NEWLINE,.... *)
END putSAL.
```

Procedures newLabelSequence and restoreLabelSequence will be useful in Chapter 14 when we deal with separate compilation of modules. The implementation module of put SAL is included in the Appendix.

10.3 Types

10.3.1 Representation of types

Until we reach Chapter 12 we will use CARDINALs to represent all types, and will make our programs easier to read by having these values as named constants, using

```
CONST
    tyInteger = 1; tyBoolean = 2; tyReal = 3;
```

A Modula-2 compiler finds out the type of a variable from the declaration; but we are not yet ready to consider compilation of declarations, and meanwhile we temporarily use a simple convention which is that a variable's identifier is restricted to being a single upper-case letter: variables A..E are BOOLEAN, variables F..N are INTEGER and variables P..Z are REAL. As in Section 8.6, variables are not declared in the source program, and we assume that

```
A: DW ?
B: DW ?
```

and so on, and

```
F: DW ?
G: DW ?
```

and so on, and

```
P: DW 2 DUP
Q: DW 2 DUP
```

and so on
are already included in the SAL object program. Note that P, Q and other REALs have two words. We use the following function to return the type of a variable:

```
PROCEDURE typeOf(chOfSy:CHAR): CARDINAL;
BEGIN
  CASE chOfSy OF
  'A'..'E': RETURN tyBoolean |
  'F'..'N': RETURN tyInteger |
  'P'..'Z': RETURN tyReal
  ELSE error (19)
  END
END typeOf;
```

Our use of this function is a temporary expedient and is nothing like what happens in a fully developed Modula-2 compiler. We will introduce more practical techniques in

Chapter 12. Meanwhile, as in Section 8.5.3, chOfSy is a global variable of type CHAR. When sy = idSy, chOfSy is the actual character of the single-character identifier.

10.3.2 Type compatibility checking

Pascal allows the assignment statement x:= y + i, where x and y are REAL and i is INTEGER. To cope with this, the type of i is automatically changed to REAL. Technically, an automatic type change is known as a *coercion*, and in a Pascal compiler one of the purposes of type checking is to determine where coercion is legitimately applicable and to output object code to accomplish coercion where this is required. Modula-2 does not have automatic coercion. Instead, a Modula-2 compiler checks that both of the operands of a logic or arithmetic operator are of the same type, and that the value of an expression on the right-hand side of an assignment statement is of the same type as the variable on the left-hand side. This is known as *type compatibility checking*.

As in Chapter 8, we will be concerned with object code that pushes two operands on to the stack and then applies an operator to the appropriate number of words at the top of the stack. When operators are pushed on to the stack, our compiler notes their types. Before applying an operator it checks that the operands are of the same type.

We now use a new version of procedure factor which outputs SAL to leave the value of a factor on the top of the stack. This version of procedure factor has a VAR parameter resultType, which returns the type of the factor. For example, if procedure factor is called when sy = idSy then procedure factor outputs code to push the value of the variable identified by chOfSy on to the stack, and assigns

```
resultType:= typeOf(chOfSy);
```

In Section 8.6 procedure term conformed to the outline:

```
PROCEDURE term;
VAR
  operator: symbolType;
BEGIN
  factor;
  WHILE sy is an appropriate operator DO
    operator:= sy; inSymbol;
    factor; apply(operator)
  END
END term;
```

For checking type compatibility, we introduce a local variable nexType and our outline procedure becomes:

```
PROCEDURE term (VAR resultType: CARDINAL);
VAR
  operator: symbolType; nexType: CARDINAL;
```

```
BEGIN
  factor (resultType);
  WHILE sy is an appropriate operator DO
    operator:= sy; inSymbol; factor (nexType);
    IF resultType = nexType THEN
      apply (operator for the appropriate type)
    ELSE output type incompatibility error message
    END
  END
END term;
```

The same method of type checking is used in various other procedures in Section 10.4.

10.3.3 Resolution of overloading

We apply operators such as + and * to integers and reals although arithmetical operations on integers and real numbers are radically different because of the floating-point representation of reals. When used to signify different operations depending on the types of its operands, an operator is said to be *overloaded*. For example, in Modula-2 the operator + is overloaded because it means integer addition if the operands are INTEGER and real addition if the operands are REAL. Moreover, + means set union if the operands are sets.

Corresponding to the single operator '+' in a source program, a compiler must output different object-code instructions according as the operands are INTEGER, REAL or sets. The compiler must, therefore, find out the types of the operands, and one of the purposes of type checking is to achieve this. Another purpose of type checking is to ensure that an operator is applied to operands of appropriate type. For example, '+' cannot be applied to operands of type BOOLEAN, and NOT cannot be applied to an operand of type REAL. In Chapter 13 we will check that types of actual parameters of procedures match the types of formal parameters.

After checking for type compatibility as in Section 10.3.2, it is easy to select the appropriate operator by case analysis using a CASE statement or an IF–THEN–ELSIF–

Table 10.1 Operators that can be applied by procedure `term`

Operator	Symbol for operator
AND	andOp
*	timesOp
DIV	divOp
MOD	modOp
/	realDivOp

ELSIF–... construction. For example, in Section 10.4 a new version of procedure `term` will be able to apply the operators shown in Table 10.1. Depending on the type of the operands, the operator can be selected by the following:

```
CASE resultType OF
   tyBoolean:  IF operator = andOp THEN
                    applyOperator(andOp)
                ELSE error(21)
                END |
   tyInteger:  IF operator IN symbolSet {timesOp, divOp, modOp} THEN
                    applyOperator(operator)
                ELSE error(21)
                END |
     tyReal:   IF operator IN symbolSet {timesOp, realDivOp} THEN
                    applyRealOperator(operator)
                ELSE error(21)
                END
ELSE error(22)
END
```

In this the only example of an overloaded operator is '*'. If the operands are INTEGER, `applyOperator(timesOp)` produces SAL for integer multiplication. If, instead, the operands are REAL, `applyRealOperator(timesOp)` produces CALL REALMULT. An attempt, for example, to apply the operator AND to operands of type REAL will evoke an error message.

10.4 Compiling expressions

In Section 10.5 we will be concerned with assignment statements that have syntax defined by the following grammar:

Tenth example grammar
    Start symbol: `assignmentStatement`
    Non-terminal symbols: `expression, subExpression, term, factor, plusorminus,`
        `addoperator, mulopertor, idSy, numberSy, real, cardinal, digit`
    Terminal symbols: `idSy, +, -, OR, *, /, DIV, MOD, AND, (, ), NOT, >, <, =, <=,`
        `>=, #, :=, ., A,B,..,Z, 0,..,9`
    Productions:

```
assignmentStatement ->  idSy ":=" expression.
expression     ->  subExpression [relop subExpression].
relop          ->  ">" | "<" | "=" | "<=" | ">=".
subExpression  ->  [plusorminus] term {addoperator term}.
plusorminus    ->  "+" | " -".
addoperator    ->  plusorminus | "OR".
```

```
term         ->  factor {muloperator factor}.
muloperator  ->  "*" | "/" | "DIV" | "MOD" | "AND".
factor       ->  idSy | numberSy | (expression) | "NOT" factor.
idSy         -> "A" | "B" | .. | "Z".
number       ->  real | cardinal.
cardinal     ->  digit {digit}.
real         ->  cardinal.cardinal.
digit        ->  "0" | "1" |..|"9".
```

An example of a sentence in the language defined by this grammar is

```
B:= (I >= 3) AND (X < Y * (Z + 6.729)) OR NOT C
```

Much of this grammar defines the internal syntax of expressions, which are simpler than expressions in Modula-2: for example, identifiers are restricted to being single letters that imply an identifier's type, as explained in Section 10.3.1, and functions are not yet allowed. To compile an assignment statement we have a procedure assignmentStatement, which calls a procedure expression to compile the right-hand side. Procedure expression, together with various procedures that it calls, is in a separate module expressn:

```
DEFINITION MODULE expressn;
FROM symbols IMPORT symbolType;
PROCEDURE expression(VAR resultType: CARDINAL);
PROCEDURE typeOf(chOfSy: CHAR): CARDINAL;
END expressn.


IMPLEMENTATION MODULE expressn;
FROM InOut IMPORT WriteString, WriteLn, Write, WriteCard;
FROM symbols IMPORT symbolType;
FROM strinTab IMPORT stringInfo;
FROM scanner IMPORT inSymbol, error, accept, valueRecord, sy, ind;
FROM putSAL IMPORT applyOperator, applyRelationalOp, applyRealOperator;
CONST
  tyInteger = 1;  tyBoolean = 2;  tyReal = 3;
TYPE
  symbolSet = SET OF symbolType;
VAR
  chOfSy: CHAR;


PROCEDURE typeOf(chOfSy:CHAR): CARDINAL;
BEGIN
  CASE chOfSy OF
  'A'..'E': RETURN tyBoolean |
  'F'..'N': RETURN tyInteger |
  'P'..'Z': RETURN tyReal
  ELSE error (19)
```

```
   END
END typeOf;


PROCEDURE expression (VAR resultType: CARDINAL);
VAR
  operator:  symbolType;
  nexType: CARDINAL;
BEGIN
  subExpression (resultType);
  IF sy IN symbolSet {equOp..greatEquOp} THEN
    operator:= sy;  inSymbol;
    subExpression (nexType);
    IF resultType = nexType THEN
       IF resultType = tyReal THEN applyRealOperator(operator)
       ELSE  applyRelationalOp(operator)
       END;
       resultType:= tyBoolean
    ELSE error(20) END;
  END
END expression;


PROCEDURE subExpression (VAR resultType: CARDINAL);
VAR
  operator: symbolType;
  nexType: CARDINAL;
BEGIN
   IF sy = plussOp THEN
     inSymbol; term (resultType);
   ELSIF sy = minusOp THEN
     inSymbol; term (resultType);
     IF resultType = tyInteger THEN applyOperator(negOp)
     ELSIF resultType = tyReal THEN applyRealOperator(negOp)
     ELSE error(20)
     END
   ELSE term (resultType)
   END;
   WHILE sy IN symbolSet{plussOp,minusOp,orOp} DO
     operator:= sy; inSymbol; term (nexType);
     IF nexType = resultType THEN
       CASE operator OF
         orOp:  IF resultType = tyBoolean THEN
                   applyOperator(orOp)
                ELSE error(20)
                END |
         plussOp, minusOp:
```

```
                        IF resultType = tyInteger THEN
                            applyOperator(operator)
                        ELSIF resultType = tyReal THEN
                            applyRealOperator(operator)
                        ELSE error(20)
                        END
            END (* CASE *)
        ELSE error(20)
        END
    END (* WHILE *)
END subExpression;


PROCEDURE term (VAR resultType: CARDINAL);
VAR
    operator: symbolType;
    nexType: CARDINAL;
BEGIN
    factor (resultType);
    WHILE sy IN symbolSet{timesOp,realDivOp, divOp, modOp, andOp} DO
        operator:= sy; inSymbol;
        factor (nexType);
        IF resultType = nexType THEN
            CASE resultType OF
            tyBoolean:  IF operator = andOp THEN
                        applyOperator(andOp) ELSE error(21) END |
            tyInteger:  IF operator IN symbolSet {timesOp, divOp, modOp} THEN
                        applyOperator(operator) ELSE error(21) END |
             tyReal:  IF operator IN symbolSet {timesOp, realDivOp} THEN
                        applyRealOperator(operator) ELSE error(21) END
            ELSE error(22)
            END
        ELSE error(20)
        END
    END (* WHILE *)
END term;


PROCEDURE factor (VAR resultType: CARDINAL);
BEGIN
  CASE sy OF
  idSy: chOfSy:= stringInfo.initialChar; resultType:= typeOf(chOfSy);
        IF (resultType = tyInteger) OR (resultType = tyBoolean) THEN
            WriteString('    PUSH  '); Write(chOfSy); WriteLn;
        ELSIF resultType = tyReal THEN
            WriteString('    LEA BX, '); Write(chOfSy); WriteLn;
            WriteString('    PUSH [BX]'); WriteLn;
```

```
        WriteString('    PUSH [BX + 1]'); WriteLn;
      ELSE error(20)
      END; inSymbol |
  numberSy: WriteString('    MOV  AX, '); WriteCard(valueRecord.val1, 5); WriteLn;
      WriteString('    PUSH AX'); WriteLn;
      IF valueRecord.valType = tyReal THEN
        WriteString('    MOV  AX, '); WriteCard(valueRecord.val2, 5); WriteLn;
        WriteString('    PUSH AX'); WriteLn;
        resultType:= tyReal
      ELSE resultType:= tyInteger
      END; inSymbol |
  notOp: inSymbol; factor(resultType);
      IF resultType # tyBoolean THEN error(20)
      ELSE applyOperator(notOp)
      END |
  openRndBrktSy: inSymbol; expression(resultType); accept(closeRndBrktSy)
  END
END factor;

BEGIN
END expressn.
```

Procedure `expression` is not the same as in Section 8.6: instead it corresponds to the production

```
expression -> subExpression [relop subExpression]
```

which is in our tenth example grammar, but not in our ninth. Procedure `subExpression` in module `expressn` corresponds to procedure `expression` in module `toSAL` in Section 8.6, which does not deal with relational operators. If an expression includes a relational operation on type-compatible operands, then procedure `expression` returns `resultType:= tyBoolean`, regardless of the type of the operands. This is because the result of a relational operation is always BOOLEAN.

If procedure `factor` is called when `sy = idSy`, then the type of the variable is ascertained by looking at its single-letter identifier. If it is of type INTEGER or BOOLEAN, and therefore occupies a single word, `factor` outputs SAL to push this word on to the stack. If, instead, it is REAL, then `factor` outputs SAL to push two words on to the stack. This is done by assigning to `BX` the address corresponding to the single-letter identifier, and then using the two instructions

```
    PUSH [BX]
    PUSH [BX + 1]
```

If `factor` is called when `sy = numberSy`, then `factor` outputs SAL to push the appropriate number of fields of `valueRecord` on to the stack. In the CASE statement in procedure `factor` there are two further possibilities, `notOp` and `openRndBrktSy`, for which the action is self-explanatory.

10.5 Compiling simple assignment statements

The following progam compiles simple assignment statements in the language defined by the tenth example grammar. We now use a semicolon as an end marker, just as we used '$' in Section 8.6. The input expression is read from a file named `sourceIn` via the lexical analyzer:

```
MODULE typAssin;

FROM InOut IMPORT WriteString, WriteLn, Write, WriteCard;

FROM symbols IMPORT symbolType;

FROM strinTab IMPORT stringInfo;

FROM scanner IMPORT inSymbol, error, accept, valueRecord, sy, ind;

FROM expressn IMPORT expression, typeOf;

CONST
   tyInteger = 1;  tyBoolean = 2;  tyReal = 3;

PROCEDURE assignmentStatement;
VAR
   charOfLHS: CHAR; lhsType, resultType: CARDINAL;
BEGIN
   charOfLHS:= stringInfo.initialChar; (* single-character identifier *)
   lhsType:= typeOf(charOfLHS);
   inSymbol; accept(assignOp); expression(resultType);
   IF lhsType = resultType THEN
     IF lhsType = tyReal THEN
       WriteString('   LEA BX, '); Write(charOfLHS); WriteLn;
       WriteString('   POP [BX + 1]'); WriteLn;
       WriteString('   POP [BX]'); WriteLn
     ELSE  WriteString('   POP   '); Write(charOfLHS); WriteLn;
     END
   ELSE error(20)
   END
END assignmentStatement;


BEGIN
   inSymbol;
   IF sy = idSy THEN assignmentStatement ELSE error(5) END;
   IF sy = semiColonSy THEN WriteString('Correct syntax'); WriteLn ELSE
     error (3)
   END
END typAssin.
```

Procedure `assignmentStatement` calls procedure `expression` to produce object code to evaluate the expression on the right-hand side and return the type of the result via `resultType`. If the result is REAL, this comprises the top two words of the stack, and procedure `assignmentStatement` outputs code to pop the top word into `charOfLHS` and to pop the next word off the stack into the word following that which is labelled `charOfLHS`. If, instead, the result of the right-hand-side expression is INTEGER or BOOLEAN, then only a single word is popped off the stack into the word labelled `charOfLHS`. The assignment operator is overloaded, in that the number of words assigned to the left-hand side depends on the type of the operands.

When, for example, the input to module `typAssin` is `A := (I > J + 7) AND (X > Y + 7.7);` the output is:

```
      PUSH   I
      PUSH   J
      MOV  AX,      7
      PUSH AX          ; push operand 7
      POP  AX
      MOV DI, SP
      ADD [DI], AX    ; stack top:= J + 7
      MOV AX, 1       ; AX:= TRUE
      POP BX
      POP CX
      CMP CX, BX
      JG  ZAAB        ; jump if I > J + 7
      DEC AX          ; AX:= FALSE
ZAAB: PUSH AX
      LEA BX, X
      PUSH [BX]       ; first word of X
      PUSH [BX + 1]   ; second word of X
      LEA BX, Y
      PUSH [BX]       ; first word of Y
      PUSH [BX + 1]   ; second word of Y
      MOV  AX, 26214 ; first word of operand 7.7
      PUSH AX
      MOV AX, 16630   ; second word of operand 7.7
      PUSH AX
      CALL REALADD
      CALL REALGREATER
      POP  AX         ; AX:= (X > Y + 7.7)
      MOV DI, SP
      AND  [DI], AX   ; AND with previous BOOLEAN result
      POP   A         ; assign result of AND to A
   Correct syntax
```

This output is not a complete program, but just a fragment. In Chapter 12 we will begin to produce executable SAL programs.

10.6 Discussion

Syntax analysis is only concerned with formal structure, not with types of operands. For example, the tree in Figure 7.1 would be unchanged if some of the operands were REAL and some INTEGER. In the present chapter we have introduced type checking, which is required *as well as* syntax checking. Because the type of a variable is related to its meaning, and because the term *semantic* means *related to meaning*, type checking is an example of *semantic checking*. From the viewpoint of compiler theory (see, for example, Fischer and LeBlanc 1988; Waite and Goos 1984), semantic checking is performed by some of the semantic actions that are associated with productions in an attribute grammar.

Our procedures `assignmentStatement` and `factor` are specialized for some kind of *stack machine*. A *stack machine* is a processor that applies operators to operands that are on a stack. An 8086 is not a stack machine because operands can be in registers or in main memory. In the early 1960s several computers were designed that really were stack machines, for example the Burroughs B5500 and the English Electric KDF9. To assign `V := X * (Y + Z)`, KDF9 assembly language only required the six instructions

```
X; Y; Z; +; *; = V;
```

The first three push successive operands on to the stack, the next two apply operators to the top two words of the stack, pushing the result on to the stack, and the last pops the result off the stack into `V`. KDF9 assembly language, which was very close to postfix notation, is an example of a *zero-address code*, because no operand addresses are associated with operators. Operators always operate on the top words of the stack, and therefore there is no need to specify addresses.

If we were to change module `putSAL` to output KDF9 assembly language, or any other stack machine assembly language, module `expressn` would require scarcely any modification. This is because we are using SAL instructions that perform operations on operands that are always on a stack.

For purposes of optimization and to achieve useful independence of the details of an object language, some compilers compile into an intermediate code, such as p-code (Welsh and Hay 1986) or EM (Bal and Tanenbaum 1986), which is the assembly language of a hypothetical stack machine, and subsequently translate this into object language. SAL is the assembly lanquage of a non-existent computer, and is in this sense hypothetical. A hypothetical stack machine intermediate language looks like the language of a stack machine and is designed to be easy to compile into. It is *hypothetical* because this stack machine does not exist; the intermediate language has to be interpreted or be translated into object code executable on a real machine. If our module `putSAL` were changed to output hypothetical stack-machine instructions instead of SAL, it would be simplified, and there would be very little requirement for change within module `expressn`.

On the other hand, if our compiler were to be changed to output quadruples, as in Exercise 6 in Section 8.8, or instead to output a parse tree as a linked data structure, together with associated attribute values, then modules `expressn` and `typAssin` would require substantial revision. In SAL only a few registers are available, and it is therefore sensible to make heavy use of a stack, but for processors that have many registers it may be best to compile into triples or quadruples and make good use of the registers when the intermediate code is translated into object code. We will very briefly return to this in Section 16.6.

SAL is a hypothetical compiler target code that is over-simple in that it does not make provision for run-time errors such as division by zero, overflow and underflow. In a CPU such as the 8086 an interrupt is generated when there is an attempt to divide by zero, and the compiler writer does not have to do anything to ensure that this is the case. The 8086 has an overflow flag that is set if an operation such as ADD causes overflow and is cleared by arithmetic operations that do not cause overflow. Object code should include instructions to check the overflow flag after each integer operation. It is generally not practical to arrange for an interrupt to occur whenever this overflow flag is set because it may be set during address calculation where no error has occurred. In processors such as the i860 that have separate floating-point units, the programmer can arrange that an interrupt will occur if there is overflow or underflow in a floating-point operation, and in this regime there is no need for instructions in the object code to check for overflow and underflow explicitly after each floating-point operation.

Farnum (1988) reviews practical requirements for production of code for floating-point arithmetic, which is beyond the scope of the present book.

10.7 Exercises

1. Write in Modula-2 an interpreter that reads an expression from the keyboard and outputs the value of that expression. For example if the expression 7.0 * (8.1 − 9.0/2.6) is typed on the keyboard, the output should be 32.469 231 approximately. The input is to be an expression in the language defined by the tenth example grammar in Section 10.4, except that identifiers are disallowed.

    Your program should declare and use a stack for the evaluation of expressions. For example, to evaluate x + y * z, your program should push the values of x, y and z on to this stack, then pop off y and z and instead push on the value of y * z. Then pop off x and the value of y * z, add these together, and push on the value of x + y * z. The value that is output by your program is to be the value that was left on the stack after evaluation of the input expression.

2. Modify procedures `subExpression` and `term` so that if the source code is of the form `term1 OR term2` then the object code will not evaluate `term2` if `term1` is true. If the source code is of the form `factor1 AND factor2` then the object code is not to evaluate `factor2` if `factor1` is false. If the source code is of the form `(factor1 AND factor2) OR term2` then `term2` is to be evaluated only if `factor1` is false or if `factor2` is false. (The technique of omitting evaluation of factors or terms that cannot affect the final result is called *short circuit evaluation* of Boolean expressions – see Fischer and LeBlanc 1988; Gough and Mohay 1988.)

CHAPTER 11

Compiling control structures

11.1 Introduction

In our step-by-step evolution of a compiler we now introduce the compilation of WHILE, REPEAT, LOOP, EXIT and IF statements as well as assignment statements. Corresponding to each of these a recursive-descent compiler has a procedure that checks syntax and semantics and outputs some kind of code or some kind of representation from which code can subsequently be produced. To determine how to program one of these procedures in detail, we start by writing a schematic outline of the code that we wish it to produce, and we then program it so as to make our wishes come true. This chapter illustrates this design process for WHILE, REPEAT, LOOP, EXIT and IF statements, using single-character identifiers as in Section 10.3.1. In Chapter 12 we will use Modula-2 identifiers.

In Modula-2 a statement sequence conforms to the production

```
statementSequence -> statement {; statement}
```

Correspondingly, our compiler includes a procedure that compiles a statement sequence:

```
PROCEDURE stmntSequence;
BEGIN
  LOOP
    statement;
    IF sy = semiColonSy THEN inSymbol ELSE EXIT END
  END
END stmntSequence;
```

In the present chapter and in Chapter 12 we will not consider all possible Modula-2 statements and instead will allow only statements such that:

```
statement -> assignmentStatement | whileStatement | repeatStatement |
             loopStatement | exitStatement | ifStatement | empty
```

Corresponding to this production we have:

```
PROCEDURE statement;
BEGIN
```

```
CASE sy OF
   idSy:     assignmentStatement    |
   whileSy:  inSymbol; whileStatement |
   loopSy:   inSymbol; loopStatement  |
   exitSy:   inSymbol; exitStatement  |
   ifSy:     inSymbol; ifStatement    |
   repeatSy: inSymbol; repeatStatement
ELSE (* do nothing *)
END
END statement;
```

This is simple because the language has been designed so that the compiler can tell whether a statement is an assignment statement, a WHILE statement, or any other kind of statement, by looking at the first symbol in the sequence of symbols that consitutes the statement. Note that if procedure `statement` is called when `sy` does not match any of the labels of the CASE statement, `statement` does nothing. This means that procedure `stmntSequence` allows consecutive semicolons, for example:

```
A:= B; ; C:= D;
```

Like procedures `expression` and `assignmentStatement`, procedures `whileStatement`, `repeatStatement`, `ifStatement`, `loopStatement` and `exitStatement` achieve syntax-directed compilation, which means that object-code production hangs upon syntax analysis.

11.2 WHILE statements

A recursive-descent compiler can check the syntax of a WHILE statement

```
whileStatement -> WHILE expression DO statementSequence END
```

by calling

```
PROCEDURE whileCheck;
BEGIN
   expression(resultType); accept(doSy); stmntSequence; accept(endSy)
END whileCheck;
```

This assumes that procedure `whileCheck` is called when `sy` is the symbol that immediately follows `whileSy`. As well as checking the syntax, the following version of the procedure also checks that the expression yields a boolean result, that is, that the expression is a condition:

```
PROCEDURE whileCheck2;
VAR
   resultType: CARDINAL;
```

```
BEGIN
  expression(resultType); IF resultType # tyBoolean THEN error (99) END;
  accept(doSy); stmntSequence; accept(endSy)
END whileCheck2;
```

To produce object code for a WHILE statement, we develop this procedure so that it includes code-producing statements. To figure out how to do this, we start by looking at the form of the object code that we would like our compiler to produce, and then we write procedure `whileStatement` so that it actually produces this code. The form of the object code corresponding to a WHILE statement is:

```
LOOPLABEL:  instructions to evaluate expression;
            POP AX     ; AX:= boolean result of expression
            CMP AX, 0  ; 0 represents FALSE
            JE AFTER   ; if result is false then jump to AFTER
            instructions corresponding statement sequence;
            JMP LOOPLABEL
AFTER:      NOP;
```

This is known as the *code skeleton* of a WHILE statement: it consists of the bare bones, without fleshing out the details of the object-code instructions that evaluate the expression or execute the statement sequence. If the condition is TRUE then the statement sequence is executed, and after execution of JMP LOOPLABEL the condition is tested again. Repetition continues until the condition is FALSE, whereupon the execution of JE AFTER prevents further iteration.

Object-code instructions to evaluate an expression are produced by calling procedure `expression`, and object-code instructions to execute a statement sequence are produced by calling procedure `stmntSequence`. Procedure `whileStatement` must also output labels corresponding to LOOPLABEL and AFTER, which is easily achieved by calling procedures `genLabel` and `putLabel`. Instead of using the actual identifier LOOPLABEL or AFTER our compiler uses labels in the series ZAAB, ZAAC, ZAAD. Putting all this together, a procedure that compiles WHILE statements is as follows:

```
PROCEDURE whileSt;
VAR
  loopLabel,after: labelString; resultType: CARDINAL;
BEGIN;
  genLabel(loopLabel);  putLabel(loopLabel);
  expression(resultType);
  genLabel(after);
  IF resultType # tyBoolean THEN error (7) END;
  putLine('    POP AX');
  putLine('    CMP AX, 0');
  putStrings('    JE ', after);
  accept(doSy); stmntSequence; accept(endSy);
  putStrings('    JMP ',loopLabel);
```

```
      putLabel(after); putLine('    NOP')
   END whileSt;
```

Procedures `putLine` and `putStrings` are imported from module `putSAL`.

We will soon see that procedures `repeatStatement` and `ifStatement` also involve checking that the result of an expression is boolean, and if it is FALSE then jumping to a label previously generated by `genLabel`. Because this material is common to `whileStatement`, `repeatStatement` and `ifStatement` we take it out and make it into a separate procedure:

```
PROCEDURE jumpIfFalse(resultType: CARDINAL; whereTo: labelString);
BEGIN
   IF resultType # tyBoolean THEN error(7) END;
   putLine('    POP AX');
   putLine('    CMP AX, 0');
   putStrings('    JE  ',whereTo)
END jumpIfFalse;
```

Using this our WHILE statement procedure is:

```
PROCEDURE whileStatement;
VAR
   loopLabel,after: labelString; resultType: CARDINAL;
BEGIN;
   genLabel(loopLabel);  putLabel(loopLabel);
   expression(resultType);
   genLabel(after);  jumpIfFalse(resultType,after);
   accept(doSy); stmntSequence; accept(endSy);
   putStrings('    JMP ',loopLabel);
   putLabel(after); putLine('    NOP');
END whileStatement;
```

If, for example, procedure `stmntSequence` is called to compile

```
   WHILE I < 12 DO I:= I + 3 END; WHILE X < 12.0 DO X:= X + 3.0 END
```

the SAL object code produced by two calls of `whileStatement` is as follows:

```
ZAAA: PUSH    I
   MOV  AX,    12
   PUSH AX
   MOV AX, 1
   POP BX
   POP CX
   CMP CX, BX
   JL  ZAAB      ; jump to ZAAB if I < 12
   DEC AX
ZAAB: PUSH AX    ; push result of expression
```

```
        POP AX
        CMP AX, 0
        JE  ZAAC       ; jump to ZAAC if result FALSE
        PUSH   I
        MOV AX,    3
        PUSH AX
        POP AX         ; AX = 3; stacktop = I
        MOV DI, SP
        ADD [DI], AX
        POP    I       ; I:= I + 3;
        JMP ZAAA       ; jump back to re-test condition of WHILE
ZAAC:   NOP            ; statement following statement sequence
ZAAD:   LEA BX, X
        PUSH [BX]
        PUSH [BX + 1] ; top two words of stack:= real X
        MOV AX,    0
        PUSH AX
        MOV AX, 16704
        PUSH AX        ; top two words of stack:= 12.0
        CALL REALLESS
        POP AX         ; AX:= (X < 12.0)
        CMP AX, 0
        JE  ZAAE       ; jump to end if condition FALSE;
        LEA BX, X
        PUSH [BX]
        PUSH [BX + 1] ; top two words of stack:= real X;
        MOV AX,    0
        PUSH AX
        MOV AX, 16448
        PUSH AX        ; top two words of stack:= 3.0
        CALL REALADD
        LEA BX, X
        POP [BX + 1]   ; first word of two-word X
        POP [BX]       ; X:= X + 3
        JMP ZAAD       ; jump back to re-test condition of WHILE
ZAAE:   NOP
```

In this and subsequent examples we have added comments to facilitate comprehension: the compiler does not produce these comments. It is worthwhile to check the visibility of the code skeletons of the two WHILE statements in this SAL fragment. Note that both the first and last statements of the object code for a WHILE statement have labels. If our compiler did not produce a NOP instruction at the end of a WHILE statement, a single SAL instruction could have two labels, which is not allowed (although this is allowed in various other assembly languages).

11.3 REPEAT statements

A REPEAT statement is compiled by procedure `repeatStatement` which checks the syntax

```
repeatStatement -> REPEAT statementSequence UNTIL expression
```

and checks that the expression yields a boolean result. To work out how to write the parts of procedure `repeatStatement` that produce code, we look at the code skeleton of a REPEAT statement:

```
LOOPLABEL:  instructions to execute statement sequence;
            instructions to evaluate expression;
            if result of expression is FALSE then jump to LOOPLABEL.
```

The following procedure calls procedure `stmntSequence` to compile the statement sequence and procedure `expression` to compile the expression. It calls `jumpIfFalse` to produce code to jump to a label placed by `putLabel` if the value of the expression is FALSE:

```
PROCEDURE repeatStatement;
VAR
  loopLabel: labelString; resultType: CARDINAL;
BEGIN
  genLabel(loopLabel); putLabel(loopLabel);
  stmntSequence;
  accept(untilSy);  expression(resultType);
  jumpIfFalse(resultType,loopLabel)
END repeatStatement;
```

For example, procedure `repeatStatement` compiles the statement REPEAT I:= J UNTIL B into the following:

```
ZAAF:  PUSH J
       POP  I     ; I:= J
       PUSH B
       POP AX     ; AX:= B
       CMP AX, 0
       JE ZAAF    ; jump back to the beginning if B is FALSE
```

In this the code skeleton for a REPEAT statement is easily visible. It is also easy to see here and in other examples that the SAL code is inefficient; for example, instead of

```
    PUSH B
    POP  AX
```

the single instruction MOV AX, B would be sufficient. We will return to this in Section 16.7.5.

11.4 IF statements

For introductory simplicity, we start by temporarily disallowing ELSIF. For a conditional statement having the form

```
IF expression THEN statementSequence1 ELSE statementSequence2 END
```

a code skeleton is as follows:

```
              instructions to evaluate expression;
              if result is FALSE then jump to AFTERTHEN;
              instructions to execute statementSequence1;
              JMP AFTERIFSTMNT;
AFTERTHEN: instructions to execute statementSequence2;
AFTERIFSTMNT:    NOP
```

This skeleton produces the desired effect because if the expression is TRUE then `statementmentsequence1` is executed, otherwise the expression must be FALSE and `statementSequence2` is executed. The instructions to execute `statementSequence1` are followed by the unconditional jump `JMP AFTERIFSTMNT` to prevent the instructions for `statementSequence2` being executed as well as the instructions for `statementSequence1`. Just as we did for WHILE and REPEAT, we write procedure `ifStmnt` so that it produces code which conforms to the code skeleton:

```
PROCEDURE ifStmnt;
VAR
  afterThen, afterIfStmnt: labelString;
  resultType: CARDINAL;
BEGIN
  genLabel(afterThen);
  expression(resultType);    accept(thenSy);
  jumpIfFalse(resultType, afterThen);
  stmntSequence;
  IF sy = elseSy THEN
    genLabel(afterIfStmnt); putStrings('    JMP  ', afterIfStmnt);
    inSymbol; putLabel(afterThen);  stmntSequence;
    putLabel(afterIfStmnt)
  ELSE putLabel(afterThen)
  END;
  putLine('    NOP'); accept(endSy)
END ifStmnt;
```

This works correctly when the ELSE part is missing and the source text has the form `IF expression THEN statementSequence END`. For example, corresponding to `IF B THEN K:= L END` the output is:

```
      PUSH   B
      POP AX
      CMP AX, 0
      JE   ZAAB   ; if NOT B then jump over assignment statement
      PUSH   L
      POP   K    ; K:= L
ZAAB:   NOP
```

Corresponding to `IF B THEN K:= L ELSE K:= M END` **the output is:**

```
      PUSH   B
      POP AX
      CMP AX, 0
      JE   ZAAB   ; if NOT B then jump to K:= M
      PUSH   L
      POP   K    ; K:= L executed if B is TRUE
      JMP   ZAAC  ; jump over K:= M
ZAAB:      PUSH   M
      POP   K
ZAAC:   NOP
```

The procedure becomes more complicated when we allow ELSIF parts. For example, corresponding to

```
IF expression1 THEN statementSequence1 ELSIF expression2 THEN statementSequence2
ELSIF expression3 THEN statementSequence3 ELSE statementSequence4 END
```

a code skeleton is:

```
            instructions to evaluate expression1;
            if result is FALSE then jump to LABEL1;
            instructions to execute statementSequence1;
            JMP AFTERIFSTMNT;
LABEL1:     instructions to evaluate expression2;
            if result is FALSE then jump to LABEL2;
            instructions to execute statementSequence2;
            JMP AFTERIFSTMNT;
LABEL2:     instructions to evaluate expression3;
            if result is FALSE then jump to LABEL3;
            instructions to execute statementSequence3;
            JMP AFTERIFSTMNT;
LABEL3:     instructions to execute statementSequence4
AFTERIFSTMNT:   NOP
```

The WHILE loop in the following procedure allows any number of ELSIFs:

```
PROCEDURE ifStatement;
VAR
   afterThen, afterIfStmnt: labelString;
```

```
    resultType: CARDINAL;
BEGIN
  genLabel(afterThen);
  expression(resultType);    accept(thenSy);
  jumpIfFalse(resultType, afterThen);
  stmntSequence;
  IF sy = endSy THEN inSymbol; putLabel(afterThen)
  ELSE
    genLabel(afterIfStmnt);
    WHILE sy = elsifSy DO
      inSymbol; putStrings('    JMP    ', afterIfStmnt);
      putLabel(afterThen); genLabel(afterThen);
      expression(resultType); accept(thenSy);
      jumpIfFalse(resultType, afterThen);
      stmntSequence
    END;
    IF sy = elseSy THEN
      inSymbol; putStrings('    JMP    ', afterIfStmnt);
      putLabel(afterThen); stmntSequence
    ELSE putLabel(afterThen); putLine('    NOP')
    END;
    putLabel(afterIfStmnt);
    accept(endSy)
  END;
  putLine('    NOP')
END ifStatement;
```

For example, if the input is IF I = J THEN K:= L ELSIF I > J THEN K:= L + 1 ELSE
K:= 0 END then the output is as follows:

```
    PUSH    I
    PUSH    J
    MOV AX, 1
    POP BX
    POP CX
    CMP CX, BX
    JE    ZAAC  ; jump if I = J
    DEC AX
ZAAC: PUSH AX
    POP AX      ; AX = (I = J)
    CMP AX, 0
    JE  ZAAB    ; jump over then part if I # J
    PUSH    L
    POP    K    ; K:= L is the then part
    JMP    ZAAD ; jump over the remaining instructions
```

```
ZAAB: PUSH    I
      PUSH    J
      MOV AX, 1
      POP BX
      POP CX
      CMP CX, BX
      JG    ZAAF  ; if I > J then jump to ZAAF
      DEC AX
ZAAF: PUSH AX
      POP AX      ;  AX:= (I > J)
      CMP AX, 0
      JE  ZAAE    ; if NOT (I > J) then jump to ZAAE
      PUSH    L
      MOV   AX, 1
      PUSH AX
      POP   AX
      MOV DI, SP
      ADD   [DI], AX
      POP    K    ;  K:= L + 1
      JMP  ZAAD   ;  jump over else part
ZAAE: MOV   AX,   0
      PUSH AX
      POP    K    ; K:= 0 is the else part
ZAAD:    NOP
```

11.5 LOOP and EXIT statements

The following is a code skeleton for a LOOP statement:

```
LOOPLABEL: instructions to execute statementSequence;
           JMP LOOPLABEL;
AFTERLOOP: NOP
```

The label AFTERLOOP is placed at the end of this so that an EXIT statement within the loop can be compiled into JMP AFTERLOOP. If we temporarily disallow the occurence of nested LOOP statements within outer LOOP statements, then a compiler procedure is as follows:

```
PROCEDURE loopStmnt;
VAR
  loopLabel: labelString;
BEGIN
  genLabel(loopLabel); putLabel(loopLabel);
  genLabel(afterLoop);
```

```
    stmntSequence;
    accept(endSy);
    putStrings('    JMP   ',loopLabel);
    putLabel(afterLoop); putLine('    NOP')
END loopStmnt;
```

Here `afterLoop` has to be a global variable so that an EXIT statement can be compiled into `JMP afterLoop`.

When the compiler comes to an EXIT statement it should check that this has been written within the statement sequence of a LOOP statement. We now introduce this check at the same time as allowing the nesting of LOOP statements one inside another. For this purpose we introduce a global variable `loopStack` that is a one-dimensional array of labels, implementing a stack of labels. The array subscript of the label at the top of this stack is `loopStackTop`. When the stack is empty, `loopStackTop = 0`. Before calling `stmntSequence`, procedure `loopStatement` generates a new label and pushes it on to this stack. An EXIT statement is compiled into

```
    JMP loopStack[loopStackTop]
```

`loopStackTop` is decremented just before the end of procedure `loopStatement`, and this in effect pops the top label off the stack. Procedure `exitStatement` checks that it has been called from within a LOOP statement by checking that `loopStackTop > 0`.

Procedures `loopStatement` and `exitStatement` are included in module `statemnt` in the Appendix. Implementation of the label stack as an array implies a limitation on the depth of nesting of LOOP statements. This limitation can be avoided by implementing the label stack as a linked list. Anyway, procedure `loopStatement` compiles, for example,

```
    LOOP
      IF A THEN EXIT END;
      LOOP
        I:= J; IF B THEN EXIT END
      END;
      IF C THEN EXIT END
    END
```

into

```
    ZAAB:    PUSH   A
      POP AX
      CMP AX, 0
      JE    ZAAD   ; if NOT A then jump to ZAAD
      JMP   ZAAC   ; else jump to instruction after outer loop
    ZAAD:    NOP
    ZAAE:    PUSH   J
      POP   I    ; I:= J;
      PUSH   B
```

```
      POP  AX
      CMP  AX, 0
      JE   ZAAG   ; if NOT B then jump to ZAAG
      JMP  ZAAF   ; else jump to instruction after inner loop
ZAAG:      NOP
      JMP  ZAAE   ; jump back to beginning of inner loop
ZAAF:      NOP    ; this is the instruction after inner loop
      PUSH   C
      POP  AX
      CMP  AX, 0
      JE   ZAAH   ; if NOT C then jump to ZAAH
      JMP  ZAAC   ; else jump to instruction after outer loop
ZAAH:      NOP
      JMP  ZAAB   ; jump back to beginning of outer loop
ZAAC:      NOP    ; this is the instruction after outer loop
```

During the compilation of the inner loop `loopStack[loopStackTop] = ZAAF` and this is why the EXIT statement in the inner loop is compiled into `JMP ZAAF`. The second call of `loopStatement` terminates when the compiler reaches END at the end of the inner LOOP, and at this time `DEC(loopStackTop)` in effect pops `ZAAF` off the loop stack and discards it, leaving `ZAAC` as the top label in the loop stack. The last EXIT statement in the outer loop is therefore compiled into `JMP ZAAC`, just the same as the first EXIT statement in the outer loop.

11.6 A compiler for simple statement sequences

Our procedures that compile statements are in a module `statemnt` that is listed in the Appendix. This module compiles a statement sequence bracketed between BEGIN and END. It is important that, for example, within a WHILE statement the statement sequence can include an IF statement in which there is a LOOP statement in which there is a WHILE statement and so on *ad infinitum*.

As in Section 10.5 the object code that is produced is not a complete SAL program. For example, the stack pointer SP is not initialized and there is no `CALL ENDPROG` to terminate execution.

11.7 Discussion

From the viewpoint of attribute grammars, the parts of procedure `whileStatement` that perform semantic checking and generate object code correspond to semantic actions that are formally associated with the production an object code skeleton is as follows:

```
                  DI:= (i - SmallestValueOfi) * 2
                  JMP JUMPTABLEBASE[DI]
JUMPTABLEBASE: JMP FIRSTLABEL
                  JMP SECONDLABEL
                  JMP SECONDLABEL
                  DW  2 DUP
                  JMP THIRDLABEL
   FIRSTLABEL: sequence of instructions for stmnts1
                  JMP AFTERCASE
  SECONDLABEL: sequence of instructions for stmnts2
                  JMP AFTERCASE
   THIRDLABEL: sequence of intructions for stmnts3
                  JMP AFTERCASE
    AFTERCASE: NOP
```

In this example the jump table is a one-dimensional array of jump instructions with the first array element located at the word labelled JUMPTABLEBASE. The instruction JMP JUMPTABLEBASE[DI] causes a jump to one of these jump instructions selected by the value of the CASE selector, which is i in this example. For i = 4, i = SmallestValueOfi, and the instruction JMP FIRSTLABEL causes a jump to a sequence of instructions that implement stmnts1. For i = 5 and i = 6, JMP SECONDLABEL causes a jump to a sequence of instructions that implement stmnts2, and so on for other values of i. In the example there is no CASE label for i = 7, and it is important that words for i = 7 are nevertheless reserved by DW 2 DUP: two words are reserved because a JMP instruction has two words. (Jump-table implementation of a CASE statement (see Fischer and LeBlanc 1988) is fast, but search-tree implementations can be more memory-efficient (see Hennessy and Mendelsohn 1982; Sale 1981).)

CHAPTER 12

Static storage

12.1 Introduction

Hitherto we have used single-letter identifiers for variables, assuming that the SAL object program already contains

```
A:  DW ?
B:  DW ?
```

and so on. We will henceforth abandon any such assumption, and instead use Modula-2 identifiers not restricted to single letters. Moreover, we will use Modula-2 identifiers for constants and types, as well as for variables. We will consider array and record types, but not pointers, subranges, sets, or enumerations. We will postpone dealing with procedures until Chapter 13.

Much of the present chapter is concerned with compiling declarations to obtain essential information about identifiers. This information is stored in a table called the *identifier table* which is introduced in more detail in Section 12.3. The use of declared identifiers has an impact on the expression and statement modules, as explained in Sections 12.5 to 12.8. In Chapters 10 and 11 a variable's predefined single-character identifier was the same in the object code as in the source code. Henceforward, the ind of a variable's identifier is stored in the identifier table: what corresponds to a variable in the object code is a numeric address of the variable within a block of consecutive words. For introductory purposes the present chapter has all variables within the same block of words that are numbered 0,1,2, ... In Chapter 13 each procedure will have its own block, and in Chapter 14 each module will have its own block.

12.2 Static allocation by the compiler

Suppose, for example, that a source program has global declarations:

```
TYPE
    anArrayType = ARRAY[1..10] OF INTEGER;
    aRecordType = RECORD
                    a1, a2: INTEGER;
```

```
                      b1: BOOLEAN
                  END;
    anotherArrayType = ARRAY[2..6] OF aRecordType;
VAR
    x, y : INTEGER;
    ar: anArrayType;
    z: REAL;
    hr: aRecordType;
    w: BOOLEAN;
    sry: anotherArrayType;
    utnm: INTEGER;
```

Table 12.1 An example of static storage allocation

word	contains
0	x
1	y
2	first element of ar
3	second element of ar
and so on up to	
11	tenth and last element of ar
12	first word of z
13	second word of z
14	hr.a1
15	hr.a2
16	hr.b1
17	w
18	a1 field of first element of sry
19	a2 field of first element of sry
20	b1 field of first element of sry
21	a1 field of second element of sry
and so on up to	
32	b1 field of last element of sry
33	utnm.

Our compiler will allocate memory to variables as shown in Table 12.1. Individual variables do not have their own labels as they did in Section 11.6: for example, there is no label corresponding to the variable w. Instead, the first word of each variable has an address relative to the first word of the block. We refer to this relative address as the variable's relAddress. For example, the relAddress of x is 0, of y is 1, of ar is 2, of z is 12, and so on. For simplicity we restrict relAddresses to 16 bits and work exclusively with 16-bit words.

This allocation of storage is said to be *static* because it remains unchanged during the execution of the entire program. The block of words that contains all the global variables is the *static block*. Storage for parameters and local variables of procedures is outside the static block and is said to be *dynamic* because it is allocated and deallocated during the execution of the program, as will be explained in Chapter 13.

12.3 The identifier table

12.3.1 Identifiers

Our compiler stores information about identifiers in a table called the *identifier table*, implemented as a chained hash table with some additional pointer links. The chained hash table consists of a one-dimensional array of linked lists of records that contain information about individual identifiers, including an identifier's `ind`. Although we are not yet ready to deal with procedures, we note that a procedure could have local identifiers x and y that are entirely distinct from global identifiers x and y. In this case the identifier table would have separate records for local variables x and y as well as separate records for global variables x and y. The general idea is that if the same identifier is used in different places to mean different things, the identifier table includes a separate record for each meaning of this identifier.

The `ind` of an identifier is stored in the identifier's record in the table. `ind` values 1..27 are allocated to standard identifiers during initialization of the string table in the lexical analyzer. The source-code module identifier has `ind = 28`, and successive programmer-defined identifiers, such as those in the example in Section 12.2, have `ind = 29,30,31, ... `. For purposes of the present chapter we only require eight standard identifiers, and a record for each of these is inserted into the identifier table by an initializing procedure `initialiseIdTable`, which is included in a listing of module `itmod` in the Appendix, not by compiling declarations.

12.3.2 The class of an identifier

One of the fields of a record in the identifier table shows the *class* of the identifier. For the purposes of the present chapter `class` is the enumeration type

```
class = (aConstant, aType, aVariable, aField, externalProc)
```

For example, if an identifier identifies a constant, its class is `aConstant`.

The object code produced by the compiler in the present chapter can be assembled, linked and interpreted by software that we have introduced previously. To be able to execute programs, we need input and output capabilities, but we are not ready to deal with this properly in the style of Modula-2. Instead, as a temporary expedient, we allow source programs to contain three unorthodox standard procedures READNUM, WRITENUM

```
whileStatement -> WHILE expression DO statementSequence END
```

Similarly, procedure `repeatStatement` embodies semantic actions associated with the production for a REPEAT statement, and the same idea is used for IF, LOOP and other statements. We have considered how to design procedures such as `whileStatement` and `repeatStatement` by looking at code skeletons. The details of the underlying semantic actions have to be determined in a similar way. In an elementary introduction to compiling it is worthwhile to note that attribute grammars provide a formal framework going beyond syntax theory. We do not need to proceed further into formal theory in order to write a recursive-descent compiler, but attribute grammar theory is important for other purposes (Aho *et al.* 1986; Fischer and LeBlanc 1988; Waite and Goos 1984).

If there is an error such as a missing semicolon in the source program then the compiler may fall out of step with the input symbol stream and therefore produce a cascade of consequential errors. In Chapter 15 we will consider detection of multiple genuine errors in a source program, and until then we will ignore the problem of errors that are unhelpfully reported as a result of previous errors.

11.8 Exercises

1. By executing procedures in module `statemnt` manually, compile the following fragment into SAL:

```
LOOP
  IF I > J THEN EXIT ELSE
    LOOP
      REPEAT I:= I + L UNTIL I > M;
      IF M >= J THEN EXIT ELSE M:= M + N END
    END;
    A:= B
  END;
  C:= D
END;
WHILE X < Y DO Y:= Y - Z END;
```

2. Write a procedure that will compile a CASE statement in which the selector is restricted to being an expression that yields a result of type INTEGER, and ELSE is disallowed. Your procedure is to produce object code that implements a CASE statement by using a jump table. For example, if an outline of a source CASE statement is

```
CASE i OF
4:   stmnts1 |
5,6: stmnts2 |
8:   smnts3
END
```

and NEWLINE. NEWLINE causes the object program to output a new line. READNUM and WRITENUM have a single parameter, which may be either INTEGER or REAL. The identifier table has one record for each of READNUM, WRITENUM and NEWLINE, and for each of these the class is externalProc.

12.3.3 Representation of types

For each type there is an identifier table record containing a field typeKind which is of type

```
kindOfType = (aStandardType, arrayType, recordType, typeAlias);
```

If an identifier identifies a standard type such as INTEGER, its record in the identifier table has typeKind = aStandardType. For a type declaration such as

```
TYPE
   fred = INTEGER;
```

the identifier table record for fred has typeKind = typeAlias, which means that fred is a new name for a type that already has a name.

A field of an identifier table record that represents a type is in fact a pointer to the identifier table record for this type. For example, Figure 12.1 includes a few fields of the records that correspond to the declarations in Section 12.2. The identifier, shown on the left, is *not* included in the identifier table, and is shown here only to facilitate understanding. As can be seen in this example, the itsType field of the record for a standard type, for an array type or for a record type is left undefined, that is, blank.

A structure like this allows us to declare a variable to be of a type that is an array of records having fields that are further arrays of further records and so on to any depth. Similarly, a record type can have fields that are arrays of records having fields that are arrays of records, and so on to any depth.

12.3.4 Identifier table record type

The identifier table is within a module called itmod, which stands for *identifier table module*. The definition module is as follows:

```
DEFINITION MODULE itmod;
FROM symbols IMPORT symbolType;
FROM putSAL IMPORT labelString;
TYPE
   class = (aConstant, aVariable, aType, aField, externalProc);
   kindOfType = (aStandardType, arrayType, recordType, typeAlias);
   idRecPtr = POINTER TO idRec;
   idRec = RECORD
```

identifier	itsInd	itsClass	itsLength	itsType
BOOLEAN	3	aType	1	
FALSE	9	aConstant		
INTEGER	14	aType	1	
REAL	20	aType	2	
TRUE	22	aConstant		
READNUM	25	externalProc		
WRITENUM	26	externalProc		
NEWLINE	27	externalProc		
anArrayType	29	aType	10	
aRecordType	30	aType	3	
a1	31	aField		
a2	32	aField		
b	33	aField		
anotherArrayType	34	aType	15	
x	35	aVariable		
y	36	aVariable		
ar	37	aVariable		
z	38	aVariable		
hr	39	aVariable		
w	40	aVariable		
sry	41	aVariable		
utnm	42	aVariable		

Figure 12.1 A few fields of the identifier table records for the example declaration in Section 12.2.

```
            itsInd: CARDINAL;
            itsType, nextSyn, nextSeq: idRecPtr;
            marked: BOOLEAN;
            CASE itsClass: class OF
              aConstant: c1, c2: CARDINAL |
              externalProc: |
              aVariable: relAddress: CARDINAL;
                 baseLabel: labelString; itsLevel: CARDINAL |
              aField: fieldAddress: CARDINAL |
              aType: itsLength: CARDINAL;
                 CASE typeKind: kindOfType OF
                   aStandardType, typeAlias:  |
                   arrayType: lowBound, upBound: INTEGER;
                       indexType, elementType: idRecPtr |
                   recordType: noOfFields: CARDINAL; fieldPtr: idRecPtr |
                 END
             END
          END;
VAR
   tyInteger, tyBoolean, tyReal: idRecPtr;
   stIndex:  ARRAY[1..3] OF idRecPtr;

PROCEDURE findItsRecord(soughtInd: CARDINAL;
             VAR recPtr: idRecPtr; VAR found: BOOLEAN);
   (* given an ind, look up a record in the identifier table *)

PROCEDURE findField(soughtInd: CARDINAL; ptr: idRecPtr;
             VAR fieldDetails: idRec; VAR found: BOOLEAN);
   (* given a field's ind, look up a field in the identifier table *)

PROCEDURE constant(VAR ofType: idRecPtr; VAR card1, card2: CARDINAL);
   (* return the type and value of a constant *)

PROCEDURE newIdRecord(VAR tabPtr: idRecPtr);
   (* create a new identifier table record *)

PROCEDURE enterIdRecord(ind: CARDINAL; VAR tablePtr: idRecPtr);
   (* enter a new record into the identifier table *)

END itmod.
```

In the identifer table record type `idRec`, `marked` is a field used in Chapter 14 which can temporarily be ignored. `nextSyn` is usually a pointer to the next record in one of the linked lists that all have the same hash function value: `nextSyn` is a kind of acronym for *next hash synonym*. Sometimes the `nextSyn` field is used instead for other purposes, as will be explained. Almost all identifier records in the identifier table are linked in a further pointer chain in sequence of their creation: `nextSeq` points to the next record in this sequence in what is really a multilist structure. Nextseq will be useful in Chapters 13 and 14, but is not used in the present chapter.

Looking now at the variant part for which the discriminator or tag field is itsClass, an identifier table record for a constant has fields C1 and C2 for a constant's value; for an integer constant field C2 is simply not used. For itsClass = aVariable there is a relAddress field and together with two further fields that need not concern us in the present chapter. For itsClass = aType the field itsLength is the number of words occupied by any variable of that type. For each dimension of an array type there is a separate identifier table record that has fields containing the lower and upper bounds and pointers to records for the types of the index and of the array elements. For a record type the identifier table record has fields containing the number of fields and a pointer to a linked list containing one record for each field.

In Chapter 11, tyInteger, tyBoolean and tyReal were CARDINAL. They are still CARDINAL in the lexical analyzer, exported via valueRecord, but in other modules they are now pointers to appropriate records in the identifier table, as in the example in Figure 12.1. These pointers are initialized as part of initialization of the identifier table module, and are exported to other modules. stIndex is a look-up table initialized so that stIndex[1] = tyInteger, stIndex[2] = tyBoolean and stIndex[3] = tyReal. stIndex is used for converting the CARDINAL representation of type in valueRecord into the pointer representation used in most modules of the compiler.

12.3.5 Identifier table module implementation

In Chapter 4 we used a label's ind as the subscript for the label's entry in the label table. This allowed the assembler to find a label's entry in the label table by direct addressing, without any search. A disadvantage of direct addressing is that the table has to have one array element for every possible ind. A well-known remedy for this is to use hashing with a table of fixed size. For simplicity we did not use this in Chapters 4 and 5, but we will use it henceforward, partly to avoid limiting the size of the identifier table, and partly because some serial search will be almost inevitable when we introduce procedures in Chapter 13, and we might as well start working with it now.

Our identifier table itself has the identifier idTable, and the identifier table module includes the global VAR declaration idTable: ARRAY[0..idTableUB] OF idRecPtr. idRecPtr is a pointer to a record of type idRec. idTableUB is chosen to be one less than a power of 2, for example idTableUB = 255.

The identifier table is organized so that the compiler can quickly find a record, given the record's ind. The compiler inserts a record at the head of a linked list pointed to by idTable[hash(ind)], and looks up a record by linearly searching the linked list pointed to by idTable[hash(ind)], where ind is the record's ind and

```
hash (ind) = ind MOD (idTableUB + 1).
```

We choose idTableUB to be one less than a power of 2 so that instead of using a MOD operator we can equivalently use

```
hash(ind) = CARDINAL(BITSET(ind) * BITSET(idTableUB))
```

which can be evaluated very quickly. Records that have the same value of hash(ind) and are therefore in the same linked list are *hash synonym* records.

For a multidimensional array type the identifier table contains one record for each dimension. The first of these records is inserted into the linked list pointed to by idTable[hash(ind)] where ind is the ind of the array type. This record points to a linked list of records for the other dimensions.

For each field of a record type there is a separate identifier table record, and this could be included in the list pointed to by idTable[hash(ind)] where ind is the field's ind, but for simplicity we have chosen not to work this way. Instead, for each record type, the identifier table record points via fieldPtr to a linked list comprising one record for each field of this record type.

To illustrate this structure, suppose, for example, that a module contains

```
TYPE
   A = ARRAY[1..3],[1..4],[1..5],[1..6] OF INTEGER; (* ind of A = 32 *)
VAR
   B, C, D, E: INTEGER;  (* ind of E = 36 *)
```

and that later in the same module the last few declarations are

```
CONST
   X = 7;               (* ind of X = 288, hash(ind of X) = 32 *)
TYPE
   Y = RECORD           (* ind of Y = 289, hash(ind of Y) = 33 *)
          P,Q: INTEGER
       END;
VAR
   Z: Y;                (* ind of Z = 292, hash(ind of Z) = 36 *)
```

Figure 12.2 outlines part of the identifier table for this example, assuming idTableUB = 255. The small squares on the left represent idTable[32]..idTable[36]. Other rectangles represent identifer table records, and show ind values were appropriate, but other fields are not shown. Records for inds 32 and 288 are in the same linked list because they have the same hash function value; the record for 288 comes first because insertion at the head of a linked list is particularly simple.

The elementType pointer in the record for ind 32, which is for four-dimensional array type A, points to a linked list of records for the other three dimensions: these records, which do not have inds, are linked by itsType pointers. ind 289 is for record type Y : its record includes a fieldPtr pointing to records for fields P and Q. Although not shown in Fig 12.2, the itsType field of the record for Z, which has ind = 292, points to the record that has ind = 289.

The identifier table module itmod, which is listed in the Appendix, includes the following procedure:

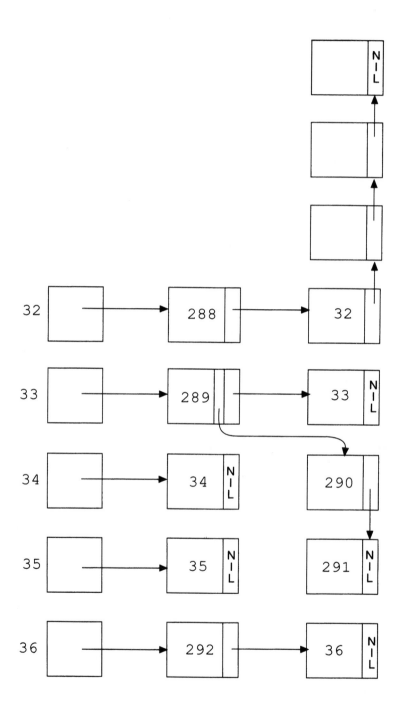

Figure 12.2 Schematic diagram showing a few incomplete records in the identifier table

```
PROCEDURE findItsRecord(soughtInd: CARDINAL; VAR recPtr: idRecPtr; VAR found:
BOOLEAN);
BEGIN
  recPtr:= idTable[CARDINAL(BITSET(soughtInd) * mask)];
  LOOP
    IF recPtr = NIL THEN found:= FALSE; RETURN
    ELSIF recPtr^.itsInd = soughtInd THEN found:= TRUE; RETURN
    ELSE recPtr:= recPtr^.nextSyn
    END
  END;
END findItsRecord;
```

which uses `mask = BITSET(idTableUB)` and linearly searches the linked list pointed to by `idTable[hash(soughtInd)]`, looking for the record that has `itsInd = soughtInd`.

Module `itmod` also exports procedure `constant` which returns the type and value of a constant defined by

```
constant -> [("+" | "-")] (numberSy | idSy);
```

The value is represented by two CARDINALs, and the second of these remains undefined if the value is not of type REAL:

```
PROCEDURE constant(VAR ofType: idRecPtr; VAR card1, card2:CARDINAL);
VAR
  recPtr: idRecPtr; negative, found: BOOLEAN;
BEGIN
  IF sy = plussOp THEN
    inSymbol; (* to get the symbol that follows '+' *)
    negative:= FALSE
  ELSIF sy = minusOp THEN negative:= TRUE; inSymbol
  ELSE negative:= FALSE  (* there was no + or - *)
  END;
  IF sy = numberSy THEN
    (* obtain type and value from valueRecord imported from lexical analyzer *)
    ofType:= stIndex[valueRecord.valType];
    card1:= valueRecord.val1; card2:= valueRecord.val2;
  ELSIF sy = idSy THEN
    findItsRecord(ind,recPtr,found);
    IF found THEN
      WITH recPtr^ DO
        IF itsClass = aConstant THEN
          ofType:= itsType; card1:= c1; card2:= c2
        ELSE found:= FALSE
        END
      END
```

```
      END;
      IF NOT found THEN error(11) END;
    ELSE error(12)
    END;
    IF negative THEN   (* make the value negative *)
      IF ofType = tyReal THEN  makeNegative(card1,card2)
      ELSIF ofType = tyInteger THEN card1:= CARDINAL(-INTEGER(card1))
      ELSE error(12)
      END
    END;
    inSymbol
END constant;
```

If, for example, procedure `constant` is called to return the type and value of `TRUE`, it calls `findItsRecord` to find the record for `TRUE` in the identifier table and obtain the type and value from this record.

12.4 Procedures that compile declarations

12.4.1 Sequence of declarations

In Modula-2 the sequence of CONST, TYPE and VAR declarations is not fixed, as it is in Pascal, and there may be more than one set of CONST, TYPE or VAR declarations; for example

```
MODULE mname;
VAR
  x,y: INTEGER;
TYPE
  wil = ARRAY[1..4] OF BOOLEAN;
CONST
  c = 6;
VAR
  a,b: BOOLEAN;
```

If a type or constant declaration refers to a constant, we require this constant to have been declared previously, and if a declaration of a variable refers to a type or to a constant, we require this, too, to have been declared previously. For introductory simplicity we do not allow constant expressions.

In the present chapter, compilation of declarations is controlled by a procedure:

```
PROCEDURE decs(VAR words: CARDINAL);
BEGIN
  words:= 3;
```

```
   LOOP
     IF sy = constSy THEN constDecs
     ELSIF sy = typeSy THEN typeDecs
     ELSIF sy = varSy THEN varDecs(words)
     ELSE EXIT
     END
   END
 END decs;
```

This calls `constDecs` to compile declarations of constants, `typeDecs` to compile declarations of types, and `varDecs` to compile declarations of variables. Each of these procedures can be called any number of times, in any sequence. These procedures, along with procedure `decs`, are in a module named `decMod`, which also contains further material required for compiling declarations. Via its VAR parameter, procedure `decs` returns the total number of words that will be required for all variables that have been declared. The variable `words` is initialized to 3 for reasons that will become clear in Chapter 13.

12.4.2 Compiling declarations of constants

The procedure that creates `idTable` records for constants is as follows:

```
PROCEDURE constDecs;
VAR
   consType, idTabPtr: idRecPtr;
   card1, card2: CARDINAL;
BEGIN
   inSymbol;      (* sy:= symbol that follows CONST *)
   WHILE sy = idSy DO
     checkDuplicateIdentifier(ind);
     enterIdRecord(ind, idTabPtr);  (* enter a new record into the
        identifier table, with idTabPtr pointing to it *)
     inSymbol; accept(equOp);
     constant(consType, card1, card2);
     WITH idTabPtr^ DO  (* assign to fields of the new record *)
       itsClass:= aConstant; itsType:= consType;
       c1:= card1; c2:= card2
     END;
     accept(semiColonSy)
   END
END constDecs;
```

There is one iteration of the WHILE loop for each individual constant in a sequence such as the following:

```
CONST
  tableUB = 36;
  stringLength = 16;
  entries = 4;
```

At the beginning of the first iteration of the WHILE loop, `sy` = `idSy` corresponding to `tableUB`, and at the start of the second iteration, `sy` = `idSy` corresponding to `stringLength`, and so on. Procedure `checkDuplicateIdentifer` calls `findItsRecord` to check whether the identifier's `ind` is already in the identifier table, and to report an error if the outcome is affirmative. Iterations of the WHILE loop continue until the symbol that follows the semicolon after a constant declaration is not `idSy`, which implies that the sequence of declared constants has terminated.

12.4.3 Named types

Most of the work for an array type declaration is done by a procedure `arrayDec`, which creates at least one `idTable` record containing information about the array. Similarly, most of the work for a record type declaration is done by a procedure `recordDec`, which creates an `idTable` record for the record type and a linked list of records for fields. One of the procedures that can call `arrayDec` and `recordDec` is procedure `typeDecs`, which is called to compile a sequence of type declarations such as

```
TYPE
  ara = ARRAY[1..4] OF INTEGER;
  recc = RECORD x,y: REAL END
```

The body of procedure `typeDecs` resembles `constDecs` in that it starts by calling `inSymbol` to get the symbol that follows `typeSy`. Each individual type declaration is dealt with by one iteration of the WHILE loop:

```
PROCEDURE typeDecs;
VAR
  typeInd: CARDINAL; found: BOOLEAN;
  typeType, idTabPtr: idRecPtr;
BEGIN
  inSymbol;
  WHILE sy = idSy DO
    checkDuplicateIdentifier(ind); typeInd:= ind;
    inSymbol;  accept(equOp);
    CASE sy OF
      idSy: findItsRecord(ind, typeType, found);
          IF found THEN
            IF typeType^.itsClass = aType THEN
              enterIdRecord(typeInd, idTabPtr);
                WITH idTabPtr^ DO
```

```
                    itsInd:=typeInd; itsType:= typeType;
                    typeKind:= typeAlias; itsLength:= typeType^.itsLength
                END;
             ELSE error(14)
             END
          ELSE error(14)
          END;   |
     arraySy:  enterIdRecord(typeInd, idTabPtr); arrayDec (idTabPtr); |
     recordSy: enterIdRecord(typeInd, idTabPtr); recordDec(idTabPtr);
   ELSE error(14)
   END;
   inSymbol;  accept(semiColonSy)
 END (* WHILE *)
END typeDecs;
```

If the symbol following `equOp` in a type declaration is `idSy` then we have something like the following:

```
TYPE
  aType = anotherType
```

If `findItsRecord` successfully finds the `ind` of this identifier, a new record is created in the `idTable`, with `typeKind = typeAlias`, and with `itsLength` the same as that of the aliased type.

12.4.4 Anonymous types

In a type declaration such as

```
TYPE
   myRecord = RECORD
                 myArray: ARRAY[1..4] OF INTEGER;
                 anotherField: anotherType
              END
or in a VAR declaration such as
VAR
  myVariable: ARRAY[1..4] OF INTEGER
```

no name is associated with the type `ARRAY[1..4] OF INTEGER`. A type that does not have a name is an *anonymous* type. Like a named type, an anonymous type has to have at least one record in the identifier table, but records for anonymous types have their `itsInd` field undefined and are not linked into a list of hash synonym records. To deal with anonymous types, and to return a pointer to the `idTable` record for a type that may or may not be anonymous, module `decMod` includes the following procedure:

```
PROCEDURE typeRecord(VAR typePtr: idRecPtr);
VAR
    typeType: CARDINAL; found: BOOLEAN;
BEGIN
  CASE sy OF
    idSy:   findItsRecord(ind, typePtr, found);
            IF NOT found THEN error(81) ELSE
              WITH typePtr^ DO
                IF itsClass # aType THEN error(82)
                ELSIF typeKind = typeAlias THEN typePtr:= itsType
                END
              END
            END   |
  arraySy: newIdRecord(typePtr); (* for an anonymous array type *)
            arrayDec(typePtr)    |
  recordSy: newIdRecord(typePtr); (* for an anonymous record type *)
            recordDec(typePtr)
  ELSE error (32)
  END
END typeRecord;
```

For example, during the compilation of an array declaration, this procedure is called just after ofSy has been accepted, so that sy is the first symbol of the array element type. Another example during the compilation of a variable declaration, typeRecord is called just after colonSy has been accepted, in order to return a pointer to the identifier table record for the variable's type.

For a named array type procedure typeDecs calls enterIdRecord to create a new record and link it into a list of hash synonym records in the chained hash table, whereas for an anonymous array type procedure typeRecord calls newIdRecord to create a new record without linking it into a list of hash synonym records.

12.4.5 Array type declarations

Procedure arrayDec creates one idTable record corresponding to each dimension of an array. If the array is only one-dimensional then the elementType field of the idTable record will contain a pointer to the idTable record for the type of the elements of the array. If the array is not one-dimensional but, for example, three-dimensional then the elementType for the idTable record for the array's first dimension is a pointer to the idTable record for the array's second dimension. The elementType for the idTable record for the array's second dimension is a pointer to the idTable record for the array's third dimension. The elementType for the idTable record for the array's third dimension is a pointer to the idTable record for the type of the elements of the three-dimensional array.

When procedure `arrayDec` begins to process an array declaration, it does not 'know' how many dimensions there will be. It counts the dimensions and creates one `idTable` record for each dimension until it comes to `ofSy`, whereupon it sets the **BOOLEAN** variable `lastDimension:= TRUE` and calls `typeRecord` to obtain a pointer to the identifier table record for the array element type:

```
PROCEDURE arrayDec(arrayRecordPtr: idRecPtr);
VAR
  v2, firstBound, secondBound, noOfDimensions, count: CARDINAL;
  lowerBoundType, upperBoundType, arrayElementType,
  currentPtr, previousPtr, recPtr: idRecPtr;
  found, lastDimension: BOOLEAN;
BEGIN
  inSymbol; accept(openSqBrktSy);
  noOfDimensions:= 0; lastDimension:= FALSE;
  REPEAT
    INC(noOfDimensions);
    constant(lowerBoundType, firstBound, v2); accept(dotDotSy);
    constant(upperBoundType, secondBound, v2);
    IF INTEGER(firstBound) > INTEGER(secondBound) THEN error(41) END;
    accept(closeSqrBrktSy);
    IF sy = ofSy THEN
      lastDimension:= TRUE;
      inSymbol; typeRecord(recPtr)
    ELSE accept(commaSy); accept(openSqBrktSy)
    END;
    IF (lowerBoundType = upperBoundType) AND
      ((lowerBoundType = tyBoolean) OR (lowerBoundType = tyInteger)) THEN
        WITH arrayRecordPtr^ DO
          itsClass:= aType; typeKind:= arrayType;
          indexType:= lowerBoundType;
          lowBound:= INTEGER(firstBound); upBound:= INTEGER(secondBound);
          IF lastDimension THEN elementType:= recPtr ELSE
            previousPtr:= arrayRecordPtr; (* points to current record *)
            newIdRecord(arrayRecordPtr); (* makes arrayRecordPtr
              point to new record *)
            elementType:= arrayRecordPtr;
            arrayRecordPtr^.nextSyn:= previousPtr
          END
        END
    ELSE error(18)
    END;
  UNTIL lastDimension;
  currentPtr:= arrayRecordPtr;
```

```
FOR count:= 1 TO noOfDimensions DO
   WITH currentPtr^ DO
      itsLength:= elementType^.itsLength * CARDINAL(upBound - lowBound + 1)
   END; currentPtr:= currentPtr^.nextSyn
END   (* FOR *)
END arrayDec;
```

There is one iteration of the REPEAT loop for each dimension. Near the end of this REPEAT loop, procedure newIdRecord is called to create an identifier table record for the next dimension of the array. The nextSyn field of this new record is made to point to the identifier table record of the previous dimension of the array, for use in the FOR statement at the end of procedure arrayDec. For a multidimensional array type, each identifier table record created by procedure arrayDec points via its elementType pointer to the next of these records, and also points via its nextSyn pointer to the previous one of these records.

The final FOR loop in procedure arrayDec fills in the itsLength fields in the idTable records that correspond to the dimensions of the array. If the array has only one dimension, then the length of the array is the number of elements of the array times the length of the array element type. The number of elements of the array is upBound - lowBound + 1. For example, the length of

```
TYPE
   x1 = ARRAY [1..3] OF REAL
```

is six words. This means that any variable of type x1 will occupy six words, as shown in Table 12.2.

Table 12.2 The six words of any variable of type ARRAY [1..3] OF REAL

Word	Contents
0	First half of first element of array
1	Second half of first element of array
2	First half of second element of array
3	Second half of second element of array
4	First half of third element of array
5	Second half of third element of array

For the two-dimensional example

```
TYPE
   x2 = ARRAY [5..8],[1..3] OF REAL
```

the idTable record for the second dimension is like that for type x1, and itsLength is the same. In this record the nextSyn field points to the record for the first dimension, for which itsLength has not yet been calculated. For the first dimension the idTable record is like that for a one-dimensional ARRAY [5..8] OF x1, and elementType is a pointer to the idTable record for the second dimension. The first dimension has four elements, each of length elementType^.itsLength, which in this example is 6. Thus the idTable record for the first dimension has itsLength = 24, which is the total length of array type x2.

For the three-dimensional example

```
TYPE
    x3 = ARRAY [-1..1], [5..8], [1..3] OF REAL
```

the first iteration of the FOR loop at the end of arrayDec assigns itsLength:= 6 in the idTable record for the third dimension, and itsLength:= 24 in the idTable record for the second dimension, because the idTable record for the second dimension is similar to that for array type x2. To fill in the itsLength field in the idTable record for the first dimension, procedure arrayDec finds this record by following the nextSyn pointer from the record for the second dimension. The idTable record for the first dimension has elementType pointing to the idTable record for the second dimension, so elementType^.itsLength = 24. For the first dimension upBound – lowBound + 1 = 3, so 3 * 24 = 72 is assigned to itsLength, which is the length of array type x3, for which the some of the fields of the three identifier table records are shown in Figure 12.3. The same ideas apply for any number of dimensions.

12.4.6 Record type declarations

For introductory simplicity we disallow variant records, so a record declaration merely contains lists of identifiers that are names of fields, and all fields in the same list are of the

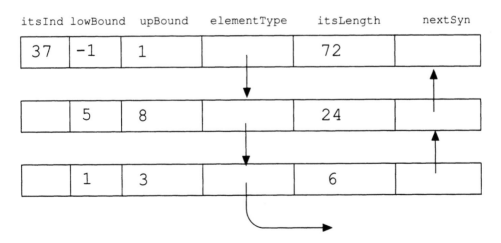

Figure 12.3 Some fields of the identifier table records for array type x3. The elementType pointer of the third record points to the record for the standard type REAL.

same type. The length of a record type is the number of words that will be occupied by any variable of this record type. This number of words is the sum of the lengths of all of the fields of the record type. Each field has a fieldAddress which is its address relative to the first of these words. For example, any variable of record type rr:

```
rr = RECORD
        a,b,c: INTEGER;
        d: ARRAY[1..4] OF INTEGER;
        e,f: REAL;
        g: BOOLEAN
     END;
```

will occupy a block of 12 words, in which the fields are as shown in Table 12.3(a). The fieldAddresses of the fields are shown in Table 12.3(b).

Table 12.3 (a) Fields of record type rr. (b) fieldAddresses of fields of record type rr.

(a)		(b)	
Word	Contents	field	fieldAddress
0	a	a	0
1	b	b	1
2	c	c	2
3	first element of array d	d	3
4	second element of array d	e	7
5	third element of array d	f	9
6	fourth element of array d	g	11
7	first half of field e		
8	second half of field e		
9	first half of field f		
10	second half of field f		
11	g		

When procedure recordDec is called, its parameter points to an idTable record for the record type, and sy is the symbol following RECORD. The outer WHILE loop is executed once for each list of fields that all have the same type. Thus the outer WHILE loop is executed four times for our example record type rr. Procedure makeList constructs a linked list of the inds of the identifiers of fields that are all of the the same type, and returns a pointer to this linked list via its VAR parameter. At the time of return from procedure makeList, sy is the first symbol following colonSy, and procedure typeRecord is called to return via its VAR parameter a pointer to the idTable record for the type of all the fields in the list. Procedure recordDec is as follows:

```
PROCEDURE recordDec (recRecPtr: idRecPtr);
VAR
  currentPtr: listRecPtr;
  newFieldPtr, fieldType, recTail: idRecPtr;
  fieldInfo: idRec; found: BOOLEAN;
  nextFieldAddress, numberOfFields, fieldLength, recordLength: CARDINAL;
BEGIN
  inSymbol; recTail:= NIL;
  nextFieldAddress:= 0; numberOfFields:= 0;
  WHILE sy = idSy DO
    makeList(currentPtr); typeRecord(fieldType);
    fieldLength:= fieldType^.itsLength;
    WHILE currentPtr # NIL DO
      findField(currentPtr^.item, recRecPtr^.nextSyn, fieldInfo, found);
      IF found THEN error (17) ELSE
        INC(numberOfFields); newIdRecord(newFieldPtr);
        WITH newFieldPtr^ DO
          itsInd:= currentPtr^.item; itsType:= fieldType;
          relAddress:= nextFieldAddress; nextSyn:= NIL
        END;
        IF recTail = NIL THEN recRecPtr^.fieldPtr:= newFieldPtr
        ELSE recTail^.nextSyn:= newFieldPtr
        END;
        recTail:= newFieldPtr;
        INC(nextFieldAddress, fieldLength)
      END; (* IF found *)
      currentPtr:= currentPtr^.next
    END; (* WHILE *)
    inSymbol;  IF sy # endSy THEN accept (semiColonSy) END;
  END; (* WHILE *)
  IF sy  # endSy THEN error (13) END;
  WITH recRecPtr^ DO
    itsClass:= aType; typeKind:= recordType;
    itsLength:= nextFieldAddress; noOfFields:= numberOfFields
  END
END recordDec;
```

The inner WHILE loop calls `findField` to check whether a field identifier is an illegal duplicate and then constructs a new record for the field. Records for successive fields are appended to the tail of the linked list pointed to by the `fieldPtr` field of the `idTable` record for the record type. The `fieldAddress` of the record's first field is 0. The `fieldAddress` of any other field is the previous `fieldAddress` plus the length of the previous field.

12.4.7 Compiling declarations of variables

Procedure `varDecs` creates one `idTable` record corresponding to each variable that is declared. The outer WHILE loop is executed once for each list of variables that all have the same type. Procedure `makeList` makes a list of the inds of these variables, and procedure `typeRecord` returns a pointer to the `idTable` record for their type.

```
PROCEDURE varDecs(VAR nextAddress: CARDINAL);
VAR
  currentPtr: listRecPtr; thisType, idTabPtr: idRecPtr;
  varInd: CARDINAL;
BEGIN
  inSymbol;
  WHILE sy = idSy DO
    makeList(currentPtr);  typeRecord(thisType);
    WHILE currentPtr # NIL DO
      varInd:= currentPtr^.item; (* ind of the variable *)
      checkDuplicateIdentifier(varInd);
      enterIdRecord(varInd, idTabPtr);
      WITH idTabPtr^ DO
        itsInd:= varInd; itsClass:= aVariable; baseLabel:= 'ZAAA';
        relAddress:= nextAddress; itsType:= thisType; itsLevel:= blockLevel
      END;
      INC(nextAddress, thisType^.itsLength); currentPtr:= currentPtr^.next
    END;
    inSymbol; accept(semiColonSy)
  END
END varDecs;
```

The inner WHILE loop creates `idTable` records for individual variables, each with a `relAddress` as explained in Section 12.2. `blockLevel` will be explained and will be useful in Chapter 13, and `baseLabel` will be important in Chapter 14. Procedure `varDecs` is included in module `decMod` which is listed in the Appendix.

12.5 The statement module

12.5.1 Compiling statements

In Chapter 11 we compiled statement sequences working with predefined single-character identifiers. We now work with declared variables and constants, and module `statemnt` in Section 11.6 is superseded by a new statement module `statmnts`. This new module, which is listed in the Appendix, has a procedure `extProc` to compile calls of `READNUM`, `WRITENUM`, etc. Module `statmnts` also has a new version of procedure `assignmentStatement` which we will consider in Section 12.5.2. Moreover, module `statmnts` has a new version of procedure `statement`:

```
PROCEDURE statement;
VAR
   idPtr: idRecPtr; found: BOOLEAN;
BEGIN
   CASE sy OF
      idSy:    findItsRecord (ind, idPtr, found);
               IF found THEN
                 CASE idPtr^.itsClass OF
                   aVariable: assignmentStatement(idPtr)   |
                   externalProc: extProc
                 ELSE error(11)
                 END
               ELSE error(101)
               END   |
      whileSy: inSymbol; whileStatement |
      loopSy:  inSymbol; loopStatement  |
      exitSy:  inSymbol; exitStatement  |
      ifSy:    inSymbol; ifStatement    |
      repeatSy: inSymbol; repeatStatement
   ELSE (* do nothing *)
   END
END statement;
```

12.5.2 Compiling assignment statements with static storage

A code skeleton for an assignment statement is:

```
Obtain the address of the left-hand-side variable;
Evaluate the right-hand-side expression;
Assign the value of the expression to the memory area of the left-hand-side variable
```

If the left-hand-side variable is an array element, we must allow for the possibility that the array subscript is a variable whose value is not available to the compiler and becomes available only during execution of the object program. Generally an array subscript is the value of an expression that cannot be evaluated at the time of compilation. The first line of our code skeleton says:

```
Obtain the address of the left-hand-side variable;
```

but does not say where this address should actually be put. Because the object-code program may have to evaluate an expression in order to obtain this `address` it is convenient to put this address on the top of the run-time stack. With this idea, a revised code skeleton for an assignment statement is:

```
Step 1:     push the address of the left-hand side onto the stack;
Step 2:     evaluate the right-hand side and leave its value on the top of the
            stack;
Step 3:     pop this value off the stack and send it to the left-hand-side
            address that was pushed on to the stack;
Step 4:     pop this address off the stack and discard it.
```

Object code for Step 1 is produced by a procedure `pushAddress`, which has as its first parameter a pointer to the first `idTable` record associated with the left-hand side of the assignment statement. The second parameter of `pushAddress` is a VAR parameter that returns the type of the left-hand-side variable. Procedure `pushAddress` is in the expression module `xpressn` because it involves expression evaluation, and we will return to this in Section 12.6.

Object code for Step 2 is produced by procedure `expression` which is also in module `xpressn`. If the type of the result of this expression differs from the type of the left-hand-side variable then procedure `assignmentStatement` reports a type-checking error:

```
PROCEDURE assignmentStatement(idPtr: idRecPtr);
VAR
  lhsTtype, resultType: idRecPtr; length: CARDINAL;
  labc: labelString;
BEGIN
  IF idPtr^.itsClass # aVariable THEN error(19); RETURN END;
  pushAddress(idPtr, lhsTtype);  accept(assignOp);
  expression (resultType);
  IF lhsTtype = resultType THEN
    length:= resultType^.itsLength;
    putStringAndVal('    MOV CX,', length);
    putLine('    MOV SI, SP ');
    putStringAndVal('    SUB SI,', length);
    putLine('    MOV DI, [SI]');
    putStringAndVal('    ADD DI,', length - 1);
    genLabel(labc); putLabel(labc);
    putLine('    POP [DI]');
    putLine('    DEC DI');
    putStrings ('    LOOP  ',labc);
    putLine('    DEC SP');
  ELSE error(20)
  END
END assignmentStatement;
```

In Section 10.4 procedure `expression` returned a result type that was either BOOLEAN, INTEGER or REAL. In the new expression module `xpressn` procedure `expression` can return a result which is an array, record, BOOLEAN, INTEGER or

REAL. In Section 10.4 the length of the result type was 1 or 2, but now there is no limit to the length of the result type. For example, if we have

```
VAR
  ay1, ay2: ARRAY [1..1000] OF INTEGER
```

and somewhere in the program we have the assignment statement `ay1 := ay2`, the result type has length 1000, and in this case the object code for the assignment statement has to copy 1000 words.

To copy a number of words, procedure `assignmentStatement` outputs object code that is a loop, starting with the number of words in register `CX`, and popping successive words off the stack into successively lower memory addresses, starting at `relAddress +` `length - 1`. Words are popped off into successively lower addresses because, as we shall see, procedure `expression` pushes on words from successively higher addresses. The sequence in which words are popped off the stack has to be the reverse of the sequence in which they were pushed on.

Before the instructions for the loop, procedure `assignmentStatment` outputs

```
MOV SI, SP
SUB SI, length
```

which leaves `SI` containing the `address` of the first word of the left-hand-side variable. The subtraction is necessary because a number (equal to `length`) of words have been pushed on to the run-time stack by the code produced by procedure `expression` after the `address` was pushed on to the run-time stack by code produced by procedure `pushAddress`. Continuing now with the detail of procedure `assignmentStatement`,

```
MOV DI, [SI]
ADD DI, length - 1
```

leaves `DI` containing the address of the last word of the left-hand-side variable. The statements `genLabel(labc); putLabel(labc)` generate and output the label for the loop that is repeated for each word assigned by the assignment statement, actually via `POP [DI]`. Near the end of procedure `assignmentStatement`, `DEC SP` corresponds to Step 4 of the code skeleton, and leaves `SP` with the same value as it had before executing the code that has been output by procedure `assignmentStatement`.

12.5.3 Name equivalence and structural equivalence

Procedure `assignmentStatement` does not produce object code to execute an assignment unless the type of the left-hand-side variable has the same name as the type of the result of the right-hand-side expression. This requirement that the names of the two types be the same is technically a requirement for *name equivalence*. In the compiler that we are considering, there is name equivalence between two types if and only if the `idTable` record for these two types is the same. For example, if we have

```
TYPE
  t = ARRAY [1..4] OF INTEGER;
VAR
  e, f: t;
  g: ARRAY [1..4] OF INTEGER;
```

our compiler will allow `e := f` but will not allow `e := g` because the types of these
variables have different names, although their structure is really the same. If two types
are really the same but only their names are different they are said to be *structurally
equivalent*. There are languages such as ALGOL 68 that allow assignment if the two
types are structurally equivalent, and do not insist upon name equivalence. In such a
language, `e := g` would be allowed and would work correctly. Structural equivalence is
more general but implementation is more complex; Modula-2 is restricted to name
equivalence.

12.6 Obtaining the address of a variable

12.6.1 Body of procedure `pushAddress`

Procedure `pushAddress`, which is in the expression module `xpressn`, produces object
code that pushes the address of a variable on to the stack. Temporarily omitting details of
two inner procedures that deal with arrays and records, procedure `pushAddress` is as
follows:

```
PROCEDURE pushAddress(idPtr: idRecPtr; VAR resultType: idRecPtr);
  PROCEDURE arrayReference; (* temporarily omitted *)
  PROCEDURE fieldReference; (* temporarily omitted *)
BEGIN (* body of pushAddress *)
  putStringAndVal ('    MOV AX,',idPtr^.relAddress);
  putLine('    ADD AX, BP');
  putLine('    PUSH AX');
  inSymbol; resultType:= idPtr^.itsType;
  WHILE sy IN symbolSet{openSqBrktSy, periodSy} DO
    IF sy = openSqBrktSy THEN
      IF resultType^.itsClass = arrayType THEN arrayReference
      ELSE error(31)
      END;
    ELSIF sy = periodSy THEN
      IF resultType^.itsClass = recordType THEN fieldReference
      ELSE error(32)
      END
    END
  END
END pushAddress;
```

Suppose, for example, that i is a variable of type INTEGER and that pushAddress has been called by assignmentStatement while dealing with the left-hand side of i:= 2. When pushAddress is called, its idPtr parameter points to the idTable record for the variable i. Procedure pushAddress obtains the relAddress and type of this variable from this record. It outputs a MOV instruction to copy this relAddress to AX. This relAddress is an address relative to the first word of the static block. The instruction ADD AX, BP adds to this relAddress the address, obtained from BP, of the first word of the static block, and PUSH AX pushes the absolute address on to the stack. The WHILE loop is not executed in this example, because i is not followed by '.' or '['.

As another example, suppose that ar is a variable of type ARRAY[4..10] OF REAL, and that procedure pushAddress has been called by procedure assignmentStatement while dealing with the left-hand side of ar[7]:= 2.1. Procedure pushAddress obtains the relAddress and type of the variable ar from its idTable record. As in the previous example, pushAddress outputs object code to push the absolute address of the first element of the array on to the run-time stack. The next input symbol is '[' so the WHILE loop is entered and procedure arrayReference is called to deal with the array subscript. As we shall see, procedure arrayReference produces code to check for array bound violation and to add

```
(array subscript - lower bound of array) * length of array element
```

to the value on top of the stack. Thus for the left-hand side of ar[7]:= 2.1, (7-4) * 2 = 6 is added to the value on top of the stack, and the result is the absolute address of ar[7], which is what is required. The total length of array variable ar is 14, and of these 14 words, the first two belong to the first element, the third and fourth to the second element, and so on.

As a further example, suppose that br is a variable of the type

```
RECORD
   x,y: REAL; u,v: INTEGER
END
```

and that procedure pushAddress has been called by procedure assignmentStatement while dealing with the left-hand side of br.u:= 2. Procedure pushAddress obtains the relAddress and type of br from its idTable record. The total length of variable br is six words, and the fieldAddress of a field is relative to the first of these words. Thus the fieldAddresses of the four fields x, y, u and v are 0, 2, 4, and 5, respectively.

For the example br.u, procedure pushAddress finds that the symbol following idSy for br is '.', and therefore calls procedure fieldReference. As we shall see, procedure fieldReference calls procedure findField to find the record that contains the fieldAddress of u, and outputs code to add this to the address that is on the top of the stack. For the example br.u, 4 is added to the address of the first word of the variable br, and the result is the address of br.u.

We can have a type that is an array of records that have fields that are arrays of records, and so on to any depth. As a simple example of this kind, suppose that cr is a variable of the type

```
RECORD
  p,q: RECORD
            x1,y1: REAL; u,v: INTEGER
        END;
  x,y: ARRAY[4..10] OF REAL
END
```

and that procedure `pushAddress` has been called by procedure `assignmentStatement` while dealing with the left-hand side of `cr.x[7]:= 2.1`. Procedure `pushAddress` starts by producing code to push on to the stack the address of the first word in the block of 40 words allocated to `cr`. For the example `cr.x[7]`, `pushAddress` finds that the symbol following `idSy` for `cr` is '.' and calls procedure `fieldReference` to produce object code to add to the address on top of the stack the `fieldAddress`, 12, of the first word of the 14-word field `x` within the block of 40 words that belong to `cr`. After the return from `fieldReference` a second execution of the WHILE loop in procedure `pushAddress` calls procedure `arrayReference` to deal with `[7]`. Procedure `arrayReference` outputs code to check for array bound violation and to add $(7 - 4) * 2$ to the address on the stack. The result is the address of the first of the two words of the REAL variable `cr.x[7]`, which is what is required.

12.6.2 Procedure `fieldReference`

When procedure `fieldReference` is called, `resultType`, which is a VAR parameter of `pushAddress`, points to the `idTable` record for the record type. Procedures `fieldReference` and `arrayReference` use `resultType` like a global variable. Procedure `fieldReference` calls `findField` to obtain the `relAddress` and other information concerning the field, and then outputs code to add this `relAddress` to the address that is currently on the top of the stack. Procedure `fieldReference` is as follows:

```
PROCEDURE fieldReference;
VAR
   fieldInfo: idRec; found: BOOLEAN;
BEGIN
  inSymbol;
  findField(ind, resultType^.fieldPtr, fieldInfo, found);
  IF found THEN
    putLine('    MOV DI, SP');
    putStringAndVal('    ADD [DI],', fieldInfo.fieldAddress);
    resultType:= fieldInfo.itsType
  ELSE  error(37)
  END;
  inSymbol
END fieldReference;
```

For example, with the declaration of record variable `cr` in Section 12.6.1, SAL object code corresponding to the assignment statement `cr.q.u:= 222` is as follows:

```
        MOV  AX,   3  ; AX:= relAddress of cr
        ADD  AX, BP   ; AX:= AX + address of first word of static block
        PUSH AX       ; push absolute address
        MOV  DI, SP
        ADD  [DI],  6 ; add relAddress of first word of field q
        MOV  DI, SP
        ADD  [DI],  4 ; add relAddress of u within field q
        MOV  AX,  222
        PUSH AX       ; push 222
        MOV  CX,   1  ; execute loop just once for an integer
        MOV  SI, SP
        SUB  SI,   1  ; lhs address is one below top of stack
        MOV  DI, [SI] ; DI:= address of lhs variable
        ADD  DI,   0
ZAAB:   POP  [DI] ; assign 222 to lhs variable
        DEC  DI       ; would be necessary for multi-word variable
        LOOP  ZAAB    ; does not jump back to ZAAB
        DEC  SP       ; in effect removes lhs address from stack
```

12.6.3 Procedure `arrayReference`

When `arrayReference` is called, `resultType` points to the `idTable` record for the array type. Procedure `arrayReference` obtains the array element length from this record, and then calls `expression` to evaluate the array subscript, for example in `ar[3 * m + n]`. If the type of the result of this expression matches the type of the array index then `arrayReference` outputs object code to check for array bound violation and add the appropriate increment to the address on the top of the stack, as has been explained previously.

Suppose, for example, that labels `no` and `yes` are `ZAAJ` and `ZAAK`, respectively, and that the lower and upper bounds are 4 and 10, respectively. In this case the array-bound checking code produced is as follows:

```
        POP DX     ; DX:= value of expression, which is subscript value
        CMP DX, 10 ; compare subscript with upper bound
        JG ZAAJ    ; jump to ZAAJ if subscript exceeds upper bound
        CMP DX, 4  ;  compare subscript with lower bound
        JGE ZAAK   ; jump to ZAAK if subscript not less than lower bound
ZAAJ:   MOV AX, 999  ;  999 is used as an error indicator
        PUSH AX    ; in preparation for calling INTWRITE
        CALL INTWRITE; output the rather crude error indicator
        CALL ENDPROG;  halt because the error is fatal
ZAAK: SUB DX,4  ;  DX:= array subscript - lower bound
        and so on.
```

Procedure `arrayReference` goes on to output code to add

```
(array subscript - lower bound) * array element length
```

to the value on the top of the stack, as has been explained previously, and to update `resultType`. Procedure `arrayReference` is as follows:

```
PROCEDURE arrayReference;
VAR
  no, yes: labelString; elementLength: CARDINAL; tyPtr: idRecPtr;
BEGIN
  REPEAT
    tyPtr:= resultType;
    elementLength:= tyPtr^.elementType^.itsLength;
    inSymbol; expression(resultType);   (* evaluates array subscript *)
    IF resultType = tyPtr^.indexType THEN
      genLabel(no); genLabel(yes);
      putLine('    POP DX');
      putStringAndVal('    CMP DX, ', tyPtr^.upBound);
      putStrings('    JG ',no);
      putStringAndVal('    CMP DX, ', tyPtr^.lowBound);
      putStrings('    JGE ', yes);
      putLabel(no);
      putLine('    MOV AX, 999');
      putLine('    PUSH AX');
      putLine('    CALL INTWRITE');
      putLine('    CALL ENDPROG');
      putLabel(yes);
      putStringAndVal('    SUB DX, ', tyPtr^.lowBound);
      putStringAndVal('    MOV AX, ', elementLength);
      putLine('    MULT DX');
      putLine('    MOV DI, SP');
      putLine('    ADD [DI], AX');
    ELSE error(36)
    END;
    resultType:= tyPtr^.elementType
  UNTIL sy # commaSy;
  accept(closeSqrBrktSy)
END arrayReference;
```

The REPEAT loop is repeated once for each dimension of a multidimensional array. Suppose, for example, that we have

```
TYPE
  ay = ARRAY [3..6], [55..57], [-2..+1] OF INTEGER;
VAR
```

```
    ry: ay;
BEGIN
    ry[5,57,-1]:= 222;
```

Corresponding to the array type `ay` procedure `arrayDec` will have created three `idTable` records, with `itsLength` 48, 12 and 4, that correspond respectively to the three dimensions. A block of 48 consecutive words is allocated by `varDecs` to any variable of type `ay`, such as the variable `ry` in our example. Each combination of values of the three subscripts of array variable `ry` corresponds to a unique one-dimensional `relAddress` relative to the first word in the block of 48 words shown in Table 12.4. The long horizontal lines demarcate the elements of the array that has elements of length 12. Within a block of 12 words, the shorter horizontal lines demarcate the elements of the middle one of the three arrays, which has elements that are one-dimensional arrays of length 4.

To access an element of the three-dimensional array, the object code uses the first subscript to choose one of the biggest blocks, and within this block uses the second subscript to choose one of the next-sized blocks, and within this block uses the third subscript to choose one of the smallest blocks, which in our example consist of one word. What 'choosing' a block actually means is that the compiler multiplies that block's size by (`subscript` - `lower bound`), and adds the product into the one-dimensional `relAddress` value that is being computed. This idea can easily be extended to any number of subscripts. An outline of procedure `arrayReference` is as follows:

```
FOR first dimension TO last dimension DO
    output code to evaluate array subscript;
    output code to check for array bound violation
    output code to add (subscript - lower bound) * array element length
    to the relAddress at the top of the stack
END
```

Referring to Table 12.4 it is easy to check that `ry[5,57,-1]` corresponds to the one-dimensional `relAddress` 33. For the assignment statement `ry [5,57,-1]:= 222` corresponding object code is as follows:

```
        MOV  AX,    3 ; AX:= relAddress of first word of ry
        ADD AX, BP
        PUSH AX        ; push absolute address of ry
        MOV AX,    5
        PUSH AX        ; push first subscript
        POP DX
        CMP DX,    6 ; check upper bound
        JG ZAAB
        CMP DX,    3 ; check lower bound
        JGE ZAAC
ZAAB:   MOV AX, 999
        PUSH AX
```

Table 12.4 Example of correspondence between three-dimensional subscripts and one one-dimensional relative address.

First subscript	Second subscript	Third subscript	One-dimensional relAddress
3	55	-2	0
3	55	-1	1
3	55	0	2
3	55	+1	3
3	56	-2	4
3	56	-1	5
3	56	0	6
3	56	+1	7
3	57	-2	8
3	57	-1	9
3	57	0	10
3	57	+1	11
4	55	-2	12
4	55	-1	13
4	55	0	14
4	55	+1	15
4	56	-2	16
4	56	-1	17
4	56	0	18
4	56	+1	19
4	57	-2	20
4	57	-1	21
4	57	0	22
4	57	+1	23
5	55	-2	24
5	55	-1	25
5	55	0	26
5	55	+1	27
5	56	-2	28
5	56	-1	29
5	56	0	30
5	56	+1	31
5	57	-2	32
5	57	-1	33
5	57	0	34
5	57	+1	35
6	55	-2	36
6	55	-1	37
6	55	0	38
6	55	+1	39
6	56	-2	40
6	56	-1	41
6	56	0	42
6	56	+1	43
6	57	-2	44
6	57	-1	45
6	57	0	46
6	57	+1	47

```
        CALL INTWRITE
        CALL ENDPROG
ZAAC:   SUB DX, 3; subtract lower bound
    MOV AX,   12
    MULT DX       ; multiply by length
    MOV DI, SP
    ADD [DI], AX ; add product to address on stack
    MOV AX,   57
    PUSH AX       ; push second subscript
    POP DX
    CMP DX,   57 ; check upper bound
    JG ZAAD
    CMP DX,   55 ; check lower bound
    JGE ZAAE
ZAAD:   MOV AX, 999
    PUSH AX
    CALL INTWRITE
    CALL ENDPROG
ZAAE:   SUB DX, 55; subtract lower bound
    MOV AX,    4
    MULT DX       ; multiply by length
    MOV DI, SP
    ADD [DI], AX ; add product to address on stack
    MOV AX,    1
    PUSH AX
    MOV  DI, SP
    NEG  [DI]     ; stack top:= third subscript
    POP DX
    CMP DX,    1 ; check upper bound
    JG ZAAF
    CMP DX, 65534; check lower bound
    JGE ZAAG
ZAAF:   MOV AX, 999
    PUSH AX
    CALL INTWRITE
    CALL ENDPROG
ZAAG:   SUB DX, 65534; subtract lower bound
    MOV AX,    1
    MULT DX       ; multiply by length
    MOV DI, SP
    ADD [DI], AX ; add product to address on top of stack
    MOV AX, 222 ; rhs value
    PUSH AX
    MOV CX,    1  ; loop will be executed once
```

```
         MOV SI, SP
         SUB SI,   1  ; lhs address is one below top of stack
         MOV DI, [SI] ; DI:= lhs address
         ADD DI,   0
 ZAAH:      POP [DI]; assign 222 to lhs variable
         DEC DI
         LOOP  ZAAH    ; not executed because length = 1
         DEC SP        ; effectively removes lhs address from stack
```

Because of the multiplication, this is known as the *multiplication method* of multidimensional array access. The more dimensions an array has, the more multiplication operations are required to map its multidimensional subscripts on to a one-dimensional relAddress, and the longer will be the total time required for array access by the object-code program.

12.7 Dereferencing a variable

In the two assignment statements

```
    x:= y; t:= x,
```

x has radically different meanings. In x:= y the meaning of x is the *address* of the variable whose identifier is x. In t:= x the meaning of x is the *value* of the variable whose identifier is x. The technical term for obtaining the value of a variable, given its address, is *dereferencing* that variable. For example, compilation of the assignment statement t:= x yields object code to dereference x and assign the value of x to t. In our compiler the object code for dereferencing a variable is produced by a procedure pushValue which is called by factor which is indirectly called by expression, as in Section 10.4.

A revised version of procedure factor is included in module xpressn in the Appendix. An outline of the body of factor is as follows:

```
CASE sy OF
   numberSy:   output code to push value of number on to the stack |
   idSy:       call procedure pushValue to push value on to the stack |
   notOp:      inSymbol; factor;
               IF globalType # tyBoolean THEN error(20) ELSE
                  applyOperator(notOp)
               END |
   openRndBrktSy: inSymbol; expression(resultType);
                  accept(closeRndBrktSy)
END;
```

The only major difference between this version of factor and the version in Section 10.4 is in the call of pushValue. Procedure pushValue would, for example, be called by factor to deal with the right-hand side of the assignment statement t:= x. An outline of the object code for this assignment statement is as follows:

```
push the address of t on to the stack;
push the value of x on to the stack;
pop the stack into the variable identified by t;
pop the address of t off the stack.
```

When pushValue is called, sy = idSy and ind is the associated ind value. Procedure pushValue calls findItsRecord to find the record for this ind in the identifier table. If this record has itsClass = aConstant then object code is produced to push the value of this constant, which may comprise one or two words, on to the stack.

Otherwise, if the idTable record has itsClass = aVariable then pushValue calls pushAddress to produce code to push the address of this variable on to the stack. This allows for the generality that a variable is a field of a record that is an element of an array that is a field of a record, and so on to any depth. Procedure pushValue is as follows:

```
PROCEDURE pushValue (VAR resultType: idRecPtr);
VAR
   multiLabel: labelString;
   idPtr: idRecPtr; found: BOOLEAN;
BEGIN
   findItsRecord(ind, idPtr, found);
   IF found THEN
     CASE idPtr^.itsClass  OF
        aConstant:  putStringAndVal('    MOV AX, ',idPtr^.c1);
                    putLine('    PUSH AX');
                    resultType:= idPtr^.itsType;
                    IF resultType = tyReal THEN (* push second word *)
                      putStringAndVal('    MOV AX, ', idPtr^.c2);
                    putLine('    PUSH AX')
                    END; inSymbol |
        aVariable:  pushAddress(idPtr, resultType);
                    putStringAndVal ('    MOV CX,', resultType^.itsLength);
                    putLine ('    POP DI ');
                    genLabel(multiLabel); putLabel(multiLabel);
                    putLine ('    PUSH [DI]');
                    putLine ('    INC DI');
                    putStrings ('    LOOP ',multiLabel)
     ELSE error(29)
     END (* CASE *);
   ELSE error (28)
   END (* IF *)
END pushValue;
```

After the call of `pushAddress`, `pushValue` produces code to dereference the variable. If the length of the variable is LENGTH and if the next label generated by `genLabel` is, for example, ZAAK, then the code that dereferences the variable is as follows:

```
        MOV CX, LENGTH
        POP DI          ; DI:= address of the first word of the variable
  ZAAK: PUSH [DI]
         INC DI         ;  for next word of variable
        LOOP ZAAC
```

This pushes successive words on to the stack. If x is of type INTEGER then LENGTH = 1 and just one word is pushed on to the stack as the result of calling `expression` which indirectly calls `factor` which calls `pushValue` for the right-hand side of t := x. Another example is that if x is an array of length 1000 then LENGTH = 1000 and 1000 words are pushed on to the stack by the object code resulting from the call of `pushValue` for the right-hand side of t := x. Because the object-code loop pushes words on to the stack in sequence of increasing address, the loop output by `assignmentStatement` to pop these words off the stack works in sequence of decreasing address.

12.8 The main module

Our simplified compiler produces a complete SAL program for which a code skeleton is:

```
        IMPORT INTREAD, INTRWRITE, NEWLINE, ENDPROG, and so on.
        LEA BP, ZAAA    ; BP:= address of first word of static block.
        LEA SP, STACKBASE ; SP:= address of first word of run-time stack.
        the object-code instructions
        are all here followed by
        CALL ENDPROG
  ZAAA: DW numberOfWords DUP  ; declaration of static block.
  STACKBASE: DW stackSize DUP ; run-time stack starts at STACKBASE.
```

Object code conforming to this skeleton is produced by the main module of our simplified compiler:

```
MODULE statMain;
FROM decMod IMPORT decs;
FROM statmnts IMPORT stmntSequence;
FROM scanner IMPORT inSymbol, ind, error, accept;
FROM symbols IMPORT symbolType;
FROM InOut IMPORT WriteString, WriteLn, WriteCard;
FROM putSAL IMPORT standardImports;
CONST
  stackSize = 64;
```

```
VAR
  numberOfWords, moduleInd: CARDINAL;
BEGIN
  standardImports; WriteLn;
  WriteString('    LEA BP, YAAA'); WriteLn;
  WriteString('    LEA SP, STACKBASE'); WriteLn;
  inSymbol; accept(moduleSy);  moduleInd:= ind;
  accept(idSy);   accept(semiColonSy);
  decs(numberOfWords); accept(beginSy); stmntSequence;
  accept(endSy); IF ind # moduleInd THEN error(17) END;
  accept(idSy); accept(periodSy);
  WriteString('    CALL ENDPROG '); WriteLn;
  WriteString('YAAA: DW '); WriteCard(numberOfWords,4); WriteString(' DUP ');
  WriteLn;
  WriteString('STACKBASE: DW '); WriteCard(stackSize, 4); WriteString(' DUP ');
  WriteLn
END statMain.
```

The call of `standardImports` in module `putSAL` outputs the line

```
IMPORT INTREAD, INTWRITE, NEWLINE, ENDPROG, and so on.
```

Procedure `decs` compiles the declarations and returns via its VAR parameter the total number of words required for variables. This number is used later for reserving the right number of words for the static block. Procedure `stmntSequence` compiles the statement sequence that constitutes the body of the source module.

For the artificially simple source program

```
MODULE test;
CONST
  Y = 2.5;  I = 25;
VAR
  A: BOOLEAN;  J: INTEGER;  X:  REAL;
BEGIN
  J:= 14; X:= 1.4;
  A:= (I > J + 7) AND (X > Y + 7.7)
END test.
```

the complete SAL object program produced by our simplified compiler is:

```
IMPORT INTREAD, INTWRITE, NEWLINE, ENDPROG, REALREAD, REALWRITE, REALNEG,
REALADD, REALSUB, REALMULT, REALDIVIDE, REALEQ, REALNOTEQ, REALLESS,
REALGREATER, REALLESSEQ, REALGREATEQ
    LEA BP, YAAA
    LEA SP, STACKBASE
    MOV AX,   4  ; relAddress of J;
    ADD AX, BP
```

```
      PUSH AX        ; absolute address of J;
      MOV AX,   14
      PUSH AX         ; push 14 on to stack
      MOV CX,   1
      MOV SI, SP
      SUB SI,   1
      MOV DI, [SI]
      ADD DI,   0
ZAAB:    POP [DI] ; J:= 14;
      DEC DI
      LOOP  ZAAB     ; does not jump to ZAAB
      DEC SP         ; discard address of J;
      MOV AX,   5  ; relAddress of X;
      ADD AX, BP
      PUSH AX        ; push absolute address of X;
      MOV AX, 13107 ; first word of 1.4
      PUSH AX
      MOV AX, 16307 ; second word of 1.4
      PUSH AX
      MOV CX,   2  ; initialize for two iterations
      MOV SI, SP
      SUB SI,   2
      MOV DI, [SI]  ; DI:= address of first word of X
      ADD DI,   1   ; DI:= address of second word of X
ZAAC:    POP [DI] ; pop into a word of X
      DEC DI         ; preparing for next word
      LOOP  ZAAC     ; jumps to ZAAC to assign second word
      DEC SP         ; discards address of X
      MOV  AX,   3
      ADD AX, BP     ; AX:= absolute address of A;
      PUSH AX
      MOV AX,   25  ; AX:= I
      PUSH AX        ; PUSH value of I
      MOV AX,   4  ; relAddress of J
      ADD AX, BP
      PUSH AX        ; absolute address of J
      MOV CX,   1  ; length of J is 1
      POP DI         ; DI:= address of J
ZAAD:    PUSH [DI]; push value of J
      INC DI         ; would be needed if J was more than one word
      LOOP ZAAD      ; jump does not take place
      MOV AX,   7
      PUSH AX        ; push 7
      POP  AX        ; AX:= 7;
```

```
      MOV DI, SP
      ADD  [DI], AX ; add 7 to top word on stack
      MOV AX, 1    ; AX:= TRUE
      POP BX        ; BX:= J + 7
      POP CX        ; CX:= I
      CMP CX, BX
      JG   ZAAE    ; IF I > J + 7 THEN jump to ZAAE
      DEC AX        ; AX:= FALSE
ZAAE: PUSH AX       ; boolean result of greater than
      MOV  AX,   5 ; relAddress of X
      ADD AX, BP
      PUSH AX        ; absolute address of X
      MOV CX,  2   ; X has two words
      POP DI         ; DI:= address of first word of X
ZAAF:    PUSH [DI]; push word of X
      INC DI         ; for next word
      LOOP ZAAF     ; jump to ZAAF for second word
      MOV AX,   0  ; first word of Y
      PUSH AX
      MOV AX, 16416 ; second word of Y
      PUSH AX
      MOV AX, 26214 ; first word of 7.7
      PUSH AX
      MOV AX, 16630 ; second word of 7.7
      PUSH AX
      CALL REALADD  ; add top two reals
      CALL REALGREATER
      POP  AX      ; AX := X > Y + 7.7
      MOV DI, SP
      AND  [DI], AX ; stack top:= first AND second subexpression
      MOV CX,  1   ; boolean result of AND has length 1
      MOV SI, SP
      SUB SI,  1
      MOV DI, [SI] ; DI:= address of A
      ADD DI,  0
ZAAG:    POP [DI] ; A:= boolean result
      DEC DI          ; not needed
      LOOP  ZAAG     ; not needed
      DEC SP         ; effectively removes address of A from stack
      CALL ENDPROG
YAAA: DW    7 DUP
STACKBASE: DW   64 DUP
```

For this the source program includes A:= (I > J + 7) AND (X > Y + 7.7) which we compiled in Section 10.5 using predefined single-character identifiers.

12.9 Discussion

The traditional name for the set of data structures used by a compiler for storing information about identifiers and other symbols is the *symbol table*. Instead of using a single monolithic symbol table we have chosen to achieve the same effect using separate string and identifier tables. The string table uniquely identifies an identifier or reserved word; the identifier table stores information about each different meaning of the same identifier.

String and identifier tables can easily be combined into a single symbol table structure. For example, we can arrange that each string table record for an identifier contains, instead of an `ind`, a pointer to a linked list of identifier table records for different meanings of this identifier. Another way of saying this is that instead of using an `ind`, or some of its least significant bits, as the subscript of a pointer in array `idTable`, we can replace the `ind` in a string table record by this pointer. An advantage is that there is no need to access an array element of `idTable`. Moreover, after finding the appropriate record in the string table there is no need to look at records for other identifiers that happen to have the same `idTable` hash function value.

If the string table and identifier tables are integrated into a single structure this is inevitably more complicated than either of these tables individually. We have kept the string and identifier tables separate not because this is efficient or logically necessary but because it is hopefully easier to explain and to understand. Separation of these tables allows character-by-character processing of strings to be encapsulated inside the lexical analyzer, and allows association of attributes with identifiers to be kept outside the lexical analyzer. The use of separate string and identifier tables facilitates modular compartmentalization. In Chapter 4 we could have combined the string, label and opCode tables into a single table, but this would have been difficult to explain.

A minor advantage of having a separate string table is that it allows reserved words to be processed inside the lexical analyzer along with symbols such as delimiters and operators. Character-by-character recognition of reserved words can be accomplished without reference to an elaborate combination of string and identifier tables. A separate identifier table does not have entries for reserved words such as BEGIN, DIV and NOT because the compiler does not need to store attributes such as `itsClass` for reserved words. The string table associates different unique `sy` values with all reserved words, whereas all entries in the identifier table have the same `sy` value, specifically, `sy = idSy`.

In the present chapter we have included actual values of constants in identifier table records, which is reasonable if these values are only one or two words in length. A fully-developed Modula-2 compiler allows string constants that are many bytes in length. Instead of storing these in the string table it may be more practical to store them in a separate area where they must be accessible at run time. The idea is similar to the idea of using `charArray` in Section 3.4, except for the requirement for run-time accessibility: an identifier table record for a constant now contains address and length information that allows retrieval of the value of the constant during execution of object code.

As in the P4 Pascal system (Pemberton and Daniels 1986), we have used a separate identifier table record for each dimension of a multidimensional array. Another classical idea is to have just a single record in the symbol table for a multidimensional array type. This record points to a *dope vector* that contains the array bounds and associated information required for efficient access to array elements (Fischer and LeBlanc 1988).

Our module `strinTbl` uses a hash tree structure for the string table. There are many alternative data structures, mainly using some kind of hashing, that would be at least as efficient. Textbooks such as Holub (1990) and Tremblay and Sorensen (1985) provide a general introduction to symbol table organization.

12.10 Exercises

1. Show the contents of the identifier table resulting from compilation of the following declarations:

```
MODULE ex1;
CONST
    a = -3;
    b = 10;
    c = 33.33;
TYPE
    d = ARRAY [a..b] OF RECORD e,f: REAL END;
    g = RECORD
            h, i: ARRAY [13..23] OF BOOLEAN;
            j: INTEGER
        END
    k = d;
VAR
    m: ARRAY [3..13] OF g;
    n: RECORD
            o: d;   p: ARRAY[a..b] OF k
        END;
```

2. Develop the compiler to allow integer subrange types. For this purpose:

   (a) List the fields of the `idTable` record for an integer subrange type.
   (b) Write a procedure `subRangeDec` to compile a subrange type declaration and produce a corresponding `idTable` record.
   (c) Modify procedures `typeDecs` and `typeRecord` to call `subRangeDec` to deal with named and anonymous integer subrange types.
   (d) Modify procedure `assignmentStatement` to allow for `t := x` where `t` is of type integer and `x` is of an integer subrange type.
   (e) Modify procedure `arrayDec` to work either with named or with anonymous subrange types for array dimensions.

3. Write a procedure `withStatement` to compile a WITH statement, and modify procedure `statement` to call `withStatement` when this is appropriate. You are free to change the access path to identifier table records for fields.

4. Include among the unorthodox external procedures further procedures INC and DEC that respectively increment and decrement an integer VAR parameter by unity. Each of these procedures is to call `pushAddress` not more than once. Explain why incrementing or decrementing an integer is more efficient via a call of one of these procedures than via an assignment statement, especially when this integer is, for example, a field of a record that is an element of an array.

5. Develop the compiler to allow casts, that is, deliberate type-conversions, in the source program. A cast looks like a call of a function procedure in which the function identifier is a type identifier. Corresponding to a cast in the object program there is to be no subroutine like that which would be required to implement an ordinary function. Instead, there is only to be object code to evaluate the expression that is the cast's parameter. If the type of the result of the expression turns out to be the same length as the type of the cast identifier, the result type of the expression becomes the type of the cast identifier. If the type of the result of the expression does not turn out to have the same length as the type of the cast-identifier, a semantic error is to be reported.

6. Develop the compiler to allow expressions in constant declarations, with operands that must either be numbers or previously declared constants, for example,

```
CONST
  a = 3 * 64;
  b = 5 + 7 * a;
```

To achieve this, incorporate into the compiler an expression interpreter like that in Exercise 1 in Section 10.6. The value and type of the result of a constant expression is to be stored in the constant's record in the identifier table.

CHAPTER 13

Procedures

13.1 Introduction

An *invocation* of a procedure is an execution of the procedure, starting with a call and ending with a return. When a procedure has been called recursively, more than one invocation of this procedure exists at a single time. Coexisting invocations of the same procedure may have different values for parameters and local variables. This implies a requirement for a separate physical storage area for the parameters and local variables for each invocation of each procedure. This storage area is given to an invocation at the time of the call and is taken away again at the time of return at the end of the invocation. Allocation of storage for invocations is said to be *dynamic* because it changes during execution of a program, wheras the allocation of storage to global variables, as in Chapter 12, is *static* because it remains fixed throughout the execution of a program.

In Section 13.6 we will introduce a *run-time model*, which is a description of the organization of memory during program execution. In Chapter 12, procedures pushValue and assignmentStatement accessed variables in the static block; we will develop these procedures so as to be able to access variables either in static or in dynamic memory.

The rule that a local variable within a procedure must not be accessible from an enclosing procedure is an example of a *scope* rule. To allow the compiler to enforce scope rules the identifier table has to be more elaborate than in Chapter 12, as we shall see in Section 13.3.1. Scope rules are based upon the textual structure of a module, which is considered in Section 13.2.

In Modula-2 a procedure can call another that occurs later in the source text. For example, there is no error in:

```
MODULE ex;

PROCEDURE S;
BEGIN
  T
END S;

PROCEDURE T;
BEGIN
  X:= 2
END T;
```

```
VAR
  X: INTEGER;
BEGIN
  S
END ex.
```

The programmer is free to write procedures in alphabetical order of their identifiers, which makes their declarations easy to find in the source text, or to group procedures and indeed other declarations together according to their meaning. For each procedure we will have a record in the identifier table as will be explained in Section 13.3.2. In our example the identifier of procedure T must be in scope while the body of procedure S is being compiled. This means that the record for T must already be in the identifier table and must be accessible while S is being compiled.

We achieve this by having the compiler scan through the entire source text twice, the first time to construct the identifier table, and the second time to generate object code. We now have a *two-pass* compiler, which allows a procedure to call procedures that are declared later, and also allows a procedure to use identifiers that are declared later; for example procedure T can access variable X that is declared after procedure T. However, in a constant declaration such as A = B, we require B to have been declared before A, and we also require a type identifier to have been declared before it can be used in any subsequent declaration, as in Pascal.

In Section 13.4 we will compile procedure declarations. The heading of a procedure will be compiled during the first pass and the body will be compiled during the second pass. To compile the body of a procedure body, most of the work is done by calling procedure stmntSequence, which compiles the sequence of statements enclosed between BEGIN and END. The compiler also has to deal with RETURN at the end of, or during, this sequence. We will consider how to compile procedure calls and returns in Section 13.9.

In our source subset of Modula-2 we will not allow procedure variables. The present chapter goes beyond Pascal in that there is no restriction on the sequence of procedure declarations and also in that we compile the RETURN statement of Modula-2; but our run-time model is a classical one which is traditional for Pascal and is sufficient for introductory purposes.

13.2 Static structure of a module

13.2.1 Textual structure

The textual organization of procedures at the outermost level of a module, the organization of procedures within procedures, and indeed the nesting of procedures to any depth, is the *static structure* of a module. The static structure is entirely determined by the organization of the source program text. This structure is *static* because it remains unchanged during program execution.

Our compiler produces object code that has similar structure to that of the source code. For example if an outline of the textual structure of the source code is:

```
MODULE moduleName;
VAR
  x: INTEGER;  (* and some other declarations *)

PROCEDURE M;
VAR
  y: INTEGER;  (* and some other declarations *)

  PROCEDURE P;

    PROCEDURE P1;
         (* rest of declaration of P1 comes here *)
    PROCEDURE P2;
         (* rest of declaration of P2 comes here *)
    PROCEDURE P3;
         (* rest of declaration of P3 comes here *)
  BEGIN
         (* body of procedure P comes here *)
  END P;

  PROCEDURE Q;
         (* rest of declaration of Q comes here *)

BEGIN
         (* body of procedure M comes here *)
END M;
PROCEDURE N;
         (* rest of declaration of N comes here *)
BEGIN
    (* body of module comes here *)
END moduleName.
```

then the object code contains subroutines that correspond to source-code procedures and is textually organized as follows:

```
JMP to body of module
static block for module
instructions for body of subroutine P1
instructions for body of subroutine P2
instructions for body of subroutine P3
instructions for body of subroutine P
instructions for body of subroutine Q
instructions for body of subroutine M
instructions for body of subroutine N
instructions for body of module
```

Instruction sequences do not include words containing variables: variables are stored elsewhere, as will be explained in Section 13.6. The object code for a subroutine remains unchanged during its execution, so that different concurrent invocations of the same procedure do not interfere with each other.

13.2.2 Block level and scope

Figure 13.1 is a tree representing the static structure of our example module moduleName. The *block level* of an identifier is the level within this tree of the procedure in which that identifier is declared. The block level of the root is zero: all identifiers declared at the outermost level are at block level zero. This includes the identifiers of procedures declared at the outermost level, so in our example the procedure identifiers M and N are at block level 0, and the integer variable x is also at block level 0.

If the identifier of a procedure is at block level k then this procedure's parameters and the identifiers declared at the outermost level within this procedure are at block level $k+1$. In our example, the variable y that is declared at the outermost level of procedure M is at block level 1. The identifiers of procedures P and Q are also at block level 1. The identifiers of procedures P1, P2 and P3 are at block level 2.

A static structure tree indicates the scope of any given identifier. Within the body of a procedure the parameters and all identifiers declared at the outermost level within this procedure are within scope. Moreover, all identifiers that are in scope at the procedure's ancestor nodes in the tree are also in scope.

For example, procedure Q can be called from within procedure P1 because the identifier of procedure Q is in scope at ancestor node M in the tree. Procedure P1 cannot be called from within procedure Q because P1 is not in scope at Q or any ancestor node of Q.

Suppose, for example, that an identifier is declared at the outer level of procedure M and is declared again at the outer level of procedure P. If this identifier is referenced within P1 the meaning at the outer level of P will be used and the meaning at the outer level of procedure M will be overridden. In Section 13.3.3 we will see in detail how this can be implemented.

Procedure parameters require special discussion. Suppose, for example, that we have the following procedure:

```
PROCEDURE R;
  PROCEDURE S (i, j: INTEGER);
  BEGIN
    (* body of S *)
  END S;
BEGIN
  S(4, 7)
END R;
```

The parameter identifiers i and j are out of scope within the body of procedure R, nevertheless procedure R can assign the value 4 to i and 7 to j at the time of calling

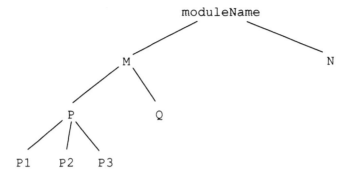

Figure 13.1 A tree representing the static structure of a module.

procedure s. At this time procedure R accesses parameters of s by using knowledge of their position in the parameter sequence, and not by using their identifiers, which are out of scope.

13.3 The identifier table

13.3.1 Structure

Henceforward the structure of the identifier table is essentially the same as in Chapter 12 except that there is one additional feature. This is that every record points to the identifier table record for the procedure that encloses it. For standard and global identifiers, which are at block level 0 and are not enclosed within any procedure, the identifier table records point to a special pseudo-procedure identifier table record that serves instead of a procedure record. The identifier table record for a procedure includes a boolean field beingCompiled which is set to TRUE while and only while the procedure is being compiled. To check whether an identifier is in scope our compiler follows the pointer from the identifier's record to the enclosing procedure's record in the identifier table. The identifier is in scope if and only if this procedure's record has beingCompiled = TRUE.

13.3.2 Identifier table definition module

To take care of procedures, parameters and scope, we replace the identifier table module itmod by a new version pritmod, which imports from a new version prSAL of putSAL. In the definition module of pritmod the identifier table record type idRec has some additional fields:

```
DEFINITION MODULE pritmod;
FROM symbols IMPORT symbolType;
```

```
FROM prSAL IMPORT labelString;
TYPE
  class = (aConstant, aType, aField, aVariable, aVARparameter, aProcedure);
  kindOfType = (aStandardType, arrayType, recordType, typeAlias);
  kindOfProc = (pureProc, functionProc, externalProc);
  idRecPtr = POINTER TO idRec;
  idRec = RECORD
            itsInd: CARDINAL;
            itsType, nextSyn, nextSeq, enclosedBy: idRecPtr;
            marked: BOOLEAN;
            CASE itsClass: class OF
              aConstant: c1, c2: CARDINAL |
              aVariable, aVARparameter: relAddress: CARDINAL;
                      baseLabel: labelString; itsLevel: CARDINAL |
              aField: fieldAddress: CARDINAL |
              aType:  itsLength: CARDINAL;
                      CASE typeKind: kindOfType OF
                        aStandardType, typeAlias: |
                        arrayType: lowBound, upBound: INTEGER;
                            indexType, elementType: idRecPtr |
                        recordType: noOfFields: CARDINAL;
                          fieldPtr: idRecPtr  |
                      END |
              aProcedure: procKind: kindOfProc;
                      procLevel, internalLevel, noOfParams,
                      varLength, paramLength: CARDINAL;
                      resultType, nextProc: idRecPtr;
                      beginLabel: labelString;
                      beingCompiled: BOOLEAN
            END
          END;
VAR
  tyInteger, tyBoolean, tyReal, tail: idRecPtr;
  stIndex: ARRAY[1..3] OF idRecPtr;
PROCEDURE findItsRecord(soughtInd: CARDINAL; VAR recPtr: idRecPtr;
  VAR found: BOOLEAN);
PROCEDURE checkDuplicateIdentifier(soughtInd: CARDINAL);
PROCEDURE findField(soughtInd: CARDINAL; ptr: idRecPtr;
  VAR fieldDetails: idRec; VAR found: BOOLEAN);
PROCEDURE constant(VAR ofType: idRecPtr; VAR card1, card2:CARDINAL);
PROCEDURE newIdRecord(VAR tabPtr: idRecPtr);
PROCEDURE enterIdRecord(ind: CARDINAL; VAR tablePtr: idRecPtr);
PROCEDURE disconnect(soughtInd: CARDINAL);
  (* removes a record from a linked list of hash synonyms *)
```

```
PROCEDURE initialiseIdTable;
  (* initialize identifier table *)
PROCEDURE pushProc(procPtr: idRecPtr);
PROCEDURE popProc;
END pritmod.
```

The enumeration `class` has additional values `aProcedure` for a procedure and `aVARparameter` for a VAR parameter. Value parameters have identifier table records that have `itsClass = aVariable`, because value parameters are treated as initialized local variables, as will be explained in Section 13.6.2. Record type `idRec` has an additional field `enclosedBy` which is a pointer to the identifier table record of the enclosing procedure.

For a procedure, `procLevel` is the block level of the procedure identifier, and `internalLevel = procLevel + 1` except that `internalLevel = 0` in the identifier table record for the pseudo-procedure that encloses all global and standard identifiers. `internalLevel` is the block level of a procedure's parameters and local variables. `noOfParams` is the number of parameters of the procedure. `paramLength` and `varLength` are, respectively, the number of words required for all parameters and the number of words required for all local variables of the procedure. When `procKind = functionProc`, `resultType` is the type of the value returned by the function procedure; otherwise the `resultType` field is unused. `beginLabel` labels the first word of the object-code subroutine that implements the procedure, except when `procKind = externalProc`.

The list of exported procedures in definition module `pritmod` also includes two new procedures `pushProc` and `popProc` that deal with a stack within the identifier table module. When starting to compile a procedure heading or body, the compiler calls `popProc` to push on to this stack a pointer to the procedure's identifier table record. When the compiler has finished compiling a procedure heading or body it calls `popProc` to pop this pointer off the stack. The pointer on the top of this stack always points to the identifier record for the procedure that is currently being compiled, except that while compiling at block level zero the pointer on the top of this stack points to the identifier table record for the pseudo-procedure that encloses global and standard identifiers.

Procedure `checkDuplicateIdentifier` no longer works by calling `findItsRecord` and has migrated from the declaration module to the identifier table module because it requires information associated with the identifier table. Procedure `checkDuplicateIdentifier` reports an error if it finds a duplicate `ind` among the records that have `recPtr^.enclosedBy = procStack[top]` and therefore belong to identifiers in the innermost procedure that is currently being compiled .

13.3.3 Enforcement of scope rules

To allow enforcement of scope rules, procedure `enterIdRecord` is now more elaborate than it was in module `itmod`. Procedure `enterIdRecord` still inserts into the same linked list all records whose `itsInd` has the same hash function value. The new development is that within this list the records are kept in decreasing order of block level of the enclosing procedure, that is, of `enclosedBy^.internalLevel`.

Procedure `newIdRecord` is the same as in module `itmod` except that it assigns to `enclosedBy` a pointer to the identifier table record for the procedure that encloses the declaration of the identifier for which the new identifier table record is being completed. This pointer is `procStack[top]`, which is the pointer on the top of the stack that we introduced in Section 13.3.2.

Procedure `findItsRecord` is the same as in module `itmod` in Section 12.3.5 except that it ignores any record for an identifier whose enclosing procedure has `beingCompiled = FALSE`:

```
PROCEDURE findItsRecord(soughtInd: CARDINAL; VAR recPtr: idRecPtr; VAR found:
BOOLEAN);
BEGIN
  recPtr:= idTable[CARDINAL(BITSET(soughtInd) * mask)];
  LOOP
    IF recPtr = NIL THEN found:= FALSE; RETURN
    ELSIF (recPtr^.itsInd = soughtInd) AND
      recPtr^.enclosedBy^.beingCompiled THEN found:= TRUE; RETURN
    ELSE recPtr:= recPtr^.nextSyn
    END
  END
END findItsRecord;
```

Suppose, for example, that an outline of the source text is as follows:

```
MODULE MN;
VAR  X: INTEGER;

PROCEDURE PA;
VAR X: INTEGER;

  PROCEDURE PB;
  VAR X: INTEGER;
  BEGIN (* body of PB *)
  END PB;

  PROCEDURE PC;
  VAR X: INTEGER;
  BEGIN (* body of PC *)
  END PC;

BEGIN (* body of PA *)
END PA;

PROCEDURE PD;
VAR X: INTEGER;
BEGIN (* body of PD *)
END PD;
```

```
BEGIN (* body of module MN *)
END MN.
```

While compiling X:= 1 in the body of module MN, findItsRecord will linearly search a linked list that includes identifier table records for all five variables X. We have ensured that this list must always be in sequence of decreasing block level. Therefore findItsRecord will first find the records for the Xs in PB and PC because these are at block level 2 and the identifier table records for PB and PC have internalLevel = 2. FindItsRecord will ignore these records because PB and PC have beingCompiled = FALSE while the body of MN is being compiled. Next findItsRecord will find the records for the Xs in PA and PD because these are at block level 1, and will ignore these because PA and PD have beingCompiled = FALSE while the body of MN is being compiled. Finally, findItsRecord will assign found:= TRUE when it finds the identifier table record for the global variable X at block level 0, because we arrange that for global identifiers enclosedBy^.beingCompiled = TRUE always.

While compiling X:= 1 in the body of PD, findItsRecord will first ignore the identifier table records for X in PB and PC because these procedures have beingCompiled = FALSE. If findItsRecord comes next to the record for X in PA it will ignore this because PA has beingCompiled = FALSE. findItsRecord will assign found:= TRUE and return a pointer to the identifier table for X in PA *because it will find this before the record for the global variable* X. We keep the records in sorted order in linked lists so as to ensure that findItsRecord will always return the innermost meaning of an identifier that is consistent with current scope.

As a final example, while compiling X:= 1 in the body of PC, if findItsRecord comes first to the record for X in PB it will ignore this because PB has beingCompiled = FALSE. It will return a pointer to the record for X in PC because this has beingCompiled = TRUE. Because PC has a higher block level, findItsRecord will not find the record for X in PA or for the global X, although both of these have enclosedBy^.beingCompiled = TRUE while PC is being compiled.

These examples illustrate how our compiler enforces scope rules. Linear search of a long linked list is inefficient, but our linked lists will not be long if idTableUB is greater than the largest ind for a module, and if the same identifier does not have more than a few different meanings.

13.4 Compiling declarations

A new module proDecs replaces the declaration module decMod that compiled declarations in Chapter 12. Module proDecs looks after the first pass and compiles CONST, TYPE and VAR declarations and procedure headings, creating identifier table records for these and for procedure parameters. Module proDecs outputs to a file the source symbol stream for statement sequences in the source module body and procedure bodies, which are compiled during the second pass. The definition module of proDecs is as follows:

```
DEFINITION MODULE proDecs;
FROM pritmod IMPORT idRecPtr;
FROM prSAL IMPORT labelString;
VAR
   moduleVarLength: CARDINAL;
PROCEDURE procInitialise(ind: CARDINAL; VAR procPtr: idRecPtr;
  VAR startLabel: labelString; VAR varWords, prmLength: CARDINAL;
  VAR resType: idRecPtr;  VAR aFunction: BOOLEAN);
END proDecs.
```

The variable `moduleVarLength` is the total number of words required for all of the module's global variables. Procedure `procInitialise` is called during the second pass just before compiling the statement sequence that constitutes a procedure body. `procInitialise` calls `findItsRecord` to find in the identifier table the record for the procedure heading, and returns information obtained from this record via its VAR parameters.

The body of the implementation module of `proDecs` begins by creating and initializing the pseudo-procedure record that will be pointed to by the records for all standard and global identifiers. A pointer to this record is pushed on to `procStack` by `pushProc`:

```
BEGIN (* body of proDecs *)
   newIdRecord(globalPtr); (* pseudo-procedure record *)
   WITH globalPtr^ DO
     itsClass:= aProcedure; internalLevel:= 0;
     beingCompiled:= TRUE
   END;
   pushProc(globalPtr); blockLevel:= 0;
   initialiseIdTable; openInterFile;
   inSymbol; outSymbol; (* MODULE symbol *)
   accept(moduleSy); outSymbol; moduleInd:= ind;
   accept(idSy); outSymbol; (* semicolon *)
   IF sy # semiColonSy THEN error(222) END;
   inSymbol;
   moduleVarLength:= 0; standardImports; WriteLn;
   block(moduleVarLength, moduleInd);
   closeInterFile; accept(periodSy)
END proDecs.
```

Procedure `openInterFile` opens the file `interFile` to which the symbol stream is written for consumption during the second pass. We use `interFile` because this is a very simple way of working, but a faster alternative is to store the symbol stream in an internal data structure if sufficient memory is available. Procedure `outSymbol` is a procedure in lexical analyzer module `scanner` that outputs to `interFile` the current value of `sy` and its associated `ind` or `valueRecord` when appropriate. Procedure `outSymbol`, which is included in the listing of module `scanner` in the Appendix, also outputs to `interFile` the current line number so that this can be used in error messages during the second pass. Procedure `block` compiles the module's procedure headings and all other declarations:

```
PROCEDURE block (VAR words: CARDINAL; endInd: CARDINAL);
BEGIN
  LOOP
    IF sy = constSy THEN constDecs
    ELSIF sy = typeSy THEN typeDecs
    ELSIF sy = varSy THEN varDecs(words)
    ELSIF sy = procedureSy THEN proceDec
    ELSE EXIT
    END
  END;
  IF sy = beginSy THEN outSymbol ELSE error (93) END;
  LOOP
    inSymbol; outSymbol;
    IF sy = endSy THEN
       REPEAT inSymbol; outSymbol UNTIL sy # endSy;
       IF sy = idSy THEN
         IF ind # endInd THEN error(94) END;
         EXIT
       END
    END
  END;
  inSymbol; outSymbol
END block;
```

The first parameter is the total number of words required for variables, and the second parameter is the `ind` of the identifier that should be found after `END` at the end of the statement sequence. The first `LOOP` is like the `LOOP` in procedure `decs` in module `decMod` except that if `sy = procedureSy` it calls `proceDec` which compiles a procedure declaration. When the first `LOOP` in procedure `block` terminates, `sy` should be `beginSy` for the statement sequence that follows all the declarations which have been compiled by the first `LOOP`. The second `LOOP` copies symbols from the lexical analyzer to `interFile` until it comes to `endSy` followed by the appropriate identifier at the end of the statement sequence. Procedure `proceDec` is:

```
PROCEDURE proceDec;
VAR
  procPtr: idRecPtr; procInd: CARDINAL;
BEGIN
  outSymbol; inSymbol; outSymbol; (* procedureSy and ind *)
  IF sy # idSy THEN error (33) ELSE
      checkDuplicateIdentifier(ind) (* check procedure identifier *)
```

```
      END;
    procInd:= ind;  (* ind of procedure identifier *)
    enterIdRecord(procInd, procPtr); (* make idTable record for
      procedure identifier *)
    INC(blockLevel); (* new block level for procedure's parameters and locally
      declared identifiers *)
    pushProc(procPtr);  (* push procPtr onto procStack *)
    procPtr^.beingCompiled:= TRUE;
    procHeading(procInd, procPtr); (* compiles the procedure heading *)
    procPtr^.varLength:= 3; (* initialization explained in Section 13.6.1 *)
    block(procPtr^.varLength, procInd); (* compiles procedure's internal
      declarations and body *)
    procPtr^.beingCompiled:= FALSE;
    DEC(blockLevel); popProc;
    accept(semiColonSy)
  END proceDec;
```

Procedure `procHeading` allows the formal parameters to comprise more than one list of parameters, such that all parameters in the same list have the same type. For example, there are three lists in

```
PROCEDURE W (a, b, c: INTEGER; VAR d, e, f: INTEGER; g, h: REAL);
```

Procedure `procHeading`, with some explanatory comments, is:

```
PROCEDURE procHeading(procInd: CARDINAL;  procPtr: idRecPtr);
VAR
  paramPtr, functionReturnType, thisType: idRecPtr;
  nextAddress, numberOfParams, count: CARDINAL;
  varParam: BOOLEAN;  currentPtr: listRecPtr;
BEGIN
  inSymbol; numberOfParams:= 0;
  nextAddress:= 0; (* parameter address *)
  IF sy = openRndBrktSy THEN (* deal with formal parameters *)
    inSymbol;
    WHILE sy IN symbolSet{idSy, varSy} DO (* FOR each list of parameters
        that are all of the same type DO *)
      IF sy = varSy THEN (* VAR parameters *)
        inSymbol; varParam:= TRUE
      ELSE varParam:= FALSE
      END;
      makeList(currentPtr); (* make currentPtr point to a list of
        parameters all of the same type.  Upon return from makeList,
        sy = parameter type identifier *)
      IF sy = idSy THEN
        typeRecord(thisType) (* thisType:= type of parameters in list *)
```

```
    ELSE error(101) (* we only allow named types *)
    END;
  IF thisType^.itsClass = aType THEN
    WHILE currentPtr # NIL DO (* for each paramter in the list *)
      checkDuplicateIdentifier(currentPtr^.item);
      enterIdRecord(currentPtr^.item,paramPtr); (* for this parameter *)
      WITH paramPtr^ DO
        IF varParam THEN itsClass:= aVARparameter
        ELSE itsClass:= aVariable (* a value parameter *)
        END;
        relAddress:= nextAddress; itsType:= thisType; itsLevel:= blockLevel
      END;
      INC(nextAddress, thisType^.itsLength); (* address of next parameter *)
      INC(numberOfParams); currentPtr:= currentPtr^.next
    END
  ELSE error(102)
  END;
  inSymbol; IF sy = semiColonSy THEN inSymbol END
END; (* WHILE *)
paramPtr:= procPtr^.nextSeq;
FOR count:= 1 TO numberOfParams DO (* this is explained in Section 13.6.2 *)
  DEC(paramPtr^.relAddress, nextAddress);
  paramPtr:= paramPtr^.nextSeq
END;
accept(closeRndBrktSy); (* at end of formal parameters *)
IF sy = colonSy THEN    (* this is a function procedure *)
  procPtr^.procKind:= functionProc; inSymbol;
  IF sy = idSy THEN typeRecord(functionReturnType)
  ELSE error(35) (* the returned type must be named *)
  END;
  IF (functionReturnType # tyBoolean) AND (functionReturnType # tyReal)
    AND (functionReturnType # tyInteger) THEN
    error (36)
  END; (* we only allow a function to return type BOOLEAN, REAL or INTEGER *)
  inSymbol
ELSE procPtr^.procKind:= pureProc (* this is not a function procedure *)
END
ELSE procPtr^.procKind:= pureProc (* there were no round brackets *)
END;
WITH procPtr^ DO (* with idTable record for procedure identifier *)
  itsClass:= aProcedure;
  procLevel:= blockLevel - 1; internalLevel:= blockLevel;
  noOfParams:= numberOfParams; paramLength:= nextAddress;
  genLabel(beginLabel);
```

```
    IF procKind = functionProc THEN resultType:= functionReturnType END
END;
  accept(semiColonSy)
END procHeading;
```

The FOR loop that traverses a list of all parameters linked by nextSeq pointers makes the relAddresses of parameters negative, as will be explained in Section 13.6.2.

13.5 The symbol stream for the second pass

During the first pass, module decMod obtains successive symbols by calling inSymbol in lexical analyzer module scanner. During the second pass successive symbols are obtained by calling a new version of inSymbol in a module named bis:

```
DEFINITION MODULE bis;
FROM symbols IMPORT symbolType;
FROM scanner IMPORT valRecType;
VAR
   valueRecord: valRecType; sy: symbolType; ind: CARDINAL;
PROCEDURE error(errNo: CARDINAL);
PROCEDURE accept(sym: symbolType);
PROCEDURE inSymbol;
PROCEDURE openInterfile;
PROCEDURE closeInterFile;
END bis.
```

Procedure inSymbol simply obtains successive symbols from the file interFile. Procedures error and accept are included in this module so that line numbers in error messages will be correct during the second pass. It is a simple exercise to develop this so as to give character positions as well as line numbers in error messages.

The introduction of procedures necessitates revision of the statement and expression modules. The revised modules import from a new module prSAL instead of putSAL: the only difference is that prSAL imports from module bis instead of module scanner, again so that line numbers in error messages will be correct during the second pass.

13.6 The run-time model

13.6.1 Activation records

We adopt a traditional run-time model that uses a single run-time stack. For each invocation of a procedure the object-code program allocates on top of the run-time stack a block of words containing all the actual parameters and local variables for that invocation. This block of consecutive words also includes sufficient words for holding temporary values during expression evaluation and for similar purposes. This block is called the *activation record* for the procedure invocation. An alternative term for an activation record is a *stack frame*.

For each recursive invocation of the same procedure a separate activation record is pushed on to the run-time stack. Within any such activation record, the local variables and actual parameters are physically separated from those within any other activation record for another invocation of the same procedure or of any other procedure. An activation record consists of four sets of consecutive words:

(a) words containing the procedure's actual parameters, and if this is a function procedure then words for the function return value are included here as well;
(b) the context part;
(c) words containing all of the procedure's local variables;
(d) words containing all of the procedure's temporary variables.

The context part consists of three words. The first of these is the *static link*, which is used in accessing variables that have a lower block-level number than those in the current procedure invocation, as will be explained in Section 13.6.4. The second word of the context part is the *dynamic link* which is used at the time of return from an invocation, as will be explained in Section 13.6.3. The third word of the context part is the subroutine return address for this invocation.

When a procedure is called, an activation record for this invocation is created for it on the top of the stack. The first word of this activation record is immediately on top of whatever was on the top of the stack at the time of the call. At the time of return from an invocation of a pure (i.e. not a function) procedure, its activation record becomes inaccessible and the top of the stack becomes exactly what it was immediately before the procedure call. The contents of this activation record are lost, in the sense that they may soon be overwritten.

In Section 13.6.5 we give a detailed example of contents of activation records. As an introductory example with details omitted, if the body of module moduleName in Section 13.2.1 calls procedure M which calls procedure P which calls procedure P2, then after this invocation of P2 an outline of the contents of the run-time stack is as shown in Figure 13.2, in which the stack grows downwards. If after the return from M procedure N is next called then the activation record for this invocation of N may overwrite the memory area that was previously occupied by M's activation record. This illustrates *dynamic*, that is to say, changing, allocation of memory.

Variables declared at block level 0 are stored within the static block of words in an area outside the run-time stack. We explained in Chapter 12 that allocation of memory to variables in the static block is *static* because it remains unchanged for the entire duration of execution of the program.

13.6.2 Addressing within an activation record

Within an activation record all addresses are expressed relative to the first word of the context part. Thus the first word of the context part has address 0. In a SAL object-code program it is convenient to have register BP, which is the *base pointer*, always containing

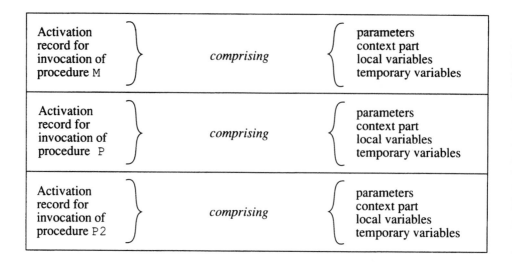

Figure 13.2 Outline of activation records for three procedure invocations.

the address of the first word of the context part of the activation record that is topmost on the stack. Thus in the topmost activation record all addresses are relative to the contents of BP. Addresses of static variables are relative to the first word of the static block.

When a procedure is called its parameters are pushed on to the run-time stack before the context part of the activation record for this invocation. The absolute addresses of parameters are therefore less than the absolute address of the first word of the context part. Because all addresses within an activation record are expressed relative to the first word of the context part, the relative addresses of parameters are actually negative. Procedure procHeading initially assigns non-negative relAddresses to parameters and subsequently makes them negative by means of a FOR loop that subtracts from each of these relAddresses the total number of words occupied by all of a procedure's parameters.

We noted in Section 12.7 that if x is a variable then in x:= y, x means the *address* of the variable whose identifier is x. In y:= x, x means the *value* stored at the address for which the identifier is x. When x is a formal parameter of a procedure in Modula-2, the programmer must resolve the ambiguity by indicating whether x is an address or a value. The programmer does this by including x in a list of VAR parameters if x is an address. If x is not included in a list of VAR parameters, the compiler assumes that x is a value. If a formal parameter x is an address, then x is said to be *called by reference*, and its idTable record has itsClass = aVARparameter. Otherwise, if x is a value, then x is said to be *called by value*, and its idTable record has itsClass = aVariable.

For a function procedure, we make space on the stack for the returned value just before the location of the first parameter. For example, for an invocation of

```
PROCEDURE pr (VAR x1: REAL; y1: REAL; VAR z1: BOOLEAN): REAL;
```

Table 13.1 First part of activation record for an invocation of function procedure pr.

relAddress	Contents
-6	first word of returned value
-5	second word of returned value
-4	address of first word of x1
-3	first word of value of y1
-2	second word of value of y1
-1	address of z1
0	static link, see Section 13.6.4
1	dynamic link, see Section 13.6.3
2	return address
3	address of first word of a
4	address of second word of a
5	address of b

```
VAR
  a: REAL; b: INTEGER;
BEGIN (* details omitted *)
END pr;
```

the activation record includes words shown in Table 13.1. If, for example, the body of procedure pr includes a reference to value parameter y1, procedure pushAddress outputs code to push the address of y1 on to the stack as follows:

```
MOV DI, -3    ;    relAddress = -3
ADD DI, BP    ;    DI:= absolute address of y1
PUSH DI       ;    push the absolute address of y1
```

As another example, if the body of procedure pr includes a reference to VAR parameter x1, procedure pushAddress outputs code to push the actual address x1 on to the stack as follows:

```
MOV DI, -4    ; relAddress of the address of the first word of x1
PUSH [BP][DI] ; pushes the word containing the address of the first word of x1
```

From within a procedure it is legitimate to reference a value parameter or a VAR parameter of a textually enclosing procedure. As will be explained in Section 13.6.4, this is done by using static links to find the appropriate activation record, and then using the parameter's negative relAddress relative to the first word of the context part of this activation record.

13.6.3 The dynamic link

The dynamic link is so called because it is used for updating BP at the time of return from a procedure invocation. The term *dynamic* is appropriate because it is associated with the changes involved in procedure call and return. Within an activation record the address of the dynamic link is [BP + 1]. The dynamic link is a word that contains the address of the first word of the context part of the immediately previous activation record on the stack. This arrangement is such that at the time of return from a procedure invocation the instruction

```
MOV BP, [BP + 1]
```

leaves BP containing the address of the first word of the context part of the activation record that is now on the top of the stack, or, if the procedure's identifier was at block level 0, BP is left containing the address of the first word of the static block. We will consider the return from a procedure further in Section 13.9.4.

13.6.4 The static link

In Section 13.6.2 we saw that for the topmost activation record, addresses are relative to BP. But we have not yet seen how the procedure that owns this activation record can access a variable that is at a lower block level and is therefore in an activation record below the topmost in the stack. The static link is used for this purpose, as will be explained in the following paragraphs. The static link is so called because it points to the activation record for the most recent invocation of the textually enclosing procedure: the structure of the source text is *static*.

As we saw in Section 13.3.2, identifier table records now include not only the relAddress but also the block level of every variable and procedure parameter. Suppose that the procedure that owns the topmost activation record has its local variables at block level k, and suppose that this procedure requires access to a variable in an outer procedure at block level $k - 2$. The stack must contain an activation record for this outer procedure because an inner procedure cannot be called except during an invocation of an outer procedure. To locate the required variable, it is necessary first to find the address of the first word of the context part of the activation record that contains it, and then to use the variable's relAddress relative to this.

To locate the activation record that contains this variable, the object program scans successive activation records from the top towards the bottom of the stack until it finds the first that is at the block level of this variable. This activation record will contain the required variable. At first sight it may not be obvious that this is the correct activation record.

This must be correct because the only procedure at block level $k-1$ that can call a procedure s at block level k is the procedure that textually encloses s. The only procedure at block level $k-1$ that can call a procedure at block level k that can call a procedure s at block level k encloses both of these procedures. The only procedure at block level $k-1$

that can indirectly call a procedure at any depth that calls procedure s at block level k encloses all of these procedures. It is not possible for a procedure at block level $k-1$ to call (directly or indirectly) some other procedure at $k-1$ that calls s at block level k and does not textually enclose s.

If, for example, a procedure at block level k requires access to a variable that is local to an enclosing procedure at block level $k-2$, the activation record for the last invocation of this enclosing procedure should be found as quickly as possible, without unnecessary linear search. To speed up this search, every activation record at block level k contains a *static link* which is the address of the first word of the context part of the activation record of the last invocation of the textually enclosing procedure at block level $k-1$.

To find the activation record for the most recent invocation of the textually enclosing procedure at block level $k-2$, we start by following the static link from the topmost activation record to the activation record of the most recent invocation of the enclosing procedure at block level $k-1$, and we follow the static link from there to the activation record of the most recent invocation of the enclosing procedure at block level $k-2$. In this example, we visit only one unwanted activation record on the way to the required one.

We now consider a more specific example, in which procedure N is called from within the body of module moduleName in Section 13.2.1. Procedure N calls procedure M which calls procedure Q which calls procedure P which calls procedure P3 which calls procedure P2, which refers to variable y that is declared in procedure M. At the time of this reference to y the run-time stack contains activation records as shown in Figure 13.3.

When compiling a reference in procedure P2 at block level 3 to variable y that is declared in procedure M, the compiler finds from the idTable that y is at block level 1. At execution time, the activation record containing y can be found by following the static link from activation record for P2 to the activation record for P, and then following the static link from this to the activation record for M, which contains the sought variable y. By not visiting two intervening activation records, access to y is faster than it would be if these activation records were visited in the course of linear search of the stack.

Let levelDifference be the difference between the block level where a variable is referenced and the block level where this variable is declared. If levelDifference = 0 then we simply use the variable's relAddress within the topmost activation record, as in the example in Section 13.6.2. If levelDifference > 0 then to push the variable's address on to the stack, detailed programming of the use of static links is as follows:

```
        MOV CX, levelDifference
        MOV BX, BP    ; BX:= address of static link in topmost activation record
ZAAL: MOV BX, [BX]; BX:= contents of static link
        LOOP ZAAL     ; Here ZAAL is just an example of label
        ADD BX, idTable[subs].relAddress; relAddress of referenced variable
        PUSH BX       ; pushes the actual address of the referenced variable
```

In the Figure 13.3 example, variable y in procedure M is referenced from within procedure P2. Just before the first iteration of the loop, BX contains the address of the static link in the activation record for P2. At the start of the second iteration, BX contains the address of the static link in the activation record for P. At the time of exit from this loop, BX contains

block level	activation record for	static link

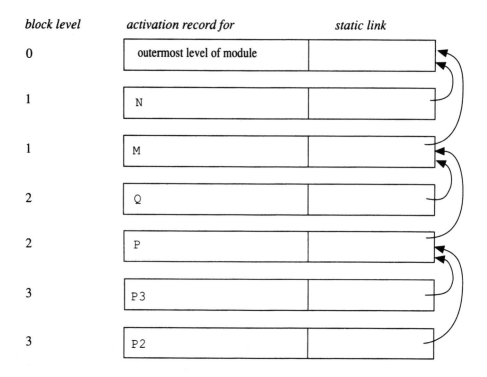

Figure 13.3 An example of static links.

the address of the first word of the context part of the activation record for M which contains variable y. The relAddress of y, obtained from the idTable, is relative to the first word of the context part of activation record for M.

To access a variable within the static block, procedure pushAddress must obtain the address of the base of the static block. We organize this in a way that will later allow multimodule operation. Specifically, for each variable, the identifier table record contains a field baseLabel, which is of type labelString. If the record has itsLevel = 0 then baseLabel labels the first word of the static block that contains this variable. Procedure pushAddress pushes the variable's address as follows:

```
LEA DI, baseLabel
ADD DI, relAddress
PUSH DI
```

The new version of procedure pushAddress is included in expression module prExprsn in the Appendix.

13.6.5 A recursive example

The *run-time model* consists of the static block, the activation records, including parameters and links, and the changing contents of the run-time stack at times of procedure invocation and return. BP and SP are also part of the run-time model. The run-time model allows recursion and mutual recursion. For example, the following program uses a recursive bubblesort routine to sort an array of integers. This is intended not as an exhibition of efficiency, but as a very simple example to illustrate recursive invocation:

```
MODULE bubbles;
FROM InOut IMPORT WriteString, WriteCard, WriteLn;
CONST
  length = 10;
TYPE
 arType = ARRAY [1..length] OF INTEGER;
VAR
  arx: arType;
  i: CARDINAL;

PROCEDURE swap(VAR p,q: INTEGER);
VAR
  temp: INTEGER;
BEGIN
  temp:= p; p:= q; q:= temp
END swap;

PROCEDURE bubbleSort(VAR thisArray:arType;  n: CARDINAL);
VAR
  lastOutOfOrder: CARDINAL;
  PROCEDURE scan(j: CARDINAL; VAR swappedAt: CARDINAL);
  BEGIN
    IF thisArray[j-1] > thisArray[j] THEN
       swappedAt:= j; swap(thisArray[j-1], thisArray[j])
    END;
    IF j < n THEN scan(j + 1, swappedAt) END
  END scan;
BEGIN (* body of bubbleSort *)
   lastOutOfOrder:= 2;
   scan (2, lastOutOfOrder);
   IF lastOutOfOrder > 2 THEN bubbleSort(thisArray, lastOutOfOrder -1) END
END bubbleSort;
BEGIN
  arx[1]:= 20; arx[2]:= 25; arx[3]:= 6; arx[4]:= 3; arx[5]:= 30;
  arx[6]:= 7;  arx[7]:= 5;  arx[8]:= 15; arx[9]:= 2; arx[10]:= 1;
  bubbleSort (arx, length);
  i:= 1;
```

```
    REPEAT WRITENUM(arx[i]); INC(i) UNTIL i > length
END bubbles.
```

Assuming, for example, that the static block starts at address 500, the contents of the static block are as shown in Table 13.2.

Table 13.2 Contents of static block for example module bubbles

Address	Contents
500	arx[1]
501	arx[2]
502	arx[3]
503	arx[4]
504	arx[5]
505	arx[6]
506	arx[7]
507	arx[8]
508	arx[9]
509	arx[10]
510	i

Suppose, for example, that bubbleSort has called itself recursively once, and scan has called itself recursively twice, so there are altogether three activation records for scan on the stack. Suppose that swap has been called by scan. Table 13.3 shows the contents of the run-time stack before the return from this invocation of swap. We assume (by way of example) that the run-time stack starts at address 1014. Of course the address and the comment are not in the stack and are shown in Table 13.3 purely to facilitate understanding. In Figure 13.3 static links were represented by pointers, whereas in Table 13.3 they are addresses. As an exercise, it is worthwhile to check the contents of Table 13.3 in detail.

13.7 Changes in the expression module

Instead of the expression module xpressn we now use a version prExprsn in which procedure pushAddress uses static links where necessary, as has been explained in detail in Section 13.6.4. Procedure pushValue has been modified so that if an idTable record has itsClass = aVARparameter then pushAddress is called to push the address of this VAR parameter onto the stack. If, instead, pushValue finds that an idTable record has itsClass = aProcedure then this should be a function procedure, and the call is compiled by procedure functionCall in a new module callRet that deals with procedure call and return. Module callRet will be considered in Section 13.9.

Table 13.3 Example of contents of activation records

Address	Contents	Comment
1014	500	actual var parameter: address of `arx[1]`
1015	10	actual value parameter `n`
1016	500	static link for `bubbleSort`
1017	500	dynamic link for `bubbleSort`
1018	233	return address for `bubbleSort`
1019	?	`lastOutOfOrder`
1020	500	actual var parameter: address of `arx[1]`
1021	9	actual value parameter `n`
1022	500	static link for `bubbleSort`
1023	1016	dynamic link for `bubbleSort`
1024	233	return address for `bubbleSort`
1025	?	`lastOutOfOrder`
1026	2	actual value parameter `j`
1027	1025	actual var param: address of `lastOutOfOrder`
1028	1022	static link for `scan`
1029	1022	dynamic link for `scan`
1030	153	return address for `scan`
1031	3	actual value parameter `j`
1032	1025	actual var param: address of `lastOutOfOrder`
1033	1022	static link for `scan`
1034	1028	dynamic link for `scan`
1035	153	return address for `scan`
1036	4	actual value parameter `j`
1037	1025	actual var param: address of `lastOutOfOrder`
1038	1022	static link for `scan`
1039	1033	dynamic link for `scan`
1040	153	return address for `scan`
1041	500	actual var param `p`
1042	501	actual var param `q`
1043	500	static link for `swap`
1044	1038	dynamic link for `swap`
1045	124	return address for `swap`
1046	?	temp: local variable in `swap`
1047	a temporary variable used in `swap`	

13.8 Changes in the statement module

The introduction of procedures has only a very small impact on the statement module, but there are two changes in procedure `statement`. One is that if the first symbol of a statement is `idSy` and the class of this identifier is found to be `aProcedure` then `procedureCall` is called to deal with this:

```
PROCEDURE procedureCall(proPtr: idRecPtr);
BEGIN (* proPtr points to idTable record for procedure identifier *)
  CASE proPtr^.procKind OF
    pureProc:     call(proPtr) (* compile a procedure call *) |
    functionProc: error(120) |
    externalProc: extProc      (* same as in module xpressn *)
  END
END procedureCall;
```

Another change is that if procedure statement is called when sy = returnSy then procedure returnStatement is called. Procedures call and returnStatement are also in the new module callRet. The new version of the statement module is prStmnt, which is included in the Appendix.

13.9 Procedure call and return

13.9.1 Distinguishing between procedure and function call

Procedure call and return are compiled during the second pass, while compiling statement sequences. Procedure call can be called either by procedure procedureCall in module prStmnt or by procedure functionCall in module callRet.

If procedure pushValue finds that the current symbol is a function identifier, it calls procedure functionCall which outputs code to add to SP the length of the function's result type. This reserves space on the stack for the value that will be returned by the function. Procedure functionCall is as follows:

```
PROCEDURE functionCall(proPtr: idRecPtr; VAR fnType: idRecPtr);
BEGIN
  WITH proPtr^ DO
    IF procKind = functionProc THEN
      fnType:= resultType;
      putStringAndVal('   ADD SP, ',resultType^.itsLength);
      call(proPtr)
    ELSE error(121)
    END
  END
END functionCall;
```

For example, for function pr in Section 13.6.2 the first word of the first parameter is at address -4 relative to the first word of the context part of an activation record for pr. Between this word and what was the top word on the stack at the time of the function call, we need to reserve two words for return of the REAL value of pr. These words are shown at relAddresses -6 and -5 in Table 13.1 but actually procedure procHeading does not assign relAddresses to these two words. Instead, procedure returnStatement addresses the last of these two words as if it has relAddress = - paramLength - 1, and then addresses the first as if its relAddress = - paramLength - 2. In effect these two relAddresses are made available by procedure functionCall, by adding two to SP before any actual parameters are pushed on to the stack by the code produced by procedure call.

13.9.2 Actual parameters

Procedure call starts by calling inSymbol to get the symbol following the procedure identifier. If the procedure has at least one formal parameter, procedure call deals with parameters by using a routine which in outline is as follows:

```
FOR each formal parameter DO
    IF this parameter is a value parameter THEN call expression to push
      the actual value of this parameter on to the stack
    ELSIF this parameter is a VAR parameter THEN
      push on to the stack the address of the actual parameter
    END
END;
```

This is implemented in detail in the first part of procedure call in module callRet in the Appendix.

13.9.3 Initialization of the context part

After producing code to push the actual parameters on to the stack, procedure call has to produce code to initialize the context part of the new activation record. When figuring out how to initialize the static link, it is important to remember that a procedure's idTable record has procLevel that is one less than the block level appropriate to the body of the procedure, because the called procedure's idTable record must be accessible during compilation of the body of the textually enclosing procedure.

Procedure call has a local variable levelDifference whose value is the difference between the block level where the procedure is called and the procLevel of the procedure's idTable record. The part of procedure call that initializes the context part starts by assigning to BX the static link for the new activation record:

```
putLine('    MOV BX, BP');
levelDifference:= blockLevel - proPtr^.procLevel;
IF levelDifference > 0 THEN
  putStringAndVal('    MOV CX,', levelDifference);
  genLabel(levelLoop); putLabel(levelLoop);
  putLine('    MOV BX, [BX]');
  putStrings('    LOOP ', levelLoop)
END;
```

The object-code instructions that follow the LOOP instruction push the contents of BX on to the stack, making this the first word of the context part of the new activation record.

Figure 13.4(a) outlines an example in which a procedure whose body is at block level 2 calls another procedure whose body is at block level 2. In this example levelDifference = 1 because the called procedure's idTable record is at block level 1, and therefore the instruction case MOV BX, [BX] is executed exactly once. This assigns to BX the contents of the word whose address was in BX, and BX is assigned to the static link of the new activation record. Thus the new activation record is given the same static link as the immediately previous activation record. This is correct because both the calling and the called procedures must be textually enclosed within the same outer procedure.

Figure 13.4(b) outlines an example in which a procedure whose body is at block level 1 calls a procedure whose body is at block level 2. The called procedure's idTable record has procLevel = 1, so levelDifference = 0. In this case MOV BX, [BX] is not executed at all. The new static link is the address, obtained from BP, of the first word of the context part of the activation record for the calling invocation.

In the detailed example given in Section 13.6.5, when swap is called by scan, levelDifference = 2, as in Figure 13.4(c), and accordingly MOV BX, [BX] is executed twice. When swap is called, BP = 1038 which is the address of the first word of the context part of the last activation record for scan in Table 13.3. Thus before MOV BX, [BX] is executed for the first time, BX = 1038. After the first execution of this instruction, BX = 1022, which is the address of the first word of the context part of the last activation

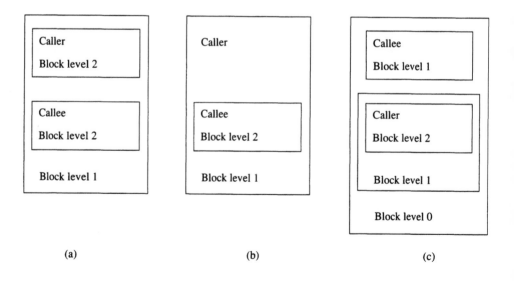

(a)   (b)   (c)

Figure 13.4 Textual relationships between caller (i.e. calling) and callee (i.e. called) procedure.

record for `bubbleSort`. After the second execution of `MOV BX, [BX]`, BX = 500, which is the address of the first word of the static block. This will be the static link for `swap`, and this is correct because `swap` should not be able to access variables in activation records at level 2 or for other procedures at level 1.

Procedure `call` is included in module `callRet` in the Appendix. After dealing with actual parameters and assigning to BX the static link for the new activation record, procedure `call` ends by outputting the intruction sequence

```
MOV SI, SP
INC SI      ; makes SI point to first word of context part
PUSH BX     ; pushes static link into context part
PUSH BP     ; pushes dynamic link into context part
MOV BP, SI; BP:= address of first word of context part
CALL proPtr^.beginLabel
```

Just before the first of these instructions is executed, SP points to the last word of the last actual parameter pushed onto the stack. The last of these instructions is the CALL that calls the procedure and pushes its return address into the third word of the context part of the newly created activation record. For the new invocation SP is initialized by the first SAL instruction in the called procedure, as we shall see in Section 13.10.

13.9.4 RETURN statements

A RETURN statement can occur anywhere within a procedure, and there may be more than one RETURN statement within the same procedure, just as there may be more than one EXIT statement within a LOOP. When starting to compile a LOOP statement, procedure `loopStatement` pushes on to the `loopStack` the label to be jumped to in order to execute an EXIT from the loop. After compiling the statement sequence within the loop, procedure `loopStatement` pops this label off the `loopStack`.

Similarly, the procedure that compiles a procedure body calls `pushRetStack` to push on to a stack, called the `retStack`, information to be used by procedure `returnStatement` for compiling RETURN statements. After compiling the statement sequence in the procedure body, this information is popped off the `retStack` by calling `popRetStack`. We implemented the `loopStack` in an array because this is very easy to understand. We implement the `retStack` in a linked list because this relieves us of having to know at compile time the maximum number of elements that the stack can contain. More specifically, `retStack` is a pointer to the top record in a stack of records that is a linked list of records of type

```
retStackRec = RECORD
                  paramLength, returnType: CARDINAL;
                  isaFunction, anyReturn: BOOLEAN;
                  next: retStackRecPtr
              END;
```

`paramLength` is the total number of words occupied by the procedure's parameters. If the procedure is a function then `isaFunction = TRUE`, otherwise `isaFunction = FALSE`. For a function procedure, `returnType` is the type of the value returned by the function, and `anyReturn` is used by the compiler to check that the function declaration includes at least one RETURN statement. `anyReturn` is initialized to FALSE before starting to compile the statement sequence in the function body, and is set to TRUE by any RETURN statement within this statement sequence. IF `anyReturn` is not TRUE at the end of the statement sequence then the compiler reports an error. For a proper (i.e. non-function) procedure, the `returnType` and `anyReturn` fields are not used.

For a function procedure, procedure `returnStatement` calls procedure `expression` to produce code to push the value of the expression on to the run-time stack. If there is no type incompatibility, procedure `returnStatement` obtains from the `idTable` the length of this type and outputs code to copy the value from the top of the stack to the area that has been reserved for the return of this value by the function, allowing for the possibility that `length > 1`.

We arrange that at run time, immediatedly after the return from a function, the value returned by the function is on the top of the stack. This is why we reserve for the returned value `length` words before the first word reserved for the function's first parameter. For example for function procedure `pr` in Section 13.6.2 we reserved `relAddresses` -6 and -5 for the returned REAL value. A RETURN statement in `pr` will call `expression` to push onto the run-time stack the REAL value that is to be returned. The two words of this REAL will have `relAddresses` 6 and 7, which follow the `relAddress` of the last local variable `b` in Table 13.1.

Procedure `returnStatement` must output code to copy the result of `expression` into the words reserved for returning the result of the function. Thus, for our example, procedure `returnStatement` must generate a loop to pop the top value off the stack into the word whose address is `BP - (paramLength + 1)`, and then pop the next value off the stack into the word whose address is `BP - paramLength`:

```
      MOV CX, length    ; length of result type
      MOV SI, BP
    SUB SI, paramLength + 1
ZAAH:   POP [SI]
      DEC SI
    LOOP ZAAH
```

Here ZAAH is a specific example of a value of `labelString` variable `furet` in procedure `returnStatement` which is included in module `callRet` in the Appendix. For function procedure `pr` (see Section 13.6.2) the total number of words for parameters is `paramLength = 4`. The first iteration of the loop pops the second word of the returned value into the word that has `relAddress` -5, and the second iteration pops the first word of the returned value into the word that has `relAddress` -6.

Procedure `returnStatement` ends by producing code to deal with return from a procedure:

```
      MOV SP, BP
```

```
SUB SP, paramLength + 1
MOV BX, [BP + 2]    ; BX:= return address
MOV BP, [BP + 1]    ; BP:= dynamic link
JMP [BX]            ; jump to return address
```

If the procedure is a not a function procedure, then the first two of these instructions make SP point to the last temporary variable, or if there are no temporary variables then the last local variable, of the previous activation record. If the procedure is a function then these two instructions make SP point to the last word of the value returned by the function. Thus SP := BP - 5 for our example procedure pr.

13.10 The main module

Before commencment of execution of the main module, proMain, the first pass has already been completed. Module proMain administers the second pass and produces object code conforming to the following skeleton:

```
LEA BP, ZAAA
LEA SP, STACKBASE
JMP ZAAB;    (* ZAAB is progStart label *)
ZAAA: DW moduleVarLength DUP  (* static block *)
    The object-code instructions for all procedures come here;
ZAAB: The object-code instructions for body of module come here;
    CALL ENDPROG
STACKBASE: DW stackSize DUP (* run-time stack *)
```

The static block starts at label ZAAA, and is followed by object code for the subroutines that implement all of the module's procedures, as in the example in Section 13.2.1. The first object-code instruction for the module body is labelled ZAAB, and the first word of the run-time stack is labelled STACKBASE. At the beginning of the skeleton, LEA BP, ZAAA initializes BP to point to the first word of the static block, and LEA SP, STACKBASE initializes SP to point to the first word of the run-time stack. JMP ZAAB is a jump to the first instruction of the module body.

The first symbol that is read from interFile should be moduleSy, and the ind associated with this symbol is copied into moduleInd. After checking the identifier symbol and semicolon at the end of the module heading, procedures are compiled by calling procBody:

```
MODULE proMain;
FROM pritmod IMPORT idRecPtr;
FROM proDecs IMPORT moduleVarLength, procInitialise;
FROM bis IMPORT inSymbol, sy, valueRecord, ind, error, accept, openInterfile,
closeInterFile;
FROM symbols IMPORT symbolType;
```

```
FROM InOut IMPORT WriteString, WriteLn, WriteCard;
FROM prSAL IMPORT labelString, genLabel, putLabel, putLine, putStrings,
  putStringAndVal;
FROM callRet IMPORT blockLevel, pushRetStack, popRetStack, noReturn,
  returnStatement;
FROM prStmnt IMPORT stmntSequence;
CONST
  stackSize = 100;
VAR
  moduleInd: CARDINAL;  progStart: labelString;

PROCEDURE  procBody;
VAR
  procedureInd, varWords, paramLength: CARDINAL;
  procPtr, resultType: idRecPtr;
  startLabel: labelString; itsaFunction: BOOLEAN;
BEGIN
  inSymbol;  procedureInd:= ind;
  procInitialise (ind, procPtr, startLabel, varWords,
                  paramLength, resultType, itsaFunction);
  inSymbol; (* end of procedure heading *)
  INC (blockLevel);
  WHILE sy = procedureSy DO procBody END;
  pushRetStack(paramLength, resultType, itsaFunction);
  accept(beginSy); putLabel(startLabel);
  putStringAndVal('    ADD SP,', varWords);
  stmntSequence; accept(endSy);
  IF (sy # idSy) OR (ind # procedureInd) THEN error(52) END;
  IF itsaFunction THEN
    putLine('    MOV AX, 998');
    putLine('    PUSH AX');
    putLine('    CALL INTWRITE');
    putLine('    CALL ENDPROG');
    IF noReturn() THEN error(51) END
  ELSE returnStatement
  END;
  popRetStack; DEC(blockLevel);
  procPtr^.beingCompiled:= FALSE;
  inSymbol; accept(semiColonSy)
END procBody;

BEGIN
  openInterfile;
  putLine('    LEA BP, ZAAA');
  putLine('    LEA SP, STACKBASE');
```

```
    genLabel(progStart);
    putStrings('     JMP ',progStart);
    WriteString('ZAAA:   DW '); WriteCard(moduleVarLength,5);
    WriteString(' DUP '); WriteLn;
    inSymbol; accept(moduleSy);  moduleInd:= ind;
    blockLevel:= 0;
    accept(idSy); accept(semiColonSy);
    WHILE sy = procedureSy DO procBody END;
    accept(beginSy); putLabel(progStart); putline('      NOP');
    stmntSequence; accept(endSy);
    IF (sy # idSy) OR (ind # moduleInd) THEN error(52) END;
    inSymbol; accept(periodSy);
    putLine('    CALL ENDPROG ');
    WriteString('STACKBASE:  DW '); WriteCard(stackSize,5);
    WriteString(' DUP'); WriteLn;
    closeInterFile
END proMain.
```

After the last procedure body, the next symbol obtained from `interFile` should be `beginSy` signifying the start of the statement sequence in the body of the source module. The first object-code instruction of this sequence is labelled `progStart`. Procedure `stmntSequence` compiles the statement sequence in the body of the module, and after checking for the period at the end of the module appends the lines

```
    CALL ENDPROG
STACKBASE: DW stackSize DUP
```

to the object-code instruction sequence.

Procedure `procBody` calls `procInitialise` to obtain information from the procedure's record in the `idTable`. This information is the procedure's start label, the total number of words occupied by all its local variables (at the outermost level within the procedure), the total number of words occupied by all its parameters, and the result type if the procedure is a function procedure. After checking `beginSy` at the start of the procedure body, `procBody` outputs an instruction, which is labelled `startLabel`, that makes SP point to the last word of the last local variable of the procedure. A call of procedure `stmntSequence` compiles the statement sequence in the procedure body.

If the procedure is a function procedure then after the object code produced by calling `stmntSequence`, procedure `procBody` appends the instructions

```
    MOV AX, 998
    PUSH AX
    CALL INTWRITE
    CALL ENDPROG
```

that cause the object program to output 998, which is a very primitive error message, and then terminate. These fatal instructions will not be executed if a RETURN statement has been executed. Unless there has been a programming error, a RETURN statement will always be executed within the body of a function procedure. Procedure `procBody` reports a compile-time error if `noReturn` returns FALSE, signifying that the source code for the function does not contain any RETURN statement.

If the source procedure is not a function then, after calling procedure `stmntSequence`, procedure `procBody` calls procedure `returnStatement` to produce object code for procedure return. This code will be executed when no RETURN statement within the procedure body has been executed. The calls of `pushRetStack` and `popRetStack` by `procBody` have been explained in Section 13.9.4.

We now give an example of a complete object-code program produced by our compiler. The source-code program is artificially simple:

```
MODULE test;
CONST
  X = 2;
VAR
  J,Y:  INTEGER;
PROCEDURE pr1(VAR K: INTEGER);
VAR
  X:  INTEGER;
  PROCEDURE pr2 (I: INTEGER): INTEGER;
  BEGIN
      RETURN X + I + J
  END pr2;
  PROCEDURE pr3 (Y: INTEGER): INTEGER;
  BEGIN
    RETURN Y + 199
  END pr3;
BEGIN
  X:= 1;
  K:= pr2(pr3(20));
END pr1;
BEGIN
  J:= X; pr1 (Y);
  WRITENUM (Y)
END test.
```

The complete object code produced by our compiler is as follows:

```
IMPORT INTREAD, INTWRITE, NEWLINE, ENDPROG, REALREAD, REALWRITE, REALNEG,
REALADD, REALSUB, REALMULT, REALDIVIDE, REALEQ, REALNOTEQ, REALLESS,
REALGREATER, REALLESSEQ, REALGREATEQ
     LEA BP, ZAAA
     LEA SP, STACKBASE
     JMP ZAAE
ZAAA: DW    2 DUP ; static block contains global J and Y
```

```
ZAAC:    ADD SP,   3; first instruction of pr2
    MOV CX,   1     ; level difference is 1
    MOV BX, BP      ; BX:= static link from pr2 to pr1
ZAAF:    MOV BX, [BX];BX:= address of first word of context part
    LOOP ZAAF
    ADD BX,   3     ; add relAddress of X local to pr1
    PUSH BX         ; push absolute address of X
    MOV CX,   1     ; X consists of one word
    POP DI
ZAAG:    PUSH [DI]  ; push value of X
    INC DI
    LOOP ZAAG       ; not needed because length = 1
    MOV DI,65535    ; DI:= CARDINAL(-1)
    ADD DI, BP      ; DI:= address of parameter I
    PUSH DI
    MOV CX,   1     ; I consists of one word
    POP DI
ZAAH:    PUSH [DI]  ; push value of I
    INC DI
    LOOP ZAAH       ; not needed because length = 1
    POP  AX
    MOV DI, SP
    ADD  [DI], AX   ; stack top:= X + I
    LEA DI,ZAAA
    ADD DI,   0     ; DI:= address of global J
    PUSH DI         ; push address
    MOV CX,   1     ; one word
    POP DI
ZAAI:    PUSH [DI]  ; push value of J
    INC DI
    LOOP ZAAI       ; not needed because length = 1
    POP  AX
    MOV DI, SP
    ADD  [DI], AX   ; stack top:= X + I + J
    MOV CX,   1     ; result has length = 1
    MOV SI, BP
    SUB SI,   2
ZAAJ:    POP [SI]   ; copy result to result word
    DEC SI
    LOOP ZAAJ       ; not needed because length = 1
    MOV SP, BP
    SUB SP,   2     ; makes SP point to result word
    MOV BX, [BP + 2]; BX:= return address
    MOV BP, [BP + 1]; BP:= dynamic link
```

```
        JMP [BX]        ; return from pr2
        MOV AX, 998     ; fail if no return
        PUSH AX
        CALL INTWRITE
        CALL ENDPROG    ; fatal failure
ZAAD:   ADD SP,  3 ; first instruction of pr3
        MOV DI,65535    ; DI:= CARDINAL(-1)
        ADD DI, BP
        PUSH DI         ; push address of value parameter Y
        MOV CX,  1      ; Y has length = 1
        POP DI
ZAAK:   PUSH [DI]       ; push value of Y
        INC DI
        LOOP ZAAK       ; unnecessary
        MOV AX, 199
        PUSH AX         ; push 199
        POP  AX
        MOV DI, SP
        ADD  [DI], AX   ; stack top:= Y + 199
        MOV CX,  1      ; result has length = 1
        MOV SI, BP
        SUB SI,   2
ZAAL:   POP [SI]        ; copy result to result word
        DEC SI
        LOOP ZAAL       ; unnecessary
        MOV SP, BP
        SUB SP,  2      ; makes SP point to result word
        MOV BX, [BP + 2]; BX:= return address
        MOV BP, [BP + 1]; BP:= dynamic link
        JMP [BX]        ; return from pr3
        MOV AX, 998     ; fail if no return
        PUSH AX
        CALL INTWRITE
        CALL ENDPROG    ; fatal failure
ZAAB:   ADD SP,  4 ; first instruction of pr1
        MOV DI,   3
        ADD DI, BP      ; DI:= address of local X
        PUSH DI         ; push address
        MOV AX,   1
        PUSH AX         ; push 1
        MOV CX,  1      ; length = 1
        MOV SI, SP
        SUB SI,   1     ; SI points to lhs address
        MOV DI, [SI]
```

```
       ADD DI,   0      ; unnecessary when length = 1
ZAAM:     POP [DI]      ; X:= 1
       DEC DI
       LOOP  ZAAM       ; unnecessary
       DEC SP
       MOV DI,65535     ; DI:= CARDINAL(-1)
       PUSH [BP][DI]    ; push actual address parameter
       ADD SP,   1      ; reserve word for value returned by pr2
       ADD SP,   1      ; reserve word for value returned by pr3
       MOV AX,   20
       PUSH AX          ; push value parameter of pr3
       MOV BX, BP       ; BX:= static link
       MOV SI, SP
       INC SI           ; SI:= address of first word of context part
       PUSH BX          ; places static link in context part
       PUSH BP          ; places dynamic link in context part
       MOV BP, SI       ; BP points to first word of context part
       CALL ZAAD        ; subroutine call for pr3
       MOV BX, BP       ; BX:= static link for pr2
       MOV SI, SP
       INC SI
       PUSH BX          ; push static link
       PUSH BP          ; push dynamic link for pr2
       MOV BP, SI       ; BP points to first word of context part
       CALL ZAAC        ; subroutine call for pr2
       MOV CX,   1      ; function result has length = 1
       MOV SI, SP
       SUB SI,   1      ; makes SI point to word containing lhs address
       MOV DI, [SI]     ; DI:= address K
       ADD DI,   0      ; unnecessary
ZAAN:     POP [DI]      ; K:= function pr2 result
       DEC DI
       LOOP  ZAAN       ; unnecessary
       DEC SP           ; discard lhs address
       MOV SP, BP
       SUB SP,   2      ; SP points at word below parameter
       MOV BX, [BP + 2]; BX:= pr1 return address
       MOV BP, [BP + 1]: BP:= dynamic link
       JMP [BX]         ; return from pr1
ZAAE:     LEA DI,ZAAA; first instruction in module body
       ADD DI,   0
       PUSH DI          ; push address of global J
       MOV AX,   2
       PUSH AX          ; push global constant X
```

```
        MOV CX,   1    ; length = 1
        MOV SI, SP
        SUB SI,   1    ; makes SI point to lhs address
        MOV DI, [SI]   ; DI:= lhs address
        ADD DI,   0
ZAAO:   POP [DI]       ; J:= X
        DEC DI
        LOOP  ZAAO     ; unnecessary
        DEC SP
        LEA DI,ZAAA
        ADD DI,   1
        PUSH DI        ; push address of global Y
        MOV BX, BP     ; BX:= new static link
        MOV SI, SP
        INC SI         ; SI:= address of first word of context part
        PUSH BX        ; place static link in context part
        PUSH BP        ; place dynamic link
        MOV BP, SI     ; reinitialize BP
        CALL ZAAB      ; call subroutine for pr1
        LEA DI,ZAAA
        ADD DI,   1    ; push address of global Y
        PUSH DI        ; push address of global Y
        MOV CX,   1    ; Y has length = 1
        POP DI
ZAAP:   PUSH [DI]      ; push value of Y
        INC DI
        LOOP ZAAP      ; unnecessary
        CALL INTWRITE  ; write Y
        CALL ENDPROG
STACKBASE: DW    100 DUP
```

As in previous examples, the object program contains many unnecessary instructions, and we will return to this in Chapter 16.

13.11 Discussion

For introductory simplicity our compiler does not check the syntax of statement sequences during the first pass, and this is satisfactory so long as a procedure identifier has not been erroneously omitted from after the END at the end of the procedure's statement sequence. To detect such errors it would be better to check the syntax of statement sequences during the first pass. The second pass could inherit a parse tree, instead of a simple sequence of symbols, from the first pass.

Our compiler allocates activation records on the run-time stack without checking that sufficient memory is available. To check that the stack will not overflow, we need to know the numbers of words for the returned value (if any), the parameters, the context part, the local variables, and the maximum number of words of the run-time stack that will be required for expression evaluation within the procedure. Brinch Hansen (1985) shows how a compiler can calculate at compile time the maximum number of words that will be required for an activation record. This enables the object program to check whether a procedure call would make the stack run out of space.

When a deeply nested procedure accesses a variable in an outer procedure at a substantially lower block level, our compiler will spend considerable time traversing a chain of successive static links. Instead of using static links, an alternative approach is to maintain at run time a one-dimensional array, traditionally called the *display*, which contains a pointer to the most recently pushed-on activation record for each block level. A variable in an enclosing procedure can be accessed after a single access to the display instead of following a succession of static links. Further details of this version of the run-time model are given in Aho *et al.* (1986), Terry (1986) and Watt (1993).

Our compiler does not impose any specific limit on the depth of textual nesting of procedures, the depth of recursion, or the length of a chain in which one procedure calls another which calls another and so on, although overall memory constraints are inevitable. In Chapter 11 we compiled control structures such as WHILE and IF–THEN that could contain further control structures nested to any depth, except that our use of an array in the implementation of the LOOP stack imposed a limitation on the depth of nesting of LOOP statements. Practical compilers may have limitations of this kind, for example on the depth to which arrays and records can contain nested arrays and records, the depth of recursion, and the length of a chain in which one module imports from another that imports from another, and so on (Pronk 1992).

13.12 Exercises

1. This exercise is concerned with the following artificially simple program:

```
MODULE ex1;
CONST
  x = 10;
TYPE
  rec = RECORD
               x: INTEGER; y: REAL
          END;
VAR
  y: INTEGER; w: REAL;

PROCEDURE p1 (VAR z: rec; w: INTEGER);
VAR
  x: INTEGER;
  PROCEDURE p11 (VAR x: REAL; y: REAL);
```

```
CONST
  e = 0.1;
VAR
  z: REAL;
BEGIN
  z:= y; x:= z - e
END p11;

PROCEDURE p12 (z: rec; VAR x: INTEGER);
BEGIN
  x:= z.x + y
END p12;

BEGIN (* body of p1 *)
  z.x:= w; p11(z.y, 2.2); p12(z, x)
END p1;

BEGIN
  y:= x; p1(w,y)
END ex1.
```

(a) Show the contents of all records in the identifier table while the body of procedure p12 is being compiled.

(b) Assuming that the stack starts at address 1000, show the contents of all activation records on the stack immediately before the address of x is pushed on to the stack at the start of execution of the assignment statement in procedure p12. Indicate the contents of each word in each activation record. For example, the contents of at least one word will be *return address* . Another example is that there will be a word containing *local variable* x. For each actual parameter you are to indicate whether it is an address or a value by writing, for example, *formal parameter z: actual parameter is address of w.* Indicate what each static link points to and what each dynamic link points to.

(c) Describe in detail the use of static links in accessing y from within the body of procedure p12.

2. For each of the following three programs show the contents of all activation records on the stack immediately before the third invocation of factorial:

(a)
```
MODULE ex2a;
CONST
  c = 4;
VAR
  result: INTEGER;

PROCEDURE factorial(n: INTEGER): INTEGER;
BEGIN
  IF n = 1 THEN RETURN 1 ELSE RETURN n * factorial(n - 1) END
```

```
     END factorial;

     BEGIN
       result:= factorial(c)
     END ex2a.
```

(b)
```
     MODULE ex2b;
     CONST
       c = 4;
     VAR
       result: INTEGER;

     PROCEDURE factorial(n: INTEGER; VAR nfac: INTEGER);
     VAR
       local: INTEGER;
     BEGIN
       IF n = 1 THEN nfac:= 1 ELSE
         factorial(n - 1, local); nfac:= n * local
       END
     END factorial;

     BEGIN
       factorial(c,result)
     END ex2b.
```

(c)
```
     MODULE ex2c;
     CONST
       c = 4;
     VAR
       result: INTEGER;

     PROCEDURE factorial (n, s: INTEGER; VAR r: INTEGER);
     BEGIN
       IF n = 1 THEN r:= s ELSE factorial (n - 1, s * n, r) END
     END factorial;

     BEGIN
       factorial(c, 1, result)
     END ex2c.
```

3. For a FOR statement that has syntax

```
ForStatement -> FOR variable:= expression TO expression DO
                     StatementSequence END
```

(a) Write a code skeleton.

(b) Write a procedure that will compile a FOR statement and include this procedure in module `prStmnt`.

The final value of the control variable is to be held in a temporary variable that is a word on the run-time stack. This word is to be reserved by INC SP near the start of the assembly language routine, and is to be deallocated by DEC SP near the end of this routine. For a FOR statement at block level 0 the address of this word is to be STACKBASE + m, and for FOR statements at higher block levels the address of this word is to be BP + 3 + varWords + m, where m = 0,1,2, ... for successively nested FOR statements. The compiler is to allow any depth of nesting of FOR statements within a procedure, and is also to allow a statement sequence in a FOR statement to call a procedure that may contain further FOR statements, and so on to any depth.

4. Develop the compiler so as to allow open array parameters as in Modula-2.
5. Develop the compiler so that after a procedure has been compiled the records for its internally declared identifiers are removed from the identifier table and their memory area is deallocated so as to be reusable for other purposes. (All such records are linked by `nextSeq` pointers, and this facilitates garbage collection.)

CHAPTER 14

Modules

14.1 Introduction

Separate compilation of modules, with strong type checking of imported identifiers, is an extremely important feature of Modula-2. This is a major advance beyond a language such as SAL which does not distinguish between different types of imports and exports. The present chapter considers the processing of exported and imported identifiers during separate compilation, and also introduces a slight development to the Chapter 5 linker to allow the compiler to use the same label sequence ZAAB, ZAAC, in the separate compilation of each module. The Chapter 4 assembler does not have to be changed at all.

The lexical analyzer and compiler modules `pritmod`, `bis`, `callRet`, `prStment` and `prExprsn` do not require any development: they already contain whatever is needed for purposes of the present chapter. The declaration module `proDecs` is replaced by a new module `moDecs` that is designed to cope, for example, with compilation of a procedure heading in a definition module and compilation of the procedure body in the corresponding implementation module. We start by considering procedure declarations because these can be understood without further discussion of import and export mechanisms.

14.2 Procedure declarations

14.2.1 Compiling declarations in a definition module

In Chapter 13 the declaration module administered the first pass, but this is not the case in the present chapter. Sections 14.3 and 14.4 introduce a new module, `frstPass`, that administers the first pass and deals with imports and exports. To compile the declarations within a definition module, the new module calls the following procedure:

```
PROCEDURE defModuleDecs (exported: BOOLEAN; VAR words: CARDINAL);
BEGIN
  LOOP
    IF sy = constSy THEN constDecs
```

```
        ELSIF sy = typeSy THEN typeDecs
        ELSIF sy = varSy THEN varDecs(words)
        ELSIF sy = procedureSy THEN procTag (exported)
        ELSE EXIT
        END
    END
END defModuleDecs;
```

This is similar to the first part of procedure `block` in Section 13.4 except that procedure `defModuleDecs` calls a new procedure `procTag` to compile the heading of a procedure whose body should be in the implementation module. As will be explained, procedure `defModuleDecs` is called to compile a definition module from which identifiers are imported and also to compile a definition module from which identifiers are exported. In these two cases the parameter `exported` is FALSE and TRUE, respectively.

As in Chapter 13, the main work of compiling a procedure heading is done by `procHeading`. Procedure `procTag` does some housekeeping before and after a call of `procHeading`:

```
PROCEDURE procTag (exported: BOOLEAN);
VAR
    procPtr: idRecPtr;  procInd: CARDINAL;
BEGIN
    inSymbol;
    IF sy # idSy THEN error (203) ELSE
        checkDuplicateIdentifier(ind)
    END;
    procInd:= ind; enterIdRecord(procInd, procPtr);
    INC(blockLevel); pushProc(procPtr);
    procPtr^.beingCompiled:= TRUE;
    procHeading(procInd, procPtr);
    DEC(blockLevel); popProc;
    IF exported THEN
        procPtr^.nextProc:= exportedProcListPtr;
        exportedProcListPtr:= procPtr
    END
END procTag;
```

Before calling procedure `procHeading`, procedure `procTag` takes preliminary steps similar to those in procedure `proceDec` in Section 13.4. While compiling an implementation module, the compiler will need to check whether a procedure's heading has been included in the corresponding definition module. For this purpose, and also to enable the compiler to check that for every procedure heading in the definition module there is a matching procedure declaration in the implementation module, if `exported` = TRUE then procedure `procTag` ends by entering the procedure's `idTable` record into a linked list that will include the records for all procedures declared in the definition module. This list is pointed to by a variable `exportedProcListPtr` that is global to the new version of the declaration module.

14.2.2 Procedure declarations in an implementation module

As in Section 13.4, procedure `block` controls the compilation of the declarations within an implementation module: procedure `block` is unchanged. To compile procedure declarations procedure `block` calls a new version of procedure `proceDec` in the new declaration module `moDecs`:

```
PROCEDURE proceDec;
VAR
  procPtr: idRecPtr; procInd: CARDINAL;
  newProc: BOOLEAN;
BEGIN
  outSymbol; inSymbol; outSymbol; (* procedureSy and ind *)
  IF blockLevel > 0 THEN
    IF sy # idSy THEN error (33) ELSE
      checkDuplicateIdentifier(ind)
    END;
    procInd:= ind; enterIdRecord(procInd, procPtr);
    INC(blockLevel); pushProc(procPtr);
    procPtr^.beingCompiled:= TRUE;
    procHeading(procInd, procPtr)
  ELSE
    checkInd(procInd, newProc, procPtr);
    IF newProc THEN enterIdRecord(procInd, procPtr) END;
    INC(blockLevel); pushProc(procPtr);
    procPtr^.beingCompiled:= TRUE;
    IF newProc THEN procHeading(procInd, procPtr)
    ELSE checkHeading(procInd, procPtr)
    END
  END;
  procPtr^.varLength:= 3;
  block(procPtr^.varLength, procInd);
  procPtr^.beingCompiled:= FALSE;
  DEC(blockLevel); popProc; accept(semiColonSy)
END proceDec;
```

IF `blockLevel > 0` then the procedure is not at the outermost level and cannot be included in the definition module: in this case the steps taken by `proceDec` are the same as in the version of this procedure in Section 13.4. If `blockLevel = 0` then `proceDec` calls a new procedure `checkInd` that linearly searches the linked list pointed to by `exportedProcListPtr` looking for a record that has the procedure's `procInd`. If this search is successful, `checkInd` returns `newProc = FALSE` to signify that this is not a new procedure in the sense that its heading was included in the definition module. In this case `checkInd` returns via `procPtr` a pointer to the identifier table record for the procedure identifier.

If the procedure was not included in the definition module, `proceDec` calls `procHeading` to compile the procedure heading, as in Section 13.4. Otherwise procedure `proceDec` calls a new procedure `checkHeading` which checks the work that was done by `procHeading` when it was called by `procTag`. Procedure `checkHeading` parallels `procHeading` so closely that a detailed explanation is unnecessary: a listing of procedure `checkHeading` in module `moDecs` is given in the Appendix. The last part of procedure `proceDec` is the same as in Section 13.4.

If procedure `checkInd` finds a procedure's identifier table record it removes it from the list pointed to by `exportedProcListPtr`. At the end of the first pass the compiler calls procedure `checkAllExportedProcsImplemented` to check that `exportedProcListPtr = NIL` signifying that all procedures in the definition module are matched by procedures in the implementation module. Detailed listings are included in module `moDecs` in the Appendix, which also exports the trivial procedure:

```
PROCEDURE enclosedByGlobalProc (ptr: idRecPtr);
BEGIN
  ptr^.enclosedBy:= globalPtr
END enclosedByGlobalProc;
```

Within module `moDecs`, `globalPtr` is a global variable that is a pointer to the `idTable` record for the pseudo-procedure that encloses global identifiers.

14.3 Exported and imported labels

14.3.1 Two-dimensional labels

In our system each module has its own separate static block that contains all variables which the module exports and also all variables which are private within the module at block level 0. For each variable in the static block, the module's identifier table has a record containing the `relAddress` of the variable and the `baseLabel` of the module's static block. If the module exports one or more variables, the `baseLabel` is included in the export list in the module's SAL object code. Moreover, for each procedure that is included in the definition module, and is therefore an exported procedure, the `beginLabel` is included in the export list in the module's SAL object code.

From any module the exported labels `beginLabel` for procedures and `baseLabel` for variables belong to the sequence ZAAA, ZAAB, ... that we have adopted in previous chapters. The linker that was introduced in Chapter 5 would be confused because this sequence is the same for all modules, so a label such as ZAAC could be exported by more than one module. To resolve this ambiguity we develop the linker and provide it with the identity of the module from which each label is imported.

From an IMPORT statement in the source program the compiler identifies the module whence an imported label comes. Our system automatically changes the first of the four letters of an imported label to indicate the exporting module. For example, while compiling a module M1 that imports from two other modules M2 and M3, the labels imported from M2 are changed by the compiler so as to belong to AAAA, AAAB, AAAC, . . . , and labels imported from M3 are changed by the compiler so as to belong to BAAA, BAAB, BAAC, ... In effect, each label is now two-dimensional: the first letter signifies the module to which the label belongs, and the remaining three letters identify the label within that module.

If module M3 imports from M2, then labels imported from M2 could, for example, be changed by the compiler to belong to AAAA, AAAB, AAAC, . . . while compiling M3. This illustrates the general fact that labels exported from a single module may have their first letter changed differently while different importing modules are being compiled. Obviously a sequence such as AAAA, AAAB, AAAC, . . . could not be reserved exclusively for exports from a single module such as M2 because this would imply that for each module that could ever be written the system would assign a unique first letter to its labels: this is unrealistic because only the 25 letters A, B, . . . , Y are available. Our compiler always uses the letter Z for a module's internal labels, as in Chapter 13 and previously.

While compiling a module our compiler makes a list of identifiers of other modules from which there are imports. For the first of these modules the compiler assigns 'A' to be the first letter of all imported labels, for the second the compiler assigns 'B' and so on. For use by the linker, the compiler outputs a table showing the identifiers of these modules and the letters that have been assigned to them. This table is actually output as a sequence of comment lines in the SAL assembly language object code. These are ignored by the assembler and are subsequently read by the linker. This information enables the linker to fill in external references correctly despite the fact that for a module's internal labels the compiler uses the same sequence ZAAB, ZAAC, ZAAD, . . . for every module.

The following is an artificially simple example of a three-module source program:

```
DEFINITION MODULE ham;
CONST
  c = 221;
VAR
  x: INTEGER;
PROCEDURE copyProc(i: INTEGER; VAR j: INTEGER);
END ham.


IMPLEMENTATION MODULE ham;
PROCEDURE copyProc(i: INTEGER; VAR j: INTEGER);
BEGIN
  j:= i
END copyProc;


BEGIN
END ham.


DEFINITION MODULE jam;
VAR
```

```
  y: INTEGER;
PROCEDURE addOne(i: INTEGER): INTEGER;
END jam.


IMPLEMENTATION MODULE jam;
FROM ham IMPORT c, copyProc;
VAR
  p: INTEGER;
PROCEDURE addOne(i: INTEGER): INTEGER;
BEGIN
  RETURN i + 1;
END addOne;
BEGIN
  p:= c; copyProc(p,y)
END jam.


MODULE main;
FROM jam IMPORT addOne, y;
FROM ham IMPORT x, copyProc;
VAR
  p: INTEGER;
BEGIN
  x:= addOne(y); copyProc(x,p); WRITENUM(p)
END main.
```

Our compiler puts in the first line of the object code a semicolon, which makes the assembler ignore this line, followed by the name of the module, which is useful to the linker. In the next comment line there is the letter S for an implementation module or M for a main module. This is followed by the number of modules from which this module imports. For module ham in our example the SAL object code is as follows:

```
  ; ham
EXPORT ZAAA, ZAAB
IMPORT INTREAD, INTWRITE, NEWLINE, ENDPROG, REALREAD, REALWRITE, REALNEG,
REALADD, REALSUB, REALMULT, REALDIVIDE, REALEQ, REALNOTEQ, REALLESS,
REALGREATER, REALLESSEQ, REALGREATEQ
  ; S    0
    LEA BP, ZAAA
    JMP ZAAC
ZAAA:  DW    1 DUP
ZAAB:    ADD SP,   3
    MOV DI,65535
    PUSH [BP][DI]
    MOV DI,65534
    ADD DI, BP
```

```
        PUSH DI
        MOV CX,   1
        POP DI
ZAAD:   PUSH [DI]
        INC DI
        LOOP ZAAD
        MOV CX,   1
        MOV SI, SP
        SUB SI,   1
        MOV DI, [SI]
        ADD DI,   0
ZAAE:   POP [DI]
        DEC DI
        LOOP  ZAAE
        DEC SP
        MOV SP, BP
        SUB SP,   3
        MOV BX, [BP + 2]
        MOV BP, [BP + 1]
        JMP [BX]
ZAAC:   NOP
```

In this the line

```
    ; S    0
```

signifies that this is an implementation module that imports from no other module. The line

```
EXPORT ZAAA, ZAAB
```

tells the assembler that ZAAA and ZAAB are exported labels. The line labelled ZAAA reserves the static block for module ham, which consists of one word for the integer x. ZAAA is exported because x is exported. The body of module ham is empty, and correspondingly the object code for the body, which starts at ZAAC, consists of a single NOP instruction. The beginLabel of procedure copyProc is ZAAB, which is exported because copyProc is exported. The cardinals 65535 and 65534, respectively, represent the integers -1 and -2 which are the relAddresses of parameters i and j in an activation record for copyProc. For module jam the SAL object code is as follows:

```
    ; jam
EXPORT ZAAA, ZAAB
IMPORT INTREAD, INTWRITE, NEWLINE, ENDPROG, REALREAD, REALWRITE, REALNEG,
REALADD, REALSUB, REALMULT, REALDIVIDE, REALEQ, REALNOTEQ, REALLESS,
REALGREATER, REALLESSEQ, REALGREATEQ, AAAB
    ; S    1
```

```
    ; ham                    ;A
        LEA BP, ZAAA
        JMP ZAAC
ZAAA:   DW      2 DUP
ZAAB:   ADD SP,   3
        MOV DI,65535
        ADD DI, BP
        PUSH DI
        MOV CX,   1
        POP DI
ZAAD:   PUSH [DI]
        INC DI
        LOOP ZAAD
        MOV AX,   1
        PUSH AX
        POP  AX
        MOV DI, SP
        ADD  [DI], AX
        MOV CX,   1
        MOV SI, BP
        SUB SI,   2
ZAAE:   POP [SI]
        DEC SI
        LOOP ZAAE
        MOV SP, BP
        SUB SP,   2
        MOV BX, [BP + 2]
        MOV BP, [BP + 1]
        JMP [BX]
        MOV AX, 998
        PUSH AX
        CALL INTWRITE
        CALL ENDPROG
ZAAC:   LEA DI,ZAAA
        ADD DI,   1
        PUSH DI
        MOV AX,   221
        PUSH AX
        MOV CX,   1
        MOV SI, SP
        SUB SI,   1
        MOV DI, [SI]
        ADD DI,   0
ZAAF:   POP [DI]
```

```
        DEC DI
        LOOP  ZAAF
        DEC SP
        LEA DI,ZAAA
        ADD DI,   1
        PUSH DI
        MOV CX,   1
        POP DI
ZAAG:       PUSH [DI]
        INC DI
        LOOP ZAAG
        LEA DI, ZAAA
        ADD DI,   0
        PUSH DI
        MOV BX, BP
        MOV SI, SP
        INC SI
        PUSH BX
        PUSH BP
        MOV BP, SI
        CALL AAAB
        NOP
```

ZAAA is exported because module jam exports a variable. ZAAB is exported because this is the beginLabel of procedure addOne that is exported by jam. The list of imported labels includes AAAB, which means label ZAAB is in the module associated with letter A. The line

```
; S    1
```

signifies that module jam is an implementation module that imports from one other module. This line is followed by a table, which in this example consists of only one line, showing for each module from which module jam imports, the letter assigned by the compiler. In this example the line

```
; ham                    ;A
```

signifies that jam imports from ham and that the compiler changes the first letter of all labels imported from ham to A. Label AAAB is included in the IMPORT list of module jam because ZAAB is the beginLabel of copyProc that is exported by ham and imported by jam.

In module jam the line labelled ZAAA reserves the static block that will contain the two integer variables y and p. ZAAB is the beginLabel of procedure addOne in module jam, and ZAAC labels the start of the instruction sequence for the module body. The fourth instruction of the module body has immediate operand 221, which is the value of the constant c exported by ham. Only the value of a constant is exported, and no label is associated with it. The penultimate instruction of the module body is CALL AAAB, which calls copyProc in module ham.

The SAL object code for module main is as follows:

```
; main
IMPORT INTREAD, INTWRITE, NEWLINE, ENDPROG, REALREAD, REALWRITE, REALNEG,
REALADD, REALSUB, REALMULT, REALDIVIDE, REALEQ, REALNOTEQ, REALLESS,
REALGREATER, REALLESSEQ, REALGREATEQ, AAAA, AAAB, BAAA, BAAB
   ;  M    2
   ; jam                     ;A
   ; ham                     ;B
     LEA BP, ZAAA
     JMP ZAAB
ZAAA:  DW     1 DUP
ZAAB:    LEA DI,BAAA
     ADD DI,   0
     PUSH DI
     ADD SP,    1
     LEA DI,AAAA
     ADD DI,   0
     PUSH DI
     MOV CX,   1
     POP DI
ZAAC:    PUSH [DI]
     INC DI
     LOOP ZAAC
     MOV BX, BP
     MOV SI, SP
     INC SI
     PUSH BX
     PUSH BP
     MOV BP, SI
     CALL AAAB
     MOV CX,   1
     MOV SI, SP
     SUB SI,   1
     MOV DI, [SI]
     ADD DI,   0
ZAAD:    POP [DI]
     DEC DI
     LOOP  ZAAD
     DEC SP
     LEA DI,BAAA
     ADD DI,   0
```

```
        PUSH DI
        MOV CX,    1
        POP DI
ZAAE:      PUSH [DI]
        INC DI
        LOOP ZAAE
        LEA DI,ZAAA
        ADD DI,    0
        PUSH DI
        MOV BX, BP
        MOV SI, SP
        INC SI
        PUSH BX
        PUSH BP
        MOV BP, SI
        CALL BAAB
        LEA DI,ZAAA
        ADD DI,    0
        PUSH DI
        MOV CX,    1
        POP DI
ZAAF:      PUSH [DI]
        INC DI
        LOOP ZAAF
        CALL INTWRITE
        NOP
        CALL ENDPROG
```

There is no EXPORT statement because the main module does not export any labels. The IMPORT list includes AAAA, AAAB, BAAA and BAAB. The M in the next line signifies that this is a main module, not an implementation module, and the 2 signifies that this module imports from two other modules. The following two lines constitute a table showing the names of the modules from which labels are imported, and also showing the letter assigned by the compiler to each of these modules. In this example the compiler has assigned letter A to jam, whereas for module jam letter A was assigned to ham. In the sixth instruction before the one labelled ZAAF, module main calls procedure copyProc in ham by CALL BAAB, wheras the body of jam called the same procedure by CALL AAAB.

In the body of jam the address of the second parameter of copyProc is the address of ZAAA, which is the start of the static block of jam, plus relative address 0, because y is the first word of the static block. In the main module the address of the same variable in the fifth and fourth instructions before ZAAC, which is dereferenced to yield the actual parameter of addOne, is the address of AAAA plus relative address 0. In AAAA the first letter has been changed from Z to A by the compiler because A is the letter associated with jam, whose static block contains y.

14.3.2 Making a list of modules from which there are imports

As will be explained in Section 14.4, the new module `frstPass` calls a procedure `imports` to deal with a clause such as `FROM moduleName IMPORT id`. Procedure `imports` obtains from the lexical analyzer the textual name, as well as the `ind` of the name, of a module from which there are imports. Procedure `imports` calls a further procedure `moduleList` to enter this name and `ind` into a list of records of type `nameRec` =

```
RECORD
   name: stringType; (* module's name *)
   modInd: CARDINAL; (* module's ind  *)
   letter: CHAR; (* will be first letter of all labels imported from module *)
   anyVariable: BOOLEAN; (* TRUE only if any variable imported from module *)
   next: nameRecPtr
END;
```

This list, which is pointed to by global variable `moduleListHead`, has one record for each module from which there are imports. Modula-2 allows more than one `FROM moduleName IMPORT` clause importing from the same module. If procedure `moduleList` finds that the list is empty or that a module's `ind` is greater than `moduleListHead^.modInd,` which is the `ind` of the most recently inserted record, then this module cannot already have a record in the list, and a new record is created, with field `letter = currentLetter`. `currentLetter`, which is a global variable of type `CHAR` in module `frstPass`, is the letter that the compiler associates with the next imported module that has not previously been encountered. After assigning `currentLetter` to the `letter` field of a module's record, procedure `moduleList` calls `INC(currentLetter)` in preparation for the next module (if any). This is how our compiler associates successive letters with successive modules from which there are imports.

If procedure `moduleList` is called to deal with the name of a module from which there have previously been imports, it linearly searches the linked list pointed to by `moduleListHead` and returns a pointer to the module's record.

14.4 Compiling imports and exports

14.4.1 Administering the first pass

The first pass is administered by the body of module `frstPass`. As in Chapter 13, the declaration module `modDecs` has a global pointer variable `globalPtr` pointing to a record that is pointed to by identifier table records for global variables. For reasons explained in Section 14.4.5, module `frstPass` has a global pointer variable `defModuleProcPtr` which is used for a similar purpose, and the body of module `frstPass` starts by creating and initializing a record pointed to by `defModuleProcPtr`.

```
BEGIN
  newIdRecord(defModuleProcPtr);
  WITH defModuleProcPtr^ DO
    itsClass:= aProcedure; internalLevel:= 0;
    beingCompiled:= TRUE; itsInd:= 255
  END;
  currentLetter:= 'A'; moduleListHead:= NIL;
  numberOfImportModules:= 0;
  initialiseIdTable; openInterfile; inSymbol;
  IF sy = implementationSy THEN (* this is an implementation module *)
    impModule:= TRUE; inSymbol
  ELSE impModule:= FALSE
  END; outSymbol; (* MODULE symbol *)
  accept(moduleSy); outSymbol; moduleInd:= ind;
  WriteString(' ; '); outputName; WriteLn;
    (* outputs name of module as a comment in SAL *)
  accept(idSy); outSymbol; (* semicolon *)
  IF sy # semiColonSy THEN error(222) END;
  moduleVarLength:= 0;
  IF impModule THEN exports(moduleInd, moduleVarLength) END;
  standardImports; inSymbol;
  WHILE sy = fromSy DO imports END; WriteLn;
  putRefTable;
  block(moduleVarLength, moduleInd);
  checkAllExportedProcsImplemented;
  closeInterFile; accept(periodSy)
END frstPass.
```

If the module being compiled is an implementation module then procedure `exports` is called to compile the definition module and to output the export table into the SAL object code as in the examples in Section 14.3.1. We will consider procedure `exports` in Section 14.4.4.

For each `FROM` clause the body of `frstPass` calls procedure `imports` to deal with imports, and we will return to this in Section 14.4.5. Procedure `putRefTable` outputs, in the form of a comment as in the examples in Section 14.3.1, a table showing the letter that the compiler has associated with each module from which there are imports, as can be seen in examples in Section 14.3.1. Procedure `block` compiles all of the module's declarations, as in Section 13.4, and procedure `checkAllExportedProcsImplemented` checks that all procedures headings in the definition module are matched in the implementation module.

14.4.2 Switching to and from definition module files

Until the compiler has read `IMPLEMENTATION` at the beginning of an implementation module file, it does not know that the file contains an implementation module. We have seen in Section 14.4.1 that for an implementation module the compiler calls procedure `exports` to compile the corresponding definition module. This requires suspending the reading of the implementation module file, then reading the definition module file, and then resuming the reading of the implementation module file. Similarly, to deal with `FROM moduleName IMPORT` the compiler has to suspend the reading of the current file, read a definition module file, and then resume the reading of the current file.

Before calling procedure `defModule` to compile a definition module, our compiler calls procedure `toDefModule` which opens the definition module file and calls procedure `switchStreamTo` (in module `scanner`) to stack information that can subsequently be used to restore reading from the current file. When procedure `defModule` has finished compiling a definition module it calls procedure `restoreStream` in module `scanner` to resume reading from the file that was most recently interrupted.

14.4.3 Compiling a definition module

To compile a definition module, procedure `defModule` starts by checking the syntax of the heading and then calls `imports` to deal with imports. The declarations in the definition module are compiled by procedure `defModuleDecs` which was introduced in Section 14.2.1:

```
PROCEDURE defModule (moduleInd: CARDINAL; exported: BOOLEAN;  VAR words: CARDINAL);
VAR
  i,j: CARDINAL;
BEGIN
  inSymbol; IF sy # definitionSy THEN error(200) END;
  inSymbol; IF sy # moduleSy THEN error (200) END;
  inSymbol; IF ind # moduleInd THEN error (201) END;
  accept(idSy); accept(semiColonSy);
  WHILE sy = fromSy DO imports END;
  defModuleDecs(exported, words);
  accept(endSy); IF ind # moduleInd THEN error(202) END;
  accept(idSy); accept(periodSy); restoreStream
END defModule;
```

Procedure `defModule` ends by checking the syntax of the end of the definition module, and calling `restoreStream` to resume reading from a previous file.

14.4.4 Exports

We saw in Section 14.4.1 that the body of module `frstPass` calls a procedure `exports` to compile the definition module that is associated with the current implementation module. Procedure `exports` calls `defModule` to enter a record into the identifier table for each identifier declared in the definition module. For any procedure included in the definition module, the `beginLabel` must be included in an `EXPORT` list at the beginning of the assembly language object program. Furthermore, if the definition module includes any variable, then the `baseLabel` of the module's static block must be included in the `EXPORT` list. For example, at the beginning of module `jam` in Section 14.3.1 there is `EXPORT ZAAA, ZAAB`.

Identifier table records created as a result of calling `defModule` are in a list linked by `nextSeq` pointers which are included in the `idRec` record type declaration in Section 13.3.2. Successive records are linked into this list by procedure `newIdRecord` in module `pritmod`. (We have previously used `nextSeq` pointers only for linking the parameters of procedures.) Before the call of `defModule`, `tail` points to the identifier table record that was most recently inserted. Procedure `exports` is as follows:

```
PROCEDURE exports(moduleInd: CARDINAL; VAR words: CARDINAL);
VAR
   startPtr, currentPtr: idRecPtr; anyVariable: BOOLEAN;
   numberOfExports, length: CARDINAL;
   moduleName: stringType;

   PROCEDURE writeLabel(label: labelString);
   BEGIN
     INC(numberOfExports);
     IF numberOfExports = 1 THEN WriteString('EXPORT ')
     ELSE WriteString(', ')
     END; WriteString(label);
   END writeLabel;

BEGIN (* body of exports *)
   startPtr:= tail;  numberOfExports:= 0; anyVariable:= FALSE;
   nameIs(moduleName, length); (* moduleName:= textual name of module *)
   toDefModule(moduleName, length); (* length = number of chars in name *)
   defModule(moduleInd, TRUE, words);
   IF tail = startPtr THEN RETURN (* no exports *) END;
   currentPtr:= startPtr;
   REPEAT
     currentPtr:= currentPtr^.nextSeq;
     CASE currentPtr^.itsClass OF
     aVariable: IF NOT anyVariable THEN
                   anyVariable:= TRUE; writeLabel ('ZAAA')
                END |
     aProcedure:     writeLabel(currentPtr^.beginLabel)
     ELSE (* do nothing *)
     END
   UNTIL currentPtr = tail;
   IF numberOfExports > 0 THEN WriteLn END
END exports;
```

Starting at the first identifier table record created by procedure `defModule`, the REPEAT loop traverses the list of all such records. When it finds a record for a procedure it outputs the procedure's `beginLabel` in the EXPORT list. When it finds a record for a variable it ensures that `'ZAAA'`, which is the base label of the module's static block, is output exactly once in the EXPORT list. The BOOLEAN variable `anyVariable` is used for preventing the base label being output more than once in the same EXPORT list. If a definition module contains only constant and type declarations, there is no need for an EXPORT statement in the object code, because no labels are exported.

As will be seen in Section 14.5.1, the base label of the static block of every module is always `'ZAAA'`, even if the static block is empty. As a result of calling `defModule`, procedures included in the definition module have `beginLabels` `'ZAAB'`, `'ZAAC'`, ... Suppose, for example, that the last of these `beginLabels` is `'ZAAD'`. In this case after the return from `defModule`, while compiling the implementation module, successive labels will be `'ZAAE'`, `'ZAAF'`, ..., simply continuing the same sequence.

After the first pass of compiling an implementation module and its associated definition module, the identifier table contains a record for every identifier that has been declared either in the definition module or in the implementation module. Identifier table records for identifiers in the definition module have the same block level, i.e. zero, as global identifiers in the implementation module.

14.4.5 Imports

Procedure `imports`, which is called to compile a FROM `moduleName` IMPORT clause, has three effects:

(a) For every imported identifier a record is inserted into the identifier table of the importing module.

(b) For every anonymous type required in support of (a) a record is inserted into the identifier table of the importing module.

(c) For every imported procedure the `beginLabel` is appended to the IMPORT list in the SAL object program, and if at least one variable is imported from an exporting module then the `baseLabel` of the exporting module's static block is also appended to the IMPORT list in the SAL object program. For example, labels AAAA, AAAB, BAAA and BAAB are appended to the IMPORT list at the head of the SAL program for module `main` in Section 14.3.1. As explained in Section 14.3.1, each imported label has had its first letter changed to indicate the module whence it comes.

Effect (b) requires explanation. Suppose, for example, that the definition module of module M1 declares a variable `threeArray` to be of the three-dimensional array type `threeDArrayType`, and that module M2 includes FROM M1 IMPORT `threeArray`. Suppose that `threeDArrayType` is not included in the list of identifiers imported into M2 from M1. Module M2 will not be able to access elements of array `threeArray` unless M2's identifier table contains one record for each dimension of `threeDArrayType`. An example of effect (b) is that procedure `import` creates three identifier table records for threeDArrayType as anonymous records in M2's identifier table, and makes M2's identifier table record for threeArray point to the first of these three threeDArrayType records.

Similarly, if M2 imports a record type identifier from M1, then effect (b) creates identifier table records for every one of the record's fields: otherwise M2 would be unable to access fields of the variables of the imported record type. Yet another example is that if M2 imports a procedure from M1 then effect (b) gives M2 an identifier table record for every parameter of the procedure.

To achieve effects (a) and (b), procedure imports calls procedure defModule to create an identifier table record for every identifier declared in the exporting definition module, and subsequently removes from the table every record that is not included in the list in FROM moduleName IMPORT ... and is not required for achieving effect (b). For example, when module jam in Section 14.3.1 is compiled, defModule puts into jam's identifier table all the records for ham's definition module. jam does not import x from ham, and therefore procedure imports deletes the record for x from jam's identifier table.

While compiling a module M2, identifiers that are included in M1's definition module but are not included in a list such as FROM M1 IMPORT ... may legitimately be duplicates of identifiers that are already in M2's identifier table. To prevent legitimate duplicates from being reported as illegal duplicates while declarations in the exporting definition module are compiled by procedure defModuleDecs, procedure imports calls pushProc to push defModuleProcPtr on to the procStack before calling defModule. The effect is that all identifier table records created via defModuleDecs have enclosedBy = defModuleProcPtr, which is a pointer that was initialized for this purpose at the beginning of the body of module frstPass, as we saw in Section 14.4.1. Because all records in the identifier table prior to the call of defModuleDecs have enclosedBy = globalPtr, and during the invocation of defModuleDecs procStack[top] = defModuleProcPtr, procedure checkDuplicateIdentifier (in module pritmod) does not report an illegal duplicate when one of these has an identifier that is the same as an identifier in the definition module being compiled by defModuleDecs.

After the call of defModule, procedure imports calls popProc, which in effect makes procStack[top] = globalPtr, and enters a WHILE loop that is repeated once for each identifier in a list that follows FROM moduleName IMPORT. For each of these identifiers findItsRecord is called to find the record that should have been created in the identifier table as a result of the call of defModule. Procedure checkDuplicateIdentifier reports an error if the identifier is the same as any that was in the identifier table before the call of defModule. Procedure enclosedByGlobalProc simply assigns globalPtr to the enclosedBy field of the record that was found by findItsRecord, which makes this field the same as in records for global variables in the importing module. Procedure mark assigns TRUE to the marked field of every identifier table record that must be preserved in the identifier table in order to achieve effect (b) for the identifier being processed in the current iteration of the WHILE loop in procedure imports. We will say more about procedure mark in Section 14.4.6. Procedure imports is as follows:

```
PROCEDURE imports;
VAR
  words, moduleInd, length: CARDINAL; found: BOOLEAN;
  currentPtr, recPtr, startPtr: idRecPtr;
  moduleName: stringType; modRecPtr: nameRecPtr;
  oldLabel, varLabel: labelString;
BEGIN
  inSymbol; IF sy # idSy THEN error(212); RETURN END;
  newLabelSequence(oldLabel);
  startPtr:= tail; words:= 0; moduleInd:= ind;
  nameIs(moduleName, length); moduleList(moduleInd, moduleName, modRecPtr);
  toDefModule(moduleName, length); pushProc(defModuleProcPtr);
  defModule(moduleInd, FALSE, words); popProc;
  inSymbol; accept(importSy);
  WHILE sy = idSy DO
    findItsRecord(ind, recPtr, found);
    IF NOT found THEN error(214)
    ELSE
      checkDuplicateIdentifier(ind);
      enclosedByGlobalProc (recPtr);
      mark(recPtr, FALSE)
    END;
    inSymbol; IF sy = commaSy THEN inSymbol END
  END;
  accept (semiColonSy);
  IF startPtr # tail THEN
    currentPtr:= startPtr^.nextSeq;
    LOOP
      IF NOT currentPtr^.marked THEN disconnect(currentPtr^.itsInd)
      ELSE
        CASE currentPtr^.itsClass OF
          aProcedure: currentPtr^.beginLabel[0]:= modRecPtr^.letter;
                WriteString(', '); WriteString(currentPtr^.beginLabel); |
          aVariable: currentPtr^.baseLabel[0]:= modRecPtr^.letter;
                modRecPtr^.anyVariable:= TRUE;
                varLabel:= currentPtr^.baseLabel
        ELSE (* do nothing *)
        END
      END;
      currentPtr:= currentPtr^.nextSeq;
      IF currentPtr = tail THEN EXIT END
    END  (* LOOP *)
  END; (* IF *)
  IF modRecPtr^.anyVariable THEN
```

```
     WriteString(', '); WriteString(varLabel)
   END;
   restoreLabelSequence(oldLabel)
 END imports;
```

The LOOP in procedure `imports` traverses the linked list of all identifier table records created as a result of the call of `defModuleDecs` that compiled the imported definition module. If a record has `marked = FALSE` then procedure `disconnect` removes this record from a list linked by `nextSyn` pointers, so the record will not be accessible via the hash table. Otherwise, for a record that has `marked = TRUE`, if this is for a procedure then its `beginLabel` is appended to the list of labels in the IMPORT statement near the beginning of the object-code program. If a record has `marked = TRUE` and is the first record for an imported variable, then the `baseLabel` of the exporting module's static block is appended to the list of labels in the IMPORT statement in the object program. Labels appended to this list have their first letter changed by procedure `imports` to indicate the module whence they are imported.

Our compiler finds out everything that it needs to know about imports by reading the source text of the definition module whence they come. This definition module does not contain the `beginlabels` of procedures. Instead, the compiler works out which `beginLabel` will belong to which imported procedure by using `defModule` in exactly the same way as in the compilation of the exporting module. To make this work correctly, the sequence ZAAB, ZAAC, ... must be started afresh for each module from which there are imports. After dealing with imports from a given module, the label sequence that was reinitialized to deal with this module must be restored to what it was just before reinitialization. The reinitialization is done by calling `newLabelSequence(oldLabel)`, and subsequently the label sequence is restored by calling `restoreLabelSequence(oldLabel)`. These two procedures are module `putSAL`.

For an exported variable, the exporting definition module does not contain the variable's `relAddress`. During compilation of the importing module, the exporting definition module is compiled and `varDecs` gives `relAddress`es to exported variables. We make this work correctly by ensuring that when an implementation module is compiled the `relAddress`es of its global variables start from one beyond the last `relAddress` assigned when the corresponding definition module was compiled. Procedure `block` *adds* to the value of `moduleVarLength` that is returned by procedure `exports`.

14.4.6 Marking records

The first parameter of procedure `mark` points to a record that is to have TRUE assigned to its `marked` field. The second parameter is TRUE if this record is to be anonymous, which means that it is not to be accessible via the hash table, that is, procedure `findItsRecord` is not to be able to find this record given its `ind`. From within a CASE statement, procedure `mark` is called recursively to mark array element type records that cannot be eliminated, record field records that cannot be eliminated, a variable's type record that cannot be eliminated, or a procedure's parameter records that cannot be eliminated:

```
PROCEDURE mark(tabPtr: idRecPtr; anonymous: BOOLEAN);
VAR
  fPtr: idRecPtr; paramPtr: idRecPtr;
  count: CARDINAL;
BEGIN
  IF (tabPtr^.itsClass = aType) AND (tabPtr^.typeKind = aStandardType) THEN
    RETURN
  END;
  IF anonymous AND NOT tabPtr^.marked THEN disconnect(tabPtr^.itsInd); RETURN
  END;
  tabPtr^.marked:= TRUE;
  CASE tabPtr^.itsClass OF
      aType: CASE tabPtr^.typeKind OF
                arrayType:  mark(tabPtr^.elementType,TRUE) |
                recordType: fPtr:= tabPtr^.fieldPtr;
                            WHILE fPtr # NIL DO
                                mark(fPtr^.itsType, TRUE); fPtr:= fPtr^.nextSyn
                            END |
                typeAlias:  mark(tabPtr^.itsType, TRUE)
              END |
      aVariable, aConstant: mark(tabPtr^.itsType, TRUE) |
      aProcedure: paramPtr:= tabPtr^.nextSeq;
                  FOR count:= 1 TO tabPtr^.noOfParams DO
                    mark(paramPtr^.itsType,TRUE); paramPtr:= paramPtr^.nextSeq
                  END
  ELSE error(213)
  END
END mark;
```

14.5 The second pass of the compiler

For an implementation module the skeleton of the object code is as follows:

```
      LEA BP, ZAAA        ; BP:= address of first word of static block
      JMP ZAAH            ; ZAAH is an example of a progStart label
ZAAA: DW moduleVarLength DUP ; static block for this module
      Instructions for module's procedures
ZAAH: Instructions for the body (if any) of the module
      NOP
```

If the body of the module is empty then the instruction that has the `progStart` label is the final NOP. The example object-code programs for `ham` and `jam` in Section 14.3.1 conform to this skeleton. For a main module the skeleton is the same except that CALL ENDPROG is appended after the final NOP.

Individual modules do not have their own individual run-time stack. Instead, after the linking of a multimodule program, the resulting machine code program uses a single run-time stack. It is convenient to put this stack into a separate module that is the first in the sequence of linked modules. As well as containing the memory area for the stack, this module also initializes the stack pointer. For our system the stack module is as follows:

```
    LEA SP, STACKBASE
    JMP CONTINUE
STACKBASE: DW 1000 DUP
CONTINUE: NOP
```

Here 1000 is an example for a small stack. The instruction labelled CONTINUE will be followed by the first instruction of the next module.

In our system the layout of the linked machine code program is as follows:

```
stack module
implementation module
implementation module
       .
       .
implementation module
main module
salSubs module
```

After the instruction labelled CONTINUE in the stack module, the first instruction LEA BP, ZAAA of the next module is executed, and then the instructions for the body of that module are executed. At the end of the instruction sequence for the body of the module, the first instruction LEA BP, ZAAA of the next module follows immediately, and this next module is entered as soon as the body of its predecessor module has been executed. This arrangement is repeated throughout the entire sequence of modules, except that the main module is terminated by CALL ENDPROG. The salSubs module contains INTREAD, INTWRITE, etc.

The main module, moMain, of our compiler is listed in the Appendix and is sufficiently similar to our previous main module proMain that detailed explanation is unnecessary. Differences are due to modification of code skeletons.

14.6 Automatic make

14.6.1 File names

This book avoids doing anything that is specific to any particular operating system, and therefore does not use commands with parameters. This means that we have to work laboriously by copying and/or renaming files. Our simplified compiler obtains its input from a file named `sourceIn`, and the source file has to be copied to `sourceIn` before the compiler program is executed. Whatever the operating system, we can arrange that the output from the compiler goes to a specified named file. Our linker expects to find the SAL assembly language program output from the compiler in a file whose name is the module name with `'.SAL'` appended to it.

The assembler in Chapter 4 takes its input from a file `salAssin`, so a file such as `jam.SAL` has to be copied to `salAssin` before being assembled. The assembler sends its output to a file named `salAsout`. The linker in the present chapter expects the contents of `salAsout` to have been copied to a file whose name is the module name with `'.SBS'`. The suffix `'.SBS'` stands for *SAL binary symbolic*. Copying or renaming files is crude and not nice but can all be done easily by a script in UNIX or a batch file in DOS.

In the present chapter the linker expects to find the source program of the main module in a file named `main.mod`. When this module is compiled the linker expects the compiler output to have been copied to a file named `main.SAL`, and when this is assembled the linker expects the binary symbolic output to be copied into a file named `main.SBS`.

14.6.2 Making a list of modules to be linked

In Section 5.2 the linker module `mcModule` read from a file the names of the modules to be linked and entered their names into a linked list. We now replace module `mcModule` by a new module `mcMake` that automatically builds up a list of files to be linked, instead of merely obtaining this list from a ready-made file. This is possible because source modules declare which other modules they import from. Module `mcMake` builds up the list by reading the comments that have been inserted into assembly language output files by the compiler. To illustrate this the three-module example in Section 14.3.1 is too simple, and instead we use a five-module example in which the names of the compiler output files are `main.SAL`, `alpha.SAL`, `beta.SAL`, `gamma.SAL` and `delta.SAL`. Module `mcMake` only reads the comments from these files, which are as follows:

```
File main.SAL:
    ; main
    ; M   3
    ; alpha ; A
    ; beta  ; B
    ; gamma ; C
```

```
File alpha.SAL:
    ; alpha
    ; S  2
    ; delta ; A
    ; gamma ; B

File beta.SAL:
    ; beta
    ; S 3
    ; gamma  ; A
    ; alpha  ; B
    ; delta  : C

File gamma.SAL
    ; gamma
    ; S 2
    ; alpha  ; A
    ; delta  ; B

File delta.SAL
    ; delta
    ; S 0
```

Module `mcMake` produces a list of files to be linked: we call this list the *module list*. It is a linked list of records of type

```
modRec = RECORD
              moduleName: stringType;
              nameLength, moduleInd, numberOfImportModules: CARDINAL;
              letterIndex: ARRAY['A'..'Y'] OF CARDINAL;
              next: modRecPtr
          END;
```

The fields are the module's name, the number of characters in the name, the module's `ind`, and the number of modules from which this module imports. `letterIndex` shows, for each letter, the `ind` of the module that is associated with this letter by the compiler. When the construction of the module list has been completed, the first entry is for the stack module, and the last is for `salSubs`, because modules are always linked in this order in our system: see Section 14.5.

While building up the module list, module `mcMake` inserts records at the head of the list because this is the simplest arrangement to program. Because `salSubs` will be the last module linked, it is the first whose record is inserted into the module list. Module `mcMake` also uses a second list called the *waiting list*, which contains information about modules whose records have not yet been entered into the module list. The waiting list is initialized to contain a single record which contains information about the main module. Most of the work of building up the module list is done by a procedure `makeRecordForModule` of which a simplified outline is the following:

```
WHILE waiting list is not empty DO
  remove first record from waiting list;
  obtain the module name from this record and append .SAL to it;
  check that the module's name is in the first comment in the .SAL file;
  if the next comment starts with an M this is a main module file which cannot
    export, so report an error;
  create a record for this module at the head of the module list;
  read the next cardinal from the file into variable j;
  FOR i:= 1 TO j DO (* FOR each imported module DO *)
    read a module's name and letter from the .SAL file;
    if there is no record for this module name in the module list or in the
    waiting list then insert a record for it at the head of the waiting list;
  END (* FOR *)
END (* WHILE *)
```

For our five-module example, identifiers `main, alpha, beta, gamma, delta` have inds 1, 2, 3, 4 and 5, respectively. The first iteration of the WHILE loop removes the record for the main module from the waiting list and inserts a record for it at the head of the module list. The record for the main module has `letterIndex['A'] = 2`, `letterIndex['B'] = 3` and `letterIndex['C'] = 4`. For example `letterIndex['B'] = 3` means that when the main module is compiled, all labels imported from the module whose ind = 3 will have their first letter changed to `'B'` by the compiler. Moreover, after the first iteration, the waiting list contains records for `alpha, beta` and `gamma`, as indicated in Table 14.1.

Table 14.1 Contents of module list and waiting list after successive iterations.

Iteration	Module list	Waiting list
1	main	gamma, beta, alpha
2	gamma, main	delta, beta, alpha
3	delta, gamma, main	beta, alpha
4	beta, delta, gamma, main	alpha
5	alpha, beta, delta, gamma, main	empty

After the second iteration of the WHILE loop, a record for module `gamma` has been inserted at the head of the module list. From file `gamma.SAL` mcMake sees that `gamma` imports from `alpha` and `delta`. There is already a record for `alpha` in the waiting list, so nothing more is done about `alpha` at this stage. There is no record for `delta` in either list, so a record for `delta` is created at the head of the waiting list. In the record for `gamma` at the head of the module list, `letterIndex['A'] = 2` because while compiling `gamma` the compiler has associated `'A'` with `alpha`. Moreover, `letterIndex['B'] = 5`, because while compiling module `gamma` the compiler has associated `'B'` with module `delta`.

After the third iteration of the WHILE loop a record for module `delta` has been inserted at the head of the module list, and no new record has been inserted into the waiting list because `delta` does not import. After the fourth iteration of the WHILE loop a record for module `beta` has been inserted at the head of the module list, and no new record has been inserted into the waiting list because for each of the three modules from which `beta` imports there is already a record in one or other of the lists.

14.6.3 The make module

The definition module is as follows:

```
DEFINITION MODULE mcMake;
PROCEDURE mcList;
PROCEDURE startFile(VAR noneLeft: BOOLEAN; VAR modInd: CARDINAL);
PROCEDURE moduleForLetter(ch: CHAR): CARDINAL;
PROCEDURE restart;
END mcMake.
```

Procedure `mcList` calls procedure `makeRecordForModule` repeatedly to construct a list of all modules that are to be linked, and ends by inserting at the head of this list a record for the stack module.

Procedures `startFile` and `restart` are similar to those in Section 5.2: procedure `startFile` makes `currentModPtr` point to the record for the next module in the list of modules that are to be linked. Procedure `startFile` appends `'.SBS'` to the file name in the record pointed to by `currentModPtr` and causes the linker to start reading from this binary symbolic file.

Function `moduleForLetter` looks up a letter in the letter index in the record pointed to by `currentModPtr`, which will be the record corresponding to the module currently being linked, and returns the `ind` of the module that is associated with this letter. For our five-module example, if `moduleForLetter('B')` is called while module `alpha` is being linked, `moduleForLetter` returns 4 because this is the `ind` of module `gamma`, showing that while compiling module `alpha` the compiler has associated letter `'B'` with module `gamma`.

14.7 Linking

14.7.1 Two-dimensional global label table

As in Section 5.3, our linker builds up a global label table during a first pass that reads only header information from binary symbolic files. The linker uses this table to translate addresses during a second pass that achieves relocation and linking. In binary symbolic the exported labels are in the same series ZAAA, ZAAB, ZAAC, ... for every module. If two different modules exported the same label, module `expTable` in Chapter 5 would report an illegal duplicate label. We deal with this by developing the global label table so that it is two-dimensional.

While building up the global label table, the linker knows which module it is currently processing. It uses the `ind` of this module as the first subscript, and uses the `ind` of an exported label as the second subscript, of an entry in the two-dimensional global label table. The module's `ind` is returned via the second parameter of procedure `startFile` in module `mcMake` when the linker starts reading from a module's file. Module `gLabTab` is now used instead of module `expTable` that was introduced in Section 5.3; the ideas are the same, except that `gLabTab` uses a two-dimensional global label table. The definition module is as follows:

```
DEFINITION MODULE gLabTab;
CONST
  relocatingConst = 64;   (* this is just an example *)
PROCEDURE getExports;
PROCEDURE whichAddress(letter: CHAR; labelInd: CARDINAL): CARDINAL;
END gLabTab.
```

An outline of procedure getExports is given below:

```
PROCEDURE getExports;
VAR
  n, relocatingVar: CARDINAL;
BEGIN
  relocatingVar:= relocatingConst; n:= 0;
  FOR each module that is to be linked DO
    open this module's file;
    moduleInd:= this module's ind;
    INC(relocatingVar, n); (* relocatingVAR is relocated address of module's
          first word *)
    read from the module's header the number, n, of words of machine code in
          the module (* for use in initializing the relocating var for the
          next module *);
    FOR each entry in the module's export table DO
      read exported label as a text string;
      enter string into the string table and obtain a unique ind value for the
          label;
      ReadCard(refAddress); (* exported label's non-relocated address *)
      gLabelTable[modulInd, ind]:= refAddress + relocatingVar (* =  relocated
          address *)
    END;
    close this module's file
  END
END getExports;
```

During the second pass of the linker, function procedure whichAddress looks up an imported label's relocated address in the global label table. An imported label has had its letter changed to indicate the module whence it is imported. Function procedure moduleForLetter returns the ind of the module associated with a given letter *for the module that is currently being processed by the linker*. This ind is used as the first subscript of globalLabelTable, and the imported label's ind is used as the second subscript:

```
PROCEDURE whichAddress(letter: CHAR; labelInd: CARDINAL): CARDINAL;
BEGIN
   IF letter = '@' THEN RETURN globalLabelTable[0,labelInd] ELSE
      RETURN  globalLabelTable[moduleForLetter(letter), labelInd]
   END
END whichAddress;
```

Labels in module salSubs are mnemonics such as INTREAD and INTWRITE, which do not belong to ZAAA, ZAAB, ... We do not apply to salSubs the trick of using an initial letter to signify the module, and this means that salSubs has to be treated in a special way. We arrange that when whichAddress is called to return the relocated address of a label imported from salSubs, the first parameter of whichAddress is '@'. Module mcMake has assumed that the module ind of salSubs is 0, and this is why for the call whichAddress('@', labelInd) function procedure whichAddress returns globalLabelTable[0, labelInd].

14.7.2 Translation of imported labels

The main module of the linker is moLink, which is identical to module salLink in Section 5.4 except that it imports from mcMake instead of mcModule and gLabTab instead of expTable, and procedure relocate is slightly modified. In Section 5.4 procedure relocate calls a procedure inText to read an imported label as a text string and look up this string in the string table to find the label's ind. Function procedure whichAddress returns the relocated address of the label that has this ind in the module associated with the first letter of the imported label. In the new version of procedure relocate, the second actual parameter of whichAddress is the imported label's ind after the first letter of the imported label has been changed back to 'Z' to make the label the same as it was when it was exported. Module moLink includes a new version of inText that changes an imported label's first letter back to 'Z' unless the label is imported from salSubs.

To figure out whether an imported label comes from salSubs, the new version of procedure inText uses the fact that every label in salSubs has more than four characters. If a label comes from salSubs procedure inText does not change the first letter to 'Z' but returns the character '@' via a VAR parameter, to be used as the first parameter of the call whichAddress(ch,ind) in procedure relocate.

14.8 Discussion

Modules provide the convenience of separate compilation and the security of encapsulation. In Chapter 13 we saw that scope rules are enforced by disallowing access to appropriate records in the identifier table. In the present chapter we have seen that an identifier that is not included in an exporting module's definition module cannot be included in an importing module's identifier table and therefore cannot be referenced from within the importing module. A definition module provides sufficient information to allow the same strength of type checking for imported identifiers as for a module's internal identifiers.

We have seen that types and constants are imported by creating records in the identifier table of the importing module, without any need for entries in the import table of the module's binary symbolic object code. For variables and procedures the compiler has to place labels in the binary symbolic import table as well as including appropriate records in the identifier table. Instead of using the first letter of an imported label to identify its home module, we could use more than one letter, or we could make imported labels explicitly two-dimensional. Another possibility is that, instead of accessing a two-dimensional global label table at link time, we can fill in external references at execution time (Gough and Mohay 1988), using two-dimensional addresses as in a segmented memory management system (Deitel 1990; Peterson and Silberschatz 1982). We have accessed a two-dimensional global label table by direct addressing because this is maximally simple; memory efficiency can easily be improved by hashing with a combined string table and global label table.

Our linker links modules listed by procedure mcList without performing any check on the times when they were compiled. If a definition module has been edited, the chance of errors can be reduced by insisting that the corresponding implementation module be recompiled before it can export to a further module. If a definition module has been edited it is safer to link a later version of the object code from the corresponding implementation module. This is safer because of the risk that an earlier version may have become obsolete. Restrictions on relative times of compilation can be implemented by means of time stamping (Bron *et al.* 1985).

14.9 Exercises

1. Modify the system so that standard procedures READNUM, WRITENUM and NEWLINE no longer exist and there is now only one standard procedure, which is HALT. HALT is simply a new name for ENDPROG. In the modified system, instead of READNUM there are to be two procedures READINTEGER and READREAL, and instead of WRITENUM there are to be two procedures WRITEINTEGER and WRITEREAL. These four new procedures, and also NEWLINE, are not to be standard procedures, but instead are to be imported from a module SimpleIO. Write a definition module for

SimpleIO and write the implementation module directly in SAL, so that it does not have to be compiled. The SAL program for SimpleIO is to call subroutines in module salSubs.

2. Develop the system so that as well as linking salSubs, the stack module, and binary symbolic modules produced as compiler SAL output, it will also link with these any number of binary symbolic modules produced by assembling programs written directly in SAL.

3. Develop the system so that as well as allowing a list of imported identifiers after the reserved word IMPORT it also allows IMPORT to be followed immediately by a semicolon, in which case imported identifiers are to be qualified by the name of the exporting module. For example, if module M includes

```
FROM N IMPORT;
```

and if module N exports identifiers p, q and r then these are to be referenced in module M with the name of N as a qualifier. Thus p, q and r are to be designated within module M by N.p, N.q and N.r.

CHAPTER 15

Error recovery

15.1 Introduction

Hitherto our compiler has reported errors in the source program but has taken no action to avoid consequent chaos. We will not attempt to make our compiler correct errors automatically, because this would be difficult with recursive descent. But in this chapter we will give our compiler some *error recovery* capability. With this the occurrence of an error may cause some further errors to be missed, but soon the compiler will recover so as to detect and report errors that occur later in the source program. Moreover, we will try to ensure that an error cannot have a devastating effect, such as causing the compiler to be stuck in a loop or to ignore a large part of the source program.

An error may put the sequence of source symbols expected by the compiler out of step with the actual sequence in the source text, which may cause an unhelpful torrent of error messages. In recursive-descent compilers, the usual method of error recovery is *panic mode* error recovery. This means that if the compiler finds that errors have put it out of step, it skips input symbols until it finds one that will probably serve as a starting point for useful continuation of parsing, with the compiler now in step with the source symbol stream. An obvious disadvantage of panic mode recovery is that the compiler fails to report errors that occur among skipped symbols.

If our compiler finds that it is out of step with the source symbol stream it calls procedure `skipTo`, which starts by calling procedure `error` to report the error:

```
PROCEDURE skipTo(sys: symbolSet; n: CARDINAL);
BEGIN
  error(n); WHILE NOT (sy IN sys) DO inSymbol END;
  IF sy = endOfTextSy THEN
    WriteString('Unable to recover from error'); WriteLn; HALT
  END
END skipTo;
```

Type `symbolSet` is SET OF `symbolType`, and `symbolType` is declared in lexical analyzer module `symbols`.

Before we have made any provision for error recovery, an outline of the recursive-descent procedure corresponding to the production whose left-hand side is the non-terminal symbol N is as follows:

```
PROCEDURE N;
BEGIN
  appropriateStatements
END N;
```

270

If `sy` is not in FIRST(N) when procedure N is called, the compiler is out of step, and there is no point in attempting to execute `appropriateStatements`. In this case it may be possible to recover by calling `skipTo` to ensure that `sy` is in FIRST(N) before commencing execution of `appropriateStatements`:

```
PROCEDURE N;
BEGIN
  IF NOT (sy IN FIRST(N)) THEN skipTo(FIRST(N), 100) END;
  appropriateStatements;
  IF NOT (sy in FOLLOW(N)) THEN skipTo(FOLLOW(N), 101) END
END N;
```

Similarly, if `sy` is not in FOLLOW(N) after `appropriateStatements`, then `skipTo` is called to attempt recovery so that the procedure that called procedure N may be able to continue usefully.

These ideas require development. If a symbol in FIRST(N) is not found where one is expected, and if the next symbol in FIRST(N) occurs very much later in the source symbol stream, then all the intervening symbols will be skipped, and this may mean that an excessively large part of the program is missed. A remedy is to skip to a symbol in the union of the sets FIRST(N), FOLLOW(N) and

```
synchSys:= symbolSet {constSy, typeSy, varSy, procedureSy, beginSy, ifSy,
         whileSy, repeatSy, loopSy, exitSy, returnSy, endOfTextSy};
```

`synchSys` is a set of major synchronizing symbols: if one of these it is reached it is best to stop skipping, so as to avoid skipping too far. Moreover, `synchSys` consists of symbols from which resumption of parsing may be straightforward. With this development, we have

```
PROCEDURE N;
BEGIN
  IF NOT (sy IN FIRST(N)) THEN skipTo(FIRST(N) + FOLLOW(N) + synchSys, 100);
    IF NOT(sy in FIRST(N)) THEN RETURN (* no point in continuing *) END
  END;
  appropriateStatements;
  IF NOT (sy in FOLLOW(N)) THEN skipTo(FOLLOW(N) + synchSys, 101) END
END N;
```

Instead of skipping to FOLLOW(N) we can take account of the context of non-terminal N. To do this we give procedure N a parameter:

```
PROCEDURE N (followSys: symbolSet);
BEGIN
  IF NOT (sy IN FIRST(N)) THEN skipTo(FIRST(N) + followSys, 100);
    IF NOT(sy IN FIRST(N)) THEN RETURN (* no point in continuing *) END
  END;
  appropriateStatements;
```

```
    IF NOT (sy in followSys)) THEN skipTo(followSys, 101) END
END N;
```

For example, procedure A that corresponds to

```
A -> MNP
```

calls N (FIRST(P) + synchSys) . Procedure B that corresponds to

```
B -> HNK
```

calls N (FIRST(K) + synchSys) .

To achieve satisfactory error recovery it is not necessary to check synchronization at the beginning and end of every recursive-descent procedure. Synchronization may be checked only at the beginning of some procedures, only at the end of others, and in some not at all. Instead of being placed only at beginning and end of procedures, synchronization checks are in some cases most usefully placed at other strategic points, as in examples given below, which are derived from the P4 Pascal compiler (Pemberton and Daniels 1986). Moreover, a set of symbols to be skipped to may be determined to some extent by the compiler writer's judgement, based on experience, rather than being determined rigidly by syntactic rules.

15.2 Recovery from errors during the first pass

For error recovery we insert synchronization checks at the beginning and end of procedure constant:

```
PROCEDURE constant(VAR ofType: idRecPtr; VAR card1, card2:CARDINAL; followSys:
symbolSet);
VAR
   recPtr: idRecPtr; negative, found: BOOLEAN;
BEGIN
  IF NOT (sy IN symbolSet{plussOp, minusOp, numberSy, idSy}) THEN
      skipTo(followSys + symbolSet{plussOp, minusOp, numberSy, idSy}, 301);
      IF NOT (sy IN symbolSet{plussOp, minusOp, numberSy, idSy}) THEN RETURN END
  END;
  IF sy = plussOp THEN inSymbol; negative:= FALSE
  ELSIF sy = minusOp THEN
     negative:= TRUE; inSymbol
  ELSE negative:= FALSE END;
  IF sy = numberSy THEN
      ofType:= stIndex[valueRecord.valType];
      card1:= valueRecord.val1; card2:= valueRecord.val2;
  ELSIF sy = idSy THEN
      findItsRecord(ind,recPtr,found);
```

```
          IF found THEN WITH recPtr^ DO
              IF itsClass = aConstant THEN
                  ofType:= itsType; card1:= c1; card2:= c2
              ELSE found:= FALSE END
          END END;
          IF NOT found THEN error(11) END;
      ELSE error(12) END;
      IF negative THEN
          IF ofType = tyReal THEN  makeNegative(card1,card2)
          ELSIF ofType = tyInteger THEN card1:= CARDINAL(-INTEGER(card1))
          ELSE error(12)
          END
      END;
      inSymbol;
      IF NOT (sy IN followSys) THEN skipTo (followSys, 302) END
  END constant;
```

There is a synchronization check at the beginning of procedure `constDecs` and also at the end of the WHILE loop, but not at the end of the procedure:

```
PROCEDURE constDecs;
VAR
   consType, idTabPtr: idRecPtr;
   card1, card2: CARDINAL;
BEGIN
   inSymbol;
   IF sy # idSy THEN skipTo(synchSys + symbolSet{idSy}, 303) END;
   WHILE sy = idSy DO
      checkDuplicateIdentifier(ind);
      enterIdRecord(ind, idTabPtr);
      inSymbol; accept(equOp);
      constant(consType, card1, card2, synchSys + symbolSet{semiColonSy});
      WITH idTabPtr^ DO
         itsClass:= aConstant; itsType:= consType;
         c1:= card1; c2:= card2
      END;
      accept(semiColonSy);
      IF NOT (sy IN synchSys + symbolSet{idSy}) THEN
         skipTo(synchSys + symbolSet{idSy},304)
      END
   END
END constDecs;
```

This calls procedure `constant` with fourth actual parameter `synchSys + symbolSet(semiColonSy)` because in constant declarations a semicolon is expected to follow a constant.

In Section 12.4.5 procedure `arrayDec` could be stuck in the REPEAT loop if OF is absent or misspelt. The following version avoids this:

```
PROCEDURE arrayDec(arrayRecordPtr: idRecPtr);
VAR
  v2, firstBound, secondBound, noOfDimensions, count: CARDINAL;
  lowerBoundType, upperBoundType, arrayElementType,
  currentPtr, previousPtr, recPtr: idRecPtr;
  found, lastDimension: BOOLEAN;
BEGIN
  inSymbol; accept(openSqBrktSy);
  noOfDimensions:= 0; lastDimension:= FALSE;
  REPEAT
    INC(noOfDimensions);
    constant(lowerBoundType, firstBound, v2, synchSys + symbolSet{dotDotSy,
    closeSqrBrktSy, ofSy, semiColonSy} ); accept(dotDotSy);
    constant(upperBoundType, secondBound, v2, synchSys + symbolSet{closeSqrBrktSy,
    ofSy, commaSy, semiColonSy});
    IF INTEGER(firstBound) > INTEGER(secondBound) THEN error(41) END;
    accept(closeSqrBrktSy);
    IF sy = ofSy THEN
      lastDimension:= TRUE; inSymbol; typeRecord(recPtr);
    ELSIF sy = commaSy THEN inSymbol; accept(openSqBrktSy)
    ELSE error(321); RETURN
    END;
    IF (lowerBoundType = upperBoundType) AND
      ((lowerBoundType = tyBoolean) OR (lowerBoundType = tyInteger)) THEN
      WITH arrayRecordPtr^ DO
        itsClass:= arrayType; indexType:= lowerBoundType;
        lowBound:= INTEGER(firstBound); upBound:= INTEGER(secondBound);
        IF lastDimension THEN elementType:= recPtr ELSE
          previousPtr:= arrayRecordPtr;
          newIdRecord(arrayRecordPtr); elementType:= arrayRecordPtr;
          arrayRecordPtr^.nextSyn:= previousPtr
        END
      END
    ELSE error(18)
    END
  UNTIL lastDimension;
  currentPtr:= arrayRecordPtr;
  FOR count:= 1 TO noOfDimensions DO
    WITH currentPtr^ DO
      itsLength:= elementType^.itsLength * CARDINAL(upBound - lowBound + 1);
    END; currentPtr:= currentPtr^.nextSyn
  END   (* FOR *)
END arrayDec;
```

This provides two further examples of calls of procedure constant. For the first call the fourth actual parameter includes symbolSet{dotDotSy, closeSqrBrktSy, ofSy, semiColonSy}: a lower bound should be followed by dotDotSy but if something is wrong it would be better not to skip beyond ']', OF, or ';'. For the second call of constant the fourth actual parameter includes symbolSet {closeSqrBrktSy, ofSy, commaSy, semiColonSy}, omitting dotDotSy because '..' is not expected to follow the upper bound of an array. commaSy is included because a comma should follow the square bracket that follows the upper bound of a dimension that is not the last dimension of an array. For both of the calls of procedure constant in procedure arrayDec the fourth actual parameter is different to that for the call in procedure constDecs.

Although procedure arrayDec does not include any synchronization check, it is called by procedure typeDecs or procedure typeRecord, which do include checks. The checks in procedure typeDecs are analogous to those in procedures constDecs and varDecs:

```
PROCEDURE varDecs(VAR nextAddress: CARDINAL);
VAR
   currentPtr: listRecPtr; thisType, idTabPtr: idRecPtr;
   varInd: CARDINAL;
BEGIN
   inSymbol;
   IF sy # idSy THEN skipTo(synchSys + symbolSet{idSy}, 311) END;
   WHILE sy = idSy DO
     makeList(currPtr);  typeRecord(thisType);
     WHILE currentPtr # NIL DO
       varInd:= currentPtr^.item;
       checkDuplicateIdentifier(varInd);
       enterIdRecord(varInd, idTabPtr);
       WITH idTabPtr^ DO
         itsInd:= varInd; itsClass:= aVariable; baseLabel:= 'ZAAA';
         relAddress:= nextAddress; itsType:= thisType; itsLevel:= blockLevel
       END;
       INC(nextAddress, thisType^.itsLength); currentPtr:= currentPtr^.next
     END;
     inSymbol; accept(semiColonSy);
     IF NOT (sy IN synchSys + symbolSet{idSy}) THEN
             skipTo(synchSys + symbolSet{idSy}, 312)
     END
   END
END varDecs;
```

Procedure varDecs calls procedure makeList which is an example of a procedure that has a synchronization check only at the end. Procedure makeList makes a list of identifiers separated by commas and terminated by a colon. At the end of procedure makeList we now replace accept(colonSy) by:

```
IF sy = colonSy THEN inSymbol....
ELSE skipTo(synchSys + symbolSet{colonSy, semiColonSy}, 323)
END
```

If the colon is missing the compiler may be out of step with the source symbol stream. Procedure `makeList` calls `skipTo(synchSys + symbolSet{colonSy, semiColonSy}, 323)` instead of `skipTo(symbolSet {colonSy}, 323)` because the next colon might be a great deal further ahead along the source symbol sequence, or might not be found at all, so the rest of the program would be skipped. We have included `semiColonSy` in the union `synchSys + symbolSet{colonSy, semiColonSy}` because a semicolon would be a sensible place to stop skipping if a colon were not found. If a semicolon occurs in the source symbol stream earlier than the next colon then there is an error anyway, and the compiler should try to check the syntax that follows the semicolon.

In Section 13.4 a version of procedure `block` was written without worrying about the effect of possible errors in the source program. In the following source program fragment, a semicolon is missing after the second END:

```
WHILE condition1 DO
 IF condition2 THEN statement1 END
END
a:= b;
furtherStatements;
```

The absence of this semicolon would cause an exit from the second LOOP in procedure `block` and this would have the devastating effect that the remainder of the statement sequence would not be copied to `interFile` and would therefore be missed during the second pass. To prevent this we use a more robust version of procedure `block`:

```
PROCEDURE block (VAR words: CARDINAL; endInd: CARDINAL);
BEGIN
  IF NOT (sy IN symbolSet{constSy, typeSy, varSy, procedureSy, beginSy})
    THEN skipTo(synchSys, 331)
  END;
  LOOP
    IF sy = constSy THEN constDecs
    ELSIF sy = typeSy THEN typeDecs
    ELSIF sy = varSy THEN varDecs(words)
    ELSIF sy = procedureSy THEN proceDec
    ELSE EXIT
    END
  END;
  IF sy = beginSy THEN outSymbol ELSE skipTo(synchSys, 313) END;
  LOOP
    inSymbol; outSymbol;
    IF sy = endSy THEN
```

```
      REPEAT inSymbol; outSymbol UNTIL sy # endSy;
      IF sy = idSy THEN
        IF ind # endInd THEN  error(94); EXIT END;
        inSymbol; outSymbol;
        IF sy IN symbolSet {semiColonSy, periodSy, endOfTextSy} THEN EXIT END;
      ELSIF sy = endOfTextSy THEN error(90); EXIT
      END
    END
  END
END block;
```

15.3 Recovery from errors during the second pass

With the version of procedure stmntSequence in Section 11.1, erroneous omission of a semicolon after a statement in the source code will cause subsequent statements in a sequence to be missed by the compiler. To allow for missing semicolons we now give procedure stmntSequence a parameter that is the set of symbols which may terminate a statement sequence:

```
PROCEDURE stmntSequence(stopSys: symbolSet);
VAR i: CARDINAL;
BEGIN
  LOOP
    statement;
    IF sy = semiColonSy THEN inSymbol
    ELSIF sy IN stopSys THEN EXIT
    ELSE
      skipTo(synchSys + stopSys + symbolSet{semiColonSy, periodSy}, 9);
      IF NOT (sy IN symbolSet{idSy, semiColonSy, whileSy,
          loopSy, exitSy, ifSy, repeatSy, returnSy}) THEN EXIT
      END
    END
  END
END stmntSequence;
```

If there is no error the LOOP is repeated until sy is one of the stopSys; but if there is an error that causes loss of synchronization with the source symbol stream, procedure stmntSequence tries to skip to a symbol that could be the first symbol of a statement or a semicolon which will be ignored by procedure statement. For the various calls of procedure stmntSequence the actual parameter is shown in Table 15.1.

To allow recovery of synchronization during compilation of expressions, we now give procedure factor a second parameter:

Table 15.1 Actual stop symbols for various calls of procedure stmntSequence

Where called	Parameter stopSys
whileStatement	{endSy}
ifStatement (first call)	{elseSy, elsifSy, endSy}
ifStatement (second call)	{elseSy, elsifSy, endSy}
ifStatement (third call)	{endSy}
loopStatement	{endSy}
repeatStatement	{untilSy}
procBody	{endSy}
body of main module	{endSy}

```
PROCEDURE factor(VAR resultType: idRecPtr;  followSys: symbolSet);
BEGIN
  IF NOT (sy IN symbolSet{numberSy, idSy, notOp, openRndBrktSy})
  THEN skipTo(followSys + symbolSet{numberSy, idSy, notOp, openRndBrktSy}, 19)
  END;
  CASE sy OF
  numberSy:  WITH valueRecord DO
                 putStringAndVal('   MOV AX, ', val1);
                 putLine('   PUSH AX');
                 IF valType = 3 THEN (* REAL *)
                   putStringAndVal('   MOV AX, ',val2);
                   putLine('   PUSH AX');
                 END;
                 resultType:= stIndex[valType];
             END;
             inSymbol |
  idSy:      pushValue (resultType) |
  notOp:     inSymbol; factor(resultType, followSys);
             IF globalType # tyBoolean THEN error(20) ELSE
               applyOperator(notOp)
             END |
 openRndBrktSy: inSymbol;
             expression(resultType, followSys + symbolSet{closeRndBrktSy});
             accept(closeRndBrktSy)
  ELSE RETURN
  END;
  IF NOT (sy IN followSys + symbolSet {plussOp..greatEquOp}) THEN
    skipTo(followSys + symbolSet {plussOp..greatEquOp}, 24)
  END;
END factor;
```

Procedure `factor` starts by checking that the current symbol is one that could be the first symbol of a factor, and ends by checking that the current symbol is one that could legitimately follow immediately after a factor. Procedure `factor` is always called as an indirect result of calling procedure `expression`. The actual parameter of `factor` depends upon the call of `expression`, as shown in Table 15.2. We give procedures `expression`, `subExpression` and `term` a second parameter `followSys`. Procedure `expression` always calls procedure `subExpression` which calls procedure `term` which calls procedure `factor` so that all four of these procedures have the same actual parameter `followSys`. Apart from this development, and the consequent amendment to all calls of procedure `expression`, there is no other change in the expession module. Moreover, apart from the change in procedure `stmntSequence` and the introduction of parameters for procedures `expression` and `stmntSequence`, there are no other changes in the statement module. Versions of compiler modules developed to provide error recovery are available on the diskette that accompanies this book, but are not included in the Appendix.

Table 15.2 Actual parameter `followSys` for various calls of procedure `expression`

Where called	Parameter `followSys`
`arrayReference`	`synchSys + symbolSet{commaSy, closeSqrBrktSy}`
`factor`	`followSys + symbolSet{closeRndBrktSy}`
`assignmentStatement`	`synchSys + symbolSet {semiColonSy, endSy,` `untilSy, elseSy, elsifSy}`
`whileStatement`	`synchSys + symbolSet{doSy}`
`ifStatement` (both calls)	`synchSys + symbolSet{thenSy}`
`repeatStatement`	`synchSys + symbolSet{semiColonSy, endSy,` `untilSy}`
`call`	`synchSys + symbolSet {commaSy, closeRndBrktSy}`
`returnStatement`	`synchSys + symbolSet{semiColonSy, endSy,` `untilSy}`

15.4 Discussion

In this chapter we have been concerned only with error recovery without attempting to reduce the number of errors that are reported uninformatively as a consequence of a single error. A simple idea is to restrict the number of errors reported in a single line of the source program, but an obvious disadvantage is that a single line may contain many genuine errors.

An error in a declaration may cause *unknown identifier* errors to be reported later in the program. When procedure `findItsRecord` returns `found = FALSE` the compiler could create an identifier table record for the unexpected identifier, which would have to have a special type, say `tyWrong`, to allow the compiler to recognize that consequent type-checking failures were due to previous errrors and need not be reported again. All of the compiler's type-checking routines would have to be developed to take this on board, thus slowing down the compiler. If, for example, the call of `findItsRecord` in procedure `statement` returned `found = FALSE` there might be an error in the identifier of a variable or of a procedure, and different action would have to be taken in these two cases to avoid unhelpful reporting of consequent errors.

For the table-driven parser in Section 8.2 there were blank entries in the parse table corresponding to syntax errors. For table-driven parsers, whether LL(1) or LR(1), error recovery is normally handled by replacing such blank entries by calls to error recovery routines that are written using specific knowledge of the state of play of the parsing process at the point of occurence of an error (Schreiner and Friedman 1985). This knowledge provides table-driven parsers with scope for repairing errors as well as recovering so as to be able to continue parsing (Backhouse 1979; Tremblay and Sorensen 1985). *Error repair* is a technical term for automatic correction of errors. For example, a successful method of error repair would automatically insert the missing close-bracket in `myarray[6 := 7`.

15.5 Exercises

1. Develop procedure `call` to provide recovery from errors in a procedure call, for example, from errors in parameters.
2. Develop procedures `imports` and `exports` to provide error recovery.
3. Identify and propose a remedy for a problem that arises when definition module `M0` imports from definition module `M1` which imports from definition module `M2` which imports from ... which imports from definition module `Mn` which imports from definition module `M0`.

CHAPTER 16

A brief introduction to compiler optimization

16.1 Introduction

The intended effect of compiler optimization is to streamline object code so that it can be executed faster and preferably with less utilization of memory. The term *optimization* is used in other disciplines, such as mathematics and chemical engineering, to mean attainment of a result that in some sense cannot be improved. In the compiler literature the term *optimization* usually means something more like *improvement* than *perfection*.

Compilers attempt optimization by applying a portfolio of techniques that yield different improvements. In this brief final chapter we indicate some of the improvements that can be made, though their practical implementation is beyond the scope of this book. Much of the detail of compiler optimization is far too complex for an introductory text; moreover, various classical techniques have a starting point different from that of a stack-oriented compiler. For a general introduction to compiler optimization see Aho *et al.* (1986); Fischer and LeBlanc (1988); and Tremblay and Sorensen (1985).

In this book we have compiled directly into an assembly language because this makes it easy for the reader to see what is being achieved. If, instead, the compiler first translates the source program into an intermediate representation (Ottenstein 1984) and subsequently translates from the intermediate representation into object code, this opens up an opportunity for optimizing the intermediate representation, which may be the easiest way to work. For this reason the present chapter will have more to say about the intermediate representation and about overall organization of a compiler.

In earlier chapters we have given examples of compiled code that is flagrantly inefficient. In some cases inefficiency can be removed or reduced by optimization techniques. In many other cases inefficiency can be removed by rewriting the code-producing routines to take account of the specific context instead of being naively general: detailed examples are given in exercises in Section 16.9.

In Chapter 13 we introduced two-pass compiling in which all or part of the source symbol stream was processed symbol by symbol. The main work of optimization usually commences after completion of the second pass and translates an intermediate representation into an improved intermediate representation without being constrained to make a single straightforward pass through the initial intermediate representation. A compiler's work may possibly be completed faster if code generation and optimization are integrated, thus avoiding duplication of housekeeping required when optimization and code generation are separate operations applied in turn to an intermediate representation (Fraser and Wendt 1986).

Optimization is costly in processor time. For this reason some compilers only attempt optimization that cannot be implemented by the source-code programmer. In some compilers optimization can optionally be omitted and in others it is simply not available. It is desirable to be able to control the trade-off between run-time efficiency and processor time spent on optimization.

16.2 Elimination of common subexpressions

One of the aims of optimization is to expurgate unnecessary object code such as that which computes a value that has already been computed. For example, in the expression

```
(x - y * (pi * v/180.0))/(z + pi * v/180.0)
```

the subexpression `pi * v/180` occurs twice. It is better to rewrite the expression as

```
(x - y * t)/(z + t)
```

following the assignment `t:= pi * v/180.0`, where `t` is a temporary variable. Elimination of the common subexpression changes the parse tree shown in Figure 16.1(a) into the *directed acyclic graph* (DAG) shown in Figure 16.1(b), in which the second occurrence of the repeated subexpression has been replaced by an arc pointing to the first occurrence.

Common subexpressions can be local or global (Fischer and LeBlanc 1988). Repetition of subexpressions within the same expression, as in Figure 16.1(a), provides an example of a local common subexpression. Global common subexpressions differ from local ones in that they are separated by program fragments which may or may not assign values to referenced variables, for example:

```
p:= x - y * (pi * v/180.0);
statementSequence;
q:= r - s * (pi * v/180.0);
```

It would be safe to compute `(pi * v/180.0)` just once, instead of twice, only if the compiler could be sure that the values of `pi` and `v` would always be the same in both occurrences of the common subexpression. This can be checked by data-flow analysis (Aho *et al.* 1986; Fischer and LeBlanc 1988). Local common subexpression elimination may be performed on stack-based intermediate code (Bal and Tanenbaum 1986) and even on object code (Davidson and Fraser 1984).

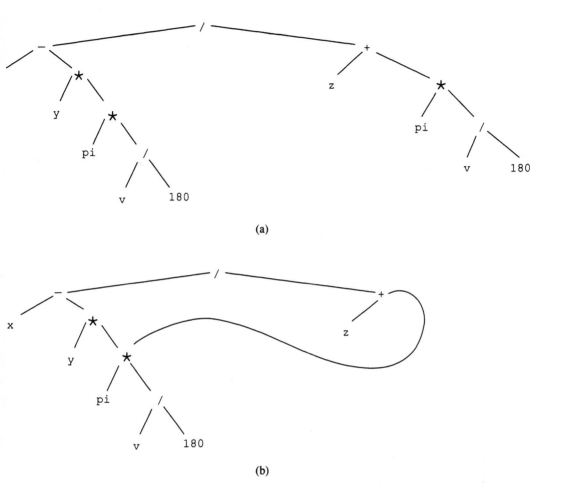

(a)

(b)

Figure 16.1 (a) Parse tree for an expression. (b) DAG for the same expression after elimination of a common subexpression.

16.3 Loop optimization

16.3.1 Frequency reduction

Consider, for example:

```
FOR s:= 10 TO 20 DO w:= s * 3.0 + pi * v/180.0 END;
```

Instead of producing object code that re-evaluates `pi * v/180.0` during each repetition of the loop, it is better to evaluate this subexpression just once before commencement of the loop:

```
t:= pi * v/180.0;
FOR:= 10 TO 20 DO w:=  s * 3.0 + t END;
```

This amendment is an example of *frequency reduction* because it reduces the frequency of evaluation of `pi * v/180.0`. This amendment is satisfactory only if the values of `pi` and `v` remain unchanged during all repetitions of the loop. Another example of frequency reduction, which is also known as *loop invariant code motion*, is that we can amend

```
WHILE sum < p + q * s DO sum:= sum + r END;
```

to

```
m:= p + q * s;   WHILE sum < m DO sum:= sum + r END;
```

after checking that the statement sequence enclosed between DO and END does not change p, q or s.

A more sophisticated example occurs in the following matrix multiplication routine:

```
FOR i:= 1 TO m DO
  FOR j:= 1 TO m DO
    c[i,j]:= a[i,1] * b[1,j];
    FOR k:= 2 TO n DO c[i,j]:= c[i,j] + a[i,k] * b[k,j] END
  END
END
```

There are n assignments to `c[i,j]`, and each of these involves the multiplication that is usual in multidimensional array access. To avoid this repetition of multiplication within the innermost loop, it is more efficient to reorganize the program so as to make just one assignment to each element of the matrix `c`:

```
FOR i:= 1 TO m DO
  FOR j:= 1 TO m DO
    sum:= a[i,1] * b[1,j];
    FOR k:= 2 TO n DO sum:= sum + a[i,k] * b[k,j] END;
    c[i,j]:= sum
  END
END
```

Unless a formidable optimizer is available it is safer for the programmer to implement this within the source code.

The routine

```
FOR i1:= lb1 TO ub1 DO
  FOR i2:= lb2 TO ub2 DO
    FOR i3:= lb3 to ub3 DO array[i1,i2,i3]:= 0 END
  END
END
```

assigns zero to the elements of `array: ARRAY [lb1..ub1], [lb2..ub2], [lb3..ub3] OF CARDINAL`. Corresponding object code uses a one-dimensional array, which we will name `oneDarray`, like this:

```
FOR i1:= lb1 TO ub1 DO
  FOR i2:= lb2 TO ub2 DO
    FOR i3:= lb3 to ub3 DO
       oneDarray[(i3 - lb3) * length3 + (i2-lb2) * length2 + (i3-lb3) * length3]:= 0
    END
  END
END
```

where

```
length3 = 1;
length2 = (ub2-lb2 + 1) * length3;
length1 = (ub2-lb2 + 1) * length2;
```

Preferably this triple loop should be reorganized so that, for example, `(i3 - lb3) * length3 + (i2-lb2) * length2` is not re-evaluated during each iteration of `FOR i3:= lb3 TO ub3 DO..END`.

16.3.2 Loop unrolling

If `p` is small, for example, if `p = 3`, it is better to compile

```
FOR i:= 1 TO 3 DO q[i]:= 0 END
```

into object code equivalent to

```
q[1]:= 0; q[2]:= 0; q[3]:= 0;
```

This may make the object code occupy more memory but execution will be much faster because `i` is not incremented, there is no testing of a condition and no conditional jump. This is an example of *loop unrolling*.

16.4 Pruning unnecessary code

16.4.1 Dead code elimination

Unreachable code, for example code that follows an unconditional jump and is not jumped into, can simply be deleted so as to reduce memory occupied by machine code. For example, in the object-code program at the end of Section 13.10 the four instructions preceding that which is labelled `ZAAB` can be deleted because they will never be executed. Another example is that if the source program and its translations contain the equivalent of

```
IF traceRequired THEN FOR i:= 1 TO n DO WriteCard(contents[i],4) END
```

this can be deleted if there is no doubt at compile time that `traceRequired` = FALSE, for example because `traceRequired` is a constant. Similarly, an optimizer can delete a WHILE loop whose condition will certainly never be TRUE.

16.4.2 Tail merging

For example, in stack-oriented object code for

```
IF condition THEN p(a,b,c) ELSE p(d,e,f) END
```

unnecessary duplication of code associated with a procedure call can be eliminated as follows:

```
IF condition THEN push a, b and c on to stack ELSE push d, e and f on to STACK
END; initialize activation record for call of p; CALL p.
```

Like dead-code elimination, this simply prunes the object-code program but otherwise does not improve efficiency.

16.4.3 Constant propagation

If, for example, an optimizer finds that `pi` is a constant then `t := pi * v/180.0` can be replaced by `t := v * (value of (pi/180.0))`, where the value of `pi/180.0` has been computed at compile time, thus avoiding a division operation at execution time. If `v` is also constant then `t` can be evaluated at compile time and if, for example, the optimizer finds later in the program `u := t + 1.414` then `u` can be evaluated at compile time. After this, `v := u * 3.0` can be evaluated at compile time. These are examples of *constant propagation* (Wegman and Zadeck 1991).

16.4.4 Copy propagation

The idea of copy propagation (see, for example, Bal and Tanenbaum 1986) is that if there is no assignment to x or to y subsequent to `y := x` then an optimizer can eliminate the assignment `y := x` and replace all references to y by references to x. There can be a propagation effect in that if there is no assignment to x, y or z during or after `y := x; statementSequence; z := y` then an optimizer can also eliminate `z := y` and replace all references to z by references to x.

16.5 In-line substitution of procedures

We saw in Chapter 13 that a procedure call incurs the overhead of creating and initializing an activation record, and a return involves updating SP and BP as well as jumping to the return address. These overheads can be avoided by treating a procedure call like a macro, that is, replacing the call by code for the body of the procedure, and making appropriate parameter substitutions. For short procedures called within inner loops it may be worthwhile to use this idea to improve the speed of execution of the object code at the cost of increasing the overall length of the program.

16.6 Register allocation

A machine such as a VAX or an MC68000 has many more CPU registers than an 8086, and run-time efficiency can be improved by making full use of these. For example, instead of using a stack outside the CPU it is faster to compile i + j - g * h into something like

```
register1:= i;
register1:= register1 + j;
register2:= g;
register2:= register2 * h;
register1:= register1 - register2.
```

Moreover, if the source program includes successive assignments that include read-only references to the same variable, as in k:= i; m:= i + 2, then it is preferable to load this variable just once into a register, thus avoiding a *redundant load* (Davidson and Fraser 1984)

Techniques for allocating registers to variables are most easily applied to basic blocks of an intermediate representation. A *basic block* is a sequence of instructions such that it is always true that when any instruction in the block is executed then every instruction in the block is executed. Let us say, for example, that the intermediate representation consists of quadruples as in Exercise 7 in Section 7.6 using an unlimited supply of temporary variables T1, T2, ... as in Section 7.2.2, along with variables declared by the programmer. A variable is said to be *dead* when the next reference to it is an assignment to it or when there will be no further reference to it. When a variable is not dead it is *live*.

A simple idea is to work along a basic block. When a variable is encountered for the first time we allocate a register that is hitherto unallocated or contains a value that will not subsequently be read. If there is no such register we spill the register whose next use is furthest ahead and allocate this to the variable (Tremblay and Sorensen 1985, p. 697). *Spilling* a register means copying its contents to a variable in main memory outside the CPU unless this register contains an unchanged copy of the contents of this variable.

An alternative idea is to construct an *interference graph* in which there is a node corresponding to each variable that is referenced within a basic block and an arc linking the nodes for each pair of variables that are ever both live at the same time. If there is any time when a pair of variables are both live then a single register cannot be allocated to both of them: they must obviously have separate registers. Let n be the number of registers available for allocation, and suppose that the node corresponding to variable v has arcs to n other nodes that correspond to a set s of n variables. In this case it will not be possible to allocate separate registers to v and also to all the variables in s, because this would require $n+1$ registers. Instead we can only allocate a register to a variable whose node has less than n arcs. The following is an outline of a register-allocating routine:

```
WHILE the interference graph is not empty DO
   IF there is no node that has less than n arcs THEN
      choose a node, say the node for variable v, and insert code to spill a
         register that will be used while v is referenced, allocate this register
         temporarily to v and, after v has been referenced, copy v back to memory
         if necessary, and restore the contents of this register;
      remove node v and its arcs from the interference graph;
   ELSE
      select any node that has less than n arcs, say the node for variable w;
      allocate to variable w a register that has not been allocated to any of
      the variables whose nodes have arcs to w's node;
      remove node w and its arcs from the interference graph
   END
END;
```

This is a simple *register-colouring* routine, so called because of its relationship to the fundamental problem of graph-colouring (Briggs *et al.* 1989; Chow and Hennessy 1990; Dhamdhere 1988). A register allocation technique that minimizes transfers between registers and main memory is given in (Hsu *et al.* 1989).

16.7 Peephole optimization

16.7.1 Peepholes

The optimization techniques that we have mentioned hitherto are to some extent global in that they involve consideration of more than a few consecutive instructions, and indeed may involve data-flow analysis of an intermediate representation of an entire program. Peephole optimization techniques differ in that at any one time they look only at a few consecutive instructions of an intermediate representation, or of an object-code program. For example, a peephole optimizer might look at the first, second, third and fourth instructions and try to improve them; then examine the second, third, fourth and fifth instructions, and try to improve them; and so on. It is as if the optimizer looks at the program through a window that is, say, four instructions long, and moves this window along the program, progressing by one instruction at each step. Such a window is known as a *peephole*.

Peephole optimization, which is usually simpler and faster than global optimisation, can be applied to an intermediate representation such as a stack-based intermediate code (Davidson and Whalley 1989; McKenzie 1989; Tanenbaum *et al.* 1982), or to object code, or to both of these in turn. Some well-known peephole optimization techniques are as follows.

16.7.2 Constant folding

Suppose that `tableUB` has been declared as a constant, and its value is therefore known at compile time; for example, `tableub = 10`. If, for example, the object code includes instructions equivalent to `last:= tableUB - 1`, a peephole optimizer can replace this by `last:= 9`, so that the subtraction is not done, perhaps repeatedly, during program execution, but is instead done just once at compile time.

A reference to field `f` of a record variable `r` typically involves adding the relative address of `f` within the record to the relative address of `r` within a block. This is an addition of constants that can be done at compile time. Similarly, if array subscript `i` is a constant then access to `a[i]` involves adding (`i - lower` bound of array `a`) to the relative address of array variable `a` within a block. This addition and subtraction can all be done at compile time so as to speed up execution of the program.

Constant folding, which means evaluation of constant expressions at compile time, can be done with or without the global technique of constant propagation that was introduced in Section 16.4.3. It is possible for a compiler's code-generating routines, instead of a separate peephole optimizer, to implement constant folding.

16.7.3 Strength reduction

Strength reduction means replacing an operation by a faster one in special cases. For example, `2 * x` can be replaced by `shift x left one bit`, which is advantageous because left shift is considerably faster than multiplication. Similarly, instead of multiplying `y` by 32, the object program can be amended to shift `y` left 5 bits. Although left shift is not available in SAL it is normally available in practical assembly languages.

Addition is a faster operation than multiplication, and we might therefore consider having a peephole optimizer replace `2 * x` by `x + x`. Annotated with comments, SAL code (without optimization) for `2 * x` is as follows:

```
LEA DI,ZAAA
ADD DI,  0    ; DI:= address of x in static block
PUSH DI       ; push address
```

```
        MOV CX,    1
        POP DI          ; DI:= address of x
ZAAC:      PUSH [DI] ; push value of x
        INC DI
        LOOP ZAAC       ; no repetition for integer x
        MOV AX,    2
        PUSH AX         ; push operand 2 on to stack
        POP BX          ; BX:= 2
        POP AX          ; AX:= x
        MULT BX         ; AX := least significant half of 2 * x
        PUSH AX         ; PUSH product on to stack
```

Here there are 14 instructions, including one MULT. SAL code for x + x, by comparison, consists of the following 19 instructions, with no MULT:

```
        LEA DI,ZAAA
        ADD DI,    0    ;  DI:= address of x in static block
        PUSH DI         ;  push address of first operand
        MOV CX,    1
        POP DI          ;  DI:= address of x
ZAAE:      PUSH [DI]    ;  push value of x
        INC DI
        LOOP ZAAE       ;  no repetion for integer x
        LEA DI,ZAAA
        ADD DI,    0    ;  DI:= address of x in static block
        PUSH DI         ;  push address of second operand
        MOV CX,    1
        POP DI
ZAAF:      PUSH [DI]    ;  push value of x
        INC DI
        LOOP ZAAF       ;  no repetition for integer x
        POP  AX
        MOV DI, SP
        ADD  [DI], AX   ;  stacktop:= x + x
```

In this example, 2 * x is considerably faster than x + x, because pushing the value of a constant on to the stack is faster than pushing first the address and then the value of a variable on to the stack.

16.7.4 Algebraic simplification

Obviously x:= y + 0 can be replaced by x:= y, and x:= y * 1 can be replaced by x:= y. Suppose, for example, that tableub has been declared as a constant and that tableub = 10. In this case, x:= y + tableub - 10 can be replaced by x:= y. Algebraic simplification is another example of a technique that can be implemented by a compiler's code-generating routines rather than by a separate peephole optimizer.

16.7.5 Eliminate unnecessary instructions

An instruction such as

```
ADD DI, 0
```

can be eliminated because it achieves nothing. Moreover, our compiler sometimes produces two successive instructions:

```
PUSH AX
POP AX
```

and these can simply be deleted, even if one or more instructions, which do not affect this, come between the PUSH and the POP. For example, in the SAL fragments in Section 16.7.3

```
PUSH DI
MOV CX,   1
POP DI
```

can be replaced by

```
MOV CX, 1
```

To take another example, the SAL object code for integer multiplication 2 * 3 includes

```
MOV AX, 2
PUSH AX
MOV AX, 3
PUSH AX
POP BX
POP AX
MULT BX
```

which should preferably be replaced by

```
MOV AX, 2
MOV BX, 3
MULT BX
```

or, even better, by

```
MOV AX, 6
```

16.7.6 Make full use of machine code instruction set

It is better to compile, for example, x := x + 1 into something like INC x instead of the general object code for an assignment statement, which pushes the address of x on to the stack, then dereferences it, and then adds a constant. To take a very different example, the 8086 has a special machine code and assembly languange instruction for array bound checking, and it is more efficient to use this than to manage without.

16.8 Retargetability

In this book we have introduced a compiler that translates directly from a source language into an object language. Working like this, if we needed to compile from n different source languages into m different object languages we would need nm different compilers. This number could be reduced by having n compilers that all compile into the same intermediate code: because these compilers go no further they are said to be *front-end* compilers. For this standard intermediate code we would have m *back ends*, that is, code generators, one for each of the m different object languages, (see, for example, Tanenbaum *et al.* 1989)

In practice this standardization has not been completely accomplished (Tremblay and Sorensen 1985). Even so, if a single intermediate representation language is useful for a worthwhile number of source-language–object-language pairs, compiler optimization should ideally be performed on this intermediate representation, so that the optimizer does not have to be redeveloped unnecessarily for different source and/or object languages (Bal and Tanenbaum 1986).

A compiler that is not committed to a single object language but instead can readily switch between different object languages is said to be *retargetable* (Ganapathi *et al.* 1982). A peephole optimizer may, and an object code generator certainly will, require substantial machine specific knowlege. Retargetability can be improved by representing this knowledge declaratively in an expert system knowledge base, so that a switch to a new object language can be accomplished by amending the contents of the knowledge base instead of rewriting procedures (Warfield and Bauer 1988).

16.9 Exercises

1. Modify the compiler introduced in this book so that:

(a) in procedure `arrayReference` (Section 12.6.3) multiplication by `elementLength` is omitted when `elementLength = 1`; and

(b) loops output by procedures `pushValue` (Section 12.8) `assignmentStatement` (Section 12.5.1) and `returnStatement` (Section 13.9.5) to copy successive words are unrolled if `length < 5`; and

(c) loops output when `levelDifference > 0` by procedures `pushAddress` (Section 13.7) and `call` (Sections 13.9.3 and 13.9.5) are unrolled whatever the value of `levelDifference`.

2. For SAL assembly language write a peephole optimizer that will:

(a) eliminate instructions of the form ADD <operand>, 0;
(b) delete pairs of consecutive instructions

```
PUSH AX
POP AX
```

(c) replace a pair of instructions

```
PUSH <register1>
POP  <register2>
```

by

```
MOV <register2>, <register1>
```

(d) replace the three instructions

```
MOV AX, <integerConstant>
PUSH AX
POP <register>
```

by

```
MOV <register>, <integerConstant>
```

(e) delete any NOP instruction that is not labelled;
(f) if a NOP instruction has a label and the following instruction has no label, move this label forward one line and then delete the NOP instruction.

3. In Section 12.5.2 procedure assignmentStatement assigns a record or an array by first pushing all of its words on to the stack, and then popping these words off into successive words of the destination variable. To avoid this inefficiency, modify the compiler so that procedure pushValue does not push all the words of an array or record on to the stack, but instead simply leaves the address of the first of these words on top of the stack. Modify procedure assignmentStatement so that if the right-hand side of an assignment statement is an array or a record, successive words are copied directly from the right-hand-side variable to the destination variable, not via the stack.

Modules listed in alphabetic sequence

```
DEFINITION MODULE alexInit;
PROCEDURE lexInitialise;
END alexInit.

IMPLEMENTATION MODULE alexInit;
FROM symbType IMPORT symbolType;
FROM strinTbl IMPORT insertString, enter;
CONST
  ax = 0; bx = 3; cx = 1; dx = 2; sp = 4; bp = 5; si = 6; di = 7;

VAR
  nextInd: CARDINAL;

PROCEDURE opEnter(str: ARRAY OF CHAR);
BEGIN
  enter(str, opCodeSy, nextInd); INC(nextInd)
END opEnter;

PROCEDURE lexInitialise;
BEGIN
  opEnter ('MOV ');  opEnter ('ADD '); opEnter ('SUB ');
  opEnter ('CMP ');  opEnter ('AND '); opEnter ('OR ');
  opEnter ('DEC ');  opEnter ('INC '); opEnter ('NEG ');
  opEnter ('MULT '); opEnter ('DIV '); opEnter ('PUSH ');
  opEnter ('POP ');  opEnter ('JMP '); opEnter ('JE ');
  opEnter ('JG ');   opEnter ('JL '); opEnter ('JNE ');
  opEnter ('JLE ');  opEnter ('JGE '); opEnter ('JC ');
  opEnter ('CALL '); opEnter ('RET '); opEnter ('LEA ');
  opEnter ('LOOP '); opEnter ('NOP '); opEnter ('DW ');
  enter ('AX ', registerSy, ax); enter ('BX ', registerSy, bx);
  enter ('CX ', registerSy, cx); enter ('DX ', registerSy, dx);
  enter ('SP ', registerSy, sp); enter ('BP ', registerSy, bp);
  enter ('SI ', registerSy, si); enter ('DI ', registerSy, di);
  enter ('DUP ', dupSy, 0);      enter ('IMPORT ', importSy, 0);
```

```
   enter ('EXPORT ', exportSy, 0)
END lexInitialise;

BEGIN
   nextInd:= 0
END alexInit.


DEFINITION MODULE assLex is included in Section 3.3.

IMPLEMENTATION MODULE assLex is included in Section 3.3


DEFINITION MODULE bis is included in Section 13.5.

IMPLEMENTATION MODULE bis;
FROM InOut IMPORT WriteString, WriteCard, ReadCard, WriteLn, Read, Write;
FROM symbols IMPORT symbolType;
FROM pritmod IMPORT idRecPtr;
FROM SYSTEM IMPORT WORD;
FROM FileSystem IMPORT File, Lookup, Reset, Close, ReadWord;
VAR
   lineNumber: CARDINAL;
   interFile: File;

PROCEDURE error(errNo: CARDINAL);
BEGIN
   WriteString('error no:' ); WriteCard(errNo,4);
   WriteString('   at line no: '); WriteCard(lineNumber,4); WriteLn
END error;

PROCEDURE accept(sym: symbolType);
BEGIN
   IF sy = sym THEN inSymbol ELSE
     WriteString('Accept failed WITH ORD(sy) = ');
     WriteCard(ORD(sy),3); WriteString(' AND ORD(sym) = ');
     WriteCard(ORD(sym),3); WriteLn; error(1)
   END
END accept;

PROCEDURE openInterFile;
BEGIN
   Lookup(interFile, 'interFile', TRUE);
   Reset(interFile)
END openInterFile;
```

```
PROCEDURE closeInterFile;
BEGIN
  Close(interFile)
END closeInterFile;

PROCEDURE inSymbol;
VAR
  w: WORD; n: CARDINAL;
BEGIN
  ReadWord(interFile, w); n:= CARDINAL(w);
  sy:= VAL(symbolType, n);
  IF sy = idSy THEN ReadWord(interFile, w); ind:= CARDINAL(w);
  ELSIF sy = numberSy THEN
    WITH valueRecord DO
      ReadWord(interFile, valType);
      ReadWord(interFile, w); val1:= CARDINAL(w);
      ReadWord(interFile, w); val2:= CARDINAL(w)
    END
  END;
  ReadWord(interFile, w); lineNumber:= CARDINAL(w);
  (* trace; *)
END inSymbol;

PROCEDURE trace;
BEGIN
  WriteString('Lineno = '); WriteCard(lineNumber, 3);
  WriteString(' ORD(sy) = '); WriteCard(ORD(sy), 3);
  IF sy = idSy THEN WriteString('  ind = '); WriteCard(ind, 3);
  ELSIF sy = numberSy THEN WriteString(' val1 = ');
    WriteCard(valueRecord.val1,4);
  END; WriteLn
END trace;

BEGIN
END bis.


DEFINITION MODULE callRet;
FROM pritmod IMPORT idRecPtr;
VAR
  blockLevel: CARDINAL;
PROCEDURE pushRetStack(prmLength: CARDINAL; resType: idRecPtr;
itsaFunction: BOOLEAN);
PROCEDURE popRetStack;
PROCEDURE noReturn(): BOOLEAN;
PROCEDURE call(proPtr: idRecPtr);
PROCEDURE functionCall(proPtr: idRecPtr; VAR fnType: idRecPtr );
PROCEDURE returnStatement;
```

```
END callRet.

IMPLEMENTATION MODULE callRet;
FROM bis IMPORT error, inSymbol, sy, ind, valueRecord, accept;
FROM symbols IMPORT symbolType;
FROM Storage IMPORT ALLOCATE, DEALLOCATE;
FROM InOut IMPORT WriteString, WriteCard, WriteLn;
FROM prExprsn IMPORT expression, pushAddress;
FROM prSAL IMPORT labelString, genLabel, putLabel, putLine,
  putStringAndVal, putStrings;
FROM pritmod IMPORT idRecPtr, class, kindOfProc, findItsRecord;
TYPE
   retStackRecPtr = POINTER TO retStackRec;
   retStackRec = RECORD
                    paramLength: CARDINAL; returnType: idRecPtr;
                    isaFunction, anyReturn: BOOLEAN;
                    next: retStackRecPtr
                 END;
   classSet = SET OF class;
VAR
   retStack: retStackRecPtr;

PROCEDURE pushRetStack (prmLength: CARDINAL; resType: idRecPtr;
   itsaFunction: BOOLEAN);
VAR
   newRecPtr: retStackRecPtr;
BEGIN
   ALLOCATE (newRecPtr, SIZE(retStackRec));
   WITH newRecPtr^ DO
     paramLength:= prmLength; returnType:= resType;
     isaFunction:= itsaFunction; anyReturn:= FALSE; next:= retStack
   END;
   retStack:= newRecPtr
END pushRetStack;

PROCEDURE popRetStack;
VAR
   oldRecPtr: retStackRecPtr;
BEGIN
   oldRecPtr:= retStack; retStack:= retStack^. next;
   DEALLOCATE(oldRecPtr, SIZE(retStackRec))
END popRetStack;

PROCEDURE noReturn(): BOOLEAN;
BEGIN
   RETURN NOT retStack^.anyReturn
END noReturn;
```

```
PROCEDURE call (proPtr: idRecPtr);
VAR
  levelLoop: labelString; found: BOOLEAN;
  itsSubs, count, levelDifference: CARDINAL;
  resultType, paramPtr, varParamPtr: idRecPtr;
BEGIN
  inSymbol;
  IF proPtr^.noOfParams > 0 THEN
    IF sy = openRndBrktSy THEN inSymbol ELSE error (104) END;
    paramPtr:= proPtr^.nextSeq;
    FOR count:= 1 TO proPtr^.noOfParams DO
      WITH paramPtr^ DO
        IF itsClass = aVariable THEN
          expression(resultType);
          IF resultType # itsType THEN error(105) END
        ELSIF itsClass = aVARparameter THEN
          findItsRecord(ind, varParamPtr, found);
          IF found AND (varParamPtr^.itsClass IN
            classSet {aVariable, aVARparameter})
          THEN pushAddress(varParamPtr, resultType);
            IF resultType # itsType THEN error(106) END
          ELSE error(106)
          END
        ELSE error(107)
        END
      END
      paramPtr:= paramPtr^.nextSeq;
      IF sy = commaSy THEN inSymbol
      ELSIF sy # closeRndBrktSy THEN error (108)
      END;
    END; (* FOR *)
    accept(closeRndBrktSy)
  ELSIF sy = openRndBrktSy THEN inSymbol; accept(closeRndBrktSy)
  END; (* IF *)
  putLine('    MOV BX, BP');
  levelDifference:= blockLevel - proPtr^.procLevel;
  IF levelDifference > 0 THEN
    putStringAndVal('    MOV CX,', levelDifference);
    genLabel(levelLoop); putLabel(levelLoop);
    putLine('    MOV BX, [BX]');
    putStrings('    LOOP ', levelLoop)
  END;
  putLine('    MOV SI, SP');
  putLine('    INC SI');
  putLine('    PUSH BX');
  putLine('    PUSH BP ');
  putLine('    MOV BP, SI');
  putStrings('    CALL ', proPtr^.beginLabel)
```

```
END call;

PROCEDURE functionCall(proPtr: idRecPtr; VAR fnType: idRecPtr);
BEGIN
  WITH proPtr^ DO
    IF procKind = functionProc THEN
      fnType:= resultType;
      putStringAndVal('    ADD SP, ',resultType^.itsLength);
      call(proPtr)
    ELSE error(121)
    END
  END
END functionCall;

PROCEDURE returnStatement;
VAR
  resultType: idRecPtr; length: CARDINAL; furet: labelString;
BEGIN
  WITH retStack^ DO
    IF isaFunction THEN
      expression(resultType);
      IF resultType = returnType THEN
        length:= resultType^.itsLength;
        putStringAndVal('    MOV CX, ', length);
        putLine('   MOV SI, BP');
        putStringAndVal('    SUB SI, ', paramLength + 1);
        genLabel(furet); putLabel(furet);
        putLine('    POP [SI] ');
        putLine('    DEC SI ');
        putStrings('    LOOP ', furet);
        anyReturn:= TRUE
      ELSE error(48)
      END
    END;
    putLine('   MOV SP, BP');
    putStringAndVal('    SUB SP,', paramLength + 1);
    putLine('   MOV BX, [BP + 2]');
    putLine('   MOV BP, [BP + 1]');
    putLine('   JMP [BX] ')
  END (* WITH *)
END returnStatement;

BEGIN
  retStack:= NIL
END callRet.
```

```
DEFINITION MODULE decMod;
PROCEDURE decs(VAR words: CARDINAL);
END decMod.


IMPLEMENTATION MODULE decMod;
FROM scanner IMPORT error, inSymbol, accept, sy, ind;
FROM symbols IMPORT symbolType;
FROM Storage IMPORT ALLOCATE;
FROM itmod IMPORT class, kindOfType, idRec, idRecPtr, constant, tyInteger,
    tyBoolean, tyReal, findItsRecord, enterIdRecord, newIdRecord, findField;
CONST
  blockLevel = 0;
TYPE
  symbolSet = SET OF symbolType;
  listRecPtr = POINTER TO listRec;
  listRec = RECORD
              item: CARDINAL;
              next: listRecPtr
            END;
PROCEDURE makeList(VAR head: listRecPtr);
VAR
  n: INTEGER;  tail: listRecPtr;
BEGIN
  head:= NIL; tail:= NIL;
  IF sy # idSy THEN error(44); RETURN END;
  ALLOCATE(head, SIZE(listRec)); head^.item:= ind;
  head^.next:= NIL; tail:= head;
  inSymbol;
  WHILE sy = commaSy DO
    inSymbol;
    IF sy = idSy THEN
      ALLOCATE(tail^.next, SIZE(listRec));
      tail:= tail^.next;
      tail^.item:= ind; tail^.next:= NIL
    ELSE error(44)
    END; inSymbol
  END;
  accept(colonSy)
END makeList;


PROCEDURE checkDuplicateIdentifier(soughtInd:CARDINAL);
VAR
  found: BOOLEAN; soughtRecPtr: idRecPtr;
BEGIN
  findItsRecord(soughtInd, soughtRecPtr, found);
  IF found THEN error(9) END
END checkDuplicateIdentifier;
```

```
PROCEDURE constDecs;
VAR
  consType, idTabPtr: idRecPtr;
  card1, card2: CARDINAL;
BEGIN
  inSymbol;
  WHILE sy = idSy DO
    checkDuplicateIdentifier(ind);
    enterIdRecord(ind, idTabPtr);
    inSymbol; accept(equOp);
    constant(consType, card1, card2);
    WITH idTabPtr^ DO
      itsClass:= aConstant; itsType:= consType;
      c1:= card1; c2:= card2
    END;
    accept(semiColonSy)
  END
END constDecs;

PROCEDURE arrayDec(arrayRecordPtr: idRecPtr);
VAR
  v2, firstBound, secondBound, noOfDimensions, count: CARDINAL;
  lowerBoundType, upperBoundType, arrayElementType,
  currentPtr, previousPtr, recPtr: idRecPtr;
  found, lastDimension: BOOLEAN;
BEGIN
  inSymbol; accept(openSqBrktSy);
  noOfDimensions:= 0; lastDimension:= FALSE;
  REPEAT
    INC(noOfDimensions);
    constant(lowerBoundType, firstBound, v2); accept(dotDotSy);
    constant(upperBoundType, secondBound, v2);
    IF INTEGER(firstBound) > INTEGER(secondBound) THEN error(41) END;
    accept(closeSqrBrktSy);
    IF sy = ofSy THEN
      lastDimension:= TRUE; inSymbol; typeRecord(recPtr)
    ELSE accept(commaSy); accept(openSqBrktSy)
    END;
    IF (lowerBoundType = upperBoundType) AND
      ((lowerBoundType = tyBoolean) OR (lowerBoundType = tyInteger)) THEN
      WITH arrayRecordPtr^ DO
        itsClass:= aType; typeKind:= arrayType; indexType:= lowerBoundType;
        lowBound:= INTEGER(firstBound); upBound:= INTEGER(secondBound);
        IF lastDimension THEN elementType:= recPtr ELSE
          previousPtr:= arrayRecordPtr;
          newIdRecord(arrayRecordPtr); elementType:= arrayRecordPtr;
          arrayRecordPtr^.nextSyn:= previousPtr
        END;
```

```
        END
      ELSE error(18)
      END;
    UNTIL lastDimension;
    currentPtr:= arrayRecordPtr;
    FOR count:= 1 TO noOfDimensions DO
      WITH  currentPtr^ DO
        itsLength:= elementType^.itsLength *
          CARDINAL(upBound - lowBound + 1)
      END; currentPtr:= currentPtr^.nextSyn
    END (* FOR *)
END arrayDec;

PROCEDURE recordDec (recRecPtr: idRecPtr);
VAR
  currentPtr: listRecPtr;
  newFieldPtr, fieldType, recTail: idRecPtr;
  fieldInfo: idRec; found: BOOLEAN;
  nextFieldAddress, numberOfFields, fieldLength, recordLength: CARDINAL;
BEGIN
  inSymbol; recTail:= NIL;
  nextFieldAddress:= 0; numberOfFields:= 0;
  WHILE sy = idSy DO
    makeList(currentPtr); typeRecord(fieldType);
    fieldLength:= fieldType^.itsLength;
    WHILE currentPtr # NIL DO
      findField(currentPtr^.item, recRecPtr^.nextSyn, fieldInfo, found);
      IF found THEN error (17) ELSE
        INC(numberOfFields); newIdRecord(newFieldPtr);
        WITH newFieldPtr^ DO
          itsInd:= currentPtr^.item; itsType:= fieldType;
          fieldAddress:= nextFieldAddress; nextSyn:= NIL;
        END;
        IF recTail = NIL THEN recRecPtr^.fieldPtr:= newFieldPtr
        ELSE recTail^.nextSyn:= newFieldPtr
        END;
        recTail:= newFieldPtr;
        INC(nextFieldAddress, fieldLength)
      END; (* IF found *)
      currentPtr:= currentPtr^.next
    END; (* WHILE *)
    inSymbol;  IF sy # endSy THEN accept (semiColonSy) END
  END; (* WHILE *)
  IF sy  # endSy THEN error (13) END;
  WITH recRecPtr^ DO
    itsClass:= aType; typeKind:= recordType;
    itsLength:= nextFieldAddress; noOfFields:= numberOfFields;
  END;
```

```
END recordDec;

PROCEDURE typeRecord(VAR typePtr: idRecPtr);
VAR
  typeType: CARDINAL; found: BOOLEAN;
BEGIN
  CASE sy OF
    idSy: findItsRecord(ind, typePtr, found);
          IF NOT found THEN error(81) ELSE
            WITH typePtr^ DO
              IF itsClass # aType THEN error (82)
              ELSIF typeKind = typeAlias THEN typePtr:= itsType
              END
            END
          END   |
    arraySy:  newIdRecord(typePtr);  arrayDec(typePtr)   |
    recordSy: newIdRecord(typePtr); recordDec(typePtr)
  ELSE error (32)
  END
END typeRecord;

PROCEDURE typeDecs;
VAR
  typeInd: CARDINAL; found: BOOLEAN;
  typeType, idTabPtr: idRecPtr;
BEGIN
  inSymbol;
  WHILE sy = idSy DO
    checkDuplicateIdentifier(ind); typeInd:= ind;
    inSymbol;  accept(equOp);
    CASE sy OF
      idSy: findItsRecord(ind, typeType, found);
            IF found THEN
              IF typeType^.itsClass = aType THEN
                enterIdRecord(typeInd, idTabPtr);
                WITH idTabPtr^ DO
                  itsType:= typeType; itsClass:= aType;
                  typeKind:= typeAlias;
                  itsLength:= typeType^.itsLength
                END
              ELSE error(14)
              END
            ELSE error(14)
            END   |
      arraySy:  enterIdRecord(typeInd, idTabPtr); arrayDec (idTabPtr) |
      recordSy: enterIdRecord(typeInd, idTabPtr); recordDec(idTabPtr)
    ELSE error(14)
    END;
```

```
    inSymbol;   accept(semiColonSy)
  END (* WHILE *)
END typeDecs;

PROCEDURE varDecs(VAR nextAddress: CARDINAL);
VAR
  currentPtr: listRecPtr; thisType, idTabPtr: idRecPtr;
  varInd: CARDINAL;
BEGIN
  inSymbol;
  WHILE sy = idSy DO
    makeList(currentPtr);   typeRecord(thisType);
    WHILE currentPtr # NIL DO
      varInd:= currentPtr^.item;
      checkDuplicateIdentifier(varInd);
      enterIdRecord(varInd, idTabPtr);
      WITH idTabPtr^ DO
        itsInd:= varInd; itsClass:= aVariable; baseLabel:= 'ZAAA';
        relAddress:= nextAddress; itsType:= thisType; itsLevel:= blockLevel
      END;
      INC(nextAddress, thisType^.itsLength); currentPtr:= currentPtr^.next
    END;
    inSymbol; accept(semiColonSy);
  END;
END varDecs;

PROCEDURE decs(VAR words: CARDINAL);
BEGIN
  words:= 3;
  LOOP
    IF sy = constSy THEN constDecs
    ELSIF sy = typeSy THEN typeDecs
    ELSIF sy = varSy THEN varDecs(words)
    ELSE EXIT
    END
  END
END decs;

BEGIN
END decMod.


DEFINITION MODULE expressn is included in Section 10.4.
IMPLEMENTATION MODULE expressn is included in Section 10.4.


DEFINITION MODULE expTable is included in Section 5.3.
```

```
IMPLEMENTATION MODULE expTable;
FROM InOut IMPORT  Read, Write, WriteString, WriteCard, WriteLn, ReadCard,
RedirectInput, CloseInput, Done;
FROM strinTbl IMPORT searchStringTable, insertString, stringType;
FROM symbType IMPORT symbolType;
FROM mcModule IMPORT startFile;
CONST
  endOfFile = 32C; endOfLine = 36C; maxLabelInd = 100;
TYPE
  charSet = SET OF CHAR;
VAR
  ch: CHAR;  sy: symbolType;
  nextInd, ind: CARDINAL;
  globalLabelTable: ARRAY [0..maxLabelInd] OF CARDINAL;

PROCEDURE inText (ch: CHAR);
VAR
  length: CARDINAL; found: BOOLEAN;
  inString: stringType;
BEGIN
  length:= 0;
  REPEAT
    inString[length]:= ch;
    INC (length); Read(ch)
  UNTIL NOT (ch IN charSet{'A'..'Z'});
  searchStringTable (inString, length, sy, ind, found);
  IF NOT found THEN
    insertString (inString, length, labelSy, nextInd);
    sy:= labelSy; ind:= nextInd; INC(nextInd)
  ELSE WriteString('Error: duplicate export of label ');
    WriteString(inString); WriteLn
  END
END inText;

PROCEDURE getExports;
VAR
  i, n, eNumber, refAddress, relocatingVar: CARDINAL;
  ch: CHAR; noneLeft: BOOLEAN;
BEGIN
  nextInd:= 0; relocatingVar:= relocatingConst; n:= 0;
  LOOP
    startFile(noneLeft); IF noneLeft THEN EXIT END;
    INC(relocatingVar, n);
    Read(ch); IF ch # 'N' THEN WriteString ('Missing N'); WriteLn END;
    ReadCard(n);
    Read(ch); IF ch # 'E' THEN WriteString ('Missing E'); WriteLn END;
    ReadCard(eNumber);
```

```
   FOR i:= 1 TO eNumber DO
     Read(ch); inText(ch); ReadCard(refAddress);
     globalLabelTable[ind]:= refAddress + relocatingVar
   END;
   CloseInput
 END
END getExports;

PROCEDURE whichAddress(letter: CHAR; ind: CARDINAL): CARDINAL;
BEGIN
  RETURN  globalLabelTable[ind]
END whichAddress;

BEGIN
END expTable.


DEFINITION MODULE frstPass;
VAR
  moduleVarLength: CARDINAL;
  impModule: BOOLEAN;
END frstPass.

IMPLEMENTATION MODULE frstPass;
FROM scanner IMPORT error, accept, inSymbol, sy, ind, valueRecord,
  makeNegative, outSymbol, openInterFile, closeInterFile, switchStreamTo,
restoreStream;
FROM symbols IMPORT symbolType;
FROM strinTab IMPORT nameIs, outputName, stringType;
FROM Storage IMPORT ALLOCATE, DEALLOCATE;
FROM FileSystem IMPORT File, Lookup, Response;
FROM InOut IMPORT WriteString, WriteCard, ReadCard, WriteLn, Write;
FROM prSAL IMPORT labelString, genLabel, putLabel, newLabelSequence,
standardImports,
  restoreLabelSequence, putLine, putStringAndVal, putStrings;
FROM moDecs IMPORT defModuleDecs, block, checkAllExportedProcsImplemented,
enclosedByGlobalProc;
FROM pritmod IMPORT class, kindOfType, idRecPtr, findItsRecord,
checkDuplicateIdentifier, newIdRecord,
  pushProc, popProc, idRec, initialiseIdTable, tail, disconnect,
printTable, checkTable;
TYPE
  nameRecPtr = POINTER TO nameRec;
```

```
  nameRec = RECORD
               name: stringType;
               modInd: CARDINAL;
               letter: CHAR;
               anyVariable: BOOLEAN;
               next: nameRecPtr
            END;
VAR
  currentLetter: CHAR; moduleListHead: nameRecPtr;
  numberOfImportModules, moduleInd: CARDINAL;
  defModuleProcPtr: idRecPtr;


PROCEDURE toDefModule (inString: stringType; length: CARDINAL);
VAR
  i: CARDINAL; newFile: File;
BEGIN
  i:= length; inString[i]:= '.'; INC(i); inString[i]:= 'D';
  INC(i); inString[i]:= 'E'; INC(i); inString[i]:= 'F';
  Lookup(newFile, inString, FALSE);
  IF newFile.res = notdone THEN
    WriteString('Failed to open definition module file. File name = ');
    WriteString (inString); WriteLn; HALT
  END;
  switchStreamTo(newFile)
END toDefModule;


PROCEDURE defModule(moduleInd: CARDINAL; exported: BOOLEAN;  VAR words:
CARDINAL);
VAR
  i,j: CARDINAL;
BEGIN
  inSymbol; IF sy # definitionSy THEN error(200) END;
  inSymbol; IF sy # moduleSy THEN error (200) END;
  inSymbol; IF ind # moduleInd THEN error (201) END;
  accept(idSy); accept(semiColonSy);
  WHILE sy = fromSy DO imports END;
  defModuleDecs(exported, words);
  accept(endSy); IF ind # moduleInd THEN error(202) END;
  accept(idSy); accept(periodSy); restoreStream
END defModule;


PROCEDURE moduleList(moduleInd: CARDINAL; moduleName: stringType; VAR
modRecPtr: nameRecPtr);
VAR
  newRecPtr, currentPtr: nameRecPtr;
BEGIN
  IF (moduleListHead = NIL) OR (moduleInd > moduleListHead^.modInd) THEN
    INC(numberOfImportModules);
```

```
    ALLOCATE(newRecPtr, SIZE(nameRec));
    WITH newRecPtr^ DO
      name:= moduleName; modInd:= moduleInd; letter:= currentLetter;
      next:= moduleListHead; anyVariable:= FALSE
    END;
    moduleListHead:= newRecPtr; modRecPtr:= newRecPtr;
    INC(currentLetter)
  ELSE currentPtr:= moduleListHead;
    LOOP
      IF currentPtr = NIL THEN error(432); EXIT
      ELSIF currentPtr^.modInd = moduleInd THEN
        modRecPtr:= currentPtr; EXIT
      ELSE currentPtr:= currentPtr^.next
      END
    END
  END
END moduleList;

PROCEDURE mark(tabPtr: idRecPtr; anonymous: BOOLEAN);
VAR
  fPtr: idRecPtr; paramPtr: idRecPtr;
  count: CARDINAL;
BEGIN
  IF (tabPtr^.itsClass = aType) AND (tabPtr^.typeKind = aStandardType) THEN
    RETURN
  END;
  IF anonymous AND NOT tabPtr^.marked THEN
    disconnect(tabPtr^.itsInd); RETURN
  END;
  tabPtr^.marked:= TRUE;
  CASE tabPtr^.itsClass OF
      aType: CASE tabPtr^.typeKind OF
                arrayType:  mark(tabPtr^.elementType,TRUE) |
                recordType: fPtr:= tabPtr^.fieldPtr;
                            WHILE fPtr # NIL DO
                                mark(fPtr^.itsType, TRUE);
                                fPtr:= fPtr^.nextSyn
                            END |
                typeAlias:  mark(tabPtr^.itsType, TRUE)
              END |
      aVariable, aConstant: mark(tabPtr^.itsType, TRUE) |
      aProcedure: paramPtr:= tabPtr^.nextSeq;
                FOR count:= 1 TO tabPtr^.noOfParams DO
                  mark(paramPtr^.itsType,TRUE);
                  paramPtr:= paramPtr^.nextSeq
                END
  ELSE error(213)
  END
```

```
END mark;

PROCEDURE imports;
VAR
  words, moduleInd, length: CARDINAL; found: BOOLEAN;
  currentPtr, recPtr, startPtr: idRecPtr;
  moduleName: stringType; modRecPtr: nameRecPtr;
  oldLabel, varLabel: labelString;
BEGIN
  inSymbol; IF sy # idSy THEN error(212); RETURN END;
  newLabelSequence(oldLabel);
  startPtr:= tail; words:= 0; moduleInd:= ind;
  nameIs(moduleName, length); moduleList(moduleInd, moduleName, modRecPtr);
  toDefModule(moduleName, length); pushProc(defModuleProcPtr);
  defModule(moduleInd, FALSE, words); popProc;
  inSymbol; accept(importSy);
  WHILE sy = idSy DO
    findItsRecord(ind, recPtr, found);
    IF NOT found THEN error(214)
    ELSE
      checkDuplicateIdentifier(ind);
      enclosedByGlobalProc(recPtr); mark(recPtr, FALSE)
    END;
    inSymbol; IF sy = commaSy THEN inSymbol END
  END;
  accept(semiColonSy);
  IF startPtr # tail THEN
    currentPtr:= startPtr^.nextSeq;
    LOOP
      IF NOT currentPtr^.marked THEN
        disconnect(currentPtr^.itsInd)
      ELSE
        CASE currentPtr^.itsClass OF
        aProcedure: currentPtr^.beginLabel[0]:= modRecPtr^.letter;
          WriteString(', ');
          WriteString(currentPtr^.beginLabel) |
        aVariable: currentPtr^.baseLabel[0]:= modRecPtr^.letter;
          modRecPtr^.anyVariable:= TRUE; varLabel:= currentPtr^.baseLabel
        ELSE (* do nothing *)
        END
      END;
      currentPtr:= currentPtr^.nextSeq;
      IF currentPtr = tail THEN EXIT END
    END (* LOOP *)
  END; (* IF *)
  IF modRecPtr^.anyVariable THEN
    WriteString(', '); WriteString(varLabel)
  END;
```

```
    restoreLabelSequence(oldLabel)
END imports;


PROCEDURE exports(moduleInd: CARDINAL; VAR words: CARDINAL);
VAR
    startPtr, currentPtr: idRecPtr; anyVariable: BOOLEAN;
    numberOfExports, length: CARDINAL;
    moduleName: stringType;

    PROCEDURE writeLabel(label: labelString);
    BEGIN
      INC(numberOfExports);
      IF numberOfExports = 1 THEN WriteString('EXPORT ')
      ELSE WriteString(', ')
      END; WriteString(label)
    END writeLabel;

BEGIN (* body of exports *)
    startPtr:= tail;  numberOfExports:= 0; anyVariable:= FALSE;
    nameIs(moduleName, length);  toDefModule(moduleName, length);
    defModule(moduleInd, TRUE, words);
    IF tail = startPtr THEN RETURN END;
    currentPtr:= startPtr;
    REPEAT
      currentPtr:= currentPtr^.nextSeq;
      CASE currentPtr^.itsClass OF
        aVariable:  IF NOT anyVariable THEN anyVariable:= TRUE;
                       writeLabel ('ZAAA')
                    END |
        aProcedure: writeLabel(currentPtr^.beginLabel)
      ELSE (* do nothing *)
      END
    UNTIL currentPtr = tail;
    IF numberOfExports > 0 THEN WriteLn END
END exports;


PROCEDURE putRefTable;
  PROCEDURE reverseOutput(ptr: nameRecPtr);
  BEGIN
      IF ptr^.next # NIL THEN reverseOutput(ptr^.next) END;
      WriteString(' ; '); WriteString(ptr^.name);
      WriteString(' ;'); Write(ptr^.letter); WriteLn
  END reverseOutput;
BEGIN
  IF NOT impModule THEN
    putStringAndVal(' ;  M ', numberOfImportModules)
  ELSE putStringAndVal(' ; S ', numberOfImportModules)
  END;
```

```
    IF numberOfImportModules > 0 THEN reverseOutput(moduleListHead) END
END putRefTable;

BEGIN
  ALLOCATE (defModuleProcPtr, SIZE(idRec));
  WITH defModuleProcPtr^ DO
    itsClass:= aProcedure; internalLevel:= 0;
    beingCompiled:= TRUE; itsInd:= 255;
  END;
  currentLetter:= 'A'; moduleListHead:= NIL;
  numberOfImportModules:= 0;
  initialiseIdTable; openInterFile; inSymbol;
  IF sy = implementationSy THEN impModule:= TRUE; inSymbol
  ELSE impModule:= FALSE
  END; outSymbol; (* MODULE symbol *)
  accept(moduleSy); outSymbol; moduleInd:= ind;
  WriteString('  ; '); outputName; WriteLn;
  accept(idSy); outSymbol; (* semicolon *)
  IF sy # semiColonSy THEN error(222) END;
  moduleVarLength:= 0;
  IF impModule THEN exports(moduleInd, moduleVarLength) END;
  standardImports; inSymbol;
  WHILE sy = fromSy DO imports END; WriteLn;
  putRefTable;
  block(moduleVarLength, moduleInd);
  checkAllExportedProcsImplemented;
  accept(periodSy); outSymbol; closeInterFile
END frstPass.


DEFINITION MODULE gLabTab is included in Section 14.7.1.

IMPLEMENTATION MODULE gLabTab;
FROM InOut IMPORT  Read, Write, WriteString, WriteCard, WriteLn, ReadCard,
RedirectInput, CloseInput, Done;
FROM strinTbl IMPORT searchStringTable, insertString, stringType;
FROM symbType IMPORT symbolType;
FROM mcMake IMPORT moduleForLetter, startFile;
CONST
  endOfFile = 32C; endOfLine = 36C;
  maxModInd =  10; maxLabelInd = 50;
TYPE
  charSet = SET OF CHAR;
VAR
  ch: CHAR;  sy: symbolType;
  nextInd, ind: CARDINAL;
  globalLabelTable: ARRAY [0..maxModInd],[0..maxLabelInd] OF CARDINAL;
```

```
PROCEDURE inText (ch: CHAR);
VAR
  length: CARDINAL;
  found: BOOLEAN;
  inString: stringType;
BEGIN
  length:= 0;
  REPEAT
    inString[length]:= ch;
    INC (length); Read(ch);
  UNTIL NOT (ch IN charSet{'A'..'Z'});
  searchStringTable (inString, length, sy, ind, found);
  IF NOT found THEN
    insertString (inString, length, labelSy, nextInd);
    sy:= labelSy; ind:= nextInd; INC(nextInd)
  END
END inText;


PROCEDURE getExports;
VAR
  n, i,  eNumber, refAddress, relocatingVar, moduleInd: CARDINAL;
  ch: CHAR;  noneLeft: BOOLEAN;
BEGIN
  nextInd:= 0; relocatingVar:= relocatingConst; n:= 0;
  LOOP
    startFile(noneLeft, moduleInd); IF noneLeft THEN EXIT END;
    INC(relocatingVar, n);
    Read(ch); IF ch # 'N' THEN WriteString ('Missing N'); WriteLn END;
    ReadCard(n);
    Read(ch); IF ch # 'E' THEN WriteString ('Missing E'); WriteLn END;
    ReadCard(eNumber);
    FOR i:= 1 TO eNumber DO
      Read(ch); inText(ch); ReadCard(refAddress);
      globalLabelTable[moduleInd,ind]:= refAddress + relocatingVar
    END;
    CloseInput
  END
END getExports;


PROCEDURE whichAddress(letter: CHAR; labelInd: CARDINAL): CARDINAL;
BEGIN
  IF letter = '@' THEN RETURN globalLabelTable[0,labelInd] ELSE
    RETURN  globalLabelTable[moduleForLetter(letter), labelInd]
  END
END whichAddress;


BEGIN
END gLabTab.
```

```
DEFINITION MODULE instrns;
PROCEDURE instruction;
END instrns.

IMPLEMENTATION MODULE instrns;
FROM machCode IMPORT enter, incAddressBy;
FROM labels IMPORT labelReference;
FROM symbType IMPORT symbolType;
FROM assLex IMPORT  sy, ind, val, error, accept, inSymbol;
FROM InOut IMPORT WriteString, WriteLn;
CONST
  opCodeUB = 26;
  bx = 3; bp = 5; di = 7; si = 6;
TYPE
  regCode = [0..7];
  regSet = SET OF regCode;
  symbolSet = SET OF symbolType;
  statusType = (displacementIsLabel, displacementNoLabel, noDisplacement);
  catType = (twoOperandCategory, singleOperandCategory,
             leaInstructionCategory, jumpInsCategory,
             noOperandInsCategory, pseudoOp);
  opCodeRecord  = RECORD
                     category: catType;
                     opCode: CARDINAL
                  END;
  operandKind = (mem, reg);
VAR
  opWord: CARDINAL;
  opCodeTable: ARRAY[0..opCodeUB] OF opCodeRecord;
  rm1array: ARRAY [bx..di] OF regCode;
  rm2array: ARRAY [bx..bp],[si..di] OF regCode;
  displacement: INTEGER;
  labelInd:  CARDINAL;
  displacementStatus: statusType;

PROCEDURE registerOperand;
BEGIN
  INC (opWord, ind * 8); (* register field of opWord *)
  inSymbol
END registerOperand;

PROCEDURE memoryOperand (VAR opWord: CARDINAL);
VAR
  noOfRegisters, reg1, reg2: CARDINAL;
  negative: BOOLEAN;
BEGIN
```

```
    noOfRegisters:= 0;
    IF sy = labelSy THEN
      displacementStatus:= displacementIsLabel;   labelInd:= ind;
      inSymbol
    ELSE   displacementStatus:= noDisplacement
    END;
    IF sy = leftSqBrktSy THEN
      inSymbol;
      noOfRegisters:= 1;   reg1:= ind;
      accept(registerSy);
      IF sy IN symbolSet {plussOp,minusOp} THEN
        negative:= (sy = minusOp);
        inSymbol;
        IF (sy # numberSy) OR
          (displacementStatus = displacementIsLabel) THEN error(7)
        END;
        displacementStatus:= displacementNoLabel;
        IF negative THEN displacement:= -INTEGER(val)
        ELSE displacement:= INTEGER(val)
        END;
        IF NOT (reg1 IN regSet{bx,bp}) THEN error (8) END;
        inSymbol
      END;
      accept(rightSqBrktSy);
      IF sy = leftSqBrktSy THEN (* based indexed address *)
        IF (displacementStatus = displacementNoLabel) OR NOT
          (reg1 IN regSet {bx,bp}) THEN error (10)
        END;
        accept (leftSqBrktSy);   reg2:= ind;
        IF NOT (reg2 IN regSet{si,di}) THEN error (11) END;
        noOfRegisters:= 2;
        accept (registerSy); accept(rightSqBrktSy)
      END;
      IF noOfRegisters = 2 THEN INC (opWord, rm2array[reg1,reg2])
      ELSIF (noOfRegisters = 1) AND (reg1 IN
        regSet{si, di, bx, bp}) THEN INC(opWord, rm1array[reg1])
      END
    END;
    IF (displacementStatus # noDisplacement) THEN
      IF (noOfRegisters > 0) THEN INC (opWord, 128)
      ELSE INC (opWord, 64)
      END
    END
END memoryOperand;

PROCEDURE secondOperand (firstOperand: operandKind;
  VAR immediate: BOOLEAN; VAR immedVal: CARDINAL);
BEGIN
```

```
  accept (commaSy); (* sy:= first symbol of second operand *)
  CASE sy  OF
  numberSy:  (* immediate addressing *)
    immediate:= TRUE; immedVal:= val;
    INC (opWord, 1024);  (* immediate bit:= 1 *)
    inSymbol |
  minusOp: inSymbol;
    IF sy = numberSy THEN (* immediate addressing *)
      immediate:= TRUE; immedVal:= CARDINAL(-INTEGER(val));
      INC (opWord, 1024);  (* immediate bit:= 1 *)
      inSymbol
    ELSE error(12) (* sign must be followed by a number *)
    END |
  registerSy:
    IF firstOperand = reg THEN  (* r/m field will select second register *)
      INC (opWord, ind);  (* r/m field of opWord:= register's ind *)
      INC (opWord, 0C0H); (* m bits:= 11 in binary *)
      inSymbol
    ELSE  (* only one register operand *)
      registerOperand
    END |
  labelSy, leftSqBrktSy: (* second operand is <memory> *)
    IF firstOperand = reg THEN
      memoryOperand (opWord);
      INC (opWord, 256); (* memRef bit:= 1 *)
    ELSE error(12) (* cannot have two memory operands *)
    END
  END
END secondOperand;


PROCEDURE enterDisplacement;
BEGIN
  IF displacementStatus = displacementIsLabel THEN labelReference(labelInd)
  ELSIF displacementStatus = displacementNoLabel THEN
    enter(CARDINAL(displacement), 0)
  END
END enterDisplacement;


PROCEDURE twoOp;
VAR
  immediate: BOOLEAN; immedVal: CARDINAL;
BEGIN
  immediate:= FALSE; displacementStatus:= noDisplacement;
  IF sy = registerSy THEN
    registerOperand;
    INC (opWord,512); (* destination bit:= 1 *)
    secondOperand(reg, immediate, immedVal);
```

```
    ELSIF sy IN symbolSet {labelSy, leftSqBrktSy} THEN
      memoryOperand (opWord);
      INC (opWord, 256); (* memRef bit:= 1 *)
      secondOperand(mem, immediate, immedVal)
    ELSE error (20)
    END;
    enter(opWord, 0);
    IF immediate THEN enter(immedVal, 0) END;
    enterDisplacement
END twoOp;


PROCEDURE singleOp;
BEGIN
  displacementStatus:= noDisplacement;
  IF sy = registerSy THEN registerOperand
  ELSIF sy IN symbolSet {labelSy, leftSqBrktSy} THEN
    memoryOperand (opWord);
    INC (opWord, 256) (* memRef bit:= 1 *)
  ELSE error (14)
  END;
  enter(opWord, 0);  enterDisplacement
END singleOp;


PROCEDURE jumpInstructions;
BEGIN
  displacementStatus:= noDisplacement;
  IF sy IN symbolSet {labelSy, leftSqBrktSy} THEN
    memoryOperand (opWord)
  ELSE error (15)
  END;
  enter(opWord, 0); enterDisplacement
END jumpInstructions;


PROCEDURE leaInstruction;
BEGIN
  IF sy = registerSy THEN registerOperand
  ELSE error (16)
  END;
  accept (commaSy);
  IF sy IN symbolSet {labelSy, leftSqBrktSy} THEN
    memoryOperand (opWord) ELSE error (17)
  END;
  enter (opWord, 0); enterDisplacement
END leaInstruction;


PROCEDURE dw;
VAR
  number: CARDINAL;
```

```
BEGIN
  IF sy = questionSy THEN
    incAddressBy (1); inSymbol
  ELSIF sy = numberSy THEN
    number:= val;  inSymbol;
    IF sy = dupSy THEN
      incAddressBy (number); inSymbol
    ELSE  enter (val, 0)
    END;
  ELSE error (19)
  END
END dw;


PROCEDURE instruction;
VAR
  opInd: CARDINAL;
BEGIN
  opInd:= ind; inSymbol;
  opWord:= opCodeTable[opInd].opCode;
  CASE opCodeTable[opInd].category OF
    twoOperandCategory:     twoOp                |
    singleOperandCategory:  singleOp             |
    leaInstructionCategory: leaInstruction       |
    jumpInsCategory:        jumpInstructions     |
    noOperandInsCategory:   enter(opWord, 0)     |
    pseudoOp:               dw
  END
END instruction;


PROCEDURE opInit(subscript, decimal: CARDINAL; cat: catType);
BEGIN
  WITH opCodeTable[subscript] DO
    category:= cat; opCode:= decimal
  END
END opInit;


BEGIN (* initialization of opCode table *)
  opInit(0, 4000H,  twoOperandCategory);
  opInit(1, 4800H,  twoOperandCategory);
  opInit(2, 5000H,  twoOperandCategory);
  opInit(3, 5800H,  twoOperandCategory);
  opInit(4, 6000H,  twoOperandCategory);
  opInit(5, 6800H,  twoOperandCategory);
  opInit(6, 1000H,  singleOperandCategory);
  opInit(7, 1200H,  singleOperandCategory);
  opInit(8, 1600H,  singleOperandCategory);
  opInit(9, 1800H,  singleOperandCategory);
  opInit(10, 1A00H, singleOperandCategory);
```

```
    opInit(11, 1C00H, singleOperandCategory);
    opInit(12, 1E00H, singleOperandCategory);
    opInit(13, 2000H, jumpInsCategory);
    opInit(14, 2800H, jumpInsCategory);
    opInit(15, 2C00H, jumpInsCategory);
    opInit(16, 2A00H, jumpInsCategory);
    opInit(17, 2B00H, jumpInsCategory);
    opInit(18, 2D00H, jumpInsCategory);
    opInit(19, 2E00H, jumpInsCategory);
    opInit(20, 2F00H, jumpInsCategory);
    opInit(21, 3000H, jumpInsCategory);
    opInit(22, 0800H, noOperandInsCategory);
    opInit(23, 0400H, leaInstructionCategory);
    opInit(24, 2900H, jumpInsCategory);
    opInit(25, 0F00H, noOperandInsCategory);
    opInit(26, 0, pseudoOp);
    rm1array[si]:= 4; rm1array[di]:= 5;
    rm1array[bp]:= 6; rm1array[bx]:= 7;
    rm2array[bx,si]:= 0; rm2array[bx,di]:= 1;
    rm2array[bp,si]:= 2; rm2array[bp,di]:= 3
END instrns.


MODULE interpret;
FROM progCode IMPORT catType, opWordFields,
   getWord, getOp, jumpIP, dereference, assignTo, ipAddress;
FROM InOut IMPORT WriteString, WriteLn, WriteCard, ReadInt, WriteInt;
FROM RealInOut IMPORT ReadReal, WriteReal;
FROM  SYSTEM IMPORT WORD;
CONST
  AX = 0; CX = 1; DX = 2; BX = 3; SP = 4; BP = 5; SI = 6; DI = 7;

VAR
  register: ARRAY[0..7] OF CARDINAL;
  opRec: opWordFields;
  halted: BOOLEAN;
  carryFlag: [0..1];
  resultValue: CARDINAL;

PROCEDURE indexing (rmField: CARDINAL; VAR refAddress: CARDINAL);
BEGIN
  CASE rmField OF
  0: refAddress:= refAddress + register[BX] + register[SI] |
  1: refAddress:= refAddress + register[BX] + register[DI] |
  2: refAddress:= refAddress + register[BP] + register[SI] |
  3: refAddress:= refAddress + register[BP] + register[DI] |
  4: INC(refAddress, register[SI]) |
  5: INC(refAddress, register[DI]) |
```

```
      6: INC(refAddress, register[BP]) |
      7: INC(refAddress, register[BX])
      END
END indexing;


PROCEDURE twoOperandInstruction(opRec: opWordFields);
VAR
   destinationAddress, destinationValue, sourceValue: CARDINAL;
BEGIN
   IF opRec.immediate = 1 THEN getWord(sourceValue)
   ELSIF opRec.destination = 1 THEN
      IF opRec.m = 3 THEN sourceValue:= register[opRec.rm]
      ELSIF opRec.memRef = 1 THEN
         sourceValue:= dereference(formAddress(opRec))
      END
   ELSIF opRec.memRef = 1 THEN sourceValue:= register[opRec.reg]
   END;
   IF opRec.destination = 0 THEN
      IF opRec.memRef = 1 THEN
         destinationAddress:= formAddress(opRec);
         destinationValue:= dereference(destinationAddress);
      ELSE WriteString('Error: memRefBit should be set'); WriteLn
      END
   ELSE destinationValue:= register[opRec.reg]
   END;
   CASE opRec.opCode OF
   0: (* MOV *)  resultValue:= sourceValue  |
   1: (* ADD *)  resultValue:= sourceValue + destinationValue  |
   2: (* SUB *)  resultValue:= CARDINAL(INTEGER(destinationValue) -
      INTEGER(sourceValue))  |
   3: (* CMP *)  resultValue:= CARDINAL(INTEGER(destinationValue) -
      INTEGER(sourceValue))  |
   4: (* AND *)  resultValue:= CARDINAL(BITSET(destinationValue) *
      BITSET(sourceValue))  |
   5: (* OR  *)  resultValue:= CARDINAL(BITSET(destinationValue) +
      BITSET(sourceValue))
   END;
   IF opRec.opCode # 3 THEN (* not CMP so assign result to destination *)
      IF opRec.destination = 1 THEN register[opRec.reg]:= resultValue
      ELSE assignTo(destinationAddress, resultValue)
      END
   END
END twoOperandInstruction;


PROCEDURE singleOperandInstruction(opRec: opWordFields);
VAR
   operandAddress, opValue, result: CARDINAL;
   temp, twoToThe16: REAL;
```

```
BEGIN
  IF opRec.opCode < 4 THEN (* DEC, INC, or NEG *)
    IF opRec.memRef = 1 THEN
       operandAddress:= formAddress(opRec);
       opValue:=dereference(operandAddress)
    ELSE opValue:= register[opRec.reg]
    END;
    CASE opRec.opCode OF
       0: (* DEC *) result:= CARDINAL(INTEGER(opValue) - 1)|
       1: (* INC *) result:= CARDINAL(INTEGER(opValue) + 1)|
       2: WriteString('Illegal opCode for One op instruction'); WriteLn|
       3: (* NEG *) result:= CARDINAL(-INTEGER(opValue))
    END;
    IF opRec.memRef = 1 THEN assignTo(operandAddress,result)
    ELSE register[opRec.reg]:= result
    END;
  ELSIF (opRec.opCode >= 4) AND (opRec.opCode <= 6) THEN
    IF opRec.memRef = 1 THEN opValue:= dereference(formAddress(opRec))
    ELSE opValue:= register[opRec.reg]
    END;
    CASE opRec.opCode OF
       4: (* MULT *) temp:= FLOAT(opValue) * FLOAT(register[AX]);
          twoToThe16:= FLOAT(8000H) * 2.0;
          register[DX]:= TRUNC (temp/twoToThe16);
          register[AX]:= TRUNC (temp - twoToThe16 * FLOAT(register[DX]));
          IF register[DX] = 0 THEN carryFlag:= 0 ELSE carryFlag:= 1 END |
       5: (* DIV *)  twoToThe16:= FLOAT(8000H) * 2.0;
          temp:= FLOAT(register[AX]) + twoToThe16 * FLOAT(register[DX]);
          temp:= temp / FLOAT(opValue);
          register[AX]:= TRUNC (temp);
          register[DX]:= TRUNC ((temp - FLOAT(register[AX])) *
            FLOAT(opValue)) |
       6: (* PUSH *) INC(register[SP]); assignTo(register[SP],opValue)
    END;
  ELSIF opRec.opCode = 7 THEN (* POP *)
    IF opRec.memRef = 1 THEN
       assignTo(formAddress(opRec),dereference(register[SP]))
    ELSE register[opRec.reg]:= dereference(register[SP])
    END;  DEC(register[SP])
  ELSE WriteString('Error: singleOp opCode exceeds 7'); WriteLn
  END
END singleOperandInstruction;

PROCEDURE leaInstruction (opRec: opWordFields);
BEGIN
  register[opRec.reg]:= formAddress(opRec)
END leaInstruction;
```

```
PROCEDURE jumpInstructions (opRec: opWordFields);
VAR
  jumpAddress: CARDINAL;
BEGIN
  jumpAddress:= formAddress(opRec);
  CASE opRec.opCode OF
  0: (* JMP *) jumpIP(jumpAddress) |
  8: (* JE *) IF resultValue = 0 THEN jumpIP(jumpAddress) END |
  12: (* JG *) IF INTEGER(resultValue) > 0 THEN jumpIP(jumpAddress) END |
  9:  (* LOOP *) DEC(register[CX]);
    IF register[CX] # 0 THEN jumpIP (jumpAddress) END |
  10: (* JL *) IF INTEGER(resultValue) < 0 THEN jumpIP(jumpAddress) END |
  11: (* JNE *) IF resultValue # 0 THEN jumpIP(jumpAddress) END |
  13: (* JLE *) IF INTEGER(resultValue) <= 0 THEN jumpIP(jumpAddress) END |
  14: (* JGE *) IF INTEGER(resultValue) >= 0 THEN jumpIP(jumpAddress) END |
  15: (* JC  *) IF carryFlag = 1 THEN jumpIP(jumpAddress) END |
  16: (* CALL *) INC(register[SP]); assignTo(register[SP],ipAddress());
    jumpIP(jumpAddress)
  ELSE WriteString('Error: illegal JPINS opCode')
  END
END jumpInstructions;


PROCEDURE noOperandInstructions (opRec: opWordFields);
BEGIN
  IF opRec.opCode = 0 THEN (* RET *)
    jumpIP(dereference(register[SP])); DEC(register[SP])
  END (* else if NOP then do nothing *)
END noOperandInstructions;


PROCEDURE extraIns (opRec: opWordFields);
TYPE
  convert = ARRAY[0..1] OF WORD;
VAR
  returnAddress: CARDINAL; I: INTEGER; x, y: REAL;

  PROCEDURE pushCard (c: CARDINAL);
  BEGIN
    INC(register[SP]); assignTo(register[SP],c)
  END pushCard;

  PROCEDURE pushReal (y: REAL);
  VAR
    conVar: convert;
  BEGIN
    conVar:= convert(y);
    pushCard(CARDINAL(conVar[0]));
    pushCard(CARDINAL(conVar[1]))
  END pushReal;
```

```
  PROCEDURE popReal(): REAL;
  VAR
    conVar: convert;
  BEGIN
    conVar[1]:= WORD(dereference(register[SP])); DEC(register[SP]);
    conVar[0]:= WORD(dereference(register[SP])); DEC(register[SP]);
    RETURN REAL(conVar)
  END popReal;

  PROCEDURE realOperands(VAR first, second: REAL);
  BEGIN
    second:= popReal(); first:= popReal()
  END realOperands;

BEGIN
  returnAddress:= dereference(register[SP]); DEC(register[SP]);
  CASE opRec.lsByte OF
  1: (* INTREAD *) ReadInt(I); pushCard(CARDINAL(I)) |
  2: (* INTWRITE *)
     WriteInt(INTEGER(dereference(register[SP])),6);
     DEC(register[SP]) |
  3: (* NEWLINE *)  WriteLn |
  4: (* ENDPROG *)  halted:= TRUE |
  5: (* REALREAD *) ReadReal(x); pushReal(x) |
  6: (* WRITEREAL *) x:= popReal(); WriteReal(x, 10) |
  7: (* REALNEG *) pushReal(-popReal()) |
  8: (* REALADD *) realOperands(x,y); pushReal(x + y) |
  9: (* REALSUB *) realOperands(x,y); pushReal(x - y) |
  10: (* REALMULT *) realOperands (x,y); pushReal(x * y) |
  11: (* REALDIVIDE *) realOperands(x,y); pushReal (x/y) |
  12: (* REALEQ *) realOperands(x,y);
     IF x = y THEN pushCard(1) ELSE pushCard(0) END |
  13: (* REALNOTEQ *) realOperands(x,y);
     IF x # y THEN pushCard(1) ELSE pushCard(0) END |
  14: (* REALLESS *) realOperands(x,y);
     IF x < y THEN pushCard(1) ELSE pushCard(0) END |
  15: (* REALGREATER *) realOperands(x,y);
     IF x > y THEN pushCard(1) ELSE pushCard(0) END |
  16: (* REALLESSEQ *) realOperands(x,y);
     IF x <= y THEN pushCard(1) ELSE pushCard(0) END |
  17: (* REALGREATEQ *) realOperands(x,y);
     IF x >= y THEN pushCard(1) ELSE pushCard(0) END
  END;
  jumpIP(returnAddress)
END extraIns;
```

```
PROCEDURE formAddress (opRec: opWordFields): CARDINAL;
VAR
  refAddress: CARDINAL;
BEGIN
  WITH opRec DO
    CASE m OF
    0: refAddress:= 0; indexing(rm, refAddress)|
    2: getWord(refAddress); indexing(rm, refAddress)|
    1: getWord(refAddress) |
    3: WriteString('Error: attempting memory ref when r/m is a register');
       WriteLn
    END
  END;
  RETURN refAddress
END formAddress;


PROCEDURE trace;
BEGIN
  WriteString('AX = '); WriteCard(register[AX],6);
  WriteString('   BX = '); WriteCard(register[BX],6);
  WriteString('   CX = '); WriteCard(register[CX],6); WriteLn;
  WriteString('DX = '); WriteCard(register[DX],6);
  WriteString('   BP = '); WriteCard(register[BP],6);
  WriteString('   IP = '); WriteCard(ipAddress(), 6); WriteLn;
  WriteString('DI = '); WriteCard(register[DI],6);
  WriteString('   SI = '); WriteCard(register[SI],6);
  WriteString('    Result value = '); WriteCard(resultValue, 5); WriteLn;
  IF register[SP] > 68 THEN    WriteString('SP = ');
    WriteCard(register[SP],6);
    WriteString('   Stack top = ');
    WriteCard(dereference(register[SP]),6);
    WriteString('    **********')
  END;  WriteLn; WriteLn
END trace;


BEGIN
  halted:= FALSE;
  REPEAT
    getOp(opRec);
    CASE opRec.category OF
      twoOperandCategory: twoOperandInstruction(opRec) |
      singleOperandCategory: singleOperandInstruction(opRec) |
      leaInstructionCategory: leaInstruction(opRec) |
      jumpInsCategory: jumpInstructions(opRec) |
      noOperandInsCategory: noOperandInstructions(opRec) |
      extraCategory: extraIns(opRec) |
      errorCategory: halted:= TRUE
    END;
```

```
    (* trace *)
  UNTIL halted
END interpret.


DEFINITION MODULE itmod is included in Section 12.3.4.

IMPLEMENTATION MODULE itmod;
FROM scanner IMPORT error, inSymbol, accept, sy, ind, valueRecord,
makeNegative;
FROM symbols IMPORT symbolType;
FROM Storage IMPORT ALLOCATE, DEALLOCATE;
FROM InOut IMPORT WriteString, WriteCard, WriteLn;
CONST
  idTableUB = 255;
  mask = BITSET(idTableUB);
TYPE
  classSet = SET OF class;
  symbolSet = SET OF symbolType;
VAR
  head,tail: idRecPtr;
  idTable: ARRAY[0..idTableUB] OF idRecPtr;

PROCEDURE findItsRecord(soughtInd: CARDINAL; VAR recPtr: idRecPtr; VAR
found: BOOLEAN);
BEGIN
  recPtr:= idTable[CARDINAL(BITSET(soughtInd) * mask)];
  LOOP
    IF recPtr = NIL THEN found:= FALSE; RETURN
    ELSIF recPtr^.itsInd = soughtInd THEN found:= TRUE; RETURN
    ELSE recPtr:= recPtr^.nextSyn
    END
  END
END findItsRecord;

PROCEDURE findField(soughtInd: CARDINAL; ptr: idRecPtr; VAR fieldDetails:
idRec; VAR found: BOOLEAN);
BEGIN
  LOOP
    IF ptr = NIL THEN found:= FALSE; RETURN
    ELSIF ptr^.itsInd = soughtInd THEN
      fieldDetails:= ptr^; found:= TRUE; RETURN
    ELSE ptr:= ptr^.nextSyn
    END;
  END
END findField;
```

```
PROCEDURE constant(VAR ofType: idRecPtr; VAR card1, card2:CARDINAL);
VAR
  recPtr: idRecPtr; negative, found: BOOLEAN;
BEGIN
  IF sy = plussOp THEN inSymbol; negative:= FALSE
  ELSIF sy = minusOp THEN negative:= TRUE; inSymbol
  ELSE negative:= FALSE
  END;
  IF sy = numberSy THEN
    ofType:= stIndex[valueRecord.valType];
    card1:= valueRecord.val1; card2:= valueRecord.val2
  ELSIF sy = idSy THEN
    findItsRecord(ind,recPtr,found);
    IF found THEN
      WITH recPtr^ DO
        IF itsClass = aConstant THEN
          ofType:= itsType; card1:= c1; card2:= c2
        ELSE found:= FALSE
        END
      END
    END;
    IF NOT found THEN error(11) END
  ELSE error(12)
  END;
  IF negative THEN
    IF ofType = tyReal THEN  makeNegative(card1,card2)
    ELSIF ofType = tyInteger THEN card1:= CARDINAL(-INTEGER(card1))
    ELSE error(12)
    END
  END;
  inSymbol
END constant;

PROCEDURE printTable;
VAR
  i,j: CARDINAL;
  tabPtr: idRecPtr; fPtr: idRecPtr;
BEGIN
  WriteString('Idtable is:'); WriteLn;
  FOR i:= 0 TO idTableUB DO
    tabPtr:= idTable[i];
    WHILE tabPtr # NIL DO
      WriteString('Ind = '); WriteCard(tabPtr^.itsInd,3);
      WriteString('   ORD(itsClass) = ');
      WriteCard(ORD(tabPtr^.itsClass), 3); WriteLn;
      IF tabPtr^.typeKind = recordType THEN
        fPtr:= tabPtr^.fieldPtr;
```

```
          FOR j:= 1 TO tabPtr^.noOfFields DO
            WriteString ('   Field ind = ');
            WriteCard(fPtr^.itsInd,3); WriteLn;
            fPtr:= fPtr^.nextSyn;
          END
        END;
        tabPtr:= tabPtr^.nextSyn
      END
  END; (* FOR *) HALT
END printTable;


PROCEDURE newIdRecord(VAR tabPtr: idRecPtr);
BEGIN
  ALLOCATE(tabPtr, SIZE(idRec));
  tail^.nextSeq:= tabPtr;
  tail:= tabPtr; tabPtr^.marked:= FALSE;
  tabPtr^.nextSeq:= NIL; tabPtr^.nextSyn:= NIL
END newIdRecord;


PROCEDURE enterIdRecord(ind: CARDINAL; VAR tablePtr: idRecPtr);
VAR
  subscript: CARDINAL;
BEGIN
  newIdRecord(tablePtr);
  subscript:= CARDINAL(BITSET(ind) * mask);
  WITH tablePtr^ DO nextSyn:= idTable[subscript]; itsInd:= ind END;
  idTable[subscript]:= tablePtr
END  enterIdRecord;


PROCEDURE makeIdRec(ind, length: CARDINAL; cl: class);
BEGIN
  ALLOCATE(idTable[ind], SIZE(idRec));
  WITH idTable[ind]^ DO
    itsInd:= ind; itsLength:= length; itsClass:= cl;
    nextSyn:= NIL;  nextSeq:= NIL; marked:= FALSE
  END
END makeIdRec;


PROCEDURE initialiseIdTable;
VAR
  i: CARDINAL;
BEGIN
  FOR i:= 0 TO idTableUB DO idTable[i]:= NIL END;
  makeIdRec(14, 1, aType); (* INTEGER *)
  idTable[14]^.typeKind:= aStandardType;
  tyInteger:= idTable[14]; stIndex[1]:= tyInteger;
  makeIdRec(3, 1, aType); (* BOOLEAN *);
  idTable[3]^.typeKind:= aStandardType;
```

```
    tyBoolean:= idTable[3]; stIndex[2]:= tyBoolean;
    makeIdRec(20, 2, aType); (* REAL *);
    idTable[20]^.typeKind:= aStandardType;
    tyReal:= idTable[20]; stIndex[3]:= tyReal;
    makeIdRec(9, 0, aConstant); (* FALSE *);
    WITH idTable[9]^ DO cl:= 0; itsType:= tyBoolean END;
    makeIdRec(22, 0, aConstant); (* TRUE *);
    WITH idTable[22]^ DO cl:= 1; itsType:= tyBoolean END;
    makeIdRec(25, 0, externalProc); (* READNUM *)
    makeIdRec(26, 0, externalProc); (* WRITENUM *)
    makeIdRec(27, 0, externalProc); (* NEWLINE *);
    tail:= tyReal
END initialiseIdTable;

BEGIN
  initialiseIdTable
END itmod.


DEFINITION MODULE labels;
PROCEDURE labelColon;
PROCEDURE commence;
PROCEDURE finalise;
PROCEDURE labelReference (labelInd: CARDINAL);
END labels.

IMPLEMENTATION MODULE labels;
FROM machCode IMPORT numericAddress, enter, enterAt,
  backPatch, putMachineCode;
FROM assLex IMPORT ind, sy, inSymbol, accept, error;
FROM InOut IMPORT WriteString, WriteCard, Write, WriteLn;
FROM symbType IMPORT symbolType;
FROM strinTbl IMPORT stringRec, stringInfo, stringText;
FROM Storage IMPORT ALLOCATE;
CONST
  endMarker = 10000;   (* larger than any address *)
  labelTableUB = 100;
  importUB =  60;
TYPE
  importRecord = RECORD
                   whichLabelInd, address: CARDINAL
                 END;
  listRecPtr = POINTER TO listRecord;
  listRecord = RECORD
                 labelInfo: stringRec;
                 extInd: CARDINAL;
                 next: listRecPtr
               END;
```

```
   labelStatus = (notSeen, referenced, declared, imported);
   labelTableRecord = RECORD
                         status: labelStatus;
                         address: CARDINAL
                      END;
VAR
   importTable : ARRAY [0..importUB] OF importRecord;
   labelTable  : ARRAY [0..labelTableUB] OF labelTableRecord;
   importReferences: [0..importUB];
   i: [0..labelTableUB];
   importLabels, exportLabels: listRecPtr;
   noOfImports, noOfExports, lastImport, lastExport,
   unknownLabels: CARDINAL;
   initialisingRecord: labelTableRecord;


PROCEDURE labelColon;
BEGIN
   CASE labelTable[ind].status OF
     declared, imported: error(5) | (* duplicate label *)
     notSeen:    WITH labelTable[ind] DO
                    address:= numericAddress; status:= declared;
                 END |
     referenced: backPatch(labelTable[ind].address, numericAddress);
                 WITH labelTable[ind] DO
                    address:= numericAddress; status:= declared
                 END; DEC (unknownLabels)
   END;
   inSymbol; accept(colonSy)
END labelColon;


PROCEDURE labelReference (labelInd: CARDINAL);
BEGIN
   CASE labelTable[labelInd].status OF
     declared:   enter(labelTable[labelInd].address,1) |
     notSeen:    WITH labelTable[labelInd] DO
                    status:= referenced;
                    address:= numericAddress
                 END;  enter(endMarker,1);
                 INC (unknownLabels) |
     referenced: WITH labelTable[labelInd] DO
                    enter(address,1);
                    address:= numericAddress - 1
                 END |
     imported:   WITH importTable[importReferences] DO
                    address:= numericAddress; enter(0,1);
                    whichLabelInd:= labelInd
                 END;
                 INC (importReferences);
```

```
    END
END labelReference;

PROCEDURE makeList(VAR head: listRecPtr; VAR howMany, lastInd: CARDINAL);
VAR
  newPtr: listRecPtr;
BEGIN
  howMany:= 0;
  REPEAT
    inSymbol; IF sy # labelSy THEN error(22) END;
    ALLOCATE (newPtr, SIZE(listRecPtr));
    WITH newPtr^ DO
      labelInfo:= stringInfo; extInd:= ind; next:= head;
    END;
    lastInd:= ind;  head:= newPtr; INC (howMany);
    inSymbol
  UNTIL sy <> commaSy;
  accept(newLineSy)
END makeList;

PROCEDURE outputLabel (soughtInd: CARDINAL);
VAR
  currentPtr: listRecPtr; found: BOOLEAN;
BEGIN
  currentPtr:= importLabels; found:= FALSE;
  LOOP
    IF currentPtr = NIL THEN error(20); EXIT
    ELSIF currentPtr^.extInd = soughtInd THEN
      stringText(currentPtr^.labelInfo); EXIT
    ELSE currentPtr:= currentPtr^.next
    END
  END
END outputLabel;

PROCEDURE commence;
VAR
  currentPtr: listRecPtr;
BEGIN
  importLabels:= NIL; exportLabels:= NIL;  inSymbol;
  WHILE sy = newLineSy DO inSymbol END;
    (* skip blank lines and comments *)
  IF sy = exportSy THEN
    makeList (exportLabels, noOfExports, lastExport)
  END;
  IF sy = importSy THEN
    makeList (importLabels, noOfImports, lastImport);
    currentPtr:= importLabels;
```

```
      WHILE currentPtr # NIL DO
        labelTable[currentPtr^.extInd].status:= imported;
        currentPtr:= currentPtr^.next
      END
    END
END commence;


PROCEDURE finalise;
VAR
  lastExternalRef, i, labelAddress: CARDINAL;
  currentPtr: listRecPtr;
BEGIN
  IF unknownLabels > 0 THEN error(43) END;
  WriteString ('N '); WriteCard (numericAddress,  6); WriteLn;
  WriteString ('E '); WriteCard (noOfExports, 5); WriteLn;
  currentPtr:= exportLabels;
  WHILE currentPtr # NIL DO
    WITH currentPtr^ DO
      labelAddress:= labelTable[extInd].address;
      IF labelTable[extInd].status # declared THEN error(20) END;
      stringText(labelInfo); Write (' ');
      WriteCard(labelAddress, 6); WriteLn
    END;
    currentPtr:= currentPtr^.next
  END;
  WriteString ('I '); WriteCard(importReferences, 6); WriteLn;
  IF importReferences > 0 THEN
    FOR i:= 0 TO importReferences  - 1 DO
      WITH importTable [i] DO
        outputLabel (whichLabelInd); Write(' ');
        WriteCard(address, 6); WriteLn
      END
    END
  END
  putMachineCode
END finalise;


BEGIN
  importReferences:= 0; unknownLabels:= 0;
  WITH initialisingRecord DO status:= notSeen; address:= endMarker END;
  FOR i:= 0 TO labelTableUB DO labelTable[i]:= initialisingRecord END
END labels.



DEFINITION MODULE lexInit;
VAR
  nextInd: CARDINAL;
END lexInit.
```

```
IMPLEMENTATION MODULE lexInit;
FROM InOut IMPORT  Read, Write, WriteString, WriteCard, WriteLn, ReadCard;
FROM strinTab IMPORT enter;
FROM symbols IMPORT symbolType;
FROM Storage IMPORT ALLOCATE;

PROCEDURE rEnter(str: ARRAY OF CHAR; symbol: symbolType);
BEGIN
  enter(str,symbol,0)
END rEnter;


PROCEDURE sEnter(str: ARRAY OF CHAR);
BEGIN
  enter(str, idSy, nextInd); INC(nextInd)
END sEnter;


BEGIN
  rEnter('AND ',andOp); rEnter('ARRAY ',arraySy);
  rEnter('BEGIN ',beginSy); rEnter('BY ', bySy);
  rEnter('CASE ',caseSy); rEnter('CONST ', constSy);
  rEnter('DEFINITION ',definitionSy); rEnter('DIV ', divOp);
  rEnter('DO ',doSy); rEnter('ELSE ', elseSy);
  rEnter('ELSIF ',elsifSy); rEnter('END ',endSy);
  rEnter('EXIT ', exitSy); rEnter('EXPORT ',exportSy);
  rEnter('FOR ', forSy); rEnter('FROM ',fromSy);
  rEnter('IF ',ifSy); rEnter('IMPLEMENTATION ', implementationSy);
  rEnter('IMPORT ',importSy); rEnter('IN ',inSy);
  rEnter('LOOP ',loopSy); rEnter('MOD ', modOp);
  rEnter('MODULE ', moduleSy); rEnter('NOT ', notOp);
  rEnter('OF ',ofSy); rEnter('OR ', orOp);
  rEnter('POINTER ',pointerSy); rEnter('PROCEDURE ',procedureSy);
  rEnter('QUALIFIED ',qualifiedSy); rEnter('RECORD ', recordSy);
  rEnter('REPEAT ',repeatSy); rEnter('RETURN ', returnSy);
  rEnter('SET ',setSy); rEnter('THEN ',thenSy);
  rEnter('TO ', toSy); rEnter('TYPE ', typeSy);
  rEnter('UNTIL ',untilSy); rEnter('VAR ', varSy);
  rEnter('WHILE ',whileSy); rEnter('WITH ',withSy);
  nextInd:= 1;
  sEnter ('ABS '); sEnter('BITSET '); sEnter('BOOLEAN ');
  sEnter ('CARDINAL '); sEnter('CHAR '); sEnter('CHR ');
  sEnter ('DEC '); sEnter('EXCL '); sEnter('FALSE ');
  sEnter ('FLOAT '); sEnter('HIGH '); sEnter('INC ');
  sEnter ('INCL '); sEnter('INTEGER '); sEnter('MAX ');
  sEnter ('MIN '); sEnter('NIL '); sEnter('ODD ');
  sEnter ('ORD '); sEnter('REAL '); sEnter('SIZE ');
  sEnter ('TRUE '); sEnter('TRUNC '); sEnter('VAL ');
  sEnter ('READNUM '); sEnter('WRITENUM ');
```

```
  sEnter('NEWLINE ')
END lexInit.


DEFINITION MODULE machCode is included in Section 4.2.

IMPLEMENTATION MODULE machCode;
FROM InOut IMPORT WriteString, Write, WriteCard, CloseOutput, WriteLn;
CONST
  endMarker = 10000;  (* larger than any address *)
  msBit = BITSET(8000H);
VAR
  machineCode: ARRAY machineCodeRange OF CARDINAL;
  bitMap   : ARRAY machineCodeRange OF bit;

PROCEDURE incAddressBy (amount: CARDINAL);
BEGIN
  INC(numericAddress, amount)
END incAddressBy;

PROCEDURE enter(aWord: CARDINAL; b: bit);
BEGIN
  machineCode[numericAddress]:= aWord;
  bitMap [numericAddress]:= b; INC(numericAddress)
END enter;

PROCEDURE enterAt(whatAddress: machineCodeRange; aWord: CARDINAL);
BEGIN
  machineCode[whatAddress]:= aWord
END enterAt;

PROCEDURE backPatch(refAddress, displacement: CARDINAL);
VAR
  thisEntry, nextEntry: CARDINAL;
BEGIN
  thisEntry:= refAddress;
  REPEAT
    nextEntry:= machineCode[thisEntry];
    machineCode[thisEntry]:= displacement;
    thisEntry:= nextEntry
  UNTIL thisEntry = endMarker
END backPatch;

PROCEDURE putMachineCode;
VAR
  n: CARDINAL; w: BITSET; count: [1..16];
BEGIN
```

```
    FOR n:= 0 TO numericAddress - 1 DO
      WriteCard(machineCode[n], 5);
      (* binary WriteWord would be more efficient *)
      (* instead optionally output pattern of 16 bits as follows *)
      (* w:= BITSET(machineCode[n]);
      FOR count:= 15 TO 0 BY - 1 DO
        IF count IN w THEN Write('1')
        ELSE Write('0')
        END;
      END; *)  (* next line should not be commented out *)
      Write(' '); WriteCard(bitMap[n],1); WriteLn
    END;  CloseOutput
END putMachineCode;


BEGIN
  numericAddress:= 0
END machCode.
```

DEFINITION MODULE mcMake is included in Section 14.6.3.

```
IMPLEMENTATION MODULE mcMake;
FROM InOut IMPORT  Read, Write, WriteString, WriteCard, WriteLn, ReadCard,
RedirectInput, CloseInput, Done;
FROM symbols IMPORT symbolType;
FROM strinTab IMPORT searchStringTable, insertString, stringType, stringUB;
FROM Storage IMPORT ALLOCATE, DEALLOCATE;
CONST
  endOfFile = 32C; endOfLine = 36C;
  maxNoOfFiles = 16;
TYPE
  charSet = SET OF CHAR;
  modRecPtr = POINTER TO modRec;
  modRec = RECORD
              moduleName: stringType;
              nameLength, moduleInd, numberOfImportModules: CARDINAL;
              letterIndex: ARRAY['A'..'Y'] OF CARDINAL;
              next: modRecPtr;
           END;
  waitingRecPtr = POINTER TO waitingRec;
  waitingRec = RECORD
                  moduleName: stringType;
                  nameLength, moduleInd: CARDINAL;
                  next: waitingRecPtr
               END;
VAR
  moduleListHead, currentModPtr: modRecPtr;
  waitingListHead: waitingRecPtr;
```

```
    ind, nextInd, noOfModules: CARDINAL;
    firstModule: BOOLEAN;

PROCEDURE printLists;
VAR
    waitingPtr: waitingRecPtr; mcPtr: modRecPtr;
    letter: CHAR; i: CARDINAL;
BEGIN
    (*  WriteString('Waiting list: '); WriteLn; waitingPtr:= waitingListHead;
    WHILE waitingPtr # NIL DO
      WITH waitingPtr^ DO
        WriteString(moduleName); WriteString('  ');
        WriteCard(moduleInd,4); WriteLn;
        waitingPtr:= next
      END
    END; *)
    WriteString('Make list: '); WriteLn; mcPtr:= moduleListHead;
    WHILE mcPtr # NIL DO
      WITH mcPtr^ DO
        WriteString(moduleName); WriteString('   ');
        WriteCard(moduleInd, 4); WriteLn;
        (* letter:= 'A';
        FOR i:= 1 TO numberOfImportModules DO
          Write(letter); Write(' ');
          WriteCard(letterIndex[letter],4); WriteLn;
          INC(letter)
        END;*)
        mcPtr:= next
      END
    END; WriteLn
END printLists;


PROCEDURE obtainString(VAR gotString: stringType; VAR length: CARDINAL);
VAR
    i,j: CARDINAL; ch: CHAR;
BEGIN
  REPEAT Read(ch) UNTIL ch = ';';
  REPEAT Read(ch) UNTIL ch # ' ';
  IF ch IN charSet{'A'..'Z','a'..'z'} THEN
    gotString[0]:= ch; i:= 0;
  ELSE WriteString('Name character error')
  END;
  LOOP
    Read(ch); IF NOT (ch IN charSet{'A'..'Z','a'..'z'}) THEN EXIT END;
    INC(i); gotString[i]:= ch
  END;
  length:= i + 1;
  FOR j:= i + 1 TO stringUB DO gotString[j]:= ' ' END;
```

```
END obtainString;

PROCEDURE obtainChar(VAR ch: CHAR);
BEGIN
  REPEAT Read(ch) UNTIL ch = ';';
  REPEAT Read(ch) UNTIL ch # ' ';
  IF NOT (ch IN charSet{'A'..'Z','a'..'z'}) THEN
    WriteString('Letter error')
  END
END obtainChar;

PROCEDURE inText(VAR inString: stringType; VAR length: CARDINAL);
VAR
  found: BOOLEAN;  sy: symbolType;
BEGIN
  obtainString(inString, length);
  searchStringTable(inString, length, sy, ind, found);
  IF NOT found THEN
    insertString(inString, length, idSy, nextInd);
    ind:= nextInd; INC(nextInd)
  END
END inText;

PROCEDURE makeRecordForModule;
VAR
  i, length, modInd, iNameLength: CARDINAL;
  name, fileName, inputName, importModName: stringType;
  newRecPtr: modRecPtr;
  chopPtr: waitingRecPtr;
  ch, currentLetter: CHAR;
BEGIN
  WITH waitingListHead^ DO
    name:= moduleName; length:= nameLength; modInd:= moduleInd
  END;
  chopPtr:= waitingListHead; waitingListHead:= waitingListHead^.next;
  DEALLOCATE(chopPtr, SIZE(waitingRec));
  fileName:= name;  fileName[length]:= '.'; i:= length + 1;
  fileName[i]:= 'S'; INC(i); fileName[i]:= 'A'; INC(i); fileName[i]:= 'L';
  RedirectInput(fileName);
  inText(inputName, iNameLength);
  IF ind # modInd THEN
    WriteString('Name in SAL file is wrong. Seeking ');
    WriteString(name); WriteString(',  but obtained ');
    WriteString(inputName); WriteLn
  END;
  obtainChar(ch);
```

```
  IF firstModule # (ch = 'M') THEN
    WriteString('Wrong kind of module'); WriteLn
  END;
  firstModule:= FALSE;
  ALLOCATE(newRecPtr, SIZE(modRec));
  WITH newRecPtr^ DO
    moduleName:= name; moduleInd:= ind;
    nameLength:= iNameLength;
    ReadCard(numberOfImportModules);
    next:= moduleListHead
  END;
  moduleListHead:= newRecPtr; currentLetter:= 'A';
  FOR i:= 1 TO newRecPtr^.numberOfImportModules DO
    inText(importModName, iNameLength); obtainChar(ch);
    IF ch # currentLetter THEN
      WriteString('Letter error in import list'); WriteLn
    END;
    newRecPtr^.letterIndex[currentLetter]:= ind;
    checkWaitingList(importModName, iNameLength, ind);
    INC(currentLetter)
  END
END makeRecordForModule;

PROCEDURE checkWaitingList(name: stringType; length, checkInd: CARDINAL);
VAR
  moduleListPtr: modRecPtr;
  waitingListPtr, newPtr: waitingRecPtr;
BEGIN
  moduleListPtr:= moduleListHead;
  WHILE moduleListPtr # NIL DO
    IF moduleListPtr^.moduleInd = checkInd THEN RETURN END;
    moduleListPtr:= moduleListPtr^.next
  END;
  waitingListPtr:= waitingListHead;
  WHILE waitingListPtr # NIL DO
    IF waitingListPtr^.moduleInd = checkInd THEN RETURN END;
    waitingListPtr:= waitingListPtr^.next
  END;
  ALLOCATE(newPtr, SIZE(waitingRec));
  WITH newPtr^ DO
    moduleName:= name; nameLength:= length;
    moduleInd:= checkInd; next:= waitingListHead
  END;
  waitingListHead:= newPtr
END checkWaitingList;
```

```
PROCEDURE mcList;
VAR
  newPtr: modRecPtr;
BEGIN
  WHILE waitingListHead # NIL DO makeRecordForModule END;
  ALLOCATE(newPtr, SIZE(modRec));
  WITH newPtr^ DO
    moduleName:= 'stackMod                 '; nameLength:= 8;
    moduleInd:= 0; numberOfImportModules:= 0;
    next:= moduleListHead
  END;
  moduleListHead:= newPtr;
  currentModPtr:= NIL;
  printLists
END mcList;


PROCEDURE startFile(VAR noneLeft: BOOLEAN; VAR modInd: CARDINAL);
VAR
  fileName: stringType;  i: CARDINAL;
BEGIN
  IF currentModPtr = NIL THEN currentModPtr:= moduleListHead ELSE
    currentModPtr:= currentModPtr^.next
  END;
  IF currentModPtr = NIL THEN noneLeft:= TRUE; RETURN
  ELSE noneLeft:= FALSE
  END;
  modInd:= currentModPtr^.moduleInd;
  WITH currentModPtr^ DO
    fileName:= moduleName; i:= nameLength;
    fileName[i]:= '.'; INC(i); fileName[i]:= 'S';
    INC(i); fileName[i]:= 'B'; INC(i); fileName[i]:= 'S'
  END;
  RedirectInput(fileName);
  IF NOT Done THEN
    WriteString('Failed to open ');
    WriteString(fileName); WriteLn;
    noneLeft:= TRUE
  END
END startFile;


PROCEDURE moduleForLetter(ch: CHAR): CARDINAL;
BEGIN
  IF NOT (ch IN charSet{'A'..'Z'}) THEN
    WriteString('Error in module letter. ch = ');
    Write(ch); WriteLn; HALT
  END;
```

```
    WITH currentModPtr^ DO
      IF ORD(ch) - ORD('A') + 1 > numberOfImportModules THEN
        WriteString('Error: import from absent module'); WriteLn;
        WriteString('Current module ind =');
        WriteCard(currentModPtr^.moduleInd, 3);
        WriteString(' Sought letter = '); Write(ch); WriteLn
      END;
      RETURN letterIndex[ch]
    END
END moduleForLetter;


PROCEDURE restart;
BEGIN
  currentModPtr:= NIL
END restart;


BEGIN
  firstModule:= TRUE; nextInd:= 1;
  ALLOCATE(moduleListHead, SIZE(modRec));
  WITH moduleListHead^ DO
    moduleName:= 'salSubs                  ' ; nameLength:= 7;
    moduleInd:= 0; numberOfImportModules:= 0; next:= NIL
  END;
  ALLOCATE(waitingListHead, SIZE(waitingRec));
  WITH waitingListHead^ DO
    moduleName:= 'main                 ';
    nameLength:= 4; moduleInd:= 1; next:= NIL
  END
END mcMake.



DEFINITION MODULE mcModule is included in Section 5.2.

IMPLEMENTATION MODULE mcModule;
FROM Storage IMPORT ALLOCATE;
FROM InOut IMPORT  Read, Write, WriteString, WriteCard, WriteLn, ReadCard,
RedirectInput, CloseInput, Done;
CONST
  endOfFile = 32C; endOfLine = 36C; charUB = 24;
TYPE
  charString = ARRAY [1..charUB] OF CHAR;
  nameRecPtr = POINTER TO nameRec;
  nameRec = RECORD
                  moduleName: charString;
                  next: nameRecPtr
              END;
VAR
  moduleListHead, currentModPtr: nameRecPtr;
```

```
PROCEDURE mcList;
VAR
  ch: CHAR;  i,j: CARDINAL;
  newPtr, tail: nameRecPtr;
BEGIN
  RedirectInput("McFile");
  moduleListHead:= NIL; Read (ch);
  WHILE ch # endOfFile DO
    i:= 1; ALLOCATE(newPtr, SIZE(nameRec));
    WITH newPtr^ DO
      WHILE ch # endOfLine DO
        moduleName[i]:= ch; INC(i); Read(ch)
      END;
      FOR j:= i TO charUB DO moduleName[j]:= ' ' END;
      next:= NIL
    END; (* WITH *)
    IF moduleListHead = NIL THEN moduleListHead:= newPtr;
    ELSE tail^.next:= newPtr
    END;
    tail:= newPtr; Read (ch);
  END;
  CloseInput
END mcList;


PROCEDURE restart;
BEGIN
  currentModPtr:= NIL
END restart;


PROCEDURE startFile(VAR noneLeft: BOOLEAN);
BEGIN
  IF currentModPtr = NIL THEN currentModPtr:= moduleListHead
  ELSE currentModPtr:= currentModPtr^.next
  END;
  IF currentModPtr = NIL THEN noneLeft:= TRUE; RETURN
  ELSE noneLeft:= FALSE
  END;
  RedirectInput(currentModPtr^.moduleName);
  IF NOT Done THEN WriteString('Failed to open ');
    WriteString(currentModPtr^.moduleName); WriteLn
  END
END startFile;


BEGIN
END mcModule.
```

```
DEFINITION MODULE moDecs;
FROM pritmod IMPORT idRecPtr;
FROM prSAL IMPORT labelString;
PROCEDURE procInitialise(ind: CARDINAL; VAR procPtr: idRecPtr;
  VAR startLabel: labelString; VAR varWords, prmLength: CARDINAL;
  VAR resType: idRecPtr;  VAR aFunction: BOOLEAN);
PROCEDURE defModuleDecs (exported: BOOLEAN; VAR words: CARDINAL);
PROCEDURE block (VAR words: CARDINAL; endInd: CARDINAL);
PROCEDURE enclosedByGlobalProc (ptr: idRecPtr);
PROCEDURE checkAllExportedProcsImplemented;
END moDecs.


IMPLEMENTATION MODULE moDecs;
FROM scanner IMPORT error, inSymbol, outSymbol, accept,
  sy, ind;
FROM symbols IMPORT symbolType;
FROM Storage IMPORT ALLOCATE, DEALLOCATE;
FROM InOut IMPORT WriteString, WriteCard, WriteLn;
FROM prSAL IMPORT labelString, genLabel, standardImports;
FROM pritmod IMPORT class, kindOfType, kindOfProc, idRec, idRecPtr,
constant, tyInteger, tyBoolean, tyReal, findItsRecord, enterIdRecord,
newIdRecord, findField, checkDuplicateIdentifier, pushProc, popProc,
printTable (* *);
TYPE
  symbolSet = SET OF symbolType;
  listRecPtr = POINTER TO listRec;
  listRec = RECORD
                 item: CARDINAL;
                 next: listRecPtr
            END;
VAR
  globalPtr, decModPtr, exportedProcListPtr: idRecPtr;
  blockLevel: CARDINAL;


PROCEDURE makeList(VAR head: listRecPtr);
VAR
  n: INTEGER;  tail: listRecPtr;
BEGIN
  head:= NIL; tail:= NIL;
  IF sy # idSy THEN error(44); RETURN END;
  ALLOCATE(head, SIZE(listRec)); head^.item:= ind;
  head^.next:= NIL; tail:= head;
  inSymbol;
  WHILE sy = commaSy DO
    inSymbol;
```

```
    IF sy = idSy THEN
      ALLOCATE(tail^.next, SIZE(listRec));
      tail:= tail^.next;
      tail^.item:= ind; tail^.next:= NIL
    ELSE error(44)
    END;
    inSymbol
  END;
  accept(colonSy)
END makeList;


PROCEDURE constDecs;
VAR
  consType, idTabPtr: idRecPtr;
  card1, card2: CARDINAL;
BEGIN
  inSymbol;
  WHILE sy = idSy DO
    checkDuplicateIdentifier(ind);
    enterIdRecord(ind, idTabPtr);
    inSymbol; accept(equOp);
    constant(consType, card1, card2);
    WITH idTabPtr^ DO
      itsClass:= aConstant; itsType:= consType;
      c1:= card1; c2:= card2
    END;
    accept(semiColonSy);
  END
END constDecs;


PROCEDURE arrayDec(arrayRecordPtr: idRecPtr);
VAR
  v2, firstBound, secondBound, noOfDimensions, count: CARDINAL;
  lowerBoundType, upperBoundType, arrayElementType,
  currentPtr, previousPtr, recPtr: idRecPtr;
  found, lastDimension: BOOLEAN;
BEGIN
  inSymbol; accept(openSqBrktSy);
  noOfDimensions:= 0; lastDimension:= FALSE;
  REPEAT
    INC(noOfDimensions);
    constant(lowerBoundType, firstBound, v2); accept(dotDotSy);
    constant(upperBoundType, secondBound, v2);
    IF INTEGER(firstBound) > INTEGER(secondBound) THEN error(41) END;
    accept(closeSqrBrktSy);
    IF sy = ofSy THEN
      lastDimension:= TRUE; inSymbol; typeRecord(recPtr);
    ELSE accept(commaSy); accept(openSqBrktSy)
```

```
      END;
    IF (lowerBoundType = upperBoundType) AND
      ((lowerBoundType = tyBoolean) OR (lowerBoundType = tyInteger)) THEN
      WITH arrayRecordPtr^ DO
        itsClass:= aType; typeKind:= arrayType; indexType:= lowerBoundType;
        lowBound:= INTEGER(firstBound); upBound:= INTEGER(secondBound);
        IF lastDimension THEN elementType:= recPtr ELSE
          previousPtr:= arrayRecordPtr; newIdRecord(arrayRecordPtr);
          elementType:= arrayRecordPtr;
          arrayRecordPtr^.nextSyn:= previousPtr
        END
      END
    ELSE error(18)
    END;
  UNTIL lastDimension;
  currentPtr:= arrayRecordPtr;
  FOR count:= 1 TO noOfDimensions DO
    WITH  currentPtr^ DO
      itsLength:= elementType^.itsLength *
        CARDINAL(upBound - lowBound + 1)
    END; currentPtr:= currentPtr^.nextSyn
  END (* FOR *)
END arrayDec;

PROCEDURE recordDec (recRecPtr: idRecPtr);
VAR
  currentPtr: listRecPtr;
  newFieldPtr, fieldType, recTail: idRecPtr;
  fieldInfo: idRec; found: BOOLEAN;
  nextFieldAddress, numberOfFields, fieldLength, recordLength: CARDINAL;
BEGIN
  inSymbol; recTail:= NIL;
  nextFieldAddress:= 0; numberOfFields:= 0;
  WHILE sy = idSy DO
    makeList(currentPtr); typeRecord(fieldType);
    fieldLength:= fieldType^.itsLength;
    WHILE currentPtr # NIL DO
      findField(currentPtr^.item, recRecPtr^.nextSyn, fieldInfo, found);
      IF found THEN error (17) ELSE
        INC(numberOfFields); newIdRecord(newFieldPtr);
        WITH newFieldPtr^ DO
          itsInd:= currentPtr^.item; itsType:= fieldType;
          fieldAddress:= nextFieldAddress; nextSyn:= NIL
        END;
        IF recTail = NIL THEN recRecPtr^.fieldPtr:= newFieldPtr
        ELSE recTail^.nextSyn:= newFieldPtr
        END;
        recTail:= newFieldPtr;
```

```
        INC(nextFieldAddress, fieldLength)
      END; (* IF FOUND *)
      currentPtr:= currentPtr^.next
    END; (* WHILE *)
    inSymbol;  IF sy # endSy THEN accept (semiColonSy) END
  END; (* WHILE *)
  IF sy # endSy THEN error (13) END;
  WITH recRecPtr^ DO
    itsClass:= aType; typeKind:= recordType;
    itsLength:= nextFieldAddress; noOfFields:= numberOfFields
  END
END recordDec;


PROCEDURE typeRecord(VAR typePtr: idRecPtr);
VAR
  typeType: CARDINAL; found: BOOLEAN;
BEGIN
  CASE sy OF
    idSy:   findItsRecord(ind, typePtr, found);
            IF NOT found THEN error(81) ELSE
              WITH typePtr^ DO
                IF itsClass # aType THEN error (82)
                ELSIF typeKind = typeAlias THEN typePtr:= itsType
                END;
              END
            END |
    araySy:  newIdRecord(typePtr);  arrayDec(typePtr)   |
    recordSy: newIdRecord(typePtr); recordDec(typePtr)
  ELSE error (32)
  END
END typeRecord;


PROCEDURE typeDecs;
VAR
  typeInd: CARDINAL; found: BOOLEAN;
  typeType, idTabPtr: idRecPtr;
BEGIN
  inSymbol;
  WHILE sy = idSy DO
    checkDuplicateIdentifier(ind); typeInd:= ind;
    inSymbol;  accept(equOp);
    CASE sy OF
    idSy: findItsRecord(ind, typeType, found);
          IF found THEN
            IF typeType^.itsClass = aType THEN
              enterIdRecord(typeInd, idTabPtr);
```

```
              WITH idTabPtr^ DO
                itsType:= typeType; typeKind:= typeAlias;
                itsLength:= typeType^.itsLength
              END;
            ELSE error(14)
            END
          ELSE error(14)
          END  |
    arraySy:  enterIdRecord(typeInd, idTabPtr); arrayDec (idTabPtr) |
    recordSy: enterIdRecord(typeInd, idTabPtr); recordDec(idTabPtr)
    ELSE error(14)
    END;
    inSymbol;  accept(semiColonSy)
  END (* WHILE *)
END typeDecs;


PROCEDURE varDecs(VAR nextAddress: CARDINAL);
VAR
  currentPtr: listRecPtr; thisType, idTabPtr: idRecPtr;
  varInd: CARDINAL;
BEGIN
  inSymbol;
  WHILE sy = idSy DO
    makeList(currentPtr);  typeRecord(thisType);
    WHILE currentPtr # NIL DO
      varInd:= currentPtr^.item;
      checkDuplicateIdentifier(varInd);
      enterIdRecord(varInd, idTabPtr);
      WITH idTabPtr^ DO
        itsInd:= varInd; itsClass:= aVariable; baseLabel:= 'ZAAA';
        relAddress:= nextAddress; itsType:= thisType; itsLevel:= blockLevel
      END;
      INC(nextAddress, thisType^.itsLength); currentPtr:= currentPtr^.next
    END;
    inSymbol; accept(semiColonSy)
  END
END varDecs;


PROCEDURE proceDec;
VAR
  procPtr: idRecPtr; procInd: CARDINAL;
  newProc: BOOLEAN;
BEGIN
  outSymbol; inSymbol; outSymbol; (* procedureSy and ind *)
  IF blockLevel > 0 THEN
    IF sy # idSy THEN error (33) ELSE
      checkDuplicateIdentifier(ind)
    END;
```

```
      procInd:= ind; enterIdRecord(procInd, procPtr);
      INC(blockLevel); pushProc(procPtr);
      procPtr^.beingCompiled:= TRUE;
      procHeading(procInd, procPtr);
    ELSE checkInd(procInd, newProc, procPtr);
      IF newProc THEN enterIdRecord(procInd, procPtr) END;
      INC(blockLevel); pushProc(procPtr);
      procPtr^.beingCompiled:= TRUE;
      IF newProc THEN procHeading(procInd, procPtr)
      ELSE checkHeading(procInd, procPtr)
      END
    END;
    procPtr^.varLength:= 3;  block(procPtr^.varLength, procInd);
    procPtr^.beingCompiled:= FALSE;
    DEC(blockLevel); popProc; accept(semiColonSy)
  END proceDec;


  PROCEDURE procHeading(procInd: CARDINAL;  procPtr: idRecPtr);
  VAR
    paramPtr, functionReturnType, thisType: idRecPtr;
    nextAddress, numberOfParams, count: CARDINAL;
    varParam: BOOLEAN;  currentPtr: listRecPtr;
  BEGIN
    inSymbol; nextAddress:= 0; numberOfParams:= 0;
    IF sy = openRndBrktSy THEN
      inSymbol;
      WHILE sy IN symbolSet{idSy, varSy} DO
        IF sy = varSy THEN inSymbol; varParam:= TRUE ELSE
          varParam:= FALSE
        END;
        makeList(currentPtr);
        IF sy = idSy THEN typeRecord(thisType) ELSE error(101) END;
        IF thisType^.itsClass = aType THEN
          WHILE currentPtr # NIL DO
            checkDuplicateIdentifier(currentPtr^.item);
            enterIdRecord(currentPtr^.item,paramPtr);
            (* for this parameter *)
            WITH paramPtr^ DO
              IF varParam THEN itsClass:= aVARparameter
              ELSE itsClass:= aVariable
              END;
              relAddress:= nextAddress; itsType:= thisType;
              itsLevel:= blockLevel
            END;
            INC(nextAddress, thisType^.itsLength);
            INC(numberOfParams); currentPtr:= currentPtr^.next
          END
        ELSE error(102)
```

```
      END;
      inSymbol; IF sy = semiColonSy THEN inSymbol END
    END; (* WHILE *)
    paramPtr:= procPtr^.nextSeq;
    FOR count:= 1 TO numberOfParams DO
      DEC(paramPtr^.relAddress, nextAddress); paramPtr:= paramPtr^.nextSeq
    END;
    accept(closeRndBrktSy);
    IF sy = colonSy THEN
      procPtr^.procKind:= functionProc; inSymbol;
      IF sy = idSy THEN typeRecord(functionReturnType) ELSE error(35) END;
      IF (functionReturnType # tyBoolean) AND (functionReturnType # tyReal)
      AND (functionReturnType # tyInteger) THEN error (36)
      END;
      inSymbol
    ELSE procPtr^.procKind:= pureProc
    END
  ELSE procPtr^.procKind:= pureProc
  END;
  WITH procPtr^ DO
    itsClass:= aProcedure; procLevel:= blockLevel - 1;
    internalLevel:= blockLevel;
    noOfParams:= numberOfParams; paramLength:= nextAddress;
    genLabel(beginLabel);
    IF procKind = functionProc THEN resultType:= functionReturnType END
  END;
  accept(semiColonSy)
END procHeading;


PROCEDURE checkHeading(procInd: CARDINAL;  procPtr: idRecPtr);
VAR
  paramPtr, functionReturnType, thisType: idRecPtr;
  numberOfParams, count: CARDINAL;
  varParam: BOOLEAN;  currentPtr: listRecPtr;
BEGIN
  inSymbol;  numberOfParams:= 0;
  IF sy = openRndBrktSy THEN
    inSymbol; paramPtr:= procPtr^.nextSeq;
    WHILE sy IN symbolSet{idSy, varSy} DO
      IF sy = varSy THEN inSymbol; varParam:= TRUE
      ELSE varParam:= FALSE
      END;
      makeList(currentPtr);
      IF sy = idSy THEN typeRecord(thisType)
      ELSE error(206); WriteLn
      END;
```

```
      IF thisType^.itsClass = aType THEN
        WHILE currentPtr # NIL DO
          IF paramPtr = NIL THEN error(207); RETURN END;
          WITH paramPtr^ DO
            IF (itsInd # currentPtr^.item) OR
              (itsType # thisType) OR
              (itsLevel # blockLevel) OR
              (varParam # (itsClass = aVARparameter))
            THEN error(211)
            END
          END;
          INC(numberOfParams); currentPtr:= currentPtr^.next;
          paramPtr:= paramPtr^.nextSeq;
        END (* WHILE *)
      ELSE error(208)
      END;
      inSymbol; IF sy = semiColonSy THEN inSymbol END
    END; (* WHILE *)
    accept(closeRndBrktSy);
    IF sy = colonSy THEN
      inSymbol;
      IF sy = idSy THEN typeRecord(functionReturnType) ELSE error(35) END;
      WITH procPtr^ DO
        IF (procKind # functionProc) OR
          (resultType # functionReturnType) THEN error (209)
        END
      END; inSymbol
    END
  END;
  WITH procPtr^ DO
    IF (itsClass # aProcedure) OR (itsInd # procInd)
      OR (procLevel # blockLevel - 1) OR (noOfParams # numberOfParams) THEN
      error(210)
    END
  END;
  accept(semiColonSy)
END checkHeading;

PROCEDURE procTag (exported: BOOLEAN);
VAR
  procPtr: idRecPtr;  procInd: CARDINAL;
BEGIN
  inSymbol;
  IF sy # idSy THEN error (203) ELSE
    checkDuplicateIdentifier(ind)
  END;
  procInd:= ind; enterIdRecord(procInd, procPtr);
  INC(blockLevel); pushProc(procPtr);
```

```
    procPtr^.beingCompiled:= TRUE;
    procHeading(procInd, procPtr);
    DEC(blockLevel); popProc;
    IF exported THEN
      procPtr^.nextProc:= exportedProcListPtr;
      exportedProcListPtr:= procPtr;
    END
END procTag;

PROCEDURE checkInd(VAR procInd: CARDINAL; VAR newProc: BOOLEAN; VAR
procPtr: idRecPtr);
VAR
  previousPtr: idRecPtr;
BEGIN
  IF sy # idSy THEN error(205); RETURN ELSE procInd:= ind END;
  procPtr:= exportedProcListPtr; previousPtr:= NIL;
  LOOP (* search list of exported procedures *)
    IF procPtr = NIL THEN
      newProc:= TRUE;
      checkDuplicateIdentifier(procInd); RETURN
    ELSIF procPtr^.itsInd = procInd THEN
      newProc:= FALSE;
      IF previousPtr = NIL THEN
        exportedProcListPtr:= procPtr^.nextProc
      ELSE previousPtr^.nextProc:= procPtr^.nextProc
      END; EXIT
    ELSE previousPtr:= procPtr; procPtr:= procPtr^.nextProc
    END
  END;
  procPtr^.enclosedBy:= NIL;
  checkDuplicateIdentifier(procInd);
  procPtr^.enclosedBy:= globalPtr
END checkInd;

PROCEDURE defModuleDecs (exported: BOOLEAN; VAR words: CARDINAL);
BEGIN
  LOOP
    IF sy = constSy THEN constDecs
    ELSIF sy = typeSy THEN typeDecs
    ELSIF sy = varSy THEN varDecs(words)
    ELSIF sy = procedureSy THEN procTag (exported)
    ELSE EXIT
    END
  END
END defModuleDecs;
```

```
PROCEDURE block (VAR words: CARDINAL; endInd: CARDINAL);
BEGIN
  LOOP
    IF sy = constSy THEN constDecs
    ELSIF sy = typeSy THEN typeDecs
    ELSIF sy = varSy THEN varDecs(words)
    ELSIF sy = procedureSy THEN proceDec
    ELSE EXIT
    END
  END;
  IF sy = beginSy THEN outSymbol ELSE error (93) END;
  LOOP
    inSymbol; outSymbol;
    IF sy = endSy THEN
      REPEAT inSymbol; outSymbol UNTIL sy # endSy;
      IF sy = idSy THEN
        IF ind # endInd THEN  error(94) END;
        EXIT
      END
    END
  END;
  inSymbol; outSymbol
END block;

PROCEDURE procInitialise(ind: CARDINAL; VAR procPtr: idRecPtr; VAR
startLabel: labelString; VAR varWords, prmLength: CARDINAL; VAR resType:
idRecPtr;  VAR aFunction: BOOLEAN);
VAR
  found: BOOLEAN;
BEGIN
  findItsRecord(ind, procPtr, found);
  IF NOT found THEN error (66); RETURN END;
  WITH procPtr^ DO
    startLabel:= beginLabel; varWords:= varLength;
    prmLength:= paramLength;  resType:= resultType;
    aFunction:= (procKind = functionProc); beingCompiled:= TRUE
  END
END procInitialise;

PROCEDURE checkAllExportedProcsImplemented;
BEGIN
  IF exportedProcListPtr # NIL THEN error(506) END
END checkAllExportedProcsImplemented;

PROCEDURE enclosedByGlobalProc (ptr: idRecPtr);
BEGIN
  ptr^.enclosedBy:= globalPtr
END enclosedByGlobalProc;
```

```
BEGIN
  ALLOCATE (globalPtr, SIZE(idRec)); (* pseudo-procedure record *)
  WITH globalPtr^ DO
    itsClass:= aProcedure; internalLevel:= 0;
    beingCompiled:= TRUE; itsInd:= 0
  END;
  pushProc(globalPtr); blockLevel:= 0;
  exportedProcListPtr:= NIL
END moDecs.



MODULE moLink;
FROM InOut IMPORT  Read, Write, WriteString, WriteCard, WriteLn, ReadCard,
RedirectInput, CloseInput, Done;
FROM FileSystem IMPORT Lookup, Rewrite, Close, WriteWord, File;
FROM strinTbl IMPORT searchStringTable, insertString, stringType;
FROM symbType IMPORT symbolType;
FROM mcMake IMPORT mcList, restart, startFile;
FROM gLabTab IMPORT relocatingConst, getExports, whichAddress;
CONST
  endOfFile = 32C; endOfLine = 36C;
  imporTableUB = 50;
TYPE
  charSet = SET OF CHAR;
VAR
  ch: CHAR;  sy: symbolType; ind: CARDINAL;


PROCEDURE inText (VAR firstCh: CHAR);
VAR
  length: CARDINAL; found: BOOLEAN;
  inString: stringType; ch: CHAR;
BEGIN
  length:= 0; ch:= firstCh;
  REPEAT
    inString[length]:= ch;
    INC (length); Read(ch);
  UNTIL NOT (ch IN charSet{'A'..'Z'});
  IF length > 4 THEN firstCh:= '@' ELSE inString[0]:= 'Z' END;
  searchStringTable (inString, length, sy, ind, found);
  IF NOT found THEN
    WriteString('Error: label not found: ');
    WriteString(inString); WriteLn
  END
END inText;
```

```
PROCEDURE putBinary(w: CARDINAL);
VAR
  count: CARDINAL;
BEGIN
  FOR count:= 15 TO 0 BY -1 DO
    IF count IN BITSET(w) THEN Write('1') ELSE Write('0') END;
  END;
END putBinary;


PROCEDURE relocate;
VAR
  i, j, whichFile, whichEntry, n, relocatingVar, moduleInd,
  eNumber, iNumber, numericAddress, machineCodeWord, bit: CARDINAL;
  imporTable: ARRAY [1..imporTableUB] OF
                RECORD
                  where, refAddress: CARDINAL
                END;
    absBinry: File;
    noneLeft: BOOLEAN;
BEGIN
  Lookup(absBinry, 'absBinry', TRUE); Rewrite(absBinry);
  relocatingVar:= relocatingConst; n:= 0;
  LOOP
    startFile(noneLeft, moduleInd); IF noneLeft THEN EXIT END;
    INC(relocatingVar, n);
    Read(ch); IF ch # 'N' THEN WriteString ('Missing N'); WriteLn END;
    ReadCard(n);
    Read(ch); IF ch # 'E' THEN WriteString ('Missing E'); WriteLn END;
    ReadCard (eNumber); Read(ch);
    FOR i:= 1 TO eNumber DO
      WHILE ch # endOfLine DO Read(ch) END; Read(ch)
    END;
    IF ch # 'I' THEN WriteString ('Missing I'); WriteLn END;
    ReadCard(iNumber);
    FOR i:= 1 TO iNumber DO
      Read(ch); IF ch = ' ' THEN WriteString('Read a space'); HALT END;
      inText(ch);
      WITH imporTable[i] DO ReadCard(where);
        refAddress:= whichAddress(ch,ind)
      END
    END;
    whichEntry:= 1;
    FOR i:= 0 TO n-1 DO
      ReadCard(machineCodeWord);  ReadCard(bit);
      IF bit = 0 THEN WriteWord(absBinry, machineCodeWord)
```

```
    ELSIF bit = 1 THEN
      IF whichEntry <= iNumber THEN
        WITH impórTable [whichEntry] DO
          IF i = where THEN
            WriteWord(absBinry, refAddress);
            INC (whichEntry);
          ELSE WriteWord(absBinry, machineCodeWord + relocatingVar)
          END
        END
      ELSE WriteWord(absBinry, machineCodeWord + relocatingVar)
      END
    ELSE WriteString ('Error. Bit map bit = '); WriteCard(bit,3)
    END
  END;
  IF whichEntry # iNumber + 1 THEN
    WriteString('Error: Unused import.  WhichEntry = ');
    WriteCard(whichEntry, 4);
    WriteString(',   iNumber = '); WriteCard(iNumber, 4); WriteLn
  END;
  CloseInput
END; Close(absBinry)
END relocate;

BEGIN
  mcList; restart; getExports; restart; relocate
END moLink.


MODULE moMain;
FROM InOut IMPORT WriteString, WriteLn, WriteCard;
FROM pritmod IMPORT idRecPtr;
FROM moDecs IMPORT procInitialise;
FROM frstPass IMPORT moduleVarLength, impModule;
FROM bis IMPORT inSymbol, sy, valueRecord, ind, error, accept,
openInterFile, closeInterFile;
FROM symbols IMPORT symbolType;
FROM prSAL IMPORT labelString, genLabel, putLabel, putLine, putStrings,
putStringAndVal;
FROM callRet IMPORT blockLevel, pushRetStack, popRetStack, noReturn,
returnStatement;
FROM prStmnt IMPORT stmntSequence;
CONST
  stackSize = 100;
VAR
  moduleInd: CARDINAL;  progStart: labelString;
```

```
PROCEDURE procBody;
VAR
  procedureInd, varWords, paramLength: CARDINAL;
  procPtr, resultType: idRecPtr;
  startLabel: labelString; itsaFunction: BOOLEAN;
BEGIN
  inSymbol;  procedureInd:= ind;
  procInitialise (ind, procPtr, startLabel, varWords,
    paramLength, resultType, itsaFunction);
  inSymbol; (* end of procedure heading *)
  INC (blockLevel);
  WHILE sy = procedureSy DO procBody END;
  pushRetStack(paramLength, resultType, itsaFunction);
  accept(beginSy); putLabel(startLabel);
  putStringAndVal('    ADD SP,', varWords);
  stmntSequence; accept(endSy);
  IF (sy # idSy) OR (ind # procedureInd) THEN error(52) END;
  IF itsaFunction THEN
    putLine('    MOV AX, 998');
    putLine('    PUSH AX');
    putLine('    CALL INTWRITE');
    putLine('    CALL ENDPROG');
    IF noReturn() THEN error(51) END
  ELSE returnStatement
  END;
  popRetStack; DEC(blockLevel);
  procPtr^.beingCompiled:= FALSE; inSymbol; accept(semiColonSy)
END procBody;

BEGIN
  openInterFile;
  putLine('    LEA BP, ZAAA');
  genLabel(progStart);  putStrings('    JMP ',progStart);
  WriteString('ZAAA:  DW '); WriteCard(moduleVarLength,5);
  WriteString(' DUP '); WriteLn;
  inSymbol; accept(moduleSy);  moduleInd:= ind;
  blockLevel:= 0;
  accept(idSy); accept(semiColonSy);
  WHILE sy = procedureSy DO procBody END;
  accept(beginSy); putLabel(progStart); putLine('    NOP');
  stmntSequence; accept(endSy); putLine('    NOP');
  IF (sy # idSy) OR (ind # moduleInd) THEN error(52) END;
  inSymbol; accept(periodSy);
  IF NOT impModule THEN  putLine('    CALL ENDPROG ') END;
  closeInterFile
END moMain.
```

```
MODULE nonRec;
FROM InOut IMPORT WriteLn, WriteString, WriteCard, Write, Read;
CONST
  stackUB = 20;   (* stack upper bound *)
  endOfFile = 32C;
TYPE
  symbolType = (A,B,C,D,E,S,t,u,v,w,x,y,endMarker,empty);
  symbolSet = SET OF symbolType;
  terminalSymbols = [t..empty];
  nonTerminals = [A..S];
  rhsRec = RECORD
              numberOfSymbolsInRHS: CARDINAL;
              rhsSymbol: ARRAY[1..3] OF symbolType
           END;
VAR
  sy: symbolType;
  top: [0..stackUB];
  stack: ARRAY [1..stackUB] OF symbolType;
  syntaxError: BOOLEAN;
  parseTable: ARRAY nonTerminals, terminalSymbols OF rhsRec;
  terminals: symbolSet;
  q: [1..3];

PROCEDURE error(n:INTEGER);
VAR
  ch: CHAR;
BEGIN
  WriteString('Error number: '); WriteCard(n,3); WriteLn; syntaxError:=
TRUE;
  IF sy # endMarker THEN
    REPEAT Read(ch) UNTIL (ch = '$') OR (ch = endOfFile)
  END
END error;

PROCEDURE initialise;
VAR
  i: nonTerminals; j: terminalSymbols;

  PROCEDURE insert2(nont,term,first,second: symbolType);
  BEGIN
    WITH parseTable[nont, term] DO
      numberOfSymbolsInRHS:= 2;
      rhsSymbol[1]:= first; rhsSymbol[2]:= second
    END
  END insert2;
```

```
  PROCEDURE insert1(nont,term,first: symbolType);
  BEGIN
    WITH parseTable[nont, term] DO
      numberOfSymbolsInRHS:= 1;
      rhsSymbol[1]:= first
    END
  END insert1;

BEGIN
  FOR i:= A TO S DO FOR j:= t TO empty DO
    parseTable[i,j].numberOfSymbolsInRHS:= 0
  END END;
  insert2(S,v,A,B); insert2(S,x,A,B);
  insert1(A,v,v); insert2(A,x,x,E);
  insert1(B,t,C); insert1(B,u,C); insert1(B,v,D);
  insert1(B,w,D); insert1(B,x,D);
  insert2(C,t,t,x); insert2(C,u,u,w);
  insert1(D,v,A); insert1(D,w,w); insert1(D,x,A);
  FOR j:= u TO endMarker DO insert1(E,j,empty) END;
  insert2(E,y,y,E);
  terminals:= symbolSet{t..endMarker};
  syntaxError:= FALSE
END initialise;

PROCEDURE inSymbol;
VAR
  ch: CHAR;
BEGIN
  Read(ch);
  WHILE ch = ' ' DO Read(ch) END; (* skip spaces *)
  CASE ch OF
  't': sy:= t |  'u': sy:= u |
  'v': sy:= v |  'w': sy:= w |
  'x': sy:= x |  'y': sy:= y |
  '$': sy:= endMarker
  ELSE error(1)
  END
END inSymbol;

PROCEDURE charForSymbol(sm: symbolType);
VAR
  ct: CHAR;
BEGIN
  CASE sm OF
  A: ct:= 'A'| B: ct:= 'B'|  C: ct:= 'C'| D: ct:= 'D'| E: ct:= 'E'|
  S: ct:= 'S'| t: ct:= 't'|  u: ct:= 'u'|  v: ct:= 'v'| w: ct:= 'w'|
  x: ct:= 'x'| y: ct:= 'y'| empty: ct:= '@'| endMarker: ct:= '$'
  END;
```

```
    IF ct = '@' THEN WriteString('empty') ELSE Write(ct) END
END charForSymbol;

PROCEDURE outputProduction(left, term: symbolType);
VAR
  k: [1..3];
BEGIN
  charForSymbol(left); WriteString ('  ->  ');
  WITH parseTable[left, term] DO
    FOR k:=  1 TO numberOfSymbolsInRHS DO  charForSymbol(rhsSymbol[k])
    END; WriteLn
  END
END outputProduction;

BEGIN
  initialise; inSymbol;
  stack[1]:= endMarker; stack[2]:= S; (* start symbol *)
  top:= 2;  (* top of stack initially is stack[2] *)
  REPEAT
    IF stack[top] IN terminals THEN
      IF stack[top] = sy THEN
        top:= top -1;  (* discard symbol at top of stack *)
        inSymbol
      ELSE error(2)
      END
    ELSE
      WITH parseTable[stack[top],sy] DO
        IF numberOfSymbolsInRHS = 0 THEN error(3) ELSE
          outputProduction(stack[top],sy);
          top:= top - 1;  (* discard lhs from top of stack *)
          FOR q:= numberOfSymbolsInRHS TO 1 BY -1 DO
            IF rhsSymbol[q] # empty THEN
              top:= top + 1; stack[top]:= rhsSymbol[q];
            END
          END
        END
      END
    END
  UNTIL (stack[top] = endMarker) OR syntaxError;
  IF sy # endMarker THEN error(4)
  ELSE WriteString('Successfully completed'); WriteLn
  END
END nonRec.
```

```
DEFINITION MODULE prExprsn;
FROM pritmod IMPORT idRecPtr;
PROCEDURE expression(VAR resultType: idRecPtr);
PROCEDURE pushAddress(idRec: idRecPtr; VAR resultType: idRecPtr);
END prExprsn.


IMPLEMENTATION MODULE prExprsn;
FROM InOut IMPORT WriteString, WriteLn, Write, WriteCard;
FROM symbols IMPORT symbolType;
FROM bis IMPORT inSymbol, error, valueRecord, sy, ind, accept;
FROM prSAL IMPORT applyOperator, applyRelationalOp, applyRealOperator,
labelString,
   putLine, putStringAndVal, putStrings, genLabel, putLabel;
FROM pritmod IMPORT class, kindOfType, findField, findItsRecord,
   tyInteger, tyBoolean, tyReal, stIndex, idRec, idRecPtr;
FROM callRet IMPORT functionCall, blockLevel;
TYPE
   symbolSet = SET OF symbolType;


PROCEDURE expression (VAR resultType: idRecPtr);
VAR
   operator: symbolType;
   nexType: idRecPtr;
BEGIN
  subExpression (resultType);
  IF sy IN symbolSet {equOp..greatEquOp} THEN
    operator:= sy;  inSymbol;
    subExpression (nexType);
    IF resultType = nexType  THEN
      IF resultType = tyReal THEN applyRealOperator(operator)
      ELSE  applyRelationalOp(operator)
      END; resultType:= tyBoolean
    ELSE error(20)
    END
  END
END expression;


PROCEDURE subExpression(VAR resultType: idRecPtr);
VAR
   operator: symbolType; nexType: idRecPtr;
BEGIN
  IF sy = plussOp THEN inSymbol; term (resultType);
  ELSIF sy = minusOp THEN
    inSymbol; term (resultType);
    IF resultType = tyInteger THEN applyOperator(negOp)
    ELSIF resultType = tyReal THEN applyRealOperator(negOp)
    ELSE error(20)
    END
```

```
    ELSE term (resultType)
    END;
    WHILE sy IN symbolSet{plussOp,minusOp,orOp} DO
      operator:= sy;   inSymbol; term (nexType);
      IF nexType = resultType THEN
        CASE operator OF
          orOp:     IF resultType = tyBoolean THEN applyOperator(orOp)
                    ELSE error(20)
                    END |
          plussOp, minusOp:
                    IF resultType  = tyInteger THEN applyOperator(operator)
                    ELSIF resultType = tyReal THEN
                        applyRealOperator(operator)
                    ELSE error(20)
                    END;
        END (* CASE *)
      ELSE error(20)
      END
    END (* WHILE *)
END subExpression;

PROCEDURE term (VAR resultType: idRecPtr);
VAR
  operator: symbolType;
  nexType: idRecPtr;
BEGIN
  factor (resultType);
  WHILE sy IN symbolSet{timesOp,realDivOp, divOp, modOp, andOp} DO
    operator:= sy; inSymbol;
    factor (nexType);
    IF resultType = nexType THEN
      IF resultType = tyBoolean THEN
        IF operator = andOp THEN
          applyOperator(andOp) ELSE error(21)
        END
      ELSIF resultType = tyInteger THEN
        IF operator IN symbolSet {timesOp, divOp, modOp} THEN
          applyOperator(operator)
        ELSE error(21)
        END
      ELSIF resultType = tyReal THEN
        IF operator IN symbolSet {timesOp, realDivOp} THEN
          applyRealOperator(operator)
        ELSE error(21)
        END
      ELSE error(22)
      END
    ELSE error(20)
```

```
      END
    END (* WHILE *)
  END term;

  PROCEDURE factor (VAR resultType: idRecPtr);
  BEGIN
    CASE sy OF
      numberSy:
        WITH valueRecord DO
          putStringAndVal('     MOV AX, ', val1);
          putLine('     PUSH AX');
          IF valType = 3 THEN (* REAL *)
            putStringAndVal('     MOV AX, ',val2);
            putLine('     PUSH AX');
          END;
          resultType:= stIndex[valType];
        END; inSymbol |
      idSy: pushValue (resultType) |
      notOp:  inSymbol; factor (resultType);
        IF resultType # tyBoolean THEN error(20)
        ELSE applyOperator(notOp)
        END |
      openRndBrktSy: inSymbol; expression(resultType); accept(closeRndBrktSy)
    END
  END factor;


  PROCEDURE pushAddress(idPtr: idRecPtr; VAR resultType: idRecPtr);
  VAR
    levelDifference: CARDINAL; levelLoop: labelString;

   PROCEDURE arrayReference;
   VAR
     no, yes: labelString; elementLength: CARDINAL; tyPtr: idRecPtr;
   BEGIN
     REPEAT
       tyPtr:= resultType;
       elementLength:= tyPtr^.elementType^.itsLength;
       inSymbol; expression(resultType);  (* evaluates ARRAY subscript *)
       IF resultType = tyPtr^.indexType THEN
         genLabel(no); genLabel(yes);
         putLine('     POP DX');
         putStringAndVal('     CMP DX, ', tyPtr^.upBound);
         putStrings('     JG ',no);
         putStringAndVal('     CMP DX, ', tyPtr^.lowBound);
         putStrings('     JGE ', yes);
         putLabel(no);
         putLine('     MOV AX, 999');
         putLine('     PUSH AX');
```

```
        putLine('    CALL INTWRITE');
        putLine('    CALL ENDPROG');
        putLabel(yes);
        putStringAndVal('    SUB DX, ', tyPtr^.lowBound);
        putStringAndVal('    MOV AX, ', elementLength);
        putLine('    MULT DX');
        putLine('    MOV DI, SP');
        putLine('    ADD [DI], AX')
      ELSE error(36)
      END; resultType:= tyPtr^.elementType
    UNTIL sy # commaSy;
    accept(closeSqrBrktSy)
  END arrayReference;


PROCEDURE fieldReference;
VAR
    fieldInfo: idRec; found: BOOLEAN;
BEGIN
    inSymbol;
    findField(ind, resultType^.fieldPtr, fieldInfo, found);
    IF found THEN
      putLine('    MOV DI, SP');
      putStringAndVal('    ADD [DI],', fieldInfo.fieldAddress);
      resultType:= fieldInfo.itsType
    ELSE  error(37)
    END; inSymbol
  END fieldReference;

BEGIN (* body of pushAddress *)
  WITH idPtr^ DO
    levelDifference:= blockLevel - itsLevel;
    IF itsLevel = 0 THEN
      putStrings('    LEA DI,', baseLabel);
      putStringAndVal('    ADD DI,', relAddress);
      putLine('    PUSH DI')
    ELSIF levelDifference = 0 THEN
      putStringAndVal('    MOV DI,', CARDINAL(relAddress));
      IF itsClass = aVARparameter THEN
        putLine('    PUSH [BP][DI]')
      ELSE
        putLine('    ADD DI, BP');
        putLine('    PUSH DI')
      END
    ELSE
      putStringAndVal('    MOV CX,',levelDifference);
      putLine('    MOV BX, BP');
      genLabel(levelLoop); putLabel(levelLoop);
      putLine('    MOV BX, [BX]');
```

```
        putStrings('    LOOP ', levelLoop);
        IF itsClass = aVARparameter THEN
          putStringAndVal('    MOV SI,', CARDINAL(relAddress));
          putLine('    PUSH [BX][SI]')
        ELSE
          putStringAndVal('    ADD BX,', CARDINAL(relAddress));
          putLine('    PUSH BX')
        END
      END
    END; (* WITH *)
    resultType:= idPtr^.itsType;
    inSymbol;
    WHILE sy IN symbolSet{openSqBrktSy, periodSy} DO
      IF sy = openSqBrktSy THEN
        IF resultType^.typeKind = arrayType THEN arrayReference
        ELSE error(31)
        END
      ELSIF sy = periodSy THEN
        IF resultType^.typeKind = recordType THEN fieldReference
        ELSE error(32)
        END
      END
    END
END pushAddress;


PROCEDURE pushValue (VAR resultType: idRecPtr);
VAR
  multiLabel: labelString;
  idPtr: idRecPtr; found: BOOLEAN;
BEGIN
  findItsRecord(ind, idPtr, found);
  IF found THEN
    CASE idPtr^.itsClass OF
      aConstant:
          putStringAndVal('    MOV AX, ',idPtr^.c1);
          putLine('    PUSH AX');
          resultType:= idPtr^.itsType;
          IF resultType = tyReal THEN
            putStringAndVal('    MOV AX, ', idPtr^.c2);
            putLine('    PUSH AX')
          END; inSymbol |
      aVariable, aVARparameter:
          pushAddress(idPtr, resultType);
          putStringAndVal ('    MOV CX,',resultType^.itsLength);
          putLine ('    POP DI ');
          genLabel(multiLabel); putLabel(multiLabel);
          putLine ('    PUSH [DI]');
          putLine ('    INC DI');
```

```
        putStrings ('    LOOP ',multiLabel) |
    aProcedure: functionCall(idPtr, resultType)
  ELSE error(29)
  END (* CASE *);
ELSE error (28)
END (* IF *)
END pushValue;


BEGIN
END prExprsn.


DEFINITION MODULE pritmod is in Section 13.3.2.

IMPLEMENTATION MODULE pritmod;
FROM scanner IMPORT error, inSymbol, accept, sy, ind, valueRecord,
makeNegative;
FROM symbols IMPORT symbolType;
FROM Storage IMPORT ALLOCATE, DEALLOCATE;
FROM InOut IMPORT WriteString, WriteCard, WriteLn;
CONST
  idTableUB = 255;
  mask = BITSET(idTableUB);
  procStackUB = 20;
TYPE
  classSet = SET OF class;
  symbolSet = SET OF symbolType;
VAR
  head: idRecPtr;
  idTable: ARRAY[0..idTableUB] OF idRecPtr;
  procStack: ARRAY[0..procStackUB] OF idRecPtr;
  top: CARDINAL;

PROCEDURE pushProc(procPtr: idRecPtr);
BEGIN
  INC(top); procStack[top]:= procPtr
END pushProc;

PROCEDURE popProc;
BEGIN
  DEC(top)
END popProc;
```

```
PROCEDURE findItsRecord(soughtInd: CARDINAL; VAR recPtr: idRecPtr; VAR
found: BOOLEAN);
BEGIN
  recPtr:= idTable[CARDINAL(BITSET(soughtInd) * mask)];
  LOOP
    IF recPtr = NIL THEN found:= FALSE; RETURN
    ELSIF (recPtr^.itsInd = soughtInd) AND
      recPtr^.enclosedBy^.beingCompiled THEN found:= TRUE; RETURN
    ELSE recPtr:= recPtr^.nextSyn
    END
  END
END findItsRecord;


PROCEDURE checkDuplicateIdentifier(soughtInd: CARDINAL);
VAR
  recPtr: idRecPtr;
BEGIN
  recPtr:= idTable[CARDINAL(BITSET(soughtInd) * mask)];
  LOOP
    IF recPtr = NIL THEN RETURN
    ELSIF (recPtr^.itsInd = soughtInd) AND
      (recPtr^.enclosedBy = procStack[top]) THEN
      error(9); WriteString('Duplicate ind = '); WriteCard(soughtInd,3);
      WriteString(' ORD(itsClass) = ');
      WriteCard(ORD(recPtr^.itsClass), 3); WriteLn; RETURN
    ELSE recPtr:= recPtr^.nextSyn
    END
  END
END checkDuplicateIdentifier;


PROCEDURE findField(soughtInd: CARDINAL; ptr: idRecPtr; VAR fieldDetails:
idRec; VAR found: BOOLEAN);
BEGIN
  LOOP
    IF ptr = NIL THEN found:= FALSE; RETURN
    ELSIF ptr^.itsInd = soughtInd THEN
      fieldDetails:= ptr^; found:= TRUE; RETURN
    ELSE ptr:= ptr^.nextSyn
    END
  END
END findField;


PROCEDURE constant(VAR ofType: idRecPtr; VAR card1, card2:CARDINAL);
VAR
  recPtr: idRecPtr; negative, found: BOOLEAN;
BEGIN
```

```
   IF sy = plussOp THEN inSymbol; negative:= FALSE
   ELSIF sy = minusOp THEN negative:= TRUE; inSymbol
   ELSE negative:= FALSE
   END;
   IF sy = numberSy THEN
     ofType:= stIndex[valueRecord.valType];
     card1:= valueRecord.val1; card2:= valueRecord.val2;
   ELSIF sy = idSy THEN
     findItsRecord(ind,recPtr,found);
     IF found THEN
       WITH recPtr^ DO
         IF itsClass = aConstant THEN
           ofType:= itsType; card1:= c1; card2:= c2
         ELSE found:= FALSE
         END
       END
     END;
     IF NOT found THEN error(11) END
   ELSE error(12)
   END;
   IF negative THEN
     IF ofType = tyReal THEN  makeNegative(card1,card2)
     ELSIF ofType = tyInteger THEN card1:= CARDINAL(-INTEGER(card1))
     ELSE error(12)
     END
   END;
   inSymbol
END constant;


PROCEDURE printTable;
VAR
  i,j: CARDINAL;
  tabPtr: idRecPtr; fPtr: idRecPtr;
BEGIN
  WriteString('Idtable is:'); WriteLn;
  FOR i:= 0 TO idTableUB DO
    tabPtr:= idTable[i];
    WHILE tabPtr # NIL DO
      WriteString('Ind = '); WriteCard(tabPtr^.itsInd,3);
      WriteString('   ORD(itsClass) = ');
      WriteCard(ORD(tabPtr^.itsClass), 3);
      WriteString('   at level = ');
      WriteCard(tabPtr^.enclosedBy^.internalLevel, 3);
      WriteString('   enclosed by = ');
      WriteCard(tabPtr^.enclosedBy^.itsInd, 3);
      WriteLn;
```

```
      IF (tabPtr^.itsClass = aType) AND
        (tabPtr^.typeKind = recordType) THEN
        fPtr:= tabPtr^.fieldPtr;
        FOR j:= 1 TO tabPtr^.noOfFields DO
          WriteString ('   Field ind = ');
          WriteCard(fPtr^.itsInd,3); WriteLn;
          fPtr:= fPtr^.nextSyn
        END
      END;
      tabPtr:= tabPtr^.nextSyn
    END
  END (* FOR *) HALT
END printTable;


PROCEDURE checkTable;
VAR
  i: CARDINAL;
BEGIN
  FOR i:= 0 TO idTableUB DO
    IF idTable[i] # NIL THEN
      IF idTable[i]^.itsInd > 40 THEN
        WriteString('Check table fails with itsInd = ');
        WriteCard(idTable[i]^.itsInd, 4); WriteLn; HALT
      END
    END
  END
END checkTable;


PROCEDURE newIdRecord(VAR tabPtr: idRecPtr);
BEGIN
  ALLOCATE(tabPtr, SIZE(idRec));
  tail^.nextSeq:= tabPtr;  tail:= tabPtr;
  WITH tabPtr^ DO
    marked:= FALSE; enclosedBy:= procStack[top];
    tabPtr^.nextSeq:= NIL; tabPtr^.nextSyn:= NIL
  END
END newIdRecord;


PROCEDURE enterIdRecord(ind: CARDINAL; VAR tablePtr: idRecPtr);
VAR
  subscript: CARDINAL; currentPtr, previousPtr: idRecPtr;
BEGIN
  newIdRecord(tablePtr); tablePtr^.itsInd:= ind;
  subscript:= CARDINAL(BITSET(ind) * mask);
  currentPtr:= idTable[subscript];
  IF currentPtr = NIL THEN idTable[subscript]:= tablePtr; RETURN
```

```
    ELSIF  tablePtr^.enclosedBy^.internalLevel >
      currentPtr^.enclosedBy^.internalLevel THEN
      tablePtr^.nextSyn:= currentPtr;
      idTable[subscript]:= tablePtr; RETURN
    ELSE
      LOOP
        previousPtr:= currentPtr; currentPtr:= currentPtr^.nextSyn;
        IF currentPtr = NIL THEN
          previousPtr^.nextSyn:= tablePtr; RETURN
        ELSIF tablePtr^.enclosedBy^.internalLevel >
          currentPtr^.enclosedBy^.internalLevel THEN
          tablePtr^.nextSyn:= currentPtr;
          previousPtr^.nextSyn:= tablePtr; RETURN
        END
      END
    END
  END
END  enterIdRecord;

PROCEDURE makeIdRec(ind, length: CARDINAL; cl: class);
BEGIN
  ALLOCATE(idTable[ind], SIZE (idRec));
  WITH idTable[ind]^ DO
    itsInd:= ind; itsLength:= length; itsClass:= cl;
    nextSyn:= NIL; enclosedBy:= procStack[top];
    nextSeq:= NIL; marked:= FALSE
  END
END makeIdRec;

PROCEDURE disconnect(soughtInd: CARDINAL);
VAR
  currentPtr, previousPtr: idRecPtr; subscript: CARDINAL;
BEGIN
  subscript:= CARDINAL(BITSET(soughtInd) * mask);
  previousPtr:= idTable[subscript];
  IF previousPtr = NIL THEN error(515); RETURN END;
  IF previousPtr^.itsInd = soughtInd THEN
    idTable[subscript]:= previousPtr^.nextSyn; RETURN
  ELSE
    currentPtr:= previousPtr^.nextSyn;
    LOOP
      IF currentPtr = NIL THEN error(515); RETURN
      ELSIF currentPtr^.itsInd = soughtInd THEN
        previousPtr^.nextSyn:= currentPtr^.nextSyn; RETURN
      ELSE previousPtr:= currentPtr; currentPtr:= currentPtr^.nextSyn
      END
    END
  END
END disconnect;
```

```
PROCEDURE initialiseIdTable;
VAR
  i: CARDINAL;
BEGIN
  FOR i:= 0 TO idTableUB DO idTable[i]:= NIL END;
  makeIdRec(14, 1, aType); (* INTEGER *)
  idTable[14]^.typeKind:= aStandardType;
  tyInteger:= idTable[14]; stIndex[1]:= tyInteger;
  makeIdRec(3, 1, aType); (* BOOLEAN *);
  idTable[3]^.typeKind:= aStandardType;
  tyBoolean:= idTable[3]; stIndex[2]:= tyBoolean;
  makeIdRec(20, 2, aType); (* REAL *);
  idTable[20]^.typeKind:= aStandardType;
  tyReal:= idTable[20]; stIndex[3]:= tyReal;
  makeIdRec(9, 0, aConstant); (* FALSE *);
  WITH idTable[9]^ DO cl:= 0; itsType:= tyBoolean END;
  makeIdRec(22, 0, aConstant); (* TRUE *);
  WITH idTable[22]^ DO cl:= 1; itsType:= tyBoolean END;
  makeIdRec(25, 0, aProcedure); (* READNUM *)
  idTable[25]^.procKind:= externalProc;
  makeIdRec(26, 0, aProcedure); (* WRITENUM *)
  idTable[26]^.procKind:= externalProc;
  makeIdRec(27, 0, aProcedure); (* NEWLINE *);
  idTable[27]^.procKind:= externalProc;
  tail:= tyReal;
END initialiseIdTable;


BEGIN
  top:= 0; (* initialize procStack *)
END pritmod.



DEFINITION MODULE proDecs is included in Section 13.4.

IMPLEMENTATION MODULE proDecs;
FROM scanner IMPORT error, inSymbol, outSymbol, accept,
  sy, ind, openInterFile, closeInterFile;
FROM symbols IMPORT symbolType;
FROM Storage IMPORT ALLOCATE;
FROM InOut IMPORT WriteString, WriteCard, WriteLn;
FROM prSAL IMPORT labelString, genLabel, standardImports;
FROM pritmod IMPORT class, kindOfType, kindOfProc, idRec, idRecPtr,
  constant, tyInteger, tyBoolean, tyReal, findItsRecord,
  enterIdRecord, newIdRecord, findField, initialiseIdTable,
  checkDuplicateIdentifier, pushProc, popProc, printTable;
```

```
TYPE
  symbolSet = SET OF symbolType;
  listRecPtr = POINTER TO listRec;
  listRec = RECORD
                  item: CARDINAL;
                  next: listRecPtr
              END;
VAR
  globalPtr: idRecPtr;
  blockLevel, moduleInd: CARDINAL;


PROCEDURE makeList(VAR head: listRecPtr);
VAR
  n: INTEGER;  tail: listRecPtr;
BEGIN
  head:= NIL; tail:= NIL;
  IF sy # idSy THEN error(44); RETURN END;
  ALLOCATE(head, SIZE(listRec)); head^.item:= ind;
  head^.next:= NIL; tail:= head;
  inSymbol;
  WHILE sy = commaSy DO
    inSymbol;
    IF sy = idSy THEN
      ALLOCATE(tail^.next, SIZE(listRec));
      tail:= tail^.next;
      tail^.item:= ind; tail^.next:= NIL
    ELSE error(44)
    END; inSymbol
  END;
  accept(colonSy)
END makeList;


PROCEDURE constDecs;
VAR
  consType, idTabPtr: idRecPtr;
  card1, card2: CARDINAL;
BEGIN
  inSymbol;
  WHILE sy = idSy DO
    checkDuplicateIdentifier(ind);
    enterIdRecord(ind, idTabPtr);
    inSymbol; accept(equOp);
    constant(consType, card1, card2);
    WITH idTabPtr^ DO
      itsClass:= aConstant; itsType:= consType;
      c1:= card1; c2:= card2
    END;
    accept(semiColonSy);
```

```
    END
END constDecs;

PROCEDURE arrayDec(arrayRecordPtr: idRecPtr);
VAR
  v2, firstBound, secondBound, noOfDimensions, count: CARDINAL;
  lowerBoundType, upperBoundType, arrayElementType,
  currentPtr, previousPtr, recPtr: idRecPtr;
  found, lastDimension: BOOLEAN;
BEGIN
  inSymbol; accept(openSqBrktSy);
  noOfDimensions:= 0; lastDimension:= FALSE;
  REPEAT
    INC(noOfDimensions);
    constant(lowerBoundType, firstBound, v2); accept(dotDotSy);
    constant(upperBoundType, secondBound, v2);
    IF INTEGER(firstBound) > INTEGER(secondBound) THEN error(41) END;
    accept(closeSqrBrktSy);
    IF sy = ofSy THEN
      lastDimension:= TRUE; inSymbol; typeRecord(recPtr)
    ELSE accept(commaSy); accept(openSqBrktSy)
    END;
    IF (lowerBoundType = upperBoundType) AND
      ((lowerBoundType = tyBoolean) OR (lowerBoundType = tyInteger)) THEN
      WITH arrayRecordPtr^ DO
        itsClass:= aType; typeKind:= arrayType;
        indexType:= lowerBoundType;
        lowBound:= INTEGER(firstBound); upBound:= INTEGER(secondBound);
        IF lastDimension THEN elementType:= recPtr ELSE
          previousPtr:= arrayRecordPtr;
          newIdRecord(arrayRecordPtr); elementType:= arrayRecordPtr;
          arrayRecordPtr^.nextSyn:= previousPtr
        END
      END
    ELSE error(18)
    END;
  UNTIL lastDimension;
  currentPtr:= arrayRecordPtr;
  FOR count:= 1 TO noOfDimensions DO
    WITH  currentPtr^ DO
      itsLength:= elementType^.itsLength *
        CARDINAL(upBound - lowBound + 1);
    END; currentPtr:= currentPtr^.nextSyn
  END (* FOR *)
END arrayDec;
```

```
PROCEDURE recordDec (recRecPtr: idRecPtr);
VAR
  currentPtr: listRecPtr;
  newFieldPtr, fieldType, recTail: idRecPtr;
  fieldInfo: idRec; found: BOOLEAN;
  nextFieldAddress, numberOfFields, fieldLength, recordLength: CARDINAL;
BEGIN
  inSymbol; recTail:= NIL;
  nextFieldAddress:= 0; numberOfFields:= 0;
  WHILE sy = idSy DO
    makeList(currentPtr); typeRecord(fieldType);
    fieldLength:= fieldType^.itsLength;
    WHILE currentPtr # NIL DO
      findField(currentPtr^.item, recRecPtr^.nextSyn, fieldInfo, found);
      IF found THEN error (17) ELSE
        INC(numberOfFields); newIdRecord(newFieldPtr);
        WITH newFieldPtr^ DO
          itsInd:= currentPtr^.item; itsType:= fieldType;
          fieldAddress:= nextFieldAddress; nextSyn:= NIL
        END;
        IF recTail = NIL THEN recRecPtr^.fieldPtr:= newFieldPtr
        ELSE recTail^.nextSyn:= newFieldPtr
        END;
        recTail:= newFieldPtr;
        INC(nextFieldAddress, fieldLength)
      END; (* IF found *)
      currentPtr:= currentPtr^.next
    END; (* WHILE *)
    inSymbol;  IF sy # endSy THEN accept (semiColonSy) END
  END; (* WHILE *)
  IF sy  # endSy THEN error (13) END;
  WITH recRecPtr^ DO
    itsClass:= aType; typeKind:= recordType;
    itsLength:= nextFieldAddress; noOfFields:= numberOfFields
  END
END recordDec;

PROCEDURE typeRecord(VAR typePtr: idRecPtr);
VAR
  typeType: CARDINAL; found: BOOLEAN;
BEGIN
```

```
  CASE sy OF
    idSy:     findItsRecord(ind, typePtr, found);
              IF NOT found THEN error(81) ELSE
                WITH typePtr^ DO
                  IF itsClass # aType THEN error (82)
                  ELSIF typeKind = typeAlias THEN typePtr:= itsType
                  END
                END
              END   |
    arraySy:  newIdRecord(typePtr);  arrayDec(typePtr)   |
    recordSy: newIdRecord(typePtr);  recordDec(typePtr)
  ELSE error (32)
  END
END typeRecord;


PROCEDURE typeDecs;
VAR
  typeInd: CARDINAL; found: BOOLEAN;
  typeType, idTabPtr: idRecPtr;
BEGIN
  inSymbol;
  WHILE sy = idSy DO
    checkDuplicateIdentifier(ind); typeInd:= ind;
    inSymbol;  accept(equOp);
    CASE sy OF
    idSy: findItsRecord(ind, typeType, found);
          IF found THEN
            IF typeType^.itsClass = aType THEN
              enterIdRecord(typeInd, idTabPtr);
              WITH idTabPtr^ DO
                itsType:= typeType; itsClass:= aType;
                typeKind:= typeAlias; itsLength:= typeType^.itsLength
              END
            ELSE error(14)
            END
          ELSE error(14)
          END   |
    arraySy:  enterIdRecord(typeInd, idTabPtr); arrayDec (idTabPtr) |
    recordSy: enterIdRecord(typeInd, idTabPtr); recordDec(idTabPtr)
    ELSE error(14)
    END;
    inSymbol;  accept(semiColonSy)
  END (* WHILE *)
END typeDecs;
```

```
PROCEDURE varDecs(VAR nextAddress: CARDINAL);
VAR
  currentPtr: listRecPtr; thisType, idTabPtr: idRecPtr;
  varInd: CARDINAL;
BEGIN
  inSymbol;
  WHILE sy = idSy DO
    makeList(currentPtr);  typeRecord(thisType);
    WHILE currentPtr # NIL DO
      varInd:= currentPtr^.item;
      checkDuplicateIdentifier(varInd);
      enterIdRecord(varInd, idTabPtr);
      WITH idTabPtr^ DO
        itsInd:= varInd; itsClass:= aVariable; baseLabel:= 'ZAAA';
        relAddress:= nextAddress; itsType:= thisType; itsLevel:= blockLevel
      END;
      INC(nextAddress, thisType^.itsLength); currentPtr:= currentPtr^.next
    END;
    inSymbol; accept(semiColonSy)
  END
END varDecs;


PROCEDURE proceDec;
VAR
  procPtr: idRecPtr; procInd: CARDINAL;
BEGIN
  outSymbol; inSymbol; outSymbol; (* procedureSy and ind *)
  IF sy # idSy THEN error (33) ELSE
    checkDuplicateIdentifier(ind)
  END;
  procInd:= ind; enterIdRecord(procInd, procPtr);
  INC(blockLevel); pushProc(procPtr);
  procPtr^.beingCompiled:= TRUE;
  procHeading(procInd, procPtr);
  procPtr^.varLength:= 3;
  block(procPtr^.varLength, procInd);
  procPtr^.beingCompiled:= FALSE;
  DEC(blockLevel); popProc;  accept(semiColonSy)
END proceDec;


PROCEDURE procHeading(procInd: CARDINAL;  procPtr: idRecPtr);
VAR
  paramPtr, functionReturnType, thisType: idRecPtr;
  nextAddress, numberOfParams, count: CARDINAL;
  varParam: BOOLEAN;  currentPtr: listRecPtr;
BEGIN
```

```
  inSymbol; nextAddress:= 0; numberOfParams:= 0;
IF sy = openRndBrktSy THEN
  inSymbol;
  WHILE sy IN symbolSet{idSy, varSy} DO
    IF sy = varSy THEN inSymbol; varParam:= TRUE ELSE varParam:= FALSE
    END;
    makeList(currentPtr);
    IF sy = idSy THEN typeRecord(thisType) ELSE error(101) END;
    IF thisType^.itsClass = aType THEN
      WHILE currentPtr # NIL DO
        checkDuplicateIdentifier(currentPtr^.item);
        enterIdRecord(currentPtr^.item,paramPtr);
        (* for this parameter *)
        WITH paramPtr^ DO
          IF varParam THEN itsClass:= aVARparameter ELSE
            itsClass:= aVariable
          END;
          relAddress:= nextAddress; itsType:= thisType;
          itsLevel:= blockLevel
        END;
        INC(nextAddress, thisType^.itsLength);
        INC(numberOfParams); currentPtr:= currentPtr^.next
      END
    ELSE error(102)
    END;
    inSymbol; IF sy = semiColonSy THEN inSymbol END
  END; (* WHILE *)
  paramPtr:= procPtr^.nextSeq;
  FOR count:= 1 TO numberOfParams DO
    DEC(paramPtr^.relAddress, nextAddress);
    paramPtr:= paramPtr^.nextSeq
  END;
  accept(closeRndBrktSy);
  IF sy = colonSy THEN
    procPtr^.procKind:= functionProc; inSymbol;
    IF sy = idSy THEN typeRecord(functionReturnType) ELSE error(35) END;
    IF (functionReturnType # tyBoolean) AND (functionReturnType # tyReal)
    AND (functionReturnType # tyInteger) THEN error (36)
    END; inSymbol
  ELSE procPtr^.procKind:= pureProc
  END
ELSE procPtr^.procKind:= pureProc
END;
WITH procPtr^ DO
  itsClass:= aProcedure; procLevel:= blockLevel - 1;
  internalLevel:= blockLevel; noOfParams:= numberOfParams;
  paramLength:= nextAddress; genLabel(beginLabel);
  IF procKind = functionProc THEN resultType:= functionReturnType END;
```

```
  END;
  accept(semiColonSy)
END procHeading;

PROCEDURE block (VAR words: CARDINAL; endInd: CARDINAL);
BEGIN
  LOOP
    IF sy = constSy THEN constDecs
    ELSIF sy = typeSy THEN typeDecs
    ELSIF sy = varSy THEN varDecs(words)
    ELSIF sy = procedureSy THEN proceDec
    ELSE EXIT
    END
  END;
  IF sy = beginSy THEN outSymbol ELSE error (93) END;
  LOOP
    inSymbol; outSymbol;
    IF sy = endSy THEN
      REPEAT inSymbol; outSymbol UNTIL sy # endSy;
      IF (sy = idSy) AND (ind # endInd) THEN error(94) END; EXIT
    END
  END;
  inSymbol; outSymbol
END block;

PROCEDURE procInitialise(ind: CARDINAL; VAR procPtr: idRecPtr;
  VAR startLabel: labelString; VAR varWords, prmLength: CARDINAL;
  VAR resType: idRecPtr;  VAR aFunction: BOOLEAN);
VAR
  found: BOOLEAN;
BEGIN
  findItsRecord(ind, procPtr, found);
  IF NOT found THEN error (66); RETURN END;
  WITH procPtr^ DO
    startLabel:= beginLabel; varWords:= varLength;
    prmLength:= paramLength;  resType:= resultType;
    aFunction:= (procKind = functionProc); beingCompiled:= TRUE
  END
END procInitialise;

BEGIN
  ALLOCATE(globalPtr, SIZE (idRec)); (* pseudo-procedure record *)
  WITH globalPtr^ DO
    itsClass:= aProcedure; internalLevel:= 0;
    beingCompiled:= TRUE
  END;
  pushProc(globalPtr); blockLevel:= 0;
  initialiseIdTable; openInterFile;
```

```
    inSymbol; outSymbol; (* MODULE symbol *)
    accept(moduleSy); outSymbol; moduleInd:= ind;
    accept(idSy); outSymbol; (* semicolon *)
    IF sy # semiColonSy THEN error(222) END; inSymbol;
    moduleVarLength:= 0; standardImports; WriteLn;
    block(moduleVarLength, moduleInd);
    closeInterFile; accept(periodSy)
END proDecs.



DEFINITION MODULE progCode is included in Section 6.2.

IMPLEMENTATION MODULE progCode;
FROM InOut IMPORT  Write, WriteString, WriteCard, WriteLn;
FROM FileSystem IMPORT Lookup, Length, Reset, Close, ReadWord,
File;
CONST
  machineCodeUB = 2000;
  startAddress = 64;
TYPE
  leastSigByteFields = RECORD
                          bm, breg, brm: CARDINAL
                       END;
VAR
  machineCode: ARRAY [startAddress..machineCodeUB] OF CARDINAL;
  unpack:   ARRAY [0..255] OF leastSigByteFields;
  ip: CARDINAL;
  absBinry: File;

PROCEDURE initialiseUnpack;
VAR
  i,j,k, count: CARDINAL;
BEGIN
  count:= 0;
  FOR i:= 0 TO 3 DO FOR j:= 0 TO 7 DO FOR k:= 0 TO 7 DO
    WITH unpack[count] DO
      bm:= i; breg:= j; brm:= k
    END;
    INC (count);
  END END END
END initialiseUnpack;

PROCEDURE readCode;
VAR
  numericAddress,  msLength, lsLength: CARDINAL;
BEGIN
  Lookup(absBinry, 'absBinry', FALSE);  Reset(absBinry);
  Length(absBinry, msLength, lsLength);
```

```
  IF msLength > 0 THEN
    WriteString ('Absbin too long'); WriteLn
  END;
  lsLength:= lsLength DIV 2;
  IF startAddress + lsLength  > machineCodeUB THEN
    WriteString('Absbin too long'); WriteLn
  END;
  FOR numericAddress:= startAddress TO startAddress + lsLength DO
    ReadWord(absBinry, machineCode[numericAddress])
  END; Close(absBinry)
END readCode;


PROCEDURE fieldValue (opWord, bitNumber, noOfBits: CARDINAL): CARDINAL;
VAR
  count, nextBit, value: CARDINAL;  wrd: BITSET;
BEGIN
  wrd:= BITSET(opWord); value:= 0; nextBit:= 1;
  FOR count:= 1 TO noOfBits DO
    IF bitNumber IN wrd THEN INC (value, nextBit) END;
    INC(bitNumber); INC(nextBit, nextBit) (* shift left *)
  END; RETURN value
END fieldValue;


PROCEDURE getWord(VAR gotWord: CARDINAL);
BEGIN
  gotWord:= machineCode[ip]; INC (ip)
END getWord;


PROCEDURE putBinary(w: CARDINAL);
VAR
  count: CARDINAL; msBit: BITSET;
BEGIN
  msBit:= BITSET(8000H);
  FOR count:= 15 TO 0 BY -1 DO
    IF count IN BITSET (w) THEN Write('1') ELSE Write('0') END
  END; WriteLn
END putBinary;


PROCEDURE getOp (VAR opRec: opWordFields);
VAR
  wrd: BITSET; opWord, whichBit: CARDINAL;
  lsByte: leastSigByteFields;
BEGIN
```

```
WITH opRec DO
  getWord (opWord);
  wrd:= BITSET (opWord);   whichBit:= 15;
  IF whichBit IN wrd THEN
    WriteString('Error: opWord msBit 1; address = ');
    WriteCard(ip,5); WriteLn; category:= errorCategory
  ELSE
    DEC(whichBit);
    IF whichBit IN wrd THEN
      category:= twoOperandCategory;
      opCode:= fieldValue(opWord, 11, 3);
      IF 10 IN wrd THEN immediate:= 1 ELSE immediate:= 0 END;
      IF 9 IN wrd THEN destination:= 1 ELSE destination:= 0 END;
      IF 8 IN wrd THEN memRef:= 1 ELSE memRef:= 0 END
    ELSE
      DEC (whichBit);
      IF whichBit IN wrd THEN
        category:= jumpInsCategory;
        opCode:= fieldValue(opWord, 8, 5)
      ELSE
        DEC (whichBit);
        IF whichBit IN wrd THEN
          category:= singleOperandCategory;
          opCode:= fieldValue(opWord, 9, 3);
          IF 8 IN wrd THEN memRef:= 1 ELSE memRef:= 0 END
        ELSE
          DEC (whichBit);
          IF whichBit IN wrd THEN
            category:= noOperandInsCategory;
            opCode:= fieldValue(opWord, 8, 3)
          ELSE
            DEC (whichBit);
            IF whichBit IN wrd THEN
              category:= leaInstructionCategory;
              opCode:= fieldValue(opWord, 8, 2)
            ELSE
              DEC (whichBit);
              IF whichBit IN wrd THEN
                category:= extraCategory
              ELSE WriteString('Error: msByte middle 6 bits 0,');
                WriteString(' Address = ');
                WriteCard(ip, 5); WriteLn; category:= errorCategory
              END
            END
          END
        END
      END
    END
  END
```

```
    END;
    lsByte:= CARDINAL(wrd * BITSET(00FFH));
    WITH unpack[lsByte] DO
      m:= bm; reg:= breg; rm:= brm
    END
  END
END getOp;


PROCEDURE jumpIP(newAddress: CARDINAL);
BEGIN
  ip:= newAddress
END jumpIP;


PROCEDURE dereference(numericAddress:CARDINAL): CARDINAL;
BEGIN
  RETURN machineCode[numericAddress]
END dereference;


PROCEDURE assignTo (numericAddress, operand: CARDINAL);
BEGIN
  machineCode[numericAddress]:= operand
END assignTo;


PROCEDURE ipAddress (): CARDINAL;
BEGIN
  RETURN ip
END ipAddress;


BEGIN
  initialiseUnpack;  readCode;  ip:= startAddress
END progCode.



MODULE promain is included in Section 13.10.



DEFINITION MODULE prSAL is identical to DEFINITION MODULE putSAL;

IMPLEMENTATION MODULE prSAL is the same as IMPLEMENTATION MODULE putSAL
except that it imports from module bis instead of module scanner.



DEFINITION MODULE prStmnt;
PROCEDURE stmntSequence;
END prStmnt.
```

```
IMPLEMENTATION MODULE prStmnt;
FROM prSAL IMPORT labelString, genLabel, putLabel, putLine, putStrings,
putStringAndVal;
FROM InOut IMPORT WriteString, WriteLn, Write, WriteCard;
FROM symbols IMPORT symbolType;
FROM bis IMPORT inSymbol, error, accept, valueRecord, sy, ind;
FROM prExprsn IMPORT expression, pushAddress;
FROM pritmod IMPORT class, kindOfProc, findItsRecord, idRecPtr,
  tyInteger, tyBoolean, tyReal;
FROM callRet IMPORT call, returnStatement, blockLevel;
FROM Storage IMPORT ALLOCATE, DEALLOCATE;
CONST
  loopStackUB = 10;
VAR
  loopStack: ARRAY[1..loopStackUB] OF labelString;
  loopStackTop: CARDINAL;


PROCEDURE assignmentStatement(idPtr: idRecPtr);
VAR
  lhsTtype, resultType: idRecPtr; length: CARDINAL;
  labc: labelString;
BEGIN
  IF (idPtr^.itsClass # aVariable) AND
    idPtr^.itsClass # aVARparameter) THEN error (19); RETURN
  END;
  pushAddress(idPtr, lhsTtype);   accept(assignOp);
  expression (resultType);
  IF lhsTtype = resultType THEN
    length:= resultType^.itsLength;
    putStringAndVal('    MOV CX,', length);
    putLine('    MOV SI, SP ');
    putStringAndVal('    SUB SI,', length);
    putLine('    MOV DI, [SI]');
    putStringAndVal('    ADD DI,', length - 1);
    genLabel(labc); putLabel(labc);
    putLine('    POP [DI]');
    putLine('    DEC DI');
    putStrings ('    LOOP  ',labc);
    putLine('    DEC SP')
  ELSE error(20)
  END
END assignmentStatement;
```

```
PROCEDURE jumpIfFalse(resultType: idRecPtr; whereTo: labelString);
BEGIN
  IF resultType # tyBoolean THEN error(7) END;
  putLine('    POP AX');
  putLine('    CMP AX, 0');
  putStrings('    JE  ',whereTo)
END jumpIfFalse;

PROCEDURE whileStatement;
VAR
  loopLabel,after: labelString; resultType: idRecPtr;
BEGIN;
  genLabel(loopLabel);  putLabel(loopLabel);
  expression(resultType);
  genLabel(after);  jumpIfFalse(resultType,after);
  accept(doSy); stmntSequence; accept(endSy);
  putStrings('    JMP ',loopLabel);
  putLabel(after); putLine('    NOP')
END whileStatement;

PROCEDURE ifStatement;
VAR
  afterThen, afterIfStmnt: labelString;
  resultType: idRecPtr;
BEGIN
  genLabel(afterThen);
  expression(resultType);    accept(thenSy);
  jumpIfFalse(resultType, afterThen);
  stmntSequence;
  IF sy = endSy THEN inSymbol; putLabel(afterThen)
  ELSE
    genLabel(afterIfStmnt);
    WHILE sy = elsifSy DO
      inSymbol; putStrings('    JMP ', afterIfStmnt);
      putLabel(afterThen); genLabel(afterThen);
      expression(resultType); accept(thenSy);
      jumpIfFalse(resultType, afterThen);
      stmntSequence
    END;
    IF sy = elseSy THEN
      inSymbol; putStrings('    JMP ', afterIfStmnt);
      putLabel(afterThen); stmntSequence;
    ELSE putLabel(afterThen); putLine('    NOP')
    END;
    putLabel(afterIfStmnt); accept(endSy)
  END;
  putLine('    NOP')
END ifStatement;
```

```
PROCEDURE loopStatement;
VAR
  loopLabel: labelString;
BEGIN
  genLabel(loopLabel); putLabel(loopLabel);
  INC(loopStackTop); genLabel(loopStack[loopStackTop]);
  stmntSequence;   accept(endSy);
  putStrings('    JMP  ',loopLabel);
  putLabel(loopStack[loopStackTop]); DEC(loopStackTop);
  putLine('    NOP')
END loopStatement;


PROCEDURE exitStatement;
BEGIN
  IF loopStackTop = 0 THEN error(9)
  ELSE putStrings('    JMP  ', loopStack[loopStackTop])
  END
END exitStatement;


PROCEDURE repeatStatement;
VAR
  loopLabel: labelString; resultType: idRecPtr;
BEGIN
  genLabel(loopLabel); putLabel(loopLabel);
  stmntSequence;
  accept(untilSy);   expression(resultType);
  jumpIfFalse(resultType,loopLabel)
END repeatStatement;


PROCEDURE extProc;
VAR
  resultType, idPtr: idRecPtr; found: BOOLEAN;
BEGIN
  CASE ind OF
  27: putLine('    CALL NEWLINE'); inSymbol  |
  25: inSymbol; accept(openRndBrktSy);  (* READNUM *)
    findItsRecord(ind, idPtr, found);
    IF idPtr^.itsClass = aVariable THEN
      pushAddress(idPtr, resultType);
      putLine('    POP DI');
      IF resultType = tyInteger THEN
        putLine('    CALL INTREAD ');
        putLine('    POP [BP][DI] ')
      ELSIF resultType = tyReal THEN (* Read 2 words *)
        putLine('    CALL REALREAD ');
        putLine('    INC DI ');
        putLine('    POP [BP][DI] ');
```

```
          putLine('     DEC DI ');
          putLine('     POP [BP][DI] ')
        ELSE error(31)
        END
      ELSE error(31)
      END; accept (closeRndBrktSy) |
  26: inSymbol; accept(openRndBrktSy); expression(resultType);
      IF resultType = tyInteger THEN
        putLine('    CALL INTWRITE ')
      ELSIF resultType = tyReal THEN
        putLine('    CALL REALWRITE ')
      ELSE error(31)
      END; accept (closeRndBrktSy)
    ELSE error(31)
    END
END extProc;


PROCEDURE procedureCall(proPtr: idRecPtr);
BEGIN
  CASE proPtr^.procKind OF
    pureProc:     call(proPtr) |
    functionProc: error(120)   |
    externalProc: extProc
  END
END procedureCall;


PROCEDURE statement;
VAR
  idPtr: idRecPtr; found: BOOLEAN;
BEGIN
  CASE sy OF
    idSy:     findItsRecord (ind, idPtr, found);
              IF found THEN
                CASE idPtr^.itsClass OF
                  aVariable, aVARparameter: assignmentStatement(idPtr)  |
                  aProcedure: procedureCall(idPtr) |
                ELSE error(11)
                END
              ELSE error(101)
              END |
    whileSy:  inSymbol; whileStatement  |
    loopSy:   inSymbol; loopStatement   |
    exitSy:   inSymbol; exitStatement   |
    ifSy:     inSymbol; ifStatement     |
    repeatSy: inSymbol; repeatStatement|
    returnSy: inSymbol; returnStatement
  ELSE (* do nothing *)
  END
```

```
END statement;

PROCEDURE stmntSequence;
BEGIN
  LOOP
    statement;
    IF sy = semiColonSy THEN inSymbol ELSE EXIT END
  END
END stmntSequence;

BEGIN
  loopStackTop:= 0
END prStmnt.
```

DEFINITION MODULE putSAL is included in Section 10.2.4.

```
IMPLEMENTATION MODULE putSAL;
FROM InOut IMPORT WriteString, Write, WriteCard, WriteLn;
FROM symbols IMPORT symbolType;
FROM scanner IMPORT error;
TYPE symbolSet = SET OF symbolType;
VAR currentLabel: labelString;

PROCEDURE genLabel(VAR newLabel: labelString);
BEGIN
  newLabel:= currentLabel;
  IF currentLabel[3] # 'Z' THEN INC(currentLabel[3]) ELSE
    currentLabel[3]:= 'A';
    IF currentLabel[2] # 'Z' THEN INC(currentLabel[2]) ELSE
      currentLabel[2]:= 'A';
      IF currentLabel[1] # 'Z' THEN INC(currentLabel[1])
      ELSE error(0)
      END
    END
  END
END genLabel;

PROCEDURE putLabel(pLabel: labelString);
BEGIN
  WriteString(pLabel); Write(':')
END putLabel;

PROCEDURE newLabelSequence(VAR thisLabel: labelString);
BEGIN
  thisLabel:= currentLabel; currentLabel:= 'ZAAB'
END newLabelSequence;
```

```
.OCEDURE restoreLabelSequence(thisLabel: labelString);
.GIN
currentLabel:= thisLabel
D restoreLabelSequence;

.OCEDURE putLine(aLine: ARRAY OF CHAR);
.GIN
WriteString(aLine); WriteLn
D putLine;

.OCEDURE putStrings(aString, etc: ARRAY OF CHAR);
.GIN
WriteString(aString); WriteString(etc); WriteLn
D putStrings;

.OCEDURE putStringAndVal(aString: ARRAY OF CHAR; v: CARDINAL);
.GIN
WriteString(aString); WriteCard(v,4); WriteLn
D putStringAndVal;

.OCEDURE applyOperator(op:symbolType);
GIN
CASE op OF
plussOp, minusOp, andOp, orOp:
  putLine('    POP  AX');
  putLine('    MOV DI, SP');
  CASE op OF
    plussOp:    putLine('    ADD  [DI], AX') |
    minusOp:    putLine('    SUB  [DI], AX') |
    andOp:      putLine('    AND  [DI], AX') |
    orOp:       putLine('    OR   [DI], AX')
  END |
timesOp, divOp, modOp:
  putLine('    POP BX');
  putLine('    POP AX');
  IF op = timesOp THEN
  putLine('    MULT BX') ELSE
  putLine('    DIV  BX') END;
  IF op = modOp THEN
  putLine('    PUSH DX') ELSE
  putLine('    PUSH AX') END |
negOp:
  putLine('    MOV  DI, SP');
  putLine('    NEG  [DI]') |
notOp:
  putLine('    MOV AX, 1');
  putLine('    POP DX');
  putLine('    SUB AX, DX');
```

```
     putLine('    PUSH AX');
  ELSE error(5)
  END
END applyOperator;

PROCEDURE applyRelationalOp(op: symbolType);
VAR
  skipLabel: labelString;
BEGIN
  genLabel(skipLabel);
  putLine('    MOV AX, 1');
  putLine('    POP BX');
  putLine('    POP CX');
  putLine('    CMP CX, BX');
  CASE op OF
    equOp:      WriteString('    JE   ') |
    notEquOp:   WriteString('    JNE  ') |
    lessOp:     WriteString('    JL   ') |
    greaterOp:  WriteString('    JG   ') |
    lessEquOp:  WriteString('    JLE  ') |
    greatEquOp: WriteString ('    JGE  ')
  END;
  WriteString(skipLabel); WriteLn;
  putLine('    DEC AX');
  putLabel(skipLabel); putLine(' PUSH AX')
END applyRelationalOp;

PROCEDURE applyRealOperator(op: symbolType);
BEGIN
  CASE op OF
    negOp:      putLine('    CALL REALNEG') |
    plussOp:    putLine('    CALL REALADD') |
    minusOp:    putLine('    CALL REALSUB') |
    timesOp:    putLine('    CALL REALMULT')   |
    realDivOp:  putLine('    CALL REALDIVIDE') |
    equOp:      putLine('    CALL REALEQ')     |
    notEquOp:   putLine('    CALL REALNOTEQ')  |
    lessOp:     putLine('    CALL REALLESS')   |
    greaterOp:  putLine('    CALL REALGREATER') |
    lessEquOp:  putLine('    CALL REALLESSEQ') |
    greatEquOp: putLine('    CALL REALGREATEQ')
  END
END applyRealOperator;
```

```
PROCEDURE standardImports;
BEGIN
  WriteString('IMPORT INTREAD, INTWRITE, NEWLINE, ENDPROG, REALREAD,
    REALWRITE,');
  WriteString(' REALNEG,  REALADD, REALSUB, REALMULT, REALDIVIDE,');
  WriteString(' REALEQ, REALNOTEQ, REALLESS, REALGREATER, REALLESSEQ,
    REALGREATEQ')
END standardImports;


BEGIN
  currentLabel:= 'ZAAB'
END putSAL.



MODULE quads;
FROM InOut IMPORT Read, Write, WriteString, WriteCard,
  WriteLn, RedirectInput, CloseInput;
CONST
  charUB = 20;  cardUB = 12;  endOfFile = 32C;
TYPE
  charSet = SET OF CHAR;
  prandType = RECORD
                  opChar: CHAR;
                  opIndex: CARDINAL
              END;
VAR
  charStack: RECORD
                 chars: ARRAY[1..charUB] OF CHAR;
                 top: [0..charUB]
             END;
  cardStack: RECORD
                 cards: ARRAY[1..cardUB] OF CARDINAL
                 top: [0..cardUB]
             END;
  nextCard, index: CARDINAL;
  operandSet: charSet;
  operator, ch: CHAR;
  firstOperand, secondOperand: prandType;

PROCEDURE pushChar(c: CHAR);
BEGIN
  WITH charStack DO INC(top); chars[top]:= c
  END
END pushChar;
```

```
PROCEDURE pushCard(i: CARDINAL);
BEGIN
  WITH cardStack DO INC(top); cards[top]:= i
  END
END pushCard;


PROCEDURE popChar(VAR c: CHAR);
BEGIN
  WITH charStack DO c:= chars[top]; DEC(top)
  END
END popChar;


PROCEDURE popCard(VAR i: CARDINAL);
BEGIN
  WITH cardStack DO i:= cards[top]; DEC(top)
  END
END popCard;


PROCEDURE poperand(VAR operandRecord: prandType);
BEGIN
  WITH operandRecord DO
    popChar(opChar);
    IF opChar = 'T' THEN popCard(opIndex) END
  END
END poperand;


PROCEDURE outOperand(operandRecord: prandType);
BEGIN
  WITH operandRecord DO
    Write(' '); Write(opChar);
    IF opChar = 'T' THEN WriteCard(opIndex,1) END
  END; Write(' ')
END outOperand;


BEGIN
  operandSet:= charSet{'A'..'S','U'..'Z'};
  nextCard:= 0; charStack.top:= 0; cardStack.top:= 0;
  RedirectInput('sorsText');
  LOOP
    Read(ch); IF (ch = ' ') OR (ch = endOfFile) THEN EXIT END;
    IF ch IN operandSet THEN pushChar(ch) ELSE
      operator:= ch; INC(nextCard); index:= nextCard;
      Write('T'); WriteCard(index, 1); WriteString(':= ');
      poperand(secondOperand); poperand(firstOperand);
      outOperand(firstOperand); Write(operator);
      outOperand(secondOperand); WriteLn;
      pushChar('T'); pushCard(index)
    END;
```

```
  END;
  CloseInput
ND quads.


ODULE recDec is included in Section 8.5.1.


ODULE salAssem;
ROM symbType IMPORT symbolType;
ROM assLex IMPORT sy, ind, val, inSymbol, error;
ROM InOut IMPORT  Read, Write, WriteString, WriteCard, WriteLn,
 ReadCard, CloseInput, RedirectOutput, CloseOutput;
ROM labels IMPORT labelColon, commence, finalise;
ROM instrns IMPORT instruction;
EGIN
 commence;
 WHILE sy # endOfTextSy DO
   IF sy = labelSy THEN
     labelColon;
     IF sy = opCodeSy THEN instruction
     ELSE error(6)
     END;
   ELSIF sy = opCodeSy THEN instruction
   END
   IF sy = newLineSy THEN inSymbol ELSE
     error(3);
     REPEAT inSymbol
     UNTIL (sy = newLineSy) OR (sy = endOfTextSy);
     IF sy = newLineSy THEN inSymbol END;
   END
 END;
 CloseInput; RedirectOutput('salAsout'); finalise; CloseOutput
ID salAssem.


)DULE salLink;
:OM InOut IMPORT  Read, Write, WriteString, WriteCard, WriteLn, ReadCard,
:directInput, CloseInput, Done;
:OM FileSystem IMPORT Lookup, Rewrite, Close, WriteWord, File;
:OM strinTbl IMPORT searchStringTable, insertString, stringType;
:OM symbType IMPORT symbolType;
.OM mcModule IMPORT mcList, restart, startFile;
.OM expTable IMPORT relocatingConst, getExports, whichAddress;
'NST
 endOfFile = 32C; endOfLine = 36C;
 importTableUB = 50;
 PE
 charSet = SET OF CHAR;
```

```
VAR
  ch: CHAR;  sy: symbolType;
  ind: CARDINAL;

PROCEDURE inText (ch: CHAR);
VAR
  length: CARDINAL; found: BOOLEAN;
  inString: stringType;
BEGIN
  length:= 0;
  REPEAT
    inString[length]:= ch; INC (length); Read(ch)
  UNTIL NOT (ch IN charSet{'A'..'Z'});
  searchStringTable (inString, length, sy, ind, found);
  IF NOT found THEN
    WriteString('Error: missing export label ');
    WriteString(inString); WriteLn
  END
END inText;

PROCEDURE putBinary(w: CARDINAL);
VAR
  count: CARDINAL;
BEGIN
  FOR count:= 15 TO 0 BY -1 DO
    IF count IN BITSET(w) THEN Write('1') ELSE Write('0') END
  END;
END putBinary;

PROCEDURE relocate;
VAR
  i, whichEntry, n, relocatingVar, eNumber, iNumber,
  numericAddress, machineCodeWord, bit: CARDINAL;
  importTable: ARRAY [1..importTableUB] OF
  RECORD
     where, refAddress: CARDINAL
  END;
  absBinry: File;  noneLeft: BOOLEAN;
BEGIN
  Lookup(absBinry, 'absBinry', TRUE); Rewrite(absBinry);
  relocatingVar:= relocatingConst; n:= 0;
  LOOP
    startFile(noneLeft); IF noneLeft THEN EXIT END;
    INC(relocatingVar, n);
    Read(ch); IF ch # 'N' THEN WriteString ('Missing N'); WriteLn END;
    ReadCard(n);
    Read(ch); IF ch # 'E' THEN WriteString ('Missing E'); WriteLn END;
    ReadCard (eNumber); Read(ch);
```

```
   FOR i:= 1 TO eNumber DO (* skip exports *)
     WHILE ch # endOfLine DO Read(ch) END; Read(ch)
   END;
   IF ch # 'I' THEN WriteString ('Missing I'); WriteLn END;
   ReadCard(iNumber);
   FOR i:= 1 TO iNumber DO
     Read(ch); inText(ch);
     WITH importTable[i] DO
       ReadCard(where); refAddress:= whichAddress(ch, ind)
     END
   END;
   whichEntry:= 1;
   FOR i:= 0 TO n-1 DO
     ReadCard(machineCodeWord);  ReadCard(bit);
     IF bit = 0 THEN WriteWord(absBinry, machineCodeWord)
     ELSIF bit = 1 THEN
       IF whichEntry <= iNumber THEN
         WITH importTable [whichEntry] DO
           IF i = where THEN
             WriteWord(absBinry, refAddress);
             INC (whichEntry);
           ELSE WriteWord(absBinry, machineCodeWord + relocatingVar)
           END
         END
       ELSE WriteWord(absBinry, machineCodeWord + relocatingVar)
       END
     ELSE WriteString ('Error. Bit map bit = '); WriteCard(bit,3);
     END
   END;
   IF whichEntry # iNumber + 1 THEN
     WriteString('Error: Unused import.  WhichEntry = ');
     WriteCard(whichEntry, 4);
     WriteString(',   iNumber = '); WriteCard(iNumber, 4); WriteLn;
   END;
   CloseInput;
 END; Close(absBinry)
END relocate;

BEGIN
 mcList; restart; getExports; restart; relocate
END salLink.


DEFINITION MODULE salOut;
FROM synLex IMPORT symbolType;
PROCEDURE applyOperator(op: symbolType);
PROCEDURE outPush(ch: CHAR)
END salOut.
```

```
IMPLEMENTATION MODULE salOut;
FROM synLex IMPORT symbolType, error;
FROM InOut IMPORT WriteString, WriteLn, Write;
TYPE
  symbolSet = SET OF symbolType;

PROCEDURE applyOperator(op:symbolType);
BEGIN
  IF op IN symbolSet {plussOp,minusOp} THEN
    WriteString('    POP  AX'); WriteLn;
    WriteString('    MOV  DI, SP'); WriteLn;
    IF op = plussOp THEN
      WriteString('    ADD  [DI], AX'); WriteLn
    ELSE
      WriteString('    SUB  [DI], AX'); WriteLn
    END
  ELSIF op IN symbolSet {timesOp, divideOp} THEN
    WriteString('    POP BX'); WriteLn;
    WriteString('    POP AX'); WriteLn;
    IF op = timesOp THEN
      WriteString('    MULT BX'); WriteLn
    ELSE
      WriteString('    DIV  BX'); WriteLn;
      WriteString('    PUSH AX'); WriteLn
    END
  ELSIF op = negOp THEN
    WriteString('    MOV  DI, SP'); WriteLn;
    WriteString('    NEG  [DI]'); WriteLn
  ELSE error(5)
  END
END applyOperator;

PROCEDURE outPush (ch: CHAR);
BEGIN
  WriteString('    PUSH  '); Write(ch); WriteLn
END outPush;

BEGIN
END salout.
```

DEFINITION MODULE scanner is included in Section 9.3.

```
IMPLEMENTATION MODULE scanner;
FROM InOut IMPORT WriteString, WriteCard, ReadCard, WriteLn, Write,
RedirectInput;
FROM symbols IMPORT symbolType;
FROM strinTab IMPORT stringType, searchStringTable, insertString;
FROM lexInit IMPORT nextInd;
FROM SYSTEM IMPORT WORD;
FROM Storage IMPORT ALLOCATE, DEALLOCATE;
FROM FileSystem IMPORT File, Lookup, Rewrite, Close, WriteWord, ReadChar;
CONST
  endOfFile = 32C; endOfLine = 36C;
  tyInteger = 1; tyReal = 3;
TYPE
  charSet = SET OF CHAR;
  convert = ARRAY[0..1] OF WORD;
  stackRecPtr = POINTER TO stackRec;
  stackRec = RECORD
                fileRecord: File;
                oldCh: CHAR;  oldLineNumber: CARDINAL;
                next: stackRecPtr
             END;
VAR
  lineNumber, i: CARDINAL;
  ch: CHAR; noSpace, prevWasDot: BOOLEAN;
  interFile, currentFile: File;
  fileStack: stackRecPtr;

PROCEDURE error(errNo: CARDINAL);
BEGIN
  WriteString('error no:' ); WriteCard(errNo,4);
  WriteString('   at line no: '); WriteCard(lineNumber,4); WriteLn
END error;

PROCEDURE accept(sym: symbolType);
BEGIN
  IF sy = sym THEN inSymbol ELSE
    WriteString('Accept failed with ORD(sy) = ');
    WriteCard(ORD(sy), 3); WriteString('  and ORD(sym) = ');
    WriteCard(ORD(sym), 3); WriteLn; error(0)
  END
END accept;

PROCEDURE outSymbol;
BEGIN
  WriteWord(interFile, WORD(ORD(sy)));
  IF sy = idSy THEN WriteWord(interFile,WORD(ind))
```

```
  ELSIF sy = numberSy THEN
    WITH valueRecord DO
       WriteWord(interFile, WORD(valType));
       WriteWord(interFile, WORD(val1));
       WriteWord(interFile, WORD(val2))
    END
  END;
  WriteWord(interFile, WORD(lineNumber))
END outSymbol;


PROCEDURE openInterFile;
BEGIN
  Lookup(interFile, 'interFile', TRUE);
  Rewrite(interFile)
END openInterFile;


PROCEDURE closeInterFile;
BEGIN
  Close(interFile)
END closeInterFile;


PROCEDURE makeNegative(VAR v1, v2: CARDINAL);
VAR
  words: convert; realVal: REAL;
BEGIN
  words[0]:= WORD (v1); words[1]:= WORD (v2);
  realVal:= REAL(words);  realVal:= -realVal;
  words:= convert(realVal);
  v1:= CARDINAL(words[0]); v2:= CARDINAL(words[1])
END makeNegative;


PROCEDURE inChar;

  PROCEDURE skipSpaces;
  BEGIN
    WHILE (ch = ' ') AND (ch # endOfFile) DO
      ReadChar(currentFile,ch);
      IF ch = endOfLine THEN
         INC(lineNumber); ReadChar(currentFile,ch)
      END
    END
  END skipSpaces;

BEGIN    (* body of procedure inChar *)
  ReadChar(currentFile,ch);
  IF ch = endOfLine THEN
    INC (lineNumber); inChar; noSpace:= FALSE
  ELSE noSpace:= TRUE
  END;
```

```
IF ch = ' ' THEN noSpace:= FALSE;   skipSpaces END
D inChar;

OCEDURE skipComment;
R
 prevCh: CHAR;
GIN
 LOOP
   prevCh:= ch; ReadChar(currentFile,ch);
   CASE ch OF
   endOfLine:  INC(lineNumber) |
   '*':        IF prevCh = '(' THEN skipComment END |
   ')':        IF prevCh = '*' THEN inChar; inSymbol; EXIT; END |
   endOfFile:  WriteString('Fatal error: missing *)');
               WriteLn; HALT
   END
 END
D skipComment;

OCEDURE inSymbol;
PROCEDURE inNumber;
VAR
  i: [0..9]; divBy, realVal: REAL;
  words: convert;
BEGIN
  WITH valueRecord DO
     valType:= tyInteger;
     sy:= numberSy; val1:= 0;
     REPEAT
       i:= ORD (ch) - ORD ('0'); (* i:= digit value *)
       val1:= 10 * val1 + CARDINAL(i);
       ReadChar(currentFile,ch)
     UNTIL NOT(ch IN charSet {'0'..'9'});
     IF ch = '.' THEN
       ReadChar(currentFile,ch);
       IF ch = '.' THEN prevWasDot:= TRUE (* second '.' in '..' *)
       ELSE (* fractional part of a REAL *)
         valType:= tyReal; realVal:= FLOAT(val1);
         divBy:= 1.0;
         REPEAT
           i:= ORD(ch) - ORD('0'); divBy:= divBy * 10.0;
           realVal:= realVal + FLOAT(i)/divBy;
           ReadChar(currentFile, ch)
         UNTIL NOT (ch IN charSet {'0'..'9'});
         words:= convert(realVal);
         val1:= CARDINAL(words[0]); val2:= CARDINAL (words[1])
       END
     END;
```

```
      IF ch = ' ' THEN inChar
      ELSIF ch = endOfLine THEN INC(lineNumber); inChar
      END;
    END (* WITH *)
  END inNumber;

  PROCEDURE inText;
  VAR
    length: CARDINAL;
    done,  found: BOOLEAN;
    inString: stringType;
  BEGIN
    length:= 0; done:= FALSE;
    REPEAT
      inString[length]:= ch; INC(length);
      ReadChar(currentFile, ch)
    UNTIL NOT (ch IN charSet{'a'..'z','A'..'Z','0'..'9'});
    searchStringTable (inString, length, sy, ind, found);
    IF NOT found THEN
      insertString (inString, length, idSy, nextInd);
      sy:= idSy; ind:= nextInd; INC(nextInd)
    END;
    IF ch = ' ' THEN inChar ELSIF ch = endOfLine THEN
      INC(lineNumber); inChar
    END
  END inText;

BEGIN    (* body of procedure inSymbol *)
  CASE ch OF
  '0'..'9': inNumber |
  'a'..'z','A'..'Z': inText   |
  '+':  sy:= plussOp; inChar |
  '-':  sy:= minusOp; inChar |
  '*':  sy:= timesOp; inChar |
  '/':  sy:= realDivOp; inChar |
  '&':  sy:= andOp; inChar |
  '(':  sy:= openRndBrktSy; inChar;
        IF noSpace AND (ch = '*') THEN skipComment END |
  ')':  sy:= closeRndBrktSy; inChar |
  '[':  sy:= openSqBrktSy; inChar |
  ']':  sy:= closeSqrBrktSy; inChar |
  '{':  sy:= openCurlBrktSy; inChar |
  '}':  sy:= closeCurlBrktSy; inChar |
  '=':  sy:= equOp; inChar |
  '#':  sy:= notEquOp; inChar |
```

```
'>':  inChar;
      IF noSpace AND (ch = '=') THEN   (* >= *)
         sy:= greatEquOp; inChar
      ELSE sy:= greaterOp
      END |
'<':  sy:= lessOp; inChar;
      IF noSpace THEN
        IF ch = '=' THEN  sy:= lessEquOp; inChar;
        ELSIF ch = '>' THEN sy:= notEquOp; inChar;
        END
      END |
'|':  sy:= barSy; inChar |
'^':  sy:= upArrowSy; inChar |
':':  inChar;
      IF noSpace AND (ch = '=') THEN sy:= assignOp; inChar
      ELSE sy:= colonSy
      END |
'.':  inChar;
      IF prevWasDot THEN sy:= dotDotSy; prevWasDot:= FALSE
      ELSIF noSpace AND (ch = '.') THEN  sy:= dotDotSy; inChar
      ELSE sy:= periodSy
      END |
';':  sy:= semiColonSy; inChar |
',':  sy:= commaSy; inChar |
 endOfFile:  sy:= endOfTextSy;
 ELSE  error(1); inChar
 END (* of CASE *)
END inSymbol;

PROCEDURE switchStreamTo(newFile: File);
VAR
  filePtr: stackRecPtr;
BEGIN
  ALLOCATE(filePtr, SIZE(stackRec));
  WITH filePtr^ DO
    fileRecord:= currentFile; oldCh:= ch;
    oldLineNumber:= lineNumber; next:= fileStack
  END; fileStack:= filePtr;
  currentFile:= newFile;
  inChar; lineNumber:= 1
END switchStreamTo;

PROCEDURE restoreStream;
VAR
  chopPtr: stackRecPtr;
BEGIN
```

```
  Close(currentFile);
  WITH fileStack^ DO
    ch:= oldCh; lineNumber:= oldLineNumber;
    currentFile:= fileRecord
  END;
  chopPtr:= fileStack; fileStack:= fileStack^.next;
  DEALLOCATE(chopPtr, SIZE(stackRec))
END restoreStream;


BEGIN
  Lookup(currentFile ,'sourceIn', FALSE); inChar;
  lineNumber:= 1; prevWasDot:= FALSE
END scanner.


MODULE statemnt;
FROM putSAL IMPORT labelString, genLabel, putLabel, putLine, putStrings,
putStringAndVal;
FROM InOut IMPORT WriteString, WriteLn, Write, WriteCard;
FROM symbols IMPORT symbolType;
FROM strinTab IMPORT stringInfo;
FROM scanner IMPORT inSymbol, accept, error, valueRecord, sy, ind;
FROM expressn IMPORT expression, typeOf;
CONST
  tyInteger = 1;  tyBoolean = 2;  tyReal = 3;
  loopStackUB = 10;
VAR
  loopStack: ARRAY[1..loopStackUB] OF labelString;
  loopStackTop: CARDINAL;


PROCEDURE assignmentStatement;
VAR
  charOfLHS: CHAR; lhsTtype, resultType: CARDINAL;
BEGIN
  charOfLHS:= stringInfo.initialChar; (* single-character identifier *)
  lhsTtype:= typeOf(charOfLHS);
  inSymbol; accept(assignOp); expression(resultType);
  IF lhsTtype = resultType THEN
      IF lhsTtype = tyReal THEN
        WriteString('    LEA BX, '); Write(charOfLHS); WriteLn;
        WriteString('    POP [BX + 1]'); WriteLn;
        WriteString('    POP [BX]'); WriteLn
      ELSE  WriteString('    POP   '); Write(charOfLHS); WriteLn
      END
  ELSE error(20)
  END
END assignmentStatement;
```

```
PROCEDURE jumpIfFalse(resultType: CARDINAL; whereTo: labelString);
BEGIN
   IF resultType # tyBoolean THEN error(7) END;
   putLine('    POP AX');
   putLine('    CMP AX, 0');
   putStrings('    JE  ',whereTo)
END jumpIfFalse;

PROCEDURE whileStatement;
VAR
  loopLabel,after: labelString; resultType: CARDINAL;
BEGIN;
   genLabel(loopLabel);  putLabel(loopLabel);
   expression(resultType);
   genLabel(after);  jumpIfFalse(resultType,after);
   accept(doSy); stmntSequence; accept(endSy);
   putStrings('    JMP  ',loopLabel);
   putLabel(after); putLine('    NOP')
END whileStatement;

PROCEDURE ifStatement;
VAR
  afterThen, afterIfStmnt: labelString;
  resultType: CARDINAL;
BEGIN
   genLabel(afterThen);
   expression(resultType);    accept(thenSy);
   jumpIfFalse(resultType, afterThen);
   stmntSequence;
   IF sy = endSy THEN inSymbol; putLabel(afterThen)
   ELSE
     genLabel(afterIfStmnt);
     WHILE sy = elsifSy DO
        inSymbol; putStrings('    JMP  ', afterIfStmnt);
        putLabel(afterThen); genLabel(afterThen);
        expression(resultType); accept(thenSy);
        jumpIfFalse(resultType, afterThen);
        stmntSequence
     END;
     IF sy = elseSy THEN
        inSymbol; putStrings('    JMP  ', afterIfStmnt);
        putLabel(afterThen); stmntSequence;
     ELSE putLabel(afterThen); putLine('    NOP')
     END;
     putLabel(afterIfStmnt);
     accept(endSy)
  END;
  putLine('    NOP');
```

```
END ifStatement;

PROCEDURE loopStatement;
VAR
  loopLabel: labelString;
BEGIN
  genLabel(loopLabel); putLabel(loopLabel);
  INC(loopStackTop); genLabel(loopStack[loopStackTop]);
  stmntSequence;
  accept(endSy);
  putStrings('    JMP   ',loopLabel);
  putLabel(loopStack[loopStackTop]); DEC(loopStackTop);
  putLine('    NOP')
END loopStatement;

PROCEDURE exitStatement;
BEGIN
  IF loopStackTop = 0 THEN error(9)
  ELSE putStrings('    JMP  ', loopStack[loopStackTop])
  END
END exitStatement;

PROCEDURE repeatStatement;
VAR
  loopLabel: labelString; resultType: CARDINAL;
BEGIN
  genLabel(loopLabel); putLabel(loopLabel);
  stmntSequence;
  accept(untilSy);  expression(resultType);
  jumpIfFalse(resultType,loopLabel)
END repeatStatement;

PROCEDURE statement;
BEGIN
  CASE sy OF
    idSy:     assignmentStatement      |
    whileSy:  inSymbol; whileStatement |
    loopSy:   inSymbol; loopStatement  |
    exitSy:   inSymbol; exitStatement  |
    ifSy:     inSymbol; ifStatement    |
    repeatSy: inSymbol; repeatStatement
  ELSE (* do nothing *)
  END
END statement;
```

```
PROCEDURE stmntSequence;
BEGIN
    LOOP
      statement;
      IF sy = semiColonSy THEN inSymbol ELSE EXIT END
    END
END stmntSequence;


BEGIN
    loopStackTop:= 0;
    inSymbol; accept(beginSy);
    stmntSequence;
    accept(endSy); accept(periodSy)
END statemnt.
```

MODULE statMain is included in Section 12.8.


```
DEFINITION MODULE statmnts;
PROCEDURE stmntSequence;
END statmnts.

IMPLEMENTATION MODULE statmnts;
FROM putSAL IMPORT labelString, genLabel, putLabel, putLine,
  putStrings, putStringAndVal;
FROM InOut IMPORT WriteString, WriteLn, Write, WriteCard;
FROM symbols IMPORT symbolType;
FROM scanner IMPORT inSymbol, error, accept, valueRecord, sy, ind;
FROM xpressn IMPORT expression, pushAddress;
FROM itmod IMPORT class, idRecPtr, tyBoolean, tyInteger,
  tyReal, findItsRecord;
CONST
  loopStackUB = 10;
VAR
  loopStack: ARRAY[1..loopStackUB] OF labelString;
  loopStackTop: CARDINAL;

PROCEDURE assignmentStatement(idPtr: idRecPtr);
VAR
  lhsTtype, resultType: idRecPtr; length: CARDINAL;
  labc: labelString;
BEGIN
  IF idPtr^.itsClass # aVariable THEN error (19); RETURN END;
  pushAddress(idPtr, lhsTtype);   accept(assignOp);
  expression (resultType);
```

```
  IF lhsTtype = resultType THEN
    length:= resultType^.itsLength;
    putStringAndVal('   MOV CX,', length);
    putLine('   MOV SI, SP ');
    putStringAndVal('   SUB SI,', length);
    putLine('   MOV DI, [SI]');
    putStringAndVal('   ADD DI,', length - 1);
    genLabel(labc); putLabel(labc);
    putLine('   POP [DI]');
    putLine('   DEC DI');
    putStrings ('   LOOP ',labc);
    putLine('   DEC SP')
  ELSE error(20)
  END
END assignmentStatement;


PROCEDURE jumpIfFalse(resultType: idRecPtr; whereTo: labelString);
BEGIN
   IF resultType # tyBoolean THEN error(7) END;
   putLine('   POP AX');
   putLine('   CMP AX, 0');
   putStrings('   JE ',whereTo)
END jumpIfFalse;


PROCEDURE whileStatement;
VAR
  loopLabel,after: labelString; resultType: idRecPtr;
BEGIN;
   genLabel(loopLabel);  putLabel(loopLabel);
   expression(resultType);
   genLabel(after);  jumpIfFalse(resultType,after);
   accept(doSy); stmntSequence; accept(endSy);
   putStrings('   JMP ',loopLabel);
   putLabel(after); putLine('   NOP')
END whileStatement;


PROCEDURE ifStatement;
VAR
  afterThen, afterIfStmnt: labelString;
  resultType: idRecPtr;
BEGIN
   genLabel(afterThen);
   expression(resultType);   accept(thenSy);
   jumpIfFalse(resultType, afterThen);
   stmntSequence;
   IF sy = endSy THEN inSymbol; putLabel(afterThen)
```

```
    ELSE
      genLabel(afterIfStmnt);
      WHILE sy = elsifSy DO
         inSymbol; putStrings('    JMP   ', afterIfStmnt);
         putLabel(afterThen); genLabel(afterThen);
         expression(resultType); accept(thenSy);
         jumpIfFalse(resultType, afterThen);
         stmntSequence
      END;
      IF sy = elseSy THEN
         inSymbol; putStrings('    JMP   ', afterIfStmnt);
         putLabel(afterThen); stmntSequence
      ELSE putLabel(afterThen); putLine('   NOP')
      END;
      putLabel(afterIfStmnt); accept(endSy)
  END;
  putLine('   NOP')
END ifStatement;


PROCEDURE loopStatement;
VAR
  loopLabel: labelString;
BEGIN
  genLabel(loopLabel); putLabel(loopLabel);
  INC(loopStackTop); genLabel(loopStack[loopStackTop]);
  stmntSequence; accept(endSy);
  putStrings('    JMP   ',loopLabel);
  putLabel(loopStack[loopStackTop]); DEC(loopStackTop);
  putLine('   NOP')
END loopStatement;


PROCEDURE exitStatement;
BEGIN
  IF loopStackTop = 0 THEN error(9)
  ELSE putStrings('    JMP   ', loopStack[loopStackTop])
  END
END exitStatement;


PROCEDURE repeatStatement;
VAR
  loopLabel: labelString; resultType: idRecPtr;
BEGIN
   genLabel(loopLabel); putLabel(loopLabel);
   stmntSequence;
   accept(untilSy);  expression(resultType);
   jumpIfFalse(resultType,loopLabel)
END repeatStatement;
```

```
PROCEDURE extProc;
VAR
  resultType, idPtr: idRecPtr; found: BOOLEAN;
BEGIN
  CASE ind OF
  27: putLine('    CALL NEWLINE'); inSymbol  |
  25: inSymbol; accept(openRndBrktSy);   (* READNUM *)
      findItsRecord(ind, idPtr, found);
      IF idPtr^.itsClass = aVariable THEN
         pushAddress(idPtr, resultType);
         putLine('    POP DI');
         IF resultType = tyInteger THEN
           putLine('    CALL INTREAD ');
           putLine('    POP [BP][DI] ')
         ELSIF resultType = tyReal THEN (* Read 2 words *)
           putLine('    CALL REALREAD ');
           putLine('    INC DI ');
           putLine('    POP [BP][DI] ');
           putLine('    DEC DI ');
           putLine('    POP [BP][DI] ')
        ELSE error(31)
        END
     ELSE error(31)
     END; accept (closeRndBrktSy); |
  26: inSymbol; accept(openRndBrktSy); expression(resultType);
      IF resultType = tyInteger THEN
        putLine('    CALL INTWRITE ')
      ELSIF resultType = tyReal THEN
        putLine('    CALL REALWRITE ')
      ELSE error(31)
      END;
      accept (closeRndBrktSy)
    ELSE error(31)
    END
END extProc;

PROCEDURE statement;
VAR
  idPtr: idRecPtr; found: BOOLEAN;
BEGIN
```

```
    CASE sy OF
      idSy: findItsRecord (ind, idPtr, found);
          IF found THEN
            CASE idPtr^.itsClass OF
              aVariable: assignmentStatement(idPtr)  |
              externalProc: extProc
            ELSE error(11)
            END
          ELSE error(101)
          END  |
      whileSy:  inSymbol; whileStatement |
      loopSy:   inSymbol; loopStatement  |
      exitSy:   inSymbol; exitStatement  |
      ifSy:     inSymbol; ifStatement    |
      repeatSy: inSymbol; repeatStatement
      ELSE (* do nothing *)
    END
END statement;

PROCEDURE stmntSequence;
BEGIN
    LOOP
      statement;
      IF sy = semiColonSy THEN inSymbol ELSE EXIT END
    END
END stmntSequence;

BEGIN
    loopStackTop:= 0
END statmnts.
```

DEFINITION MODULE strinTab is identical to DEFINITION MODULE strinTbl
except that it imports from symbols instead of symbType.

IMPLEMENTATION MODULE strinTab is identical to IMPLEMENTATION MODULE
strinTbl except that it imports from symbols instead of symbType.

DEFINITION MODULE strinTbl is included in Section 3.2.

```
IMPLEMENTATION MODULE strinTbl;
FROM InOut IMPORT  Read, Write, WriteString, WriteCard, WriteLn,
  ReadCard;
FROM Storage IMPORT ALLOCATE;
FROM symbType IMPORT symbolType;
CONST
  charArrayUB = 1000;
```

```
TYPE
  comparison = (isGreater, isLess, isEqual);
  nodePtr = POINTER TO nodeRec;
  nodeRec = RECORD
                start, strLength: CARDINAL;
                whichSy: symbolType;
                index: CARDINAL;
                lessThan, greaterThan: nodePtr
            END;
  charSet = SET OF CHAR;
  statusType = (searching, duplicate, inserted);
VAR
  charArray: ARRAY [1..charArrayUB] OF CHAR;
  hashTable: ARRAY [0..51] OF nodePtr;
  nextTextStart: [1..charArrayUB];
  h: CARDINAL;

PROCEDURE hashSubscript(ch: CHAR): CARDINAL;
BEGIN
  IF ch IN charSet{'a'..'z'} THEN RETURN ORD(ch) - ORD('a')
  ELSE RETURN ORD(ch) - ORD('A') + 26
  END
END hashSubscript;

PROCEDURE searchStringTable (inString: stringType;
  length: CARDINAL; VAR symbol: symbolType; VAR ind: CARDINAL;
  VAR found: BOOLEAN);
VAR
  currentPtr: nodePtr;
  i, lasti:  CARDINAL;
  whichWay: comparison;
  ch, inch: CHAR;
BEGIN
  found:= FALSE;
  currentPtr:= hashTable[hashSubscript(inString[0])];
  WHILE (currentPtr <> NIL) AND NOT found DO
    WITH currentPtr^ DO
      whichWay:= isEqual;
      IF length < strLength THEN currentPtr:= lessThan;
      ELSIF length > strLength THEN currentPtr:= greaterThan;
      ELSIF length > 1 THEN  i:= 0; lasti:= length -2;
        WHILE (i <= lasti) AND (whichWay = isEqual) DO
          ch:= charArray [start + i];
          inch:= inString[i+1];
          IF inch < ch THEN whichWay:= isLess
          ELSIF inch > ch THEN whichWay:= isGreater
          END; INC (i)
        END;
      END;
```

```
      CASE whichWay OF
        isEqual:  found:= TRUE; symbol:= whichSy; ind:= index |
        isLess:   currentPtr:= lessThan |
        isGreater: currentPtr:= greaterThan
      END;  (* CASE *)
    ELSE found:= TRUE; symbol:= whichSy; ind:= index
    END;    (* IF *)
  END (* WITH *)
END; (* WHILE *)
IF found THEN
  WITH stringInfo DO initialChar:= inString[0];
    stringStart:= currentPtr^.start; stringLength:= length
  END
END
END searchStringTable;


PROCEDURE insertString (inString: stringType;
  length: CARDINAL; symbol: symbolType; ind: CARDINAL);
VAR
  currentPtr, newPtr: nodePtr;
  i, lasti: INTEGER;
  whichWay: comparison;
  ch, inch: CHAR;
  status : statusType;
BEGIN
  status:= searching;
  ALLOCATE (newPtr, SIZE(nodeRec));
  WITH newPtr^ DO
    whichSy:= symbol; index:= ind;
    start:= nextTextStart; strLength:= length;
    lessThan:= NIL; greaterThan:= NIL
  END;
  currentPtr:= hashTable[hashSubscript(inString[0])];
  IF currentPtr = NIL THEN hashTable[hashSubscript(inString[0])]:= newPtr;
    status:= inserted
    ELSE
      WHILE status = searching DO
      WITH currentPtr^ DO
        whichWay:= isEqual;
        IF length < strLength THEN whichWay:= isLess
        ELSIF length > strLength THEN whichWay:= isGreater
        ELSIF length > 1 THEN i:= 0; lasti:= length - 2;
```

```
        WHILE (i <= lasti) AND (whichWay = isEqual) DO
          ch:= charArray [start + CARDINAL(i)];
          inch:= inString[i + 1];
          IF inch < ch THEN whichWay:= isLess
          ELSIF inch > ch THEN whichWay:= isGreater
          END;  INC (i)
        END
     END; (* IF *)
     CASE whichWay OF
       isEqual:  status:= duplicate;
         WriteString('Error: string already in string table.');
         WriteString('String = ');
         WriteString(inString); WriteLn |
       isLess:   IF lessThan # NIL THEN currentPtr:= lessThan
         ELSE lessThan:= newPtr; status:= inserted
         END |
       isGreater: IF greaterThan # NIL THEN currentPtr:= greaterThan
         ELSE greaterThan:= newPtr;  status:= inserted
         END
     END  (* CASE *)
   END (* WITH *)
 END (* WHILE *)
END; (* IF *)
IF status = inserted THEN
  i:= 0; lasti:= INTEGER(length) - 2;
  WHILE i <= lasti DO
    charArray[nextTextStart + CARDINAL(i)]:= inString[i + 1];
    INC(i)
  END;
  IF nextTextStart <= charArrayUB - length + 1 THEN
    INC(nextTextStart,length -1)
  ELSE WriteString('ERROR: CharArray upper bound too small');
    WriteLn
  END;
  WITH stringInfo DO initialChar:= inString[0];
    stringStart:=newPtr^.start; stringLength:= length
  END
 END
END insertString;

PROCEDURE stringText (idString: stringRec);
VAR
  i: CARDINAL;
BEGIN
```

```
  WITH idString DO Write(initialChar);
    FOR i:= stringStart TO stringStart + stringLength - 2 DO
      Write(charArray[i])
    END
  END
END stringText;


PROCEDURE outputName;
BEGIN
  stringText(stringInfo)
END outputName;


PROCEDURE nameIs (VAR name: stringType; VAR length: CARDINAL);
VAR
  i,j: CARDINAL;
BEGIN
  WITH stringInfo DO
    i:= stringStart; name[0]:= initialChar;
    FOR j:= 1 TO stringLength - 1 DO
      name[j]:= charArray[i]; INC(i)
    END;
    FOR j:= stringLength TO stringUB DO name[j]:= ' ' END;
    length:= stringLength
  END
END nameIs;


PROCEDURE enter(str: ARRAY OF CHAR; symbol: symbolType; ind: CARDINAL);
VAR
  i,j: CARDINAL; instrns: stringType;
BEGIN
  i:= 0;
  WHILE str[i] # ' ' DO instrns[i]:= str[i]; INC(i) END;
  FOR j:= i TO stringUB DO instrns[j]:= ' ' END;
  insertString(instrns, i, symbol, ind)
END enter;


BEGIN
  nextTextStart:= 1;
  FOR h:= 0 TO 51 DO hashTable[h]:= NIL END
END strinTbl.



DEFINITION MODULE symbols is included in Section 9.2.

IMPLEMENTATION MODULE symbols;
BEGIN
END symbols.
```

DEFINITION MODULE symbType is included in Section 3.1.

```
IMPLEMENTATION MODULE symbType;
BEGIN
END symbType.
```


DEFINITION MODULE synLex is included in Section 8.5.3.

```
IMPLEMENTATION MODULE synLex;
FROM InOut IMPORT WriteString, WriteLn, WriteCard, Read, Write;
CONST
   endOfFile = 32C;
TYPE
     charSet = SET OF CHAR;

PROCEDURE error(n:CARDINAL);
VAR
    ch: CHAR;
BEGIN
    WriteString('Error number: '); WriteCard(n,3); WriteLn;
    IF sy # endMarkerSy THEN
    REPEAT Read(ch) UNTIL (ch = '$') OR (ch = endOfFile) END
END error;

PROCEDURE inSymbol;
VAR
    ch: CHAR;
BEGIN
    IF sy # endMarkerSy THEN Read(ch) END;
    WHILE ch = ' ' DO Read(ch) END; (* skip spaces *)
    CASE ch OF
        'A'..'Z':  sy:= variableSy |
        '+':  sy:= plussOp |  '-':  sy:= minusOp|
        '*':  sy:= timesOp|  '/':  sy:= divideOp|
        '(':  sy:= leftRndBrktSy| ')':  sy:= rightRndBrktSy|
        '$':  sy:= endMarkerSy
    ELSE Write(ch); WriteLn; error(1)
    END; chOfSy:= ch
END inSymbol;


BEGIN
END synLex.
```


MODULE toPostFx is included in Section 8.5.3.

```
MODULE toSAL;
FROM synLex IMPORT error, inSymbol, symbolType, sy, chOfSy;
FROM salOut IMPORT applyOperator, outPush;
CONST
  endOfFile = 32C;
TYPE
  charSet = SET OF CHAR;
  symbolSet = SET OF symbolType;

PROCEDURE expression;
VAR
  operator: symbolType;
BEGIN
  IF sy = plussOp THEN
    inSymbol; term
  ELSIF sy = minusOp THEN
    inSymbol; term; applyOperator(negOp)
  ELSE term END;
  WHILE sy IN symbolSet{plussOp, minusOp} DO
    operator:= sy; inSymbol; term;
    applyOperator(operator)
  END
END expression;

PROCEDURE term;
VAR
  operator: symbolType;
BEGIN
  factor;
  WHILE sy IN symbolSet{timesOp,divideOp} DO
    operator:= sy; inSymbol; factor;
    applyOperator(operator)
  END
END term;

PROCEDURE factor;
BEGIN
  IF sy = leftRndBrktSy THEN
    inSymbol; expression;
    IF sy # rightRndBrktSy THEN error (2) END;
    inSymbol
  ELSIF sy = variableSy THEN
    outPush(chOfSy); inSymbol
  END
END factor;
```

```
BEGIN
  inSymbol; expression;
  IF sy # endMarkerSy THEN error (3) END
END toSAL.


MODULE typAssin is included in Section 10.5.


DEFINITION MODULE xpressn;
FROM itmod IMPORT idRecPtr;
PROCEDURE expression(VAR resultType: idRecPtr);
PROCEDURE pushAddress(idPtr: idRecPtr; VAR resultType: idRecPtr);
END xpressn.

IMPLEMENTATION MODULE xpressn;
FROM InOut IMPORT WriteString, WriteLn, Write, WriteCard;
FROM symbols IMPORT symbolType;
FROM scanner IMPORT inSymbol, error, accept, valueRecord, sy, ind;
FROM putSAL IMPORT applyOperator, applyRelationalOp, applyRealOperator,
labelString,
  putLine, putStringAndVal, putStrings, genLabel, putLabel;
FROM itmod IMPORT idRecPtr, idRec, class, kindOfType, findField,
findItsRecord, tyInteger, tyBoolean, tyReal, stIndex;
TYPE
  symbolSet = SET OF symbolType;

PROCEDURE expression (VAR resultType: idRecPtr);
VAR
  operator:  symbolType;
  nexType: idRecPtr;
BEGIN
  subExpression (resultType);
  IF sy IN symbolSet {equOp..greatEquOp} THEN
    operator:= sy;  inSymbol;
    subExpression (nexType);
    IF resultType = nexType  THEN
      IF resultType = tyReal THEN applyRealOperator(operator)
      ELSE  applyRelationalOp(operator)
      END; resultType:= tyBoolean
    ELSE error(20)
    END
  END
END expression;

PROCEDURE subExpression(VAR resultType: idRecPtr);
VAR
  operator: symbolType; nexType: idRecPtr;
```

```
BEGIN
  IF sy = plussOp THEN inSymbol; term (resultType);
  ELSIF sy = minusOp THEN
    inSymbol; term (resultType);
    IF resultType = tyInteger THEN applyOperator(negOp)
    ELSIF resultType = tyReal THEN
      applyRealOperator(negOp)
    ELSE error(20)
    END
  ELSE term (resultType)
  END;
  WHILE sy IN symbolSet{plussOp,minusOp,orOp} DO
    operator:= sy;   inSymbol; term (nexType);
    IF nexType = resultType THEN
      CASE operator OF
        orOp:  IF resultType = tyBoolean THEN applyOperator(orOp)
               ELSE error(20)
               END |
        plussOp, minusOp:
               IF resultType  = tyInteger THEN  applyOperator(operator)
               ELSIF resultType = tyReal THEN   applyRealOperator(operator)
               ELSE error(20)
               END
      END (* CASE *)
    ELSE error(20)
    END
  END (* WHILE *)
END subExpression;


PROCEDURE term (VAR resultType: idRecPtr);
VAR
  operator: symbolType;
  nexType: idRecPtr;
BEGIN
  factor (resultType);
  WHILE sy IN symbolSet{timesOp,realDivOp, divOp, modOp, andOp} DO
    operator:= sy; inSymbol;
    factor (nexType);
    IF resultType = nexType THEN
      IF resultType = tyBoolean THEN
        IF operator = andOp THEN
           applyOperator(andOp) ELSE error(21)
        END
      ELSIF resultType = tyInteger THEN
        IF operator IN symbolSet {timesOp, divOp, modOp} THEN
          applyOperator(operator)
        ELSE error(21)
        END
```

```
      ELSIF resultType = tyReal THEN
        IF operator IN symbolSet {timesOp, realDivOp} THEN
          applyRealOperator(operator)
        ELSE error(21)
        END
      ELSE error(22)
      END
    ELSE error(20)
    END
  END (* WHILE *)
END term;


PROCEDURE factor (VAR resultType: idRecPtr);
BEGIN
  CASE sy OF
    numberSy:
        WITH valueRecord DO
          putStringAndVal('    MOV AX, ', val1);
          putLine('    PUSH AX');
          IF valType = 3 THEN (* REAL *)
            putStringAndVal('    MOV AX, ',val2);
            putLine('    PUSH AX')
          END;
          resultType:= stIndex[valType];
        END; inSymbol |
    idSy: pushValue (resultType) |
    notOp:  inSymbol; factor (resultType);
          IF resultType # tyBoolean THEN error(20)
          ELSE applyOperator(notOp)
          END |
    openRndBrktSy: inSymbol; expression(resultType); accept(closeRndBrktSy)
  END
END factor;


PROCEDURE pushAddress(idPtr: idRecPtr; VAR resultType: idRecPtr);
  PROCEDURE arrayReference;
  VAR
    no, yes: labelString; elementLength: CARDINAL; tyPtr: idRecPtr;
  BEGIN
    REPEAT
      tyPtr:= resultType;
      elementLength:= tyPtr^.elementType^.itsLength;
      inSymbol; expression(resultType);  (* evaluates ARRAY subscript *)
      IF resultType = tyPtr^.indexType THEN
        genLabel(no); genLabel(yes);
        putLine('    POP DX');
        putStringAndVal('    CMP DX, ', tyPtr^.upBound);
        putStrings('    JG ',no);
```

```
        putStringAndVal ('    CMP DX, ', tyPtr^.lowBound);
        putStrings ('    JGE ', yes);
        putLabel (no);
        putLine ('    MOV AX, 999');
        putLine ('    PUSH AX');
        putLine ('    CALL INTWRITE');
        putLine ('    CALL ENDPROG');
        putLabel (yes);
        putStringAndVal ('    SUB DX, ', tyPtr^.lowBound);
        putStringAndVal ('    MOV AX, ', elementLength);
        putLine ('    MULT DX');
        putLine ('    MOV DI, SP');
        putLine ('    ADD [DI], AX');
      ELSE error (36)
      END; resultType:= tyPtr^.elementType
    UNTIL sy # commaSy; accept (closeSqrBrktSy)
  END arrayReference;

  PROCEDURE fieldReference;
  VAR
      fieldInfo: idRec; found: BOOLEAN;
  BEGIN
    inSymbol;
    findField (ind, resultType^.fieldPtr, fieldInfo, found);
    IF found THEN
      putLine ('    MOV DI, SP');
      putStringAndVal ('    ADD [DI],', fieldInfo.fieldAddress);
      resultType:= fieldInfo.itsType
    ELSE  error (37)
    END; inSymbol
  END fieldReference;

BEGIN (* body of pushAddress *)
  putStringAndVal ('    MOV  AX,', idPtr^.relAddress);
  putLine ('    ADD AX, BP');
  putLine ('    PUSH AX');
  inSymbol; resultType:= idPtr^.itsType;
  WHILE sy IN symbolSet{openSqBrktSy, periodSy} DO
    IF sy = openSqBrktSy THEN
      IF resultType^.typeKind = arrayType THEN arrayReference
      ELSE error (31)
      END
    ELSIF sy = periodSy THEN
      IF resultType^.typeKind = recordType THEN fieldReference
      ELSE error (32)
      END
    END
  END
```

```
END pushAddress;

PROCEDURE pushValue (VAR resultType: idRecPtr);
VAR
  multiLabel: labelString;
  idPtr: idRecPtr; found: BOOLEAN;
BEGIN
  findItsRecord(ind, idPtr, found);
  IF found THEN
    CASE idPtr^.itsClass  OF
      aConstant: putStringAndVal('   MOV AX, ',idPtr^.c1);
                 putLine('    PUSH AX');
                 resultType:= idPtr^.itsType;
                 IF resultType = tyReal THEN
                   putStringAndVal('    MOV AX, ', idPtr^.c2);
                   putLine('    PUSH AX')
                 END; inSymbol |
      aVariable: pushAddress(idPtr, resultType);
                 putStringAndVal ('    MOV CX,', resultType^.itsLength);
                 putLine ('    POP DI ');
                 genLabel(multiLabel); putLabel(multiLabel);
                 putLine ('    PUSH [DI]');
                 putLine ('    INC DI');
                 putStrings ('    LOOP ',multiLabel)
    ELSE error(29)
    END (* CASE *)
  ELSE error (28)
  END (* IF *)
END pushValue;

BEGIN
END xpressn.
```

Bibliography

Aho, A.V. Sethi, R. and Ullman, J.D. (1986) *Compilers: Principles, Techniques and Tools*, Addison-Wesley.

Ammann, U. (1977) 'Code generation in a Pascal compiler', *Software Practice and Experience, 7*, 391–423.

Anderson, T.L. (1984) 'Seven Modula-2 compilers reviewed', *Journal of Pascal, Ada and Modula-2*, March/April, pp. 38–43.

Backhouse, R.C. (1979) *Syntax of Programming Languages: Theory and Practice*, Prentice Hall.

Bal, H.E. and Tanenbaum, A.S. (1986) 'Language and machine independent global optimisation on intermediate code', *Computer Languages*, **11** (2) 105–21.

Barrett, W.A., Bates, R.M., Gustafson, D.A.and Couch, J.D. (1986) *Compiler Construction Theory and Practice*, Science Research Associates, Chicago.

Barron, D.W. (1978) *Assemblers and Loaders*, North-Holland.

Bennett, J.P. (1990) *Introduction to Compiling Techniques: a First Course using ANSI C, LEX and YACC*, McGraw-Hill.

Briggs P., Cooper, K.D., Kennedy K. and Torczon, L. (1989) 'Colouring heuristics for register allocation', *SIGPLAN Notices*, **24** (7), 275–84.

Bron, C., Dijkstra, E.J. and Rossingh, T.J.(1985) 'A note on the checking of interfaces between separately compiled modules', *SIGPLAN Notices*, **20** (8), 60–3.

Calingaert, P. (1979) *Assemblers, Compilers and Program Translation*, Computer Science Press, Potomac, MD.

Chow F.C. and Hennessey, J.L. 'The priority based colouring approach to register allocation', *ACM Trans. on Programming Languages and Systems*, **12** (4), 501–36.

Cornelius, B.J. (1988) 'Problems with the language Modula-2', *Software Practice and Experience*, **18** (6), 529–43.

Davidson J.W. and Fraser, C.W. (1984) 'Register allocation and exhaustive peephole optimisation', *Software Practice and Experience*, **14** (9), 857–65.

Davidson J.W. and Whalley, D. B. (1989) 'Quick compilers using peephole optimisation', *Software Practice and Experience*, **19** (1), 79–97.

Dhamdhere, D.M. (1988) 'Register assignment using code placement techniques', *Computer Languages*, **13** (2), 75–93.

Deitel, H.M. (1990) *Operating Systems* (2nd edn), Addison-Wesley.

Farnum, C. (1988) 'Compiler support for floating point computation', *Software Practice and Experience*, **18** (7), 701–9.

Fischer, C.N. and LeBlanc, R.J. (1988) *Crafting a Compiler*, Benjamin/Cummings.

Fischer,B., Hammer C. and Struckmann, W. (1992) 'Aladdin: a scanner generator for incremental programming environments', *Software Practice and Experience*, **22** (11), 1011–25.

Fraser, C.W. and Wendt, A.L. (1986) 'Integrating code generation and optimisation', *SIGPLAN Notices*, **21** (7), 242–8.

Ganapathi, M., Fischer, C.N. and Hennessy, J.L. (1982) 'Retargetable compiler code generation', *Computing Surveys*, **14** (4), 573–92.

Gough, K.J. and Mohay, G.M. (1988) *Modula-2: A Second Course in Programming*, Prentice Hall.

Grosch, J. (1989) 'Efficient generation of lexical analysers', *Software Practice and Experience*, **19** (11), 1089–1105.

Brinch Hansen, P. (1985) *Brinch Hansen on Pascal Compilers*, Prentice Hall.

Hennessy, J.L. and Mendelsohn, N. (1982) 'Compilation of the Pascal Case statement', *Software Practice and Experience*, **12**, 879–82.

Holub, A.I. (1990) *Compiler Design in C*, Prentice Hall.

Hsu, W.C., Fischer, C.N. and Goodman, J.R. (1989) 'On the minimisation of loads/stores in local register allocation', *IEEE Transactions on Software Engineering*, **15** (10), 1252–60.

Louden, K. (1990) 'P-code and compiler portability', *SIGPLAN Notices*, **25** (5), 53–9.

McKenzie, B.J. (1989) 'Fast peephole optimisation techniques', *Software Practice and Experience*, **19** (12), 1151–62.

Myers, G.L. (1982) *Advances in Computer Architecture*, John Wiley.

Nori, K.V., Ammann, U., Jensen, K., Nageli, H.H. and Jacobi, C. (1981) 'Pascal-P implementation notes', in D.W. Barron (ed.), *Pascal, the Language and its Implementation*, John Wiley.

Ottenstein, K.J. (1984) 'Intermediate Program representations in compiler construction: a supplemental bibliography', *SIGPLAN NOTICES*, **19** (7), 25–7.

Pagan, F.G. (1991) *Partial Computation and the Construction of Language Processors*, Prentice Hall.

Pemberton, S. and Daniels, M.C. (1986) *Pascal Implementation: The P4 System*, Ellis Horwood.

Peterson, J.L. and Silberschatz, A. (1982) *Operating Systems Concepts*, Addison-Wesley.

Powell, M.L. (1984) 'A portable optimising compiler for Modula-2', *SIGPLAN Notices*, **19** (6), 310–18.

Pronk, C. (1992) 'Stress testing of compilers for Modula-2', *Software Practice and Experience*, **22** (10), 885–97.

Pyster, A.B. (1988) *Compiler Design and Construction*, Van Nostrand Reinhold.

Rechenberg, P. and Mössenböck, H. *A Compiler Generator for Microcomputers*, Prentice Hall.

Sale, A. (1981) 'The implementation of case statements in Pascal', *Software Practice and Experience*, **11**, 929–42.

Schreiner, A.T. and Friedman, H.G. (1985) *Introduction to Compiler Construction with UNIX*, Prentice Hall.

Tanenbaum, A.S., van Steveren, H. and Stevenson, J.H. (1982) 'Using peephole optimisation on intermediate code', *ACM Trans. on Programming Languages and Systems*, **4** (1), 21–36.

Tanenbaum, A.S., Kaashoek, M.F., Langendoen, K.C. and Jacobs, C.J. H. (1989) 'The design of very fast portable compilers', *SIGPLAN Notices*, **24** (11), 125–31.

Terry, P.D. (1986) *Programming Language Translation*, Addison-Wesley.

Tremblay, J.-P. and Sorensen, P.G. (1985) *The Theory and Practice of Compiler Writing*, McGraw-Hill.

Waite, W.M. and Goos, G. (1984) *Compiler Construction*, Springer-Verlag.

Warfield, J.W. and. Bauer, H.R (1988) 'An expert system for a retargetable peephole optimiser', *SIGPLAN NOTICES*, **23** (10), 123–30.

Watt, D.A. (1993) *Programming Language Processors*, Prentice Hall.

Wegman, M.N. and Zadeck F.K. (1991) 'Constant propagation with conditional branches', *ACM Trans. on Programming Languages and Systems*, **13** (2), 181–210.

Welsh, J. and Hay, A. (1986) *A Model Implementation of Standard Pascal*, Prentice Hall.

Wirth, N. (1985) *Programming in Modula-2* (3rd edn), Springer-Verlag.

Wirth, N. (1988) 'From Modula to Oberon', *Software Practice and Experience*, **18** (7), 661–70.

Wirth, N. and Gutknecht, J. (1992) *Project Oberon the Design of an Operating System and Compiler*, ACM Press and Addison Wesley.

Index

value of (*continued*)
  variable or parameter, 192–4, 222
value parameter, 207, 217
value record, 125, 169
VAR parameter, 207, 216, 217, 222
variables
  dead, 287
  declaration, 180

labels corresponding to, 82, 118, 134
local, 207, 215
storage allocation, 161, 180, 201
temporary, 82, 101, 215

WHILE, 147–50

YACC, 121